# 50% OFF
# ACCUPLACER Prep Course!

Dear Customer,

Thank you for your purchase of this ACCUPLACER Study Guide. Included with your purchase is **discounted access to our online ACCUPLACER Test Prep Course.** Many ACCUPLACER courses are needlessly expensive and don't deliver enough value. Our course provides the best ACCUPLACER prep material, and with discounted access, with discounted access, **you only pay half price**.

**We have structured our online course to perfectly complement your printed study guide**. The ACCUPLACER Online Course contains **in-depth lessons** that cover all the most important topics, **260+ video reviews** that explain difficult concepts, over **1,250+ practice questions** to ensure you feel prepared, and more than **550+ flashcards** so you can study on the go.

### *Online ACCUPLACER Test Prep Course*

**Topics Include:**
- Reading
  - Figurative Language & Literary Devices
- Writing
  - Sentence Structure
- Arithmetic
  - Converting Between Percentages, Fractions, and Decimals
- Quantitative Reasoning, Algebra, and Statistics
  - Cross Multiplication & Slope
- Advanced Algebra and Functions
  - Quadratics & Advanced Systems of Equations

**Course Features:**
- ACCUPLACER Study Guide
  - Get content that complements our best-selling study guide.
- 8 Full-Length Practice Tests
  - With over 1,250 practice questions, you can test yourself again and again.
- Mobile Friendly
  - If you need to study on the go, the course is easily accessible from your mobile device.
- ACCUPLACER Flashcards
  - Our course includes a flashcard mode consisting of over 550 content cards to help you study.

To lock in your discounted access, visit mometrix.com/university/accuplacer or simply scan this QR code with your smartphone. At the checkout page, enter the discount code: **accu50off**

If you have any questions or concerns, please contact us at support@mometrix.com.

# Access Your Online Resources

**Don't miss out on the Online Resources included with your purchase!**

Your purchase of this product unlocks access to our Online Resources page. Elevate your study experience with our **interactive practice test interface**, along with all of the additional resources that we couldn't include in this book.

**Flip to the Online Resources section at the end of this book to find the link and a QR code to get started!**

# ACCUPLACER
## Study Guide 2025-2026

ACCUPLACER® Test Prep Secrets Book

8 Full-Length Practice Tests

250+ Online Video Tutorials

**3rd Edition**

Copyright © 2026 by Mometrix Media LLC

All rights reserved. This product, or parts thereof, may not be reproduced, stored in a retrieval system, or transmitted in any form or by any means—electronic, mechanical, photocopy, recording, scanning, or other—except for brief quotations in critical reviews or articles, without the prior written permission of the publisher.

Written and edited by the Matthew Bowling

Printed in the United States of America

This paper meets the requirements of ANSI/NISO Z39.48-1992 (Permanence of Paper).

Mometrix offers volume discount pricing to institutions. For more information or a price quote, please contact our sales department at sales@mometrix.com or 888-248-1219.

ACCUPLACER® is a trademark registered by the College Board, which is not affiliated with, and does not endorse, this product.

Paperback
ISBN 13: 978-1-5167-2899-2
ISBN 10: 1-5167-2899-8

# Dear Future Exam Success Story

First of all, **THANK YOU** for purchasing Mometrix study materials!

Second, congratulations! You are one of the few determined test-takers who are committed to doing whatever it takes to excel on your exam. **You have come to the right place.** We developed these study materials with one goal in mind: to deliver you the information you need in a format that's concise and easy to use.

In addition to optimizing your guide for the content of the test, we've outlined our recommended steps for breaking down the preparation process into small, attainable goals so you can make sure you stay on track.

We've also analyzed the entire test-taking process, identifying the most common pitfalls and showing how you can overcome them and be ready for any curveball the test throws you.

Standardized testing is one of the biggest obstacles on your road to success, which only increases the importance of doing well in the high-pressure, high-stakes environment of test day. Your results on this test could have a significant impact on your future, and this guide provides the information and practical advice to help you achieve your full potential on test day.

**Your success is our success**

**We would love to hear from you!** If you would like to share the story of your exam success or if you have any questions or comments in regard to our products, please contact us at **800-673-8175** or **support@mometrix.com**.

Thanks again for your business and we wish you continued success!

Sincerely,
The Mometrix Test Preparation Team

---

Need more help? Check out our flashcards at:
http://MometrixFlashcards.com/ACCUPLACER

# Table of Contents

**INTRODUCTION** — 1
    Review Video Directory — 1

**SECRET KEY #1 – PLAN BIG, STUDY SMALL** — 2

**SECRET KEY #2 – MAKE YOUR STUDYING COUNT** — 3

**SECRET KEY #3 – PRACTICE THE RIGHT WAY** — 4

**SECRET KEY #4 – HAVE A PLAN FOR GUESSING** — 5

**TEST-TAKING STRATEGIES** — 8

**SEVEN-WEEK ACCUPLACER STUDY PLAN** — 12
    Week 1: Reading — 13
    Week 2: Writing — 14
    Week 3: Arithmetic — 15
    Week 4: Quantitative Reasoning, Algebra, and Statistics — 16
    Week 5: Advanced Algebra and Functions — 18
    Week 6: Practice Tests #1–4 — 19
    Week 7: Practice Tests #5–8 — 20

**READING** — 21
    Information and Ideas — 21
    Rhetoric — 50
    Synthesis — 55
    Vocabulary — 56
    Chapter Quiz — 64

**WRITING** — 65
    Development — 65
    Organization — 69
    Effective Language Use — 75
    Sentence Structure — 79
    Conventions of Usage — 95
    Conventions of Punctuation — 108
    Chapter Quiz — 113

**ARITHMETIC** — 114
    Rounding and Estimation — 114
    Operations — 114
    Subtraction with Regrouping — 117
    Order of Operations — 118
    Properties of Operations — 118
    Fractions — 120
    Decimals — 123
    Percentages — 125
    Converting Between Percentages, Fractions, and Decimals — 126
    Number Lines — 127

    COMPARING NUMBERS ......... 128
    CHAPTER QUIZ ......... 128

## QUANTITATIVE REASONING, ALGEBRA, AND STATISTICS ......... 129

    ABSOLUTE VALUE ......... 129
    RATIONAL AND IRRATIONAL NUMBERS ......... 129
    PROPORTIONS AND RATIOS ......... 130
    CROSS MULTIPLICATION ......... 131
    SLOPE ......... 131
    METRIC AND CUSTOMARY MEASUREMENTS ......... 132
    PROPERTIES OF EXPONENTS ......... 134
    SCIENTIFIC NOTATION ......... 134
    LINEAR EXPRESSIONS ......... 135
    SOLVING EQUATIONS ......... 135
    LINEAR EQUATIONS ......... 140
    INEQUALITIES ......... 141
    SOLVING INEQUALITIES ......... 141
    GRAPHING INEQUALITIES ......... 143
    SYSTEMS OF EQUATIONS ......... 146
    GRAPHING EQUATIONS ......... 148
    PROBABILITY ......... 150
    TWO-WAY FREQUENCY TABLES ......... 153
    DATA ANALYSIS ......... 154
    MEASURES OF CENTRAL TENDENCY ......... 157
    DISPLAYING INFORMATION ......... 159
    SCATTER PLOTS ......... 165
    TRIANGLES ......... 166
    QUADRILATERALS ......... 168
    CIRCLES ......... 173
    3D SHAPES ......... 174
    MIDPOINT AND DISTANCE FORMULAS ......... 177
    TRANSFORMATIONS ......... 178
    PYTHAGOREAN THEOREM ......... 180
    CHAPTER QUIZ ......... 180

## ADVANCED ALGEBRA AND FUNCTIONS ......... 181

    QUADRATICS ......... 181
    ADVANCED SYSTEMS OF EQUATIONS ......... 183
    BASICS OF FUNCTIONS ......... 185
    COMMON FUNCTIONS ......... 189
    RATIONAL AND IRRATIONAL EXPRESSIONS ......... 196
    POLYNOMIALS ......... 198
    ADVANCED FUNCTIONS ......... 201
    CONGRUENCE AND SIMILARITY ......... 204
    TRIANGLE PROPERTIES ......... 205
    TRIGONOMETRIC FUNCTIONS ......... 207
    CIRCLE PROPERTIES ......... 210
    TRIGONOMETRIC FORMULAS ......... 213
    THE UNIT CIRCLE ......... 213
    TRIGONOMETRIC IDENTITIES ......... 215

| | |
|---|---|
| Domain, Range, and Asymptotes in Trigonometry | 217 |
| Chapter Quiz | 217 |

## Practice Test #1 — 218
- Reading Placement Test — 218
- Writing Placement Test — 224
- Arithmetic Placement Test — 230
- Quantitative Reasoning, Algebra, and Statistics Placement Test — 233
- Advanced Algebra and Functions Placement Test — 238

## Answer Key and Explanations for Test #1 — 244
- Reading Placement Test — 244
- Writing Placement Test — 245
- Arithmetic Placement Test — 248
- Quantitative Reasoning, Algebra, and Statistics Placement Test — 252
- Advanced Algebra and Functions Placement Test — 255

## Practice Test #2 — 260
- Reading Placement Test — 260
- Writing Placement Test — 266
- Arithmetic Placement Test — 273
- Quantitative Reasoning, Algebra, and Statistics Placement Test — 276
- Advanced Algebra and Functions Placement Test — 281

## Answer Key and Explanations for Test #2 — 287
- Reading Placement Test — 287
- Writing Placement Test — 288
- Arithmetic Placement Test — 291
- Quantitative Reasoning, Algebra, and Statistics Placement Test — 294
- Advanced Algebra and Functions Placement Test — 297

## Six Additional Practice Tests — 303

## How to Overcome Test Anxiety — 304

## Online Resources — 310

# Introduction

**Thank you for purchasing this resource**! You have made the choice to prepare yourself for a test that could have a huge impact on your future, and this guide is designed to help you be fully ready for test day. Obviously, it's important to have a solid understanding of the test material, but you also need to be prepared for the unique environment and stressors of the test, so that you can perform to the best of your abilities.

For this purpose, the first section that appears in this guide is the **Secret Keys**. We've devoted countless hours to meticulously researching what works and what doesn't, and we've boiled down our findings to the four most impactful steps you can take to improve your performance on the test. We start at the beginning with study planning and move through the preparation process, all the way to the testing strategies that will help you get the most out of what you know when you're finally sitting in front of the test.

We recommend that you start preparing for your test as far in advance as possible. However, if you've bought this guide as a last-minute study resource and only have a few days before your test, we recommend that you skip over the first two Secret Keys since they address a long-term study plan.

If you struggle with **test anxiety**, we strongly encourage you to check out our recommendations for how you can overcome it. Test anxiety is a formidable foe, but it can be beaten, and we want to make sure you have the tools you need to defeat it.

## Review Video Directory

As you work your way through this guide, you will see numerous review video links interspersed with the written content. If you would like to access all of these review videos in one place, click on the video directory link found on the online resources page: **mometrix.com/resources719/accuplacer**

# Secret Key #1 – Plan Big, Study Small

There's a lot riding on your performance. If you want to ace this test, you're going to need to keep your skills sharp and the material fresh in your mind. You need a plan that lets you review everything you need to know while still fitting in your schedule. We'll break this strategy down into three categories.

## Information Organization

Start with the information you already have: the official test outline. From this, you can make a complete list of all the concepts you need to cover before the test. Organize these concepts into groups that can be studied together, and create a list of any related vocabulary you need to learn so you can brush up on any difficult terms. You'll want to keep this vocabulary list handy once you actually start studying since you may need to add to it along the way.

## Time Management

Once you have your set of study concepts, decide how to spread them out over the time you have left before the test. Break your study plan into small, clear goals so you have a manageable task for each day and know exactly what you're doing. Then just focus on one small step at a time. When you manage your time this way, you don't need to spend hours at a time studying. Studying a small block of content for a short period each day helps you retain information better and avoid stressing over how much you have left to do. You can relax knowing that you have a plan to cover everything in time. In order for this strategy to be effective though, you have to start studying early and stick to your schedule. Avoid the exhaustion and futility that comes from last-minute cramming!

## Study Environment

The environment you study in has a big impact on your learning. Studying in a coffee shop, while probably more enjoyable, is not likely to be as fruitful as studying in a quiet room. It's important to keep distractions to a minimum. You're only planning to study for a short block of time, so make the most of it. Don't pause to check your phone or get up to find a snack. It's also important to **avoid multitasking**. Research has consistently shown that multitasking will make your studying dramatically less effective. Your study area should also be comfortable and well-lit so you don't have the distraction of straining your eyes or sitting on an uncomfortable chair.

The time of day you study is also important. You want to be rested and alert. Don't wait until just before bedtime. Study when you'll be most likely to comprehend and remember. Even better, if you know what time of day your test will be, set that time aside for study. That way your brain will be used to working on that subject at that specific time and you'll have a better chance of recalling information.

Finally, it can be helpful to team up with others who are studying for the same test. Your actual studying should be done in as isolated an environment as possible, but the work of organizing the information and setting up the study plan can be divided up. In between study sessions, you can discuss with your teammates the concepts that you're all studying and quiz each other on the details. Just be sure that your teammates are as serious about the test as you are. If you find that your study time is being replaced with social time, you might need to find a new team.

# Secret Key #2 – Make Your Studying Count

You're devoting a lot of time and effort to preparing for this test, so you want to be absolutely certain it will pay off. This means doing more than just reading the content and hoping you can remember it on test day. It's important to make every minute of study count. There are two main areas you can focus on to make your studying count.

## Retention

It doesn't matter how much time you study if you can't remember the material. You need to make sure you are retaining the concepts. To check your retention of the information you're learning, try recalling it at later times with minimal prompting. Try carrying around flashcards and glance at one or two from time to time or ask a friend who's also studying for the test to quiz you.

To enhance your retention, look for ways to put the information into practice so that you can apply it rather than simply recalling it. If you're using the information in practical ways, it will be much easier to remember. Similarly, it helps to solidify a concept in your mind if you're not only reading it to yourself but also explaining it to someone else. Ask a friend to let you teach them about a concept you're a little shaky on (or speak aloud to an imaginary audience if necessary). As you try to summarize, define, give examples, and answer your friend's questions, you'll understand the concepts better and they will stay with you longer. Finally, step back for a big picture view and ask yourself how each piece of information fits with the whole subject. When you link the different concepts together and see them working together as a whole, it's easier to remember the individual components.

Finally, practice showing your work on any multi-step problems, even if you're just studying. Writing out each step you take to solve a problem will help solidify the process in your mind, and you'll be more likely to remember it during the test.

## Modality

*Modality* simply refers to the means or method by which you study. Choosing a study modality that fits your own individual learning style is crucial. No two people learn best in exactly the same way, so it's important to know your strengths and use them to your advantage.

For example, if you learn best by visualization, focus on visualizing a concept in your mind and draw an image or a diagram. Try color-coding your notes, illustrating them, or creating symbols that will trigger your mind to recall a learned concept. If you learn best by hearing or discussing information, find a study partner who learns the same way or read aloud to yourself. Think about how to put the information in your own words. Imagine that you are giving a lecture on the topic and record yourself so you can listen to it later.

For any learning style, flashcards can be helpful. Organize the information so you can take advantage of spare moments to review. Underline key words or phrases. Use different colors for different categories. Mnemonic devices (such as creating a short list in which every item starts with the same letter) can also help with retention. Find what works best for you and use it to store the information in your mind most effectively and easily.

# Secret Key #3 – Practice the Right Way

Your success on test day depends not only on how many hours you put into preparing, but also on whether you prepared the right way. It's good to check along the way to see if your studying is paying off. One of the most effective ways to do this is by taking practice tests to evaluate your progress. Practice tests are useful because they show exactly where you need to improve. Every time you take a practice test, pay special attention to these three groups of questions:

- The questions you got wrong
- The questions you had to guess on, even if you guessed right
- The questions you found difficult or slow to work through

This will show you exactly what your weak areas are, and where you need to devote more study time. Ask yourself why each of these questions gave you trouble. Was it because you didn't understand the material? Was it because you didn't remember the vocabulary? Do you need more repetitions on this type of question to build speed and confidence? Dig into those questions and figure out how you can strengthen your weak areas as you go back to review the material.

Additionally, many practice tests have a section explaining the answer choices. It can be tempting to read the explanation and think that you now have a good understanding of the concept. However, an explanation likely only covers part of the question's broader context. Even if the explanation makes perfect sense, **go back and investigate** every concept related to the question until you're positive you have a thorough understanding.

As you go along, keep in mind that the practice test is just that: practice. Memorizing these questions and answers will not be very helpful on the actual test because it is unlikely to have any of the same exact questions. If you only know the right answers to the sample questions, you won't be prepared for the real thing. **Study the concepts** until you understand them fully, and then you'll be able to answer any question that shows up on the test.

It's important to wait on the practice tests until you're ready. If you take a test on your first day of study, you may be overwhelmed by the amount of material covered and how much you need to learn. Work up to it gradually.

On test day, you'll need to be prepared for answering questions, managing your time, and using the test-taking strategies you've learned. It's a lot to balance, like a mental marathon that will have a big impact on your future. Like training for a marathon, you'll need to start slowly and work your way up. When test day arrives, you'll be ready.

Start with the strategies you've read in the first two Secret Keys—plan your course and study in the way that works best for you. If you have time, consider using multiple study resources to get different approaches to the same concepts. It can be helpful to see difficult concepts from more than one angle. Then find a good source for practice tests. Many times, the test website will suggest potential study resources or provide sample tests.

# Secret Key #4 – Have a Plan for Guessing

When you're taking the test, you may find yourself stuck on a question. Some of the answer choices seem better than others, but you don't see the one answer choice that is obviously correct. What do you do?

The scenario described above is very common, yet most test takers have not effectively prepared for it. Developing and practicing a plan for guessing may be one of the single most effective uses of your time as you get ready for the exam.

In developing your plan for guessing, there are three questions to address:

- When should you start the guessing process?
- How should you narrow down the choices?
- Which answer should you choose?

## When to Start the Guessing Process

Unless your plan for guessing is to select C every time (which, despite its merits, is not what we recommend), you need to leave yourself enough time to apply your answer elimination strategies. Since you have a limited amount of time for each question, that means that if you're going to give yourself the best shot at guessing correctly, you have to decide quickly whether or not you will guess.

Of course, the best-case scenario is that you don't have to guess at all, so first, see if you can answer the question based on your knowledge of the subject and basic reasoning skills. Focus on the key words in the question and try to jog your memory of related topics. Give yourself a chance to bring the knowledge to mind, but once you realize that you don't have (or you can't access) the knowledge you need to answer the question, it's time to start the guessing process.

It's almost always better to start the guessing process too early than too late. It only takes a few seconds to remember something and answer the question from knowledge. Carefully eliminating wrong answer choices takes longer. Plus, going through the process of eliminating answer choices can actually help jog your memory.

**Summary**: Start the guessing process as soon as you decide that you can't answer the question based on your knowledge.

# How to Narrow Down the Choices

The next chapter in this book (**Test-Taking Strategies**) includes a wide range of strategies for how to approach questions and how to look for answer choices to eliminate. You will definitely want to read those carefully, practice them, and figure out which ones work best for you. Here though, we're going to address a mindset rather than a particular strategy.

Your odds of guessing an answer correctly depend on how many options you are choosing from.

| Number of options left | 5 | 4 | 3 | 2 | 1 |
|---|---|---|---|---|---|
| Odds of guessing correctly | 20% | 25% | 33% | 50% | 100% |

You can see from this chart just how valuable it is to be able to eliminate incorrect answers and make an educated guess, but there are two things that many test takers do that cause them to miss out on the benefits of guessing:

- Accidentally eliminating the correct answer
- Selecting an answer based on an impression

We'll look at the first one here, and the second one in the next section.

To avoid accidentally eliminating the correct answer, we recommend a thought exercise called **the $5 challenge**. In this challenge, you only eliminate an answer choice from contention if you are willing to bet $5 on it being wrong. Why $5? Five dollars is a small but not insignificant amount of money. It's an amount you could afford to lose but wouldn't want to throw away. And while losing $5 once might not hurt too much, doing it twenty times will set you back $100. In the same way, each small decision you make—eliminating a choice here, guessing on a question there—won't by itself impact your score very much, but when you put them all together, they can make a big difference. By holding each answer choice elimination decision to a higher standard, you can reduce the risk of accidentally eliminating the correct answer.

The $5 challenge can also be applied in a positive sense: If you are willing to bet $5 that an answer choice *is* correct, go ahead and mark it as correct.

**Summary**: Only eliminate an answer choice if you are willing to bet $5 that it is wrong.

# Which Answer to Choose

You're taking the test. You've run into a hard question and decided you'll have to guess. You've eliminated all the answer choices you're willing to bet $5 on. Now you have to pick an answer. Why do we even need to talk about this? Why can't you just pick whichever one you feel like when the time comes?

The answer to these questions is that if you don't come into the test with a plan, you'll rely on your impression to select an answer choice, and if you do that, you risk falling into a trap. The test writers know that everyone who takes their test will be guessing on some of the questions, so they intentionally write wrong answer choices to seem plausible. You still have to pick an answer though, and if the wrong answer choices are designed to look right, how can you ever be sure that you're not falling for their trap? The best solution we've found to this dilemma is to take the decision out of your hands entirely. Here is the process we recommend:

**Once you've eliminated any choices that you are confident (willing to bet $5) are wrong, select the first remaining choice as your answer.**

Whether you choose to select the first remaining choice, the second, or the last, the important thing is that you use some preselected standard. Using this approach guarantees that you will not be enticed into selecting an answer choice that looks right, because you are not basing your decision on how the answer choices look.

```
X.  This is wrong.
X.  Also wrong.
(C. Maybe?)
D.  Maybe?
```

This is not meant to make you question your knowledge. Instead, it is to help you recognize the difference between your knowledge and your impressions. There's a huge difference between thinking an answer is right because of what you know, and thinking an answer is right because it looks or sounds like it should be right.

**Summary**: To ensure that your selection is appropriately random, make a predetermined selection from among all answer choices you have not eliminated.

# Test-Taking Strategies

This section contains a list of test-taking strategies that you may find helpful as you work through the test. By taking what you know and applying logical thought, you can maximize your chances of answering any question correctly!

It is very important to realize that every question is different and every person is different: no single strategy will work on every question, and no single strategy will work for every person. That's why we've included all of them here, so you can try them out and determine which ones work best for different types of questions and which ones work best for you.

## Question Strategies

### ⊘ READ CAREFULLY

Read the question and the answer choices carefully. Don't miss the question because you misread the terms. You have plenty of time to read each question thoroughly and make sure you understand what is being asked. Yet a happy medium must be attained, so don't waste too much time. You must read carefully and efficiently.

### ⊘ CONTEXTUAL CLUES

Look for contextual clues. If the question includes a word you are not familiar with, look at the immediate context for some indication of what the word might mean. Contextual clues can often give you all the information you need to decipher the meaning of an unfamiliar word. Even if you can't determine the meaning, you may be able to narrow down the possibilities enough to make a solid guess at the answer to the question.

### ⊘ PREFIXES

If you're having trouble with a word in the question or answer choices, try dissecting it. Take advantage of every clue that the word might include. Prefixes can be a huge help. Usually, they allow you to determine a basic meaning. *Pre-* means before, *post-* means after, *pro-* is positive, *de-* is negative. From prefixes, you can get an idea of the general meaning of the word and try to put it into context.

### ⊘ HEDGE WORDS

Watch out for critical hedge words, such as *likely, may, can, often, almost, mostly, usually, generally, rarely,* and *sometimes*. Question writers insert these hedge phrases to cover every possibility. Often an answer choice will be wrong simply because it leaves no room for exception. Be on guard for answer choices that have definitive words such as *exactly* and *always*.

### ⊘ SWITCHBACK WORDS

Stay alert for *switchbacks*. These are the words and phrases frequently used to alert you to shifts in thought. The most common switchback words are *but, although,* and *however*. Others include *nevertheless, on the other hand, even though, while, in spite of, despite,* and *regardless of*. Switchback words are important to catch because they can change the direction of the question or an answer choice.

### ⊘ FACE VALUE

When in doubt, use common sense. Accept the situation in the problem at face value. Don't read too much into it. These problems will not require you to make wild assumptions. If you have to go beyond creativity and warp time or space in order to have an answer choice fit the question, then you should move on and consider the other answer choices. These are normal problems rooted in reality. The applicable relationship or explanation may not be readily apparent, but it is there for you to figure out. Use your common sense to interpret anything that isn't clear.

# Answer Choice Strategies

## ⊘ ANSWER SELECTION

The most thorough way to pick an answer choice is to identify and eliminate wrong answers until only one is left, then confirm it is the correct answer. Sometimes an answer choice may immediately seem right, but be careful. The test writers will usually put more than one reasonable answer choice on each question, so take a second to read all of them and make sure that the other choices are not equally obvious. As long as you have time left, it is better to read every answer choice than to pick the first one that looks right without checking the others.

## ⊘ ANSWER CHOICE FAMILIES

An answer choice family consists of two (in rare cases, three) answer choices that are very similar in construction and cannot all be true at the same time. If you see two answer choices that are direct opposites or parallels, one of them is usually the correct answer. For instance, if one answer choice says that quantity $x$ increases and another either says that quantity $x$ decreases (opposite) or says that quantity $y$ increases (parallel), then those answer choices would fall into the same family. An answer choice that doesn't match the construction of the answer choice family is more likely to be incorrect. Most questions will not have answer choice families, but when they do appear, you should be prepared to recognize them.

## ⊘ ELIMINATE ANSWERS

Eliminate answer choices as soon as you realize they are wrong, but make sure you consider all possibilities. If you are eliminating answer choices and realize that the last one you are left with is also wrong, don't panic. Start over and consider each choice again. There may be something you missed the first time that you will realize on the second pass.

## ⊘ AVOID FACT TRAPS

Don't be distracted by an answer choice that is factually true but doesn't answer the question. You are looking for the choice that answers the question. Stay focused on what the question is asking for so you don't accidentally pick an answer that is true but incorrect. Always go back to the question and make sure the answer choice you've selected actually answers the question and is not merely a true statement.

## ⊘ EXTREME STATEMENTS

In general, you should avoid answers that put forth extreme actions as standard practice or proclaim controversial ideas as established fact. An answer choice that states the "process should be used in certain situations, if…" is much more likely to be correct than one that states the "process should be discontinued completely." The first is a calm rational statement and doesn't even make a definitive, uncompromising stance, using a hedge word *if* to provide wiggle room, whereas the second choice is far more extreme.

## ⊘ BENCHMARK

As you read through the answer choices and you come across one that seems to answer the question well, mentally select that answer choice. This is not your final answer, but it's the one that will help you evaluate the other answer choices. The one that you selected is your benchmark or standard for judging each of the other answer choices. Every other answer choice must be compared to your benchmark. That choice is correct until proven otherwise by another answer choice beating it. If you find a better answer, then that one becomes your new benchmark. Once you've decided that no other choice answers the question as well as your benchmark, you have your final answer.

### ⊘ Predict the Answer

Before you even start looking at the answer choices, it is often best to try to predict the answer. When you come up with the answer on your own, it is easier to avoid distractions and traps because you will know exactly what to look for. The right answer choice is unlikely to be word-for-word what you came up with, but it should be a close match. Even if you are confident that you have the right answer, you should still take the time to read each option before moving on.

## General Strategies

### ⊘ Tough Questions

If you are stumped on a problem or it appears too hard or too difficult, don't waste time. Move on! Remember though, if you can quickly check for obviously incorrect answer choices, your chances of guessing correctly are greatly improved. Before you completely give up, at least try to knock out a couple of possible answers. Eliminate what you can and then guess at the remaining answer choices before moving on.

### ⊘ Check Your Work

Since you will probably not know every term listed and the answer to every question, it is important that you get credit for the ones that you do know. Don't miss any questions through careless mistakes. If at all possible, try to take a second to look back over your answer selection and make sure you've selected the correct answer choice and haven't made a costly careless mistake (such as marking an answer choice that you didn't mean to mark). This quick double check should more than pay for itself in caught mistakes for the time it costs.

### ⊘ Don't Rush

It is very easy to make errors when you are in a hurry. Maintaining a fast pace in answering questions is pointless if it makes you miss questions that you would have gotten right otherwise. Test writers like to include distracting information and wrong answers that seem right. Taking a little extra time to avoid careless mistakes can make all the difference in your test score. Find a pace that allows you to be confident in the answers that you select.

### ⊘ Keep Moving

Panicking will not help you pass the test, so do your best to stay calm and keep moving. Taking deep breaths and going through the answer elimination steps you practiced can help to break through a stress barrier and keep your pace.

## Final Notes

The combination of a solid foundation of content knowledge and the confidence that comes from practicing your plan for applying that knowledge is the key to maximizing your performance on test day. As your foundation of content knowledge is built up and strengthened, you'll find that the strategies included in this chapter become more and more effective in helping you quickly sift through the distractions and traps of the test to isolate the correct answer.

Now that you're preparing to move forward into the test content chapters of this book, be sure to keep your goal in mind. As you read, think about how you will be able to apply this information on the test. If you've already seen sample questions for the test and you have an idea of the question format and style, try to come up with questions of your own that you can answer based on what you're reading. This will give you valuable practice applying your knowledge in the same ways you can expect to on test day.

**Good luck and good studying!**

# Seven-Week ACCUPLACER Study Plan

On the next few pages, we've provided an optional study plan to help you use this study guide to its fullest potential over the course of 7 weeks. If you have 14 weeks available and want to spread it out more, spend two weeks on each section of the plan.

Below is a quick summary of the subjects covered in each week of the plan.

- Week 1: Reading
- Week 2: Writing
- Week 3: Arithmetic
- Week 4: Quantitative Reasoning, Algebra, and Statistics
- Week 5: Advanced Algebra and Functions
- Week 6: Practice Tests #1–4
- Week 7: Practice Tests #5–8

Please note that not all subjects will take the same amount of time to work through.

Each chapter is followed by a short chapter quiz. These quizzes are intended to help you check your knowledge of the material one chapter at a time, but they are not necessarily representative of the questions that you will encounter on the real test. We recommend taking each chapter quiz after reading through the chapter and reviewing any notes you made along the way.

Eight full-length practice tests are included in this study guide. Take these practice tests without any reference materials a day or two before the real thing as practice runs to get yourself in the mode of answering questions at a good pace.

# Week 1: Reading

## INSTRUCTIONAL CONTENT

First, read carefully through the **Reading** chapter in this book, checking off your progress as you go:

- ❏ Information and Ideas
- ❏ Rhetoric
- ❏ Synthesis
- ❏ Vocabulary

As you read, do the following:

- Highlight any sections, terms, or concepts you think are important
- Draw an asterisk (*) next to any areas you are struggling with
- Watch the review videos to gain more understanding of a particular topic
- Take notes in your notebook or in the margins of this book

After you've read through everything, go back and review any sections that you highlighted or that you drew an asterisk next to, referencing your notes along the way.

## CHAPTER QUIZ

Once you've studied the content, take the chapter quiz. Check your answers against the provided answer key. For any questions that you got wrong, review that section of the guide once more.

# Week 2: Writing

## INSTRUCTIONAL CONTENT

First, read carefully through the **Writing** chapter in this book, checking off your progress as you go:

- ❏ Development
- ❏ Organization
- ❏ Effective Language Use
- ❏ Sentence Structure
- ❏ Conventions of Usage
- ❏ Conventions of Punctuation

As you read, do the following:

- Highlight any sections, terms, or concepts you think are important
- Draw an asterisk (*) next to any areas you are struggling with
- Watch the review videos to gain more understanding of a particular topic
- Take notes in your notebook or in the margins of this book

After you've read through everything, go back and review any sections that you highlighted or that you drew an asterisk next to, referencing your notes along the way.

## CHAPTER QUIZ

Once you've studied the content, take the chapter quiz. Check your answers against the provided answer key. For any questions that you got wrong, review that section of the guide once more.

# Week 3: Arithmetic

## INSTRUCTIONAL CONTENT

First, read carefully through the **Arithmetic** chapter in this book, checking off your progress as you go:

- ❏ Rounding and Estimation
- ❏ Operations
- ❏ Subtraction with Regrouping
- ❏ Order of Operations
- ❏ Properties of Operations
- ❏ Fractions
- ❏ Decimals
- ❏ Percentages
- ❏ Converting Between Percentages, Fractions, and Decimals
- ❏ Number Lines
- ❏ Comparing Numbers

As you read, do the following:

- Highlight any sections, terms, or concepts you think are important
- Draw an asterisk (*) next to any areas you are struggling with
- Watch the review videos to gain more understanding of a particular topic
- Take notes in your notebook or in the margins of this book

After you've read through everything, go back and review any sections that you highlighted or that you drew an asterisk next to, referencing your notes along the way.

## CHAPTER QUIZ

Once you've studied the content, take the chapter quiz. Check your answers against the provided answer key. For any questions that you got wrong, review that section of the guide once more.

# Week 4: Quantitative Reasoning, Algebra, and Statistics

## INSTRUCTIONAL CONTENT

First, read carefully through the **Quantitative Reasoning, Algebra, and Statistics** chapter in this book, checking off your progress as you go:

- ❏ Absolute Value
- ❏ Rational and Irrational Numbers
- ❏ Proportions and Ratios
- ❏ Cross Multiplication
- ❏ Slope
- ❏ Metric and Customary Measurements
- ❏ Properties of Exponents
- ❏ Scientific Notation
- ❏ Linear Expressions
- ❏ Solving Equations
- ❏ Linear Equations
- ❏ Inequalities
- ❏ Solving Inequalities
- ❏ Graphing Inequalities
- ❏ Systems of Equations
- ❏ Graphing Equations
- ❏ Probability
- ❏ Two-Way Frequency Tables
- ❏ Data Analysis
- ❏ Measures of Central Tendency
- ❏ Displaying Information
- ❏ Scatter Plots
- ❏ Triangles
- ❏ Quadrilaterals
- ❏ Circles
- ❏ 3D Shapes
- ❏ Midpoint and Distance Formulas
- ❏ Transformations
- ❏ Pythagorean Theorem

As you read, do the following:

- Highlight any sections, terms, or concepts you think are important
- Draw an asterisk (*) next to any areas you are struggling with
- Watch the review videos to gain more understanding of a particular topic
- Take notes in your notebook or in the margins of this book

After you've read through everything, go back and review any sections that you highlighted or that you drew an asterisk next to, referencing your notes along the way.

## CHAPTER QUIZ

Once you've studied the content, take the chapter quiz. Check your answers against the provided answer key. For any questions that you got wrong, review that section of the guide once more.

# Week 5: Advanced Algebra and Functions

## INSTRUCTIONAL CONTENT

First, read carefully through the **Advanced Algebra and Functions** chapter in this book, checking off your progress as you go:

- ❏ Quadratics
- ❏ Advanced Systems of Equations
- ❏ Basics of Functions
- ❏ Common Functions
- ❏ Rational and Irrational Expressions
- ❏ Polynomials
- ❏ Advanced Functions
- ❏ Congruence and Similarity
- ❏ Triangle Properties
- ❏ Trigonometric Functions
- ❏ Circle Properties
- ❏ Trigonometric Formulas
- ❏ The Unit Circle
- ❏ Trigonometric Identities
- ❏ Domain, Range, and Asymptotes in Trigonometry

As you read, do the following:

- Highlight any sections, terms, or concepts you think are important
- Draw an asterisk (*) next to any areas you are struggling with
- Watch the review videos to gain more understanding of a particular topic
- Take notes in your notebook or in the margins of this book

After you've read through everything, go back and review any sections that you highlighted or that you drew an asterisk next to, referencing your notes along the way.

## CHAPTER QUIZ

Once you've studied the content, take the chapter quiz. Check your answers against the provided answer key. For any questions that you got wrong, review that section of the guide once more.

# Week 6: Practice Tests #1-4

Your success on test day depends not only on how many hours you put into preparing, but also on whether you prepared the right way. It's good to check to see if your studying is paying off. One of the most effective ways to do this is by taking practice tests to evaluate your progress. Practice tests are useful because they show exactly where you need to improve. Every time you take a practice test, pay special attention to these three groups of questions:

- The questions you got wrong
- The questions you had to guess on, even if you guessed right
- The questions you found difficult or slow to work through

This will show you exactly what your weak areas are, and where you need to devote more study time. Ask yourself why each of these questions gave you trouble. Was it because you didn't understand the material? Was it because you didn't remember the vocabulary? Do you need more repetitions on this type of question to build speed and confidence? Dig into those questions and figure out how you can strengthen your weak areas as you go back to review the material.

As you go along, keep in mind that the practice tests are just that: practice. Memorizing these questions and answers will not be very helpful on the actual test because it is unlikely to have any of the same exact questions. If you only know the right answers to the sample questions, you won't be prepared for the real thing. **Study the concepts** until you understand them fully, and then you'll be able to answer any question that shows up on the test.

## PRACTICE TESTS #1-4

The ACCUPLACER does not have a time limit; most people complete the English (Reading and Writing) section in about 45 minutes and the math sections in about 1 hour. You may not have to take both parts on the same day, but we recommend practicing to complete the entire test in one sitting. The goal for this week is to get used to switching topics without taking more than a short break between them.

## PRACTICE TEST #1

Complete one section of this practice test at a time. Feel free to reference the applicable sections of this guide as you go. Once you've finished each section, check your answers against the provided answer key. For any questions you answered incorrectly, review the answer rationale, and then **go back and review** the applicable sections of the book.

## PRACTICE TEST #2

Complete both English sections, again referencing the guide as you go. Check your answers and review the relevant content in the guide. Then, complete all of the math sections, again referencing the guide as you go along, checking your answers, and reviewing the content for any questions you got wrong.

## PRACTICE TESTS #3 AND #4

Complete each test in its entirety, referencing the guide as needed, before checking your answers and reviewing the content.

# Week 7: Practice Tests #5–8

The goal for this week is to get used to taking the entire ACCUPLACER in one sitting, without referencing the guide or your notes. Remember that you may be allowed to take breaks between sections, and you may be allowed to take different sections on different days. If so, feel free to take these practice tests using the same rules that will be in place when you take the real test.

## PRACTICE TEST #5

Complete one section of this practice test at a time. Once you've finished each section, check your answers against the provided answer key. For any questions you answered incorrectly, review the answer rationale, and then **go back and review** the applicable sections of the book.

## PRACTICE TEST #6

Complete both English sections. Check your answers and review the relevant content in the guide. Then, complete all of the math sections, check your answers, and review the content for any questions you got wrong.

## PRACTICE TESTS #7 AND #8

Finally, complete each test in its entirety before checking your answers and reviewing the content.

# Reading

Transform passive reading into active learning! After immersing yourself in this chapter, put your comprehension to the test by taking a quiz. The insights you gained will stay with you longer this way. Scan the QR code to go directly to the chapter quiz interface for this study guide. If you're using a computer, simply visit the online resources page at **mometrix.com/resources719/accuplacer-28992** and click the Chapter Quizzes link.

## Information and Ideas

### MAIN IDEAS AND SUPPORTING DETAILS
#### IDENTIFYING TOPICS AND MAIN IDEAS

One of the most important skills in reading comprehension is the identification of **topics** and **main ideas**. There is a subtle difference between these two features. The topic is the subject of a text (i.e., what the text is all about). The main idea, on the other hand, is the most important point being made by the author. The topic is usually expressed in a few words at the most while the main idea often needs a full sentence to be completely defined. As an example, a short passage might be written on the topic of penguins, and the main idea could be written as *Penguins are different from other birds in many ways*. In most nonfiction writing, the topic and the main idea will be **stated directly** and often appear in a sentence at the very beginning or end of the text. When being tested on an understanding of the author's topic, you may be able to skim the passage for the general idea by reading only the first sentence of each paragraph. A body paragraph's first sentence is often—but not always—the main **topic sentence** which gives you a summary of the content in the paragraph.

However, there are cases in which the reader must figure out an **unstated** topic or main idea. In these instances, you must read every sentence of the text and try to come up with an overarching idea that is supported by each of those sentences.

Note: The main idea should not be confused with the thesis statement. While the main idea gives a brief, general summary of a text, the thesis statement provides a **specific perspective** on an issue that the author supports with evidence.

> **Review Video: Topics and Main Ideas**
> Visit mometrix.com/academy and enter code: 407801

#### SUPPORTING DETAILS

**Supporting details** are smaller pieces of evidence that provide backing for the main point. In order to show that a main idea is correct or valid, an author must add details that prove their point. All texts contain details, but they are only classified as supporting details when they serve to reinforce some larger point. Supporting details are most commonly found in informative and persuasive texts. In some cases, they will be clearly indicated with terms like *for example* or *for instance*, or they will be enumerated with terms like *first*, *second*, and *last*. However, you need to be prepared for texts that do not contain those indicators. As a reader, you should consider whether the author's supporting details really back up his or her main point. Details can be factual and correct, yet they may not be **relevant** to the author's point. Conversely, details can be relevant, but be ineffective because they are based on opinion or assertions that cannot be proven.

> **Review Video: Supporting Details**
> Visit mometrix.com/academy and enter code: 396297

# AUTHOR'S PURPOSE
## AUTHOR'S PURPOSE

Usually, identifying the author's **purpose** is easier than identifying his or her **position**. In most cases, the author has no interest in hiding his or her purpose. A text that is meant to entertain, for instance, should be written to please the reader. Most narratives, or stories, are written to entertain, though they may also inform or persuade. Informative texts are easy to identify, while the most difficult purpose of a text to identify is persuasion because the author has an interest in making this purpose hard to detect. When a reader discovers that the author is trying to persuade, he or she should be skeptical of the argument. For this reason, persuasive texts often try to establish an entertaining tone and hope to amuse the reader into agreement. On the other hand, an informative tone may be implemented to create an appearance of authority and objectivity.

An author's purpose is evident often in the **organization** of the text (e.g., section headings in bold font points to an informative text). However, you may not have such organization available to you in your exam. Instead, if the author makes his or her main idea clear from the beginning, then the likely purpose of the text is to **inform**. If the author begins by making a claim and provides various arguments to support that claim, then the purpose is probably to **persuade**. If the author tells a story or wants to gain the reader's attention more than to push a particular point or deliver information, then his or her purpose is most likely to **entertain**. As a reader, you must judge authors on how well they accomplish their purpose. In other words, you need to consider the type of passage (e.g., technical, persuasive, etc.) that the author has written and if the author has followed the requirements of the passage type.

> **Review Video: Understanding the Author's Intent**
> Visit mometrix.com/academy and enter code: 511819

## INFORMATIONAL TEXTS

An **informational text** is written to educate and enlighten readers. Informational texts are almost always nonfiction and are rarely structured as a story. The intention of an informational text is to deliver information in the most comprehensible way. So, look for the structure of the text to be very clear. In an informational text, the thesis statement is one or two sentences that normally appears at the end of the first paragraph. The author may use some colorful language, but he or she is likely to put more emphasis on clarity and precision. Informational essays do not typically appeal to the emotions. They often contain facts and figures and rarely include the opinion of the author; however, readers should remain aware of the possibility for bias as those facts are presented. Sometimes a persuasive essay can resemble an informative essay, especially if the author maintains an even tone and presents his or her views as if they were established fact.

> **Review Video: Informational Text**
> Visit mometrix.com/academy and enter code: 924964

## PERSUASIVE WRITING

In a persuasive essay, the author is attempting to change the reader's mind or **convince** him or her of something that he or she did not believe previously. There are several identifying characteristics of **persuasive writing**. One is **opinion presented as fact**. When authors attempt to persuade readers, they often present their opinions as if they were fact. Readers must be on guard for statements that sound factual but which cannot be subjected to research, observation, or experiment. Another characteristic of persuasive writing is **emotional language**. An author will often try to play on the emotions of readers by appealing to their sympathy or sense of morality. When an author uses colorful or evocative language with the intent of arousing the reader's passions, then the author may be attempting to persuade. Finally, in many cases, a persuasive text will give an **unfair explanation of opposing positions**, if these positions are mentioned at all.

## ENTERTAINING TEXTS

The success or failure of an author's intent to **entertain** is determined by those who read the author's work. Entertaining texts may be either fiction or nonfiction, and they may describe real or imagined people, places, and events. Entertaining texts are often narratives or poems. A text that is written to entertain is likely to contain **colorful language** that engages the imagination and the emotions. Such writing often features a great deal of figurative language, which typically enlivens the subject matter with images and analogies.

Though an entertaining text is not usually written to persuade or inform, authors may accomplish both of these tasks in their work. An entertaining text may *appeal to the reader's emotions* and cause him or her to think differently about a particular subject. In any case, entertaining texts tend to showcase the personality of the author more than other types of writing.

## DESCRIPTIVE TEXT

In a sense, almost all writing is descriptive, insofar as an author seeks to describe events, ideas, or people to the reader. Some texts, however, are primarily concerned with **description**. A descriptive text focuses on a particular subject and attempts to depict the subject in a way that will be clear to readers. Descriptive texts contain many adjectives and adverbs (i.e., words that give shades of meaning and create a more detailed mental picture for the reader). A descriptive text fails when it is unclear to the reader. A descriptive text will certainly be informative and may be persuasive and entertaining as well.

> **Review Video: Descriptive Texts**
> Visit mometrix.com/academy and enter code: 174903

## EXPRESSION OF FEELINGS

When an author intends to **express feelings**, he or she may use **expressive and bold language**. An author may write with emotion for any number of reasons. Sometimes, authors will express feelings because they are describing a personal situation of great pain or happiness. In other situations, authors will attempt to persuade the reader and will use emotion to stir up the passions. This kind of expression is easy to identify when the writer uses phrases like *I felt* and *I sense*. However, readers may find that the author will simply describe feelings without introducing them. As a reader, you must know the importance of recognizing when an author is expressing emotion and not to become overwhelmed by sympathy or passion. Readers should maintain some **detachment** so that they can still evaluate the strength of the author's argument or the quality of the writing.

> **Review Video: Emotional Language in Literature**
> Visit mometrix.com/academy and enter code: 759390

## EXPOSITORY PASSAGE

An **expository** passage aims to **inform** and enlighten readers. Expository passages are nonfiction and usually center around a simple, easily defined topic. Since the goal of exposition is to teach, such a passage should be as clear as possible. Often, an expository passage contains helpful organizing words, like *first, next, for example,* and *therefore*. These words keep the reader **oriented** in the text. Although expository passages do not need to feature colorful language and artful writing, they are often more effective with these features. For a reader, the challenge of expository passages is to maintain steady attention. Expository passages are not always about subjects that will naturally interest a reader, so the writer is often more concerned with **clarity** and **comprehensibility** than with engaging the reader. By reading actively, you can ensure a good habit of focus when reading an expository passage.

> **Review Video: Expository Passages**
> Visit mometrix.com/academy and enter code: 256515

## NARRATIVE PASSAGE

A **narrative** passage is a story that can be fiction or nonfiction. However, there are a few elements that a text must have in order to be classified as a narrative. First, the text must have a **plot** (i.e., a series of events). Narratives often proceed in a clear sequence, but this is not a requirement. If the narrative is good, then these events will be interesting to readers. Second, a narrative has **characters**. These characters could be people, animals, or even inanimate objects—so long as they participate in the plot. Third, a narrative passage often contains **figurative language** which is meant to stimulate the imagination of readers by making comparisons and observations. For instance, a *metaphor*, a common piece of figurative language, is a description of one thing in terms of another. *The moon was a frosty snowball* is an example of a metaphor. In the literal sense this is obviously untrue, but the comparison suggests a certain mood for the reader.

## TECHNICAL PASSAGE

A **technical** passage is written to *describe* a complex object or process. Technical writing is common in medical and technological fields, in which complex ideas of mathematics, science, and engineering need to be explained *simply* and *clearly*. To ease comprehension, a technical passage usually proceeds in a very logical order. Technical passages often have clear headings and subheadings, which are used to keep the reader oriented in the text. Additionally, you will find that these passages divide sections up with numbers or letters. Many technical passages look more like an outline than a piece of prose. The amount of **jargon** or difficult vocabulary will vary in a technical passage depending on the intended audience. As much as possible, technical passages try to avoid language that the reader will have to research in order to understand the message, yet readers will find that jargon cannot always be avoided.

> **Review Video: Technical Passages**
> Visit mometrix.com/academy and enter code: 478923

# COMMON ORGANIZATIONS OF TEXTS
## ORGANIZATION OF THE TEXT

The way a text is organized can help readers understand the author's intent and his or her conclusions. There are various ways to organize a text, and each one has a purpose and use. Usually, authors will organize information logically in a passage so the reader can follow and locate the information within the text. However, since not all passages are written with the same logical structure, you need to be familiar with several different types of passage structure.

> **Review Video: Sequence of Events in a Story**
> Visit mometrix.com/academy and enter code: 807512

## CHRONOLOGICAL

When using **chronological** order, the author presents information in the order that it happened. For example, biographies are typically written in chronological order. The subject's birth and childhood are presented first, followed by their adult life, and lastly the events leading up to the person's death.

## CAUSE AND EFFECT

One of the most common text structures is **cause and effect**. A **cause** is an act or event that makes something happen, and an **effect** is the thing that happens as a result of the cause. A cause-and-effect relationship is not always explicit, but there are some terms in English that signal causes, such as *since, because*, and *due to*. Furthermore, terms that signal effects include *consequently, therefore, this leads to*. As an example, consider the sentence *Because the sky was clear, Ron did not bring an umbrella*. The cause is the clear sky, and the effect is that Ron did not bring an umbrella. However, readers may find that sometimes the cause-and-effect relationship will not be clearly noted. For instance, the sentence *He was late and missed the meeting* does not contain any signaling words, but the sentence still contains a cause (he was late) and an effect (he missed the meeting).

> **Review Video: Cause and Effect**
> Visit mometrix.com/academy and enter code: 868099

> **Review Video: Rhetorical Strategy of Cause and Effect Analysis**
> Visit mometrix.com/academy and enter code: 725944

## MULTIPLE EFFECTS

Be aware of the possibility for a single cause to have **multiple effects.** (e.g., *Single cause*: Because you left your homework on the table, your dog engulfed the assignment. *Multiple effects*: As a result, you receive a failing grade, your parents do not allow you to go out with your friends, you miss out on the new movie, and one of your classmates spoils it for you before you have another chance to watch it).

## MULTIPLE CAUSES

Also, there is the possibility for a single effect to have **multiple causes.** (e.g., *Single effect*: Alan has a fever. *Multiple causes*: An unexpected cold front came through the area, and Alan forgot to take his multi-vitamin to avoid getting sick.) Additionally, an effect can in turn be the cause of another effect, in what is known as a cause-and-effect chain. (e.g., As a result of her disdain for procrastination, Lynn prepared for her exam. This led to her passing her test with high marks. Hence, her resume was accepted and her application was approved.)

## CAUSE AND EFFECT IN PERSUASIVE ESSAYS

**Persuasive essays**, in which an author tries to make a convincing argument and change the minds of readers, usually include cause-and-effect relationships. However, these relationships should not always be taken at face value. Frequently, an author will assume a cause or take an effect for granted. To read a persuasive essay effectively, readers need to judge the cause-and-effect relationships that the author is presenting. For instance, imagine an author wrote the following: *The parking deck has been unprofitable because people would prefer to ride their bikes.* The relationship is clear: the cause is that people prefer to ride their bikes, and the effect is that the parking deck has been unprofitable. However, readers should consider whether this argument is conclusive. Perhaps there are other reasons for the failure of the parking deck: a down economy, excessive fees, etc. Too often, authors present causal relationships as if they are fact rather than opinion. Readers should be on the alert for these dubious claims.

## PROBLEM-SOLUTION

Some nonfiction texts are organized to **present a problem** followed by a solution. For this type of text, the problem is often explained before the solution is offered. In some cases, as when the problem is well known, the solution may be introduced briefly at the beginning. Other passages may focus on the solution, and the problem will be referenced only occasionally. Some texts will outline multiple solutions to a problem, leaving readers to choose among them. If the author has an interest or an allegiance to one solution, he or she may fail to mention or describe accurately some of the other solutions. Readers should be careful of the author's agenda when reading a problem-solution text. Only by understanding the author's perspective and interests can one develop a proper judgment of the proposed solution.

## COMPARE AND CONTRAST

Many texts follow the **compare-and-contrast** model in which the similarities and differences between two ideas or things are explored. Analysis of the similarities between ideas is called **comparison**. In an ideal comparison, the author places ideas or things in an equivalent structure, i.e., the author presents the ideas in the same way. If an author wants to show the similarities between cricket and baseball, then he or she may do so by summarizing the equipment and rules for each game. Be mindful of the similarities as they appear in the passage and take note of any differences that are mentioned. Often, these small differences will only reinforce the more general similarity.

> **Review Video: Compare and Contrast**
> Visit mometrix.com/academy and enter code: 798319

Thinking critically about ideas and conclusions can seem like a daunting task. One way to ease this task is to understand the basic elements of ideas and writing techniques. Looking at the ways different ideas relate to each other can be a good way for readers to begin their analysis. For instance, sometimes authors will write about two ideas that are in opposition to each other. Or, one author will provide his or her ideas on a topic, and another author may respond in opposition. The analysis of these opposing ideas is known as **contrast**. Contrast is often marred by the author's obvious partiality to one of the ideas. A discerning reader will be put off by an author who does not engage in a fair fight. In an analysis of opposing ideas, both ideas should be presented in clear and reasonable terms. If the author does prefer a side, you need to read carefully to determine the areas where the author shows or avoids this preference. In an analysis of opposing ideas, you should proceed through the passage by marking the major differences point by point with an eye that is looking for an explanation of each side's view. For instance, in an analysis of capitalism and communism, there is an importance in outlining each side's view on labor, markets, prices, personal responsibility, etc. Additionally, as you read through the passages, you should note whether the opposing views present each side in a similar manner.

## SEQUENCE

Readers must be able to identify a text's **sequence**, or the order in which things happen. Often, when the sequence is very important to the author, the text is indicated with signal words like *first, then, next*, and *last*. However, a sequence can be merely implied and must be noted by the reader. Consider the sentence *He walked through the garden and gave water and fertilizer to the plants*. Clearly, the man did not walk through the garden before he collected water and fertilizer for the plants. So, the implied sequence is that he first collected water, then he collected fertilizer, next he walked through the garden, and last he gave water or fertilizer as necessary to the plants. Texts do not always proceed in an orderly sequence from first to last. Sometimes they begin at the end and start over at the beginning. As a reader, you can enhance your understanding of the passage by taking brief notes to clarify the sequence.

> **Review Video: Sequence**
> Visit mometrix.com/academy and enter code: 489027

## MAKING AND EVALUATING PREDICTIONS
### MAKING PREDICTIONS

When we read literature, **making predictions** about what will happen in the writing reinforces our purpose for reading and prepares us mentally. A **prediction** is a guess about what will happen next. Readers constantly make predictions based on what they have read and what they already know. We can make predictions before we begin reading and during our reading. Consider the following sentence: *Staring at the computer screen in shock, Kim blindly reached over for the brimming glass of water on the shelf to her side.* The sentence suggests that Kim is distracted, and that she is not looking at the glass that she is going to pick up. So, a reader might predict that Kim is going to knock over the glass. Of course, not every prediction will be accurate: perhaps Kim will pick the glass up cleanly. Nevertheless, the author has certainly created the expectation that the water might be spilled.

As we read on, we can test the accuracy of our predictions, revise them in light of additional reading, and confirm or refute our predictions. Predictions are always subject to revision as the reader acquires more information. A reader can make predictions by observing the title and illustrations; noting the structure, characters, and subject; drawing on existing knowledge relative to the subject; and asking "why" and "who" questions. Connecting reading to what we already know enables us to learn new information and construct meaning. For example, before third-graders read a book about Johnny Appleseed, they may start a KWL chart—a list of what they *Know*, what they *Want* to know or learn, and what they have *Learned* after reading.

Activating existing background knowledge and thinking about the text before reading improves comprehension.

> **Review Video: Predictive Reading**
> Visit mometrix.com/academy and enter code: 437248

*Test-taking tip*: To respond to questions requiring future predictions, your answers should be based on evidence of past or present behavior and events.

## EVALUATING PREDICTIONS

When making predictions, readers should be able to explain how they developed their prediction. One way readers can defend their thought process is by citing textual evidence. Textual evidence to evaluate reader predictions about literature includes specific synopses of the work, paraphrases of the work or parts of it, and direct quotations from the work. These references to the text must support the prediction by indicating, clearly or unclearly, what will happen later in the story. A text may provide these indications through literary devices such as foreshadowing. Foreshadowing is anything in a text that gives the reader a hint about what is to come by emphasizing the likelihood of an event or development. Foreshadowing can occur through descriptions, exposition, and dialogue. Foreshadowing in dialogue usually occurs when a character gives a warning or expresses a strong feeling that a certain event will occur. Foreshadowing can also occur through irony. However, unlike other forms of foreshadowing, the events that seem the most likely are the opposite of what actually happens. Instances of foreshadowing and irony can be summarized, paraphrased, or quoted to defend a reader's prediction.

> **Review Video: Textual Evidence for Predictions**
> Visit mometrix.com/academy and enter code: 261070

## MAKING INFERENCES AND DRAWING CONCLUSIONS

**Inferences** are logical conclusions that readers make based on their observations and previous knowledge. An inference is based on both what is found in a passage or a story and what is known from personal experience. For instance, a story may say that a character is frightened and can hear howling in the distance. Based on both what is in the text and personal knowledge, it is a logical conclusion that the character is frightened because he hears the sound of wolves. A good inference is supported by the information in a passage.

### IMPLICIT AND EXPLICIT INFORMATION

By inferring, readers construct meanings from text that are personally relevant. By combining their own schemas or concepts and their background information pertinent to the text with what they read, readers interpret it according to both what the author has conveyed and their own unique perspectives. Inferences are different from **explicit information**, which is clearly stated in a passage. Authors do not always explicitly spell out every meaning in what they write; many meanings are implicit. Through inference, readers can comprehend implied meanings in the text, and also derive personal significance from it, making the text meaningful and memorable to them. Inference is a natural process in everyday life. When readers infer, they can draw conclusions about what the author is saying, predict what may reasonably follow, amend these predictions as they continue to read, interpret the import of themes, and analyze the characters' feelings and motivations through their actions.

### EXAMPLE OF DRAWING CONCLUSIONS FROM INFERENCES

*Read the excerpt and decide why Jana finally relaxed.*

> Jana loved her job, but the work was very demanding. She had trouble relaxing. She called a friend, but she still thought about work. She ordered a pizza, but eating it did not help. Then, her kitten jumped on her lap and began to purr. Jana leaned back and began to hum a little tune. She felt better.

You can draw the conclusion that Jana relaxed because her kitten jumped on her lap. The kitten purred, and Jana leaned back and hummed a tune. Then she felt better. The excerpt does not explicitly say that this is the reason why she was able to relax. The text leaves the matter unclear, but the reader can infer or make a "best guess" that this is the reason she is relaxing. This is a logical conclusion based on the information in the passage. It is the best conclusion a reader can make based on the information he or she has read. Inferences are based on the information in a passage, but they are not directly stated in the passage.

*Test-taking tip*: While being tested on your ability to make correct inferences, you must look for **contextual clues**. An answer can be true, but not the best or most correct answer. The contextual clues will help you find the answer that is the **best answer** out of the given choices. Be careful in your reading to understand the context in which a phrase is stated. When asked for the implied meaning of a statement made in the passage, you should immediately locate the statement and read the **context** in which the statement was made. Also, look for an answer choice that has a similar phrase to the statement in question.

> **Review Video: Inference**
> Visit mometrix.com/academy and enter code: 379203
>
> **Review Video: How to Support a Conclusion**
> Visit mometrix.com/academy and enter code: 281653

## READING COMPREHENSION AND CONNECTING WITH TEXTS
### COMPARING TWO STORIES

When presented with two different stories, there will be **similarities** and **differences** between the two. A reader needs to make a list, or other graphic organizer, of the points presented in each story. Once the reader has written down the main point and supporting points for each story, the two sets of ideas can be compared. The reader can then present each idea and show how it is the same or different in the other story. This is called **comparing and contrasting ideas**.

The reader can compare ideas by stating, for example: "In Story 1, the author believes that humankind will one day land on Mars, whereas in Story 2, the author believes that Mars is too far away for humans to ever step foot on." Note that the two viewpoints are different in each story that the reader is comparing. A reader may state that: "Both stories discussed the likelihood of humankind landing on Mars." This statement shows how the viewpoint presented in both stories is based on the same topic, rather than how each viewpoint is different. The reader will complete a comparison of two stories with a conclusion.

> **Review Video: How to Compare and Contrast**
> Visit mometrix.com/academy and enter code: 833765

### OUTLINING A PASSAGE

As an aid to drawing conclusions, **outlining** the information contained in the passage should be a familiar skill to readers. An effective outline will reveal the structure of the passage and will lead to solid conclusions. An effective outline will have a title that refers to the basic subject of the text, though the title does not need to restate the main idea. In most outlines, the main idea will be the first major section. Each major idea in the passage will be established as the head of a category. For instance, the most common outline format calls for the main ideas of the passage to be indicated with Roman numerals. In an effective outline of this kind, each of the main ideas will be represented by a Roman numeral and none of the Roman numerals will designate minor details or secondary ideas. Moreover, all supporting ideas and details should be placed in the appropriate place on the outline. An outline does not need to include every detail listed in the text, but it should feature all of those that are central to the argument or message. Each of these details should be listed under the corresponding main idea.

> **Review Video: Outlining as an Aid to Drawing Conclusions**
> Visit mometrix.com/academy and enter code: 584445

## USING GRAPHIC ORGANIZERS

Ideas from a text can also be organized using **graphic organizers**. A graphic organizer is a way to simplify information and take key points from the text. A graphic organizer such as a timeline may have an event listed for a corresponding date on the timeline, while an outline may have an event listed under a key point that occurs in the text. Each reader needs to create the type of graphic organizer that works the best for him or her in terms of being able to recall information from a story. Examples include a spider-map, which takes a main idea from the story and places it in a bubble with supporting points branching off the main idea. An outline is useful for diagramming the main and supporting points of the entire story, and a Venn diagram compares and contrasts characteristics of two or more ideas.

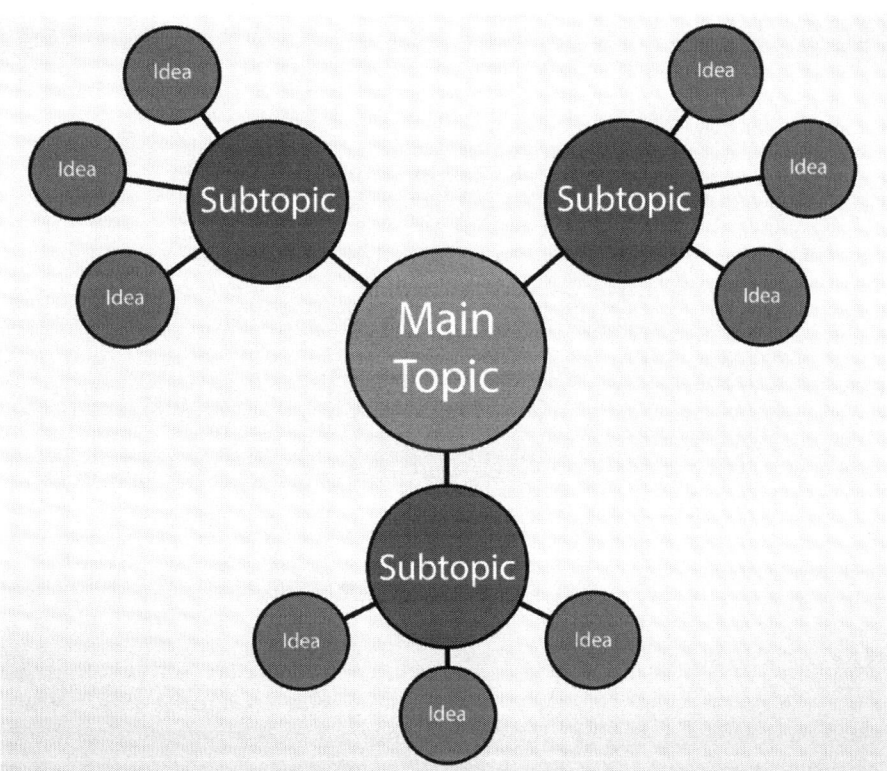

> **Review Video: Graphic Organizers**
> Visit mometrix.com/academy and enter code: 665513

## MAKING LOGICAL CONCLUSIONS ABOUT A PASSAGE

A reader should always be drawing conclusions from the text. Sometimes conclusions are **implied** from written information, and other times the information is **stated directly** within the passage. One should always aim to draw conclusions from information stated within a passage, rather than to draw them from mere implications. At times an author may provide some information and then describe a counterargument. Readers should be alert for direct statements that are subsequently rejected or weakened by the author. Furthermore, you should always read through the entire passage before drawing conclusions. Many readers are trained to expect the author's conclusions at either the beginning or the end of the passage, but many texts do not adhere to this format.

Drawing conclusions from information implied within a passage requires confidence on the part of the reader. **Implications** are things that the author does not state directly, but readers can assume based on what the author does say. Consider the following passage: *I stepped outside and opened my umbrella. By the time I got to work, the cuffs of my pants were soaked.* The author never states that it is raining, but this fact is clearly implied. Conclusions based on implication must be well supported by the text. In order to draw a solid conclusion, readers should have **multiple pieces of evidence**. If readers have only one piece, they must be assured that there is no other possible explanation than their conclusion. A good reader will be able to draw many conclusions from information implied by the text, which will be a great help on the exam.

## *Drawing Conclusions*

A common type of inference that a reader has to make is **drawing a conclusion**. The reader makes this conclusion based on the information provided within a text. Certain facts are included to help a reader come to a specific conclusion. For example, a story may open with a man trudging through the snow on a cold winter day, dragging a sled behind him. The reader can logically **infer** from the setting of the story that the man is wearing heavy winter clothes in order to stay warm. Information is implied based on the setting of a story, which is why **setting** is an important element of the text. If the same man in the example was trudging down a beach on a hot summer day, dragging a surf board behind him, the reader would assume that the man is not wearing heavy clothes. The reader makes inferences based on their own experiences and the information presented to them in the story.

*Test-taking tip*: When asked to identify a conclusion that may be drawn, look for critical "hedge" phrases, such as *likely*, *may*, *can*, and *will often*, among many others. When you are being tested on this knowledge, remember the question that writers insert into these hedge phrases to cover every possibility. Often an answer will be wrong simply because there is no room for exception. Extreme positive or negative answers (such as always or never) are usually not correct. When answering these questions, the reader **should not** use any outside knowledge that is not gathered directly or reasonably inferred from the passage. Correct answers can be derived straight from the passage.

## *Example*

Read the following sentence from *Little Women* by Louisa May Alcott and draw a conclusion based upon the information presented:

> *You know the reason Mother proposed not having any presents this Christmas was because it is going to be a hard winter for everyone; and she thinks we ought not to spend money for pleasure, when our men are suffering so in the army.*

Based on the information in the sentence, the reader can conclude, or **infer**, that the men are away at war while the women are still at home. The pronoun *our* gives a clue to the reader that the character is speaking about men she knows. In addition, the reader can assume that the character is speaking to a brother or sister, since the term "Mother" is used by the character while speaking to another person. The reader can also come to the conclusion that the characters celebrate Christmas, since it is mentioned in the **context** of the sentence. In the sentence, the mother is presented as an unselfish character who is opinionated and thinks about the wellbeing of other people.

## *Summarizing*

A helpful tool is the ability to **summarize** the information that you have read in a paragraph or passage format. This process is similar to creating an effective outline. First, a summary should accurately define the main idea of the passage, though the summary does not need to explain this main idea in exhaustive detail. The summary should continue by laying out the most important supporting details or arguments from the passage. All of the significant supporting details should be included, and none of the details included should be irrelevant or insignificant. Also, the summary should accurately report all of these details. Too often, the desire for brevity in a summary leads to the sacrifice of clarity or accuracy. Summaries are often difficult to read because they omit

all of the graceful language, digressions, and asides that distinguish great writing. However, an effective summary should communicate the same overall message as the original text.

> **Review Video: Summarizing Text**
> Visit mometrix.com/academy and enter code: 172903

## PARAPHRASING

**Paraphrasing** is another method that the reader can use to aid in comprehension. When paraphrasing, one puts what they have read into their own words by rephrasing what the author has written, or one "translates" all of what the author shared into their own words by including as many details as they can.

## EVALUATING A PASSAGE

It is important to understand the logical conclusion of the ideas presented in an informational text. **Identifying a logical conclusion** can help you determine whether you agree with the writer or not. Coming to this conclusion is much like making an inference: the approach requires you to combine the information given by the text with what you already know and make a logical conclusion. If the author intended for the reader to draw a certain conclusion, then you can expect the author's argumentation and detail to be leading in that direction.

One way to approach the task of drawing conclusions is to make brief **notes** of all the points made by the author. When the notes are arranged on paper, they may clarify the logical conclusion. Another way to approach conclusions is to consider whether the reasoning of the author raises any pertinent questions. Sometimes you will be able to draw several conclusions from a passage. On occasion these will be conclusions that were never imagined by the author. Therefore, be aware that these conclusions must be **supported directly by the text**.

## EVALUATION OF SUMMARIES

A summary of a literary passage is a condensation in the reader's own words of the passage's main points. Several guidelines can be used in evaluating a summary. The summary should be complete yet concise. It should be accurate, balanced, fair, neutral, and objective, excluding the reader's own opinions or reactions. It should reflect in similar proportion how much each point summarized was covered in the original passage. Summary writers should include tags of attribution, like "Macaulay argues that" to reference the original author whose ideas are represented in the summary. Summary writers should not overuse quotations; they should only quote central concepts or phrases they cannot precisely convey in words other than those of the original author. Another aspect of evaluating a summary is considering whether it can stand alone as a coherent, unified composition. In addition, evaluation of a summary should include whether its writer has cited the original source of the passage they have summarized so that readers can find it.

## MAKING CONNECTIONS TO ENHANCE COMPREHENSION

Reading involves thinking. For good comprehension, readers make **text-to-self**, **text-to-text**, and **text-to-world connections**. Making connections helps readers understand text better and predict what might occur next based on what they already know, such as how characters in the story feel or what happened in another text. Text-to-self connections with the reader's life and experiences make literature more personally relevant and meaningful to readers. Readers can make connections before, during, and after reading—including whenever the text reminds them of something similar they have encountered in life or other texts. The genre, setting, characters, plot elements, literary structure and devices, and themes an author uses allow a reader to make connections to other works of literature or to people and events in their own lives. Venn diagrams and other graphic organizers help visualize connections. Readers can also make double-entry notes: key content, ideas, events, words, and quotations on one side, and the connections with these on the other.

# Reading Informational Texts

## Language Use

### Literal and Figurative Language

As in fictional literature, informational text also uses both **literal language**, which means just what it says, and **figurative language**, which imparts more than literal meaning. For example, an informational text author might use a simile or direct comparison, such as writing that a racehorse "ran like the wind." Informational text authors also use metaphors or implied comparisons, such as "the cloud of the Great Depression." Imagery may also appear in informational texts to increase the reader's understanding of ideas and concepts discussed in the text.

> **Review Video: Figurative Language**
> Visit mometrix.com/academy and enter code: 584902

### Explicit and Implicit Information

When informational text states something explicitly, the reader is told by the author exactly what is meant, which can include the author's interpretation or perspective of events. For example, a professor writes, "I have seen students go into an absolute panic just because they weren't able to complete the exam in the time they were allotted." This explicitly tells the reader that the students were afraid, and by using the words "just because," the writer indicates their fear was exaggerated out of proportion relative to what happened. However, another professor writes, "I have had students come to me, their faces drained of all color, saying 'We weren't able to finish the exam.'" This is an example of implicit meaning: the second writer did not state explicitly that the students were panicked. Instead, he wrote a description of their faces being "drained of all color." From this description, the reader can infer that the students were so frightened that their faces paled.

> **Review Video: Explicit and Implicit Information**
> Visit mometrix.com/academy and enter code: 735771

### Making Inferences About Informational Text

With informational text, reader comprehension depends not only on recalling important statements and details, but also on reader inferences based on examples and details. Readers add information from the text to what they already know to draw inferences about the text. These inferences help the readers to fill in the information that the text does not explicitly state, enabling them to understand the text better. When reading a nonfictional autobiography or biography, for example, the most appropriate inferences might concern the events in the book, the actions of the subject of the autobiography or biography, and the message the author means to convey. When reading a nonfictional expository (informational) text, the reader would best draw inferences about problems and their solutions, and causes and their effects. When reading a nonfictional persuasive text, the reader will want to infer ideas supporting the author's message and intent.

### Structures or Organizational Patterns in Informational Texts

Informational text can be **descriptive**, appealing to the five senses and answering the questions what, who, when, where, and why. Another method of structuring informational text is sequence and order. **Chronological** texts relate events in the sequence that they occurred, from start to finish, while how-to texts organize information into a series of instructions in the sequence in which the steps should be followed. **Comparison-contrast** structures of informational text describe various ideas to their readers by pointing out how things or ideas are similar and how they are different. **Cause and effect** structures of informational text describe events that occurred and identify the causes or reasons that those events occurred. **Problem and solution** structures of informational texts introduce and describe problems and offer one or more solutions for each problem described.

## Determining an Informational Author's Purpose

Informational authors' purposes are why they write texts. Readers must determine authors' motivations and goals. Readers gain greater insight into a text by considering the author's motivation. This develops critical reading skills. Readers perceive writing as a person's voice, not simply printed words. Uncovering author motivations and purposes empowers readers to know what to expect from the text, read for relevant details, evaluate authors and their work critically, and respond effectively to the motivations and persuasions of the text. The main idea of a text is what the reader is supposed to understand from reading it; the purpose of the text is why the author has written it and what the author wants readers to do with its information. Authors state some purposes clearly, while other purposes may be unstated but equally significant. When stated purposes contradict other parts of a text, the author may have a hidden agenda. Readers can better evaluate a text's effectiveness, whether they agree or disagree with it, and why they agree or disagree through identifying unstated author purposes.

## Identifying Author's Point of View or Purpose

In some informational texts, readers find it easy to identify the author's point of view and purpose, such as when the author explicitly states his or her position and reason for writing. But other texts are more difficult, either because of the content or because the authors give neutral or balanced viewpoints. This is particularly true in scientific texts, in which authors may state the purpose of their research in the report, but never state their point of view except by interpreting evidence or data.

To analyze text and identify point of view or purpose, readers should ask themselves the following four questions:

1. With what main point or idea does this author want to persuade readers to agree?
2. How does this author's word choice affect the way that readers consider this subject?
3. How do this author's choices of examples and facts affect the way that readers consider this subject?
4. What is it that this author wants to accomplish by writing this text?

> **Review Video: Understanding the Author's Intent**
> Visit mometrix.com/academy and enter code: 511819
>
> **Review Video: Author's Position**
> Visit mometrix.com/academy and enter code: 827954

## Evaluating Arguments Made by Informational Text Writers

When evaluating an informational text, the first step is to identify the argument's conclusion. Then identify the author's premises that support the conclusion. Try to paraphrase premises for clarification and make the conclusion and premises fit. List all premises first, sequentially numbered, then finish with the conclusion. Identify any premises or assumptions not stated by the author but required for the stated premises to support the conclusion. Read word assumptions sympathetically, as the author might. Evaluate whether premises reasonably support the conclusion. For inductive reasoning, the reader should ask if the premises are true, if they support the conclusion, and if so, how strongly. For deductive reasoning, the reader should ask if the argument is valid or invalid. If all premises are true, then the argument is valid unless the conclusion can be false. If it can, then the argument is invalid. An invalid argument can be made valid through alterations such as the addition of needed premises.

## Use of Rhetoric in Informational Texts

There are many ways authors can support their claims, arguments, beliefs, ideas, and reasons for writing in informational texts. For example, authors can appeal to readers' sense of **logic** by communicating their reasoning through a carefully sequenced series of logical steps to help "prove" the points made. Authors can appeal to readers' **emotions** by using descriptions and words that evoke feelings of sympathy, sadness, anger, righteous indignation, hope, happiness, or any other emotion to reinforce what they express and share with their audience. Authors may appeal to the **moral** or **ethical values** of readers by using words and descriptions that can convince readers that something is right or wrong. By relating personal anecdotes, authors can supply readers with more accessible, realistic examples of points they make, as well as appealing to their emotions. They can provide supporting evidence by reporting case studies. They can also illustrate their points by making analogies to which readers can better relate.

## ORGANIZATIONAL FEATURES IN TEXTS
### TEXT FEATURES IN INFORMATIONAL TEXTS

- The **title of a text** gives readers some idea of its content.
- The **table of contents** is a list near the beginning of a text, showing the book's sections and chapters and their coinciding page numbers. This gives readers an overview of the whole text and helps them find specific chapters easily.
- An **appendix**, at the back of the book or document, includes important information that is not present in the main text.
- Also at the back, an **index** lists the book's important topics alphabetically with their page numbers to help readers find them easily.
- **Glossaries**, usually found at the backs of books, list technical terms alphabetically with their definitions to aid vocabulary learning and comprehension. Boldface print is used to emphasize certain words, often identifying words included in the text's glossary where readers can look up their definitions.
- **Headings** separate sections of text and show the topic of each.
- **Subheadings** divide subject headings into smaller, more specific categories to help readers organize information.
- **Footnotes**, at the bottom of the page, give readers more information, such as citations or links.
- **Bullet points** list items separately, making facts and ideas easier to see and understand.
- A **sidebar** is a box of information to one side of the main text giving additional information, often on a more focused or in-depth example of a topic.

### VISUAL FEATURES IN TEXTS

- **Illustrations** and **photographs** are pictures that visually emphasize important points in text.
- The **captions** below the illustrations explain what those images show.
- **Charts** and **tables** are visual forms of information that make something easier to understand quickly.
- **Diagrams** are drawings that show relationships or explain a process.
- **Graphs** visually show the relationships among multiple sets of information plotted along vertical and horizontal axes.
- **Maps** show geographical information visually to help readers understand the relative locations of places covered in the text.
- **Timelines** are visual graphics that show historical events in chronological order to help readers see their sequence.

> **Review Video: Informational Text**
> Visit mometrix.com/academy and enter code: 924964

# Technical Language

## Technical Language

Technical language is more impersonal than literary and vernacular language. Passive voice makes the tone impersonal. For example, instead of writing, "We found this a central component of protein metabolism," scientists write, "This was found a central component of protein metabolism." While science professors have traditionally instructed students to avoid active voice because it leads to first-person ("I" and "we") usage, science editors today find passive voice dull and weak. Many journal articles combine both. Tone in technical science writing should be detached, concise, and professional. While one may normally write, "This chemical has to be available for proteins to be digested," professionals write technically, "The presence of this chemical is required for the enzyme to break the covalent bonds of proteins." The use of technical language appeals to both technical and non-technical audiences by displaying the author or speaker's understanding of the subject and suggesting their credibility regarding the message they are communicating.

## Technical Material for Non-Technical Readers

Writing about **technical subjects** for **non-technical readers** differs from writing for colleagues because authors place more importance on delivering a critical message than on imparting the maximum technical content possible. Technical authors also must assume that non-technical audiences do not have the expertise to comprehend extremely scientific or technical messages, concepts, and terminology. They must resist the temptation to impress audiences with their scientific knowledge and expertise and remember that their primary purpose is to communicate a message that non-technical readers will understand, feel, and respond to. Non-technical and technical styles include similarities. Both should formally cite any references or other authors' work utilized in the text. Both must follow intellectual property and copyright regulations. This includes the author's protecting his or her own rights, or a public domain statement, as he or she chooses.

> **Review Video: Technical Passages**
> Visit mometrix.com/academy and enter code: 478923

## Non-Technical Audiences

Writers of technical or scientific material may need to write for many non-technical audiences. Some readers have no technical or scientific background, and those who do may not be in the same field as the authors. Government and corporate policymakers and budget managers need technical information they can understand for decision-making. Citizens affected by technology or science are a different audience. Non-governmental organizations can encompass many of the preceding groups. Elementary and secondary school programs also need non-technical language for presenting technical subject matter. Additionally, technical authors will need to use non-technical language when collecting consumer responses to surveys, presenting scientific or para-scientific material to the public, writing about the history of science, and writing about science and technology in developing countries.

## Use of Everyday Language

Authors of technical information sometimes must write using non-technical language that readers outside their disciplinary fields can comprehend. They should use not only non-technical terms, but also normal, everyday language to accommodate readers whose native language is different than the language the text is written in. For example, instead of writing that "eustatic changes like thermal expansion are causing hazardous conditions in the littoral zone," an author would do better to write that "a rising sea level is threatening the coast." When technical terms cannot be avoided, authors should also define or explain them using non-technical language. Although authors must cite references and acknowledge their use of others' work, they should avoid the kinds of references or citations that they would use in scientific journals—unless they reinforce author messages. They should not use endnotes, footnotes, or any other complicated referential techniques because non-technical journal publishers usually do not accept them. Including high-resolution illustrations, photos, maps, or satellite images and incorporating multimedia into digital publications will enhance non-technical writing about technical subjects. Technical authors may publish using non-technical language in e-journals, trade journals, specialty newsletters, and daily newspapers.

# Types of Technical Writing

## Types of Printed Communication

### Memo

A memo (short for *memorandum*) is a common form of written communication. There is a standard format for these documents. It is typical for there to be a **heading** at the top indicating the author, date, and recipient. In some cases, this heading will also include the author's title and the name of his or her institution. Below this information will be the **body** of the memo. These documents are typically written by and for members of the same organization. They usually contain a plan of action, a request for information on a specific topic, or a response to such a request. Memos are considered to be official documents, so they are usually written in a **formal** style. Many memos are organized with numbers or bullet points, which make it easier for the reader to identify key ideas.

### Posted Announcement

People post **announcements** for all sorts of occasions. Many people are familiar with notices for lost pets, yard sales, and landscaping services. In order to be effective, these announcements need to *contain all of the information* the reader requires to act on the message. For instance, a lost pet announcement needs to include a good description of the animal and a contact number for the owner. A yard sale notice should include the address, date, and hours of the sale, as well as a brief description of the products that will be available there. When composing an announcement, it is important to consider the perspective of the **audience**—what will they need to know in order to respond to the message? Although a posted announcement can have color and decoration to attract the eye of the passerby, it must also convey the necessary information clearly.

### Classified Advertisement

Classified advertisements, or **ads**, are used to sell or buy goods, to attract business, to make romantic connections, and to do countless other things. They are an inexpensive, and sometimes free, way to make a brief **pitch**. Classified ads used to be found only in newspapers or special advertising circulars, but there are now online listings as well. The style of these ads has remained basically the same. An ad usually begins with a word or phrase indicating what is being **sold** or **sought**. Then, the listing will give a brief **description** of the product or service. Because space is limited and costly in newspapers, classified ads there will often contain abbreviations for common attributes. For instance, two common abbreviations are *bk* for *black*, and *obo* for *or best offer*. Classified ads will then usually conclude by listing the **price** (or the amount the seeker is willing to pay), followed by **contact information** like a telephone number or email address.

### Scale Readings of Standard Measurement Instruments

The scales used on **standard measurement instruments** are fairly easy to read with a little practice. Take the **ruler** as an example. A typical ruler has different units along each long edge. One side measures inches, and the other measures centimeters. The units are specified close to the zero reading for the ruler. Note that the ruler does not begin measuring from its outermost edge. The zero reading is a black line a tiny distance inside of the edge. On the inches side, each inch is indicated with a long black line and a number. Each half-inch is noted with a slightly shorter line. Quarter-inches are noted with still shorter lines, eighth-inches are noted with even shorter lines, and sixteenth-inches are noted with the shortest lines of all. On the centimeter side, the second-largest black lines indicate half-centimeters, and the smaller lines indicate tenths of centimeters, otherwise known as millimeters.

## Visual Information in Informational Texts

### Charts, Graphs, and Visuals

#### Tables

Tables are presented in a standard format so they will be easy to read and understand. A title is at the top, a short phrase indicating the information the table or graph intends to convey. The title of a table could be something like "Median Income for Various Education Levels" or "Price of Milk Compared to Demand." A table is composed of information laid out in vertical columns and horizontal rows. Typically, each column will have a label. If "Median Income for Various Education Levels" was placed in a table format, the two columns could be labeled "Education Level" and "Median Annual Salary." Each location on the table is called a cell, which holds a piece of information. Cells are defined by their column and row (e.g., second column, fifth row).

**Median Annual Salary for Various Education Levels**

| Education Level | Median Annual Salary |
|---|---|
| Associate degree | $52,260 |
| Bachelor's degree | $74,464 |
| Master's degree | $86,372 |
| Professional degree | $108,160 |
| Doctoral degree | $108,316 |

## GRAPHS

Like a table, a graph typically has a title at the top. This title may simply state the identities of the two axes: e.g., "Income vs. Education." However, the title may also be something more descriptive, like "A comparison of average income with level of education." In any case, bar and line graphs are laid out along two perpendicular lines, or axes. The vertical axis is called the *y*-axis, and the horizontal axis is called the *x*-axis. It is typical for the *x*-axis to be the independent variable and the *y*-axis to be the dependent variable. The independent variable is the one manipulated by the researcher or creator of the graph. In the above example, the independent variable would be "education level," since the maker of the graph will define these values (associate degree, bachelor's degree, master's degree, etc.). The dependent value is not controlled by the researcher.

When selecting a graph format, it is important to consider the intention and the structure of the presentation. A bar graph is appropriate for displaying the relations between a series of distinct quantities that are on the same scale. For instance, if one wanted to display the amount of money spent on groceries during the months of a year, a bar graph would be appropriate. The vertical axis would represent values of money, and the horizontal axis would identify each month. A line graph also requires data expressed in common units, but it is better for demonstrating the general trend in that data. If the grocery expenses were plotted on a line graph instead of a bar graph, there would be more emphasis on whether the amount of money spent rose or fell over the course of the year. Whereas a bar graph is good for showing the relationships between the different values plotted, the line graph is good for showing whether the values tended to increase, decrease, or remain stable.

## PIE CHART

A pie chart, also known as a circle graph, is useful for depicting how a single unit or category is divided. The standard pie chart is a circle with designated wedges. Each wedge is **proportional** in size to a part of the whole. For instance, consider Shawna, a student at City College, who uses a pie chart to represent her budget. If she spends half of her money on rent, then the pie chart will represent that amount with a line through the center of the pie. If she spends a quarter of her money on food, there will be a line extending from the edge of the circle to the center at a right angle to the line depicting rent. This illustration would make it clear that the student spends twice the amount of money on rent as she does on food.

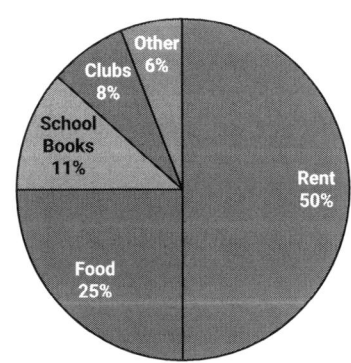

A pie chart is effective at showing how a single entity is divided into parts. They are not effective at demonstrating the relationships between parts of different wholes. For example, an unhelpful use of a pie chart would be to compare the respective amounts of state and federal spending devoted to infrastructure since these values are only meaningful in the context of the entire budget.

## BAR GRAPH

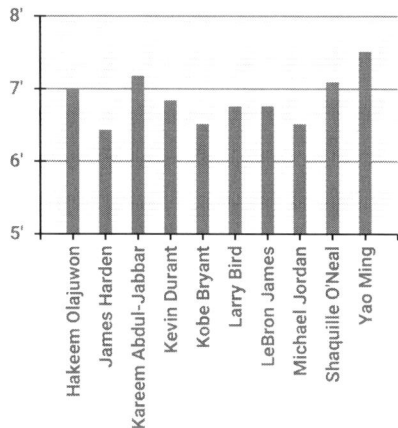

The bar graph is one of the most common visual representations of information. **Bar graphs** are used to illustrate sets of numerical **data**. The graph has a vertical axis (along which numbers are listed) and a horizontal axis (along which categories, words, or some other indicators are placed). One example of a bar graph is a depiction of the respective heights of famous basketball players: the vertical axis would contain numbers ranging from five to eight feet, and the horizontal axis would contain the names of the players. The length of the bar above the player's name would illustrate his height, and the top of the bar would stop perpendicular to the height listed along the left side. In this representation, one would see that Yao Ming is taller than Michael Jordan because Yao's bar would be higher.

## LINE GRAPH

A line graph is a type of graph that is typically used for measuring trends over time. The graph is set up along a vertical and a horizontal **axis**. The variables being measured are listed along the left side and the bottom side of the axes. Points are then plotted along the graph as they correspond with their values for each variable. For instance, consider a line graph measuring a person's income for each month of the year. If the person earned $1500 in January, there should be a point directly above January (perpendicular to the horizontal axis) and directly to the right of $1500 (perpendicular to the vertical axis). Once all of the lines are plotted, they are connected with a line from left to right. This line provides a nice visual illustration of the general **trends** of the data, if they exist. For instance, using the earlier example, if the line sloped up, then one would see that the person's income had increased over the course of the year.

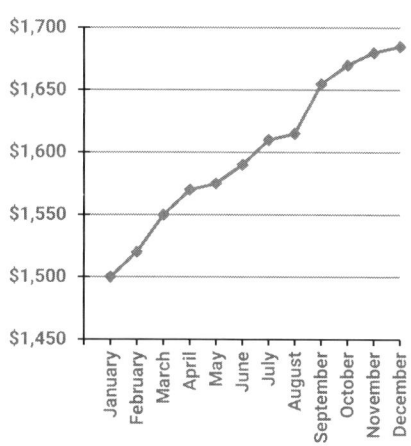

## PICTOGRAPHS

A **pictograph** is a graph, generally in the horizontal orientation, that uses pictures or symbols to represent the data. Each pictograph must have a key that defines the picture or symbol and gives the quantity each picture or symbol represents. Pictures or symbols on a pictograph are not always shown as whole elements. In this case, the fraction of the picture or symbol shown represents the same fraction of the quantity a whole picture or symbol stands for.

> **Review Video: Pictographs**
> Visit mometrix.com/academy and enter code: 147860

# Plot and Story Structure
## Plot and Story Structure

The **plot** includes the events that happen in a story and the order in which they are told to the reader. There are several types of plot structures, as stories can be told in many ways. The most common plot structure is the chronological plot, which presents the events to the reader in the same order they occur for the characters in the story. Chronological plots usually have five main parts, the **exposition, rising action**, the **climax, falling action**, and the **resolution**. This type of plot structure guides the reader through the story's events as the characters experience them and is the easiest structure to understand and identify. While this is the most common plot structure, many stories are nonlinear, which means the plot does not sequence events in the same order the characters experience them. Such stories might include elements like flashbacks that cause the story to be nonlinear.

> **Review Video: How to Make a Story Map**
> Visit mometrix.com/academy and enter code: 261719

### Exposition

The **exposition** is at the beginning of the story and generally takes place before the rising action begins. The purpose of the exposition is to give the reader context for the story, which the author may do by introducing one or more characters, describing the setting or world, or explaining the events leading up to the point where the story begins. The exposition may still include events that contribute to the plot, but the **rising action** and main conflict of the story are not part of the exposition. Some narratives skip the exposition and begin the story with the beginning of the rising action, which causes the reader to learn the context as the story intensifies.

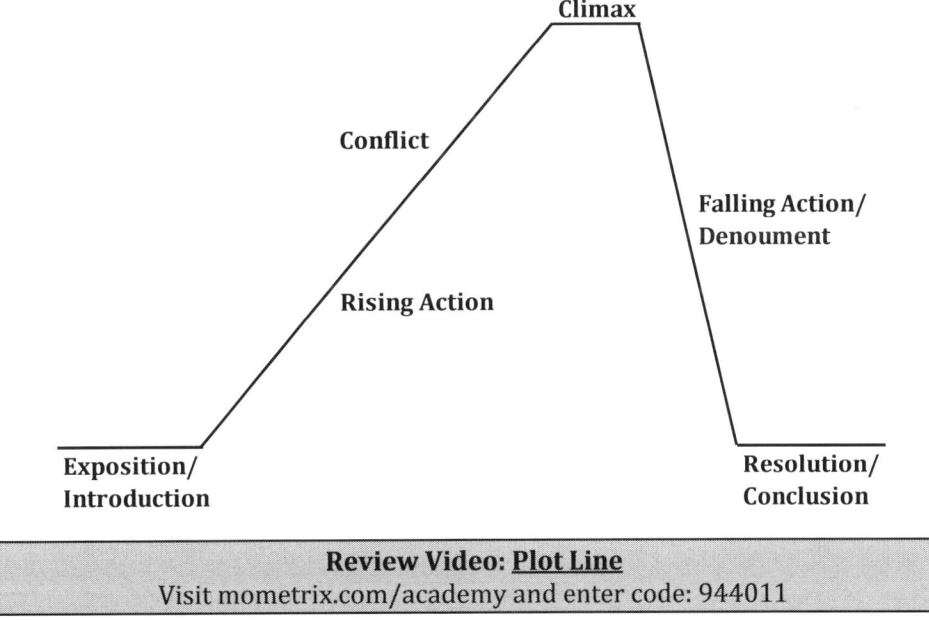

> **Review Video: Plot Line**
> Visit mometrix.com/academy and enter code: 944011

### Conflict

A **conflict** is a problem to be solved. Literary plots typically include one conflict or more. Characters' attempts to resolve conflicts drive the narrative's forward movement. **Conflict resolution** is often the protagonist's primary occupation. Physical conflicts like exploring, wars, and escapes tend to make plots most suspenseful and exciting. Emotional, mental, or moral conflicts tend to make stories more personally gratifying or rewarding for many audiences. Conflicts can be external or internal. A major type of internal conflict is some inner personal battle, or **man versus self**. Major types of external conflicts include **man versus nature, man versus man**, and **man versus society**. Readers can identify conflicts in literary plots by identifying the protagonist and antagonist and asking why they conflict, what events develop the conflict, where the climax occurs, and how they identify with the characters.

*Read the following paragraph and discuss the type of conflict present:*

> Timothy was shocked out of sleep by the appearance of a bear just outside his tent. After panicking for a moment, he remembered some advice he had read in preparation for this trip: he should make noise so the bear would not be startled. As Timothy started to hum and sing, the bear wandered away.

There are three main types of conflict in literature: **man versus man**, **man versus nature**, and **man versus self**. This paragraph is an example of man versus nature. Timothy is in conflict with the bear. Even though no physical conflict like an attack exists, Timothy is pitted against the bear. Timothy uses his knowledge to "defeat" the bear and keep himself safe. The solution to the conflict is that Timothy makes noise, the bear wanders away, and Timothy is safe.

> **Review Video: Conflict**
> Visit mometrix.com/academy and enter code: 559550
>
> **Review Video: Determining Relationships in a Story**
> Visit mometrix.com/academy and enter code: 929925

## RISING ACTION

The **rising action** is the part of the story where conflict **intensifies**. The rising action begins with an event that prompts the main conflict of the story. This may also be called the **inciting incident**. The main conflict generally occurs between the protagonist and an antagonist, but this is not the only type of conflict that may occur in a narrative. After this event, the protagonist works to resolve the main conflict by preparing for an altercation, pursuing a goal, fleeing an antagonist, or doing some other action that will end the conflict. The rising action is composed of several additional events that increase the story's tension. Most often, other developments will occur alongside the growth of the main conflict, such as character development or the development of minor conflicts. The rising action ends with the **climax**, which is the point of highest tension in the story.

## CLIMAX

The **climax** is the event in the narrative that marks the height of the story's conflict or tension. The event that takes place at the story's climax will end the rising action and bring about the results of the main conflict. If the conflict was between a good protagonist and an evil antagonist, the climax may be a final battle between the two characters. If the conflict is an adventurer looking for heavily guarded treasure, the climax may be the adventurer's encounter with the final obstacle that protects the treasure. The climax may be made of multiple scenes, but can usually be summarized as one event. Once the conflict and climax are complete, the **falling action** begins.

## FALLING ACTION

The **falling action** shows what happens in the story between the climax and the resolution. The falling action often composes a much smaller portion of the story than the rising action does. While the climax includes the end of the main conflict, the falling action may show the results of any minor conflicts in the story. For example, if the protagonist encountered a troll on the way to find some treasure, and the troll demanded the protagonist share the treasure after retrieving it, the falling action would include the protagonist returning to share the treasure with the troll. Similarly, any unexplained major events are usually made clear during the falling action. Once all significant elements of the story are resolved or addressed, the story's resolution will occur. The **resolution** is the end of the story, which shows the final result of the plot's events and shows what life is like for the main characters once they are no longer experiencing the story's conflicts.

## Resolution

The way the conflict is **resolved** depends on the type of conflict. The plot of any book starts with the lead up to the conflict, then the conflict itself, and finally the solution, or **resolution**, to the conflict. In **man versus man** conflicts, the conflict is often resolved by two parties coming to some sort of agreement or by one party triumphing over the other party. In **man versus nature** conflicts, the conflict is often resolved by man coming to some realization about some aspect of nature. In **man versus self** conflicts, the conflict is often resolved by the character growing or coming to an understanding about part of himself.

## Theme

A **theme** is a central idea demonstrated by a passage. Often, a theme is a lesson or moral contained in the text, but it does not have to be. It also is a unifying idea that is used throughout the text; it can take the form of a common setting, idea, symbol, design, or recurring event. A passage can have two or more themes that convey its overall idea. The theme or themes of a passage are often based on **universal themes**. They can frequently be expressed using well-known sayings about life, society, or human nature, such as "Hard work pays off" or "Good triumphs over evil." Themes are not usually stated **explicitly**. The reader must figure them out by carefully reading the passage. Themes are created through descriptive language or events in the plot. The events of a story help shape the themes of a passage.

## Example

*Explain why "if you care about something, you need to take care of it" accurately describes the theme of the following excerpt.*

> Luca collected baseball cards, but he wasn't very careful with them. He left them around the house. His dog liked to chew. One day, Luca and his friend Bart were looking at his collection. Then they went outside. When Luca got home, he saw his dog chewing on his cards. They were ruined.

This excerpt tells the story of a boy who is careless with his baseball cards and leaves them lying around. His dog ends up chewing them and ruining them. The lesson is that if you care about something, you need to take care of it. This is the theme, or point, of the story. Some stories have more than one theme, but this is not really true of this excerpt. The reader needs to figure out the theme based on what happens in the story. Sometimes, as in the case of fables, the theme is stated directly in the text. However, this is not usually the case.

> **Review Video: Themes in Literature**
> Visit mometrix.com/academy and enter code: 732074

## Narrator's Point of View

### Point of View

Another element that impacts a text is the author's point of view. The **point of view** of a text is the perspective from which a passage is told. An author will always have a point of view about a story before he or she draws up a plot line. The author will know what events they want to take place, how they want the characters to interact, and how they want the story to resolve. An author will also have an opinion on the topic or series of events which is presented in the story that is based on their prior experience and beliefs.

The two main points of view that authors use, especially in a work of fiction, are first person and third person. If the narrator of the story is also the main character, or *protagonist*, the text is written in first-person point of view. In first person, the author writes from the perspective of *I*. Third-person point of view is probably the most common that authors use in their passages. Using third person, authors refer to each character by using

*he* or *she*. In third-person omniscient, the narrator is not a character in the story and tells the story of all of the characters at the same time.

> **Review Video: Point of View**
> Visit mometrix.com/academy and enter code: 383336

## FIRST-PERSON NARRATION

**First-person** narratives let narrators express inner feelings and thoughts, especially when the narrator is the protagonist as Lemuel Gulliver is in Jonathan Swift's *Gulliver's Travels*. The narrator may be a close friend of the protagonist, like Dr. Watson in Sir Arthur Conan Doyle's *Sherlock Holmes*. Or, the narrator can be less involved with the main characters and plot, like Nick Carraway in F. Scott Fitzgerald's *The Great Gatsby*. When a narrator reports others' narratives, she or he is a "**frame narrator**," like the nameless narrator of Joseph Conrad's *Heart of Darkness* or Mr. Lockwood in Emily Brontë's *Wuthering Heights*. **First-person plural** is unusual but can be effective. Isaac Asimov's *I, Robot*, William Faulkner's *A Rose for Emily*, Maxim Gorky's *Twenty-Six Men and a Girl*, and Jeffrey Eugenides' *The Virgin Suicides* all use first-person plural narration. Author Kurt Vonnegut is the first-person narrator in his semi-autobiographical novel *Timequake*. Also unusual, but effective, is a **first-person omniscient** (rather than the more common third-person omniscient) narrator, like Death in Markus Zusak's *The Book Thief* and the ghost in Alice Sebold's *The Lovely Bones*.

## SECOND-PERSON NARRATION

While **second-person** address is very commonplace in popular song lyrics, it is the least used form of narrative voice in literary works. Popular serial books of the 1980s like *Fighting Fantasy* or *Choose Your Own Adventure* employed second-person narratives. In some cases, a narrative combines both second-person and first-person voices, using the pronouns *you* and *I*. This can draw readers into the story, and it can also enable the authors to compare directly "your" and "my" feelings, thoughts, and actions. When the narrator is also a character in the story, as in Edgar Allan Poe's short story "The Tell-Tale Heart" or Jay McInerney's novel *Bright Lights, Big City,* the narrative is better defined as first-person despite it also addressing "you."

## THIRD-PERSON NARRATION

Narration in the third person is the most prevalent type, as it allows authors the most flexibility. It is so common that readers simply assume without needing to be informed that the narrator is not a character in the story, or involved in its events. **Third-person singular** is used more frequently than **third-person plural**, though some authors have also effectively used plural. However, both singular and plural are most often included in stories according to which characters are being described. The third-person narrator may be either objective or subjective, and either omniscient or limited. **Objective third-person** narration does not include what the characters described are thinking or feeling, while **subjective third-person** narration does. The **third-person omniscient** narrator knows everything about all characters, including their thoughts and emotions, and all related places, times, and events. However, the **third-person limited** narrator may know everything about a particular character, but is limited to that character. In other words, the narrator cannot speak about anything that character does not know.

## ALTERNATING-PERSON NARRATION

Although authors more commonly write stories from one point of view, there are also instances wherein they alternate the narrative voice within the same book. For example, they may sometimes use an omniscient third-person narrator and a more intimate first-person narrator at other times. In J. K. Rowling's series of *Harry Potter* novels, she often writes in a third-person limited narrative, but sometimes changes to narration by characters other than the protagonist. George R. R. Martin's series *A Song of Ice and Fire* changes the point of view to coincide with divisions between chapters. The same technique is used by Erin Hunter (a pseudonym for several authors of the *Warriors, Seekers,* and *Survivors* book series). Authors using first-person narrative sometimes switch to third-person to describe significant action scenes, especially those where the narrator was absent or uninvolved, as Barbara Kingsolver does in her novel *The Poisonwood Bible*.

> **Review Video: The Narrator of a Story**
> Visit mometrix.com/academy and enter code: 742528

## SETTING, MOOD, AND TONE
### SETTING AND TIME FRAME

A literary text has both a setting and time frame. A **setting** is the place in which the story as a whole is set. The **time frame** is the period in which the story is set. This may refer to the historical period the story takes place in or if the story takes place over a single day. Both setting and time frame are relevant to a text's meaning because they help the reader place the story in time and space. An author uses setting and time frame to anchor a text, create a mood, and enhance its meaning. This helps a reader understand why a character acts the way he does, or why certain events in the story are important. The setting impacts the **plot** and character **motivations**, while the time frame helps place the story in **chronological context**.

### EXAMPLE

*Read the following excerpt from The Adventures of Huckleberry Finn by Mark Twain and analyze the relevance of setting to the text's meaning:*

> We said there warn't no home like a raft, after all. Other places do seem so cramped up and smothery, but a raft don't. You feel mighty free and easy and comfortable on a raft.

This excerpt from *The Adventures of Huckleberry Finn* by Mark Twain reveals information about the **setting** of the book. By understanding that the main character, Huckleberry Finn, lives on a raft, the reader can place the story on a river, in this case, the Mississippi River in the South before the Civil War. The information about the setting also gives the reader clues about the **character** of Huck Finn: he clearly values independence and freedom, and he likes the outdoors. The information about the setting in the quote helps the reader to better understand the rest of the text.

### SYNTAX AND WORD CHOICE

Authors use words and **syntax**, or sentence structure, to make their texts unique, convey their own writing style, and sometimes to make a point or emphasis. They know that word choice and syntax contribute to the reader's understanding of the text as well as to the tone and mood of a text.

> **Review Video: Syntax**
> Visit mometrix.com/academy and enter code: 242280

### MOOD AND TONE

Mood is a story's atmosphere, or the feelings the reader gets from reading it. The way authors set the mood in writing is comparable to the way filmmakers use music to set the mood in movies. Instead of music, though, writers judiciously select descriptive words to evoke certain **moods**. The mood of a work may convey joy, anger, bitterness, hope, gloom, fear, apprehension, or any other emotion the author wants the reader to feel. In addition to vocabulary choices, authors also use figurative expressions, particular sentence structures, and choices of diction that project and reinforce the moods they want to create. Whereas mood is the reader's emotions evoked by reading what is written, **tone** is the emotions and attitudes of the writer that she or he expresses in the writing. Authors use the same literary techniques to establish tone as they do to establish mood. An author may use a humorous tone, an angry or sad tone, a sentimental or unsentimental tone, or something else entirely.

## MOOD AND TONE IN THE GREAT GATSBY

To understand the difference between mood and tone, look at this excerpt from F. Scott Fitzgerald's *The Great Gatsby*. In this passage, Nick Caraway, the novel's narrator, is describing his affordable house, which sits in a neighborhood full of expensive mansions.

> "I lived at West Egg, the—well the less fashionable of the two, though this is a most superficial tag to express the bizarre and not a little sinister contrast between them. My house was at the very tip of the egg, only fifty yard from the Sound, and squeezed between two huge places that rented for twelve or fifteen thousand a season … My own house was an eyesore, but it was a small eyesore, and it had been overlooked, so I had a view of the water, a partial view of my neighbor's lawn, and the consoling proximity of millionaires—all for eighty dollars a month."

In this description, the mood created for the reader does not match the tone created through the narrator. The mood in this passage is one of dissatisfaction and inferiority. Nick compares his home to his neighbors', saying he lives in the "less fashionable" neighborhood and that his house is "overlooked," an "eyesore," and "squeezed between two huge" mansions. He also adds that his placement allows him the "consoling proximity of millionaires." A literal reading of these details leads the reader to have negative feelings toward Nick's house and his economic inferiority to his neighbors, creating the mood.

However, Fitzgerald also conveys an opposing attitude, or tone, through Nick's description. Nick calls the distinction between the neighborhoods "superficial," showing a suspicion of the value suggested by the neighborhoods' titles, properties, and residents. Nick also undermines his critique of his own home by calling it "a small eyesore" and claiming it has "been overlooked." However, he follows these statements with a description of his surroundings, claiming that he has "a view of the water" and can see some of his wealthy neighbor's property from his home, and a comparison between the properties' rent. While the mental image created for the reader depicts a small house shoved between looming mansions, the tone suggests that Nick enjoys these qualities about his home, or at least finds it charming. He acknowledges its shortcomings, but includes the benefits of his home's unassuming appearance.

> **Review Video: Style, Tone, and Mood**
> Visit mometrix.com/academy and enter code: 416961

## HISTORICAL AND SOCIAL CONTEXT

Fiction that is heavily influenced by a historical or social context cannot be comprehended as the author intended if the reader does not keep this context in mind. Many important elements of the text will be influenced by any context, including symbols, allusions, settings, and plot events. These contexts, as well as the identity of the work's author, can help to inform the reader about the author's concerns and intended meanings. For example, George Orwell published his novel *1984* in the year 1949, soon after the end of World War II. At that time, following the defeat of the Nazis, the Cold War began between the Western Allied nations and the Eastern Soviet Communists. People were therefore concerned about the conflict between the freedoms afforded by Western democracies versus the oppression represented by Communism. Orwell had also previously fought in the Spanish Civil War against a Spanish regime that he and his fellows viewed as oppressive. From this information, readers can infer that Orwell was concerned about oppression by totalitarian governments. This informs *1984*'s story of Winston Smith's rebellion against the oppressive "Big Brother" government, of the fictional dictatorial state of Oceania, and his capture, torture, and ultimate conversion by that government. Some literary theories also seek to use historical and social contexts to reveal deeper meanings and implications in a text.

## CHARACTER DEVELOPMENT AND DIALOGUE
### CHARACTER DEVELOPMENT
When depicting characters or figures in a written text, authors generally use actions, dialogue, and descriptions as characterization techniques. Characterization can occur in both fiction and nonfiction and is used to show a character or figure's personality, demeanor, and thoughts. This helps create a more engaging experience for the reader by providing a more concrete picture of a character or figure's tendencies and features. Characterizations also gives authors the opportunity to integrate elements such as dialects, activities, attire, and attitudes into their writing.

To understand the meaning of a story, it is vital to understand the characters as the author describes them. We can look for contradictions in what a character thinks, says, and does. We can notice whether the author's observations about a character differ from what other characters in the story say about that character. A character may be dynamic, meaning they change significantly during the story, or static, meaning they remain the same from beginning to end. Characters may be two-dimensional, not fully developed, or may be well developed with characteristics that stand out vividly. Characters may also symbolize universal properties. Additionally, readers can compare and contrast characters to analyze how each one developed.

A well-known example of character development can be found in Charles Dickens's *Great Expectations*. The novel's main character, Pip, is introduced as a young boy, and he is depicted as innocent, kind, and humble. However, as Pip grows up and is confronted with the social hierarchy of Victorian England, he becomes arrogant and rejects his loved ones in pursuit of his own social advancement. Once he achieves his social goals, he realizes the merits of his former lifestyle, and lives with the wisdom he gained in both environments and life stages. Dickens shows Pip's ever-changing character through his interactions with others and his inner thoughts, which evolve as his personal values and personality shift.

### DIALOGUE
Effectively written dialogue serves at least one, but usually several, purposes. It advances the story and moves the plot, develops the characters, sheds light on the work's theme or meaning, and can, often subtly, account for the passage of time not otherwise indicated. It can alter the direction that the plot is taking, typically by introducing some new conflict or changing existing ones. **Dialogue** can establish a work's narrative voice and the characters' voices and set the tone of the story or of particular characters. When fictional characters display enlightenment or realization, dialogue can give readers an understanding of what those characters have discovered and how. Dialogue can illuminate the motivations and wishes of the story's characters. By using consistent thoughts and syntax, dialogue can support character development. Skillfully created, it can also represent real-life speech rhythms in written form. Via conflicts and ensuing action, dialogue also provides drama.

### DIALOGUE IN FICTION
In fictional works, effectively written dialogue does more than just break up or interrupt sections of narrative. While **dialogue** may supply exposition for readers, it must nonetheless be believable. Dialogue should be dynamic, not static, and it should not resemble regular prose. Authors should not use dialogue to write clever similes or metaphors, or to inject their own opinions. Nor should they use dialogue at all when narrative would be better. Most importantly, dialogue should not slow the plot movement. Dialogue must seem natural, which means careful construction of phrases rather than actually duplicating natural speech, which does not necessarily translate well to the written word. Finally, all dialogue must be pertinent to the story, rather than just added conversation.

# FIGURATIVE LANGUAGE
## LITERAL AND FIGURATIVE MEANING

When language is used **literally**, the words mean exactly what they say and nothing more. When language is used **figuratively**, the words mean something beyond their literal meaning. For example, "The weeping willow tree has long, trailing branches and leaves" is a literal description. But "The weeping willow tree looks as if it is bending over and crying" is a figurative description—specifically, a **simile** or stated comparison. Another figurative language form is **metaphor**, or an implied comparison. A good example is the metaphor of a city, state, or city-state as a ship, and its governance as sailing that ship. Ancient Greek lyrical poet Alcaeus is credited with first using this metaphor, and ancient Greek tragedian Aeschylus then used it in *Seven Against Thebes,* and then Plato used it in the *Republic.*

## FIGURES OF SPEECH

A **figure of speech** is a verbal expression whose meaning is figurative rather than literal. For example, the phrase "butterflies in the stomach" does not refer to actual butterflies in a person's stomach. It is a metaphor representing the fluttery feelings experienced when a person is nervous or excited—or when one "falls in love," which does not mean physically falling. "Hitting a sales target" does not mean physically hitting a target with arrows as in archery; it is a metaphor for meeting a sales quota. "Climbing the ladder of success" metaphorically likens advancing in one's career to ascending ladder rungs. Similes, such as "light as a feather" (meaning very light, not a feather's actual weight), and hyperbole, like "I'm starving/freezing/roasting," are also figures of speech. Figures of speech are often used and crafted for emphasis, freshness of expression, or clarity.

> **Review Video: Figures of Speech**
> Visit mometrix.com/academy and enter code: 111295

## FIGURATIVE LANGUAGE

**Figurative language** extends past the literal meanings of words. It offers readers new insight into the people, things, events, and subjects covered in a work of literature. Figurative language also enables readers to feel they are sharing the authors' experiences. It can stimulate the reader's senses, make comparisons that readers find intriguing or even startling, and enable readers to view the world in different ways. When looking for figurative language, it is important to consider the context of the sentence or situation. Phrases that appear out of place or make little sense when read literally are likely instances of figurative language. Once figurative language has been recognized, context is also important to determining the type of figurative language being used and its function. For example, when a comparison is being made, a metaphor or simile is likely being used. This means the comparison may emphasize or create irony through the things being compared. Seven specific types of figurative language include: alliteration, onomatopoeia, personification, imagery, similes, metaphors, and hyperbole.

> **Review Video: Figurative Language**
> Visit mometrix.com/academy and enter code: 584902

### ALLITERATION AND ONOMATOPOEIA

**Alliteration** describes a series of words beginning with the same sounds. **Onomatopoeia** uses words imitating the sounds of things they name or describe. For example, in his poem "Come Down, O Maid," Alfred Tennyson writes of "The moan of doves in immemorial elms, / And murmuring of innumerable bees." The word "moan" sounds like some sounds doves make, "murmuring" represents the sounds of bees buzzing. Onomatopoeia also includes words that are simply meant to represent sounds, such as "meow," "kaboom," and "whoosh."

> **Review Video: Alliteration in Everyday Expressions**
> Visit mometrix.com/academy and enter code: 462837

## PERSONIFICATION

Another type of figurative language is **personification**. This is describing a non-human thing, like an animal or an object, as if it were human. The general intent of personification is to describe things in a manner that will be comprehensible to readers. When an author states that a tree *groans* in the wind, he or she does not mean that the tree is emitting a low, pained sound from a mouth. Instead, the author means that the tree is making a noise similar to a human groan. Of course, this personification establishes a tone of sadness or suffering. A different tone would be established if the author said that the tree was *swaying* or *dancing*. Alfred Tennyson's poem "The Eagle" uses all of these types of figurative language: "He clasps the crag with crooked hands." Tennyson used alliteration, repeating /k/ and /kr/ sounds. These hard-sounding consonants reinforce the imagery, giving visual and tactile impressions of the eagle.

> **Review Video: Personification**
> Visit mometrix.com/academy and enter code: 260066

## SIMILES AND METAPHORS

**Similes** are stated comparisons using "like" or "as." Similes can be used to stimulate readers' imaginations and appeal to their senses. Because a simile includes *like* or *as,* the device creates more space between the description and the thing being described than a metaphor does. If an author says that *a house was like a shoebox*, then the tone is different than the author saying that the house *was* a shoebox. Authors will choose between a metaphor and a simile depending on their intended tone.

Similes also help compare fictional characters to well-known objects or experiences, so the reader can better relate to them. William Wordsworth's poem about "Daffodils" begins, "I wandered lonely as a cloud." This simile compares his loneliness to that of a cloud. It is also personification, giving a cloud the human quality loneliness. In his novel *Lord Jim* (1900), Joseph Conrad writes in Chapter 33, "I would have given anything for the power to soothe her frail soul, tormenting itself in its invincible ignorance like a small bird beating about the cruel wires of a cage." Conrad uses the word "like" to compare the girl's soul to a small bird. His description of the bird beating at the cage shows the similar helplessness of the girl's soul to gain freedom.

> **Review Video: Similes**
> Visit mometrix.com/academy and enter code: 642949

A **metaphor** is a type of figurative language in which the writer equates something with another thing that is not particularly similar, instead of using *like* or *as*. For instance, *the bird was an arrow arcing through the sky*. In this sentence, the arrow is serving as a metaphor for the bird. The point of a metaphor is to encourage the reader to consider the item being described in a *different way*. Let's continue with this metaphor for a flying bird. You are asked to envision the bird's flight as being similar to the arc of an arrow. So, you imagine the flight to be swift and bending. Metaphors are a way for the author to describe an item *without being direct and obvious*. This literary device is a lyrical and suggestive way of providing information. Note that the reference for a metaphor will not always be mentioned explicitly by the author. Consider the following description of a forest in winter: *Swaying skeletons reached for the sky and groaned as the wind blew through them*. In this example, the author is using *skeletons* as a metaphor for leafless trees. This metaphor creates a spooky tone while inspiring the reader's imagination.

### LITERARY EXAMPLES OF METAPHOR

A **metaphor** is an implied comparison, i.e., it compares something to something else without using "like", "as", or other comparative words. For example, in "The Tyger" (1794), William Blake writes, "Tyger Tyger, burning bright, / In the forests of the night." Blake compares the tiger to a flame not by saying it is like a fire, but by simply describing it as "burning." Henry Wadsworth Longfellow's poem "O Ship of State" (1850) uses an extended metaphor by referring consistently throughout the entire poem to the state, union, or republic as a seagoing vessel, referring to its keel, mast, sail, rope, anchors, and to its braving waves, rocks, gale, tempest, and "false lights on the shore." Within the extended metaphor, Wordsworth uses a specific metaphor: "the anchors of thy hope!"

### TED HUGHES' ANIMAL METAPHORS

Ted Hughes frequently used animal metaphors in his poetry. In "The Thought Fox," a model of concise, structured beauty, Hughes characterizes the poet's creative process with succinct, striking imagery of an idea entering his head like a wild fox. Repeating "loneliness" in the first two stanzas emphasizes the poet's lonely work: "Something else is alive / Beside the clock's loneliness." He treats an idea's arrival as separate from himself. Three stanzas detail in vivid images a fox's approach from the outside winter forest at starless midnight—its nose, "Cold, delicately" touching twigs and leaves; "neat" paw prints in snow; "bold" body; brilliant green eyes; and self-contained, focused progress—"Till, with a sudden sharp hot stink of fox," he metaphorically depicts poetic inspiration as the fox's physical entry into "the dark hole of the head." Hughes ends by summarizing his vision of a poet as an interior, passive idea recipient, with the outside world unchanged: "The window is starless still; the clock ticks, / The page is printed."

> **Review Video: Metaphors in Writing**
> Visit mometrix.com/academy and enter code: 133295

## METONYMY

**Metonymy** is naming one thing with words or phrases of a closely related thing. This is similar to metaphor. However, the comparison has a close connection, unlike metaphor. An example of metonymy is to call the news media *the press*. Of course, *the press* is the machine that prints newspapers. Metonymy is a way of naming something without using the same name constantly.

## SYNECDOCHE

**Synecdoche** points to the whole by naming one of the parts. An example of synecdoche would be calling a construction worker a *hard hat*. Like metonymy, synecdoche is an easy way of naming something without having to overuse a name. The device allows writers to highlight pieces of the thing being described. For example, referring to businessmen as *suits* suggests professionalism and unity.

> **Review Video: Metonymy and Synecdoche**
> Visit mometrix.com/academy and enter code: 900306

## HYPERBOLE

Hyperbole is excessive exaggeration used for humor or emphasis rather than for literal meaning. For example, in *To Kill a Mockingbird*, Harper Lee wrote, "People moved slowly then. There was no hurry, for there was nowhere to go, nothing to buy and no money to buy it with, nothing to see outside the boundaries of Maycomb County." This was not literally true; Lee exaggerates the scarcity of these things for emphasis. In "Old Times on the Mississippi," Mark Twain wrote, "I... could have hung my hat on my eyes, they stuck out so far." This is not literal, but makes his description vivid and funny. In his poem "As I Walked Out One Evening", W. H. Auden wrote, "I'll love you, dear, I'll love you / Till China and Africa meet, / And the river jumps over the mountain / And the salmon sing in the street." He used things not literally possible to emphasize the duration of his love.

## UNDERSTATEMENT

**Understatement** is the opposite of hyperbole. This device discounts or downplays something. Think about someone who climbs Mount Everest. Then, they say that the journey was *a little stroll*. As with other types of figurative language, understatement has a range of uses. The device may show self-defeat or modesty as in the Mount Everest example. However, some may think of understatement as false modesty (i.e., an attempt to bring attention to you or a situation). For example, a woman is praised on her diamond engagement ring. The woman says, *Oh, this little thing?* Her understatement might be heard as stuck-up or unfeeling.

> **Review Video: Hyperbole and Understatement**
> Visit mometrix.com/academy and enter code: 308470

## LITERARY DEVICES
### LITERARY IRONY

In literature, irony demonstrates the opposite of what is said or done. The three types of irony are **verbal irony**, **situational irony**, and **dramatic irony**. Verbal irony uses words opposite to the meaning. Sarcasm may use verbal irony. One common example is describing something that is confusing as "clear as mud." For example, in his 1986 movie *Hannah and Her Sisters,* author, director, and actor Woody Allen says to his character's date, "I had a great evening; it was like the Nuremburg Trials." Notice these employ similes. In situational irony, what happens contrasts with what was expected. O. Henry's short story *The Gift of the Magi* uses situational irony: a husband and wife each sacrifice their most prized possession to buy each other a Christmas present. The irony is that she sells her long hair to buy him a watch fob, while he sells his heirloom pocket-watch to buy her the jeweled combs for her hair she had long wanted; in the end, neither of them can use their gifts. In dramatic irony, narrative informs audiences of more than its characters know. For example, in *Romeo and Juliet,* the audience is made aware that Juliet is only asleep, while Romeo believes her to be dead, which then leads to Romeo's death.

> **Review Video: Irony**
> Visit mometrix.com/academy and enter code: 374204

### IDIOMS

Idioms create comparisons, and often take the form of similes or metaphors. Idioms are always phrases and are understood to have a meaning that is different from its individual words' literal meaning. For example, "break a leg" is a common idiom that is used to wish someone luck or tell them to perform well. Literally, the phrase "break a leg" means to injure a person's leg, but the phrase takes on a different meaning when used as an idiom. Another example is "call it a day," which means to temporarily stop working on a task, or find a stopping point, rather than literally referring to something as "a day." Many idioms are associated with a region or group. For example, an idiom commonly used in the American South is "'til the cows come home." This phrase is often used to indicate that something will take or may last for a very long time, but not that it will literally last until the cows return to where they reside.

### ALLUSION

An allusion is an uncited but recognizable reference to something else. Authors use language to make allusions to places, events, artwork, and other books in order to make their own text richer. For example, an author may allude to a very important text in order to make his own text seem more important. Martin Luther King, Jr. started his "I Have a Dream" speech by saying "Five score years ago…" This is a clear allusion to President Abraham Lincoln's "Gettysburg Address" and served to remind people of the significance of the event. An author may allude to a place to ground his text or make a cultural reference to make readers feel included. There are many reasons that authors make allusions.

> **Review Video: Allusions**
> Visit mometrix.com/academy and enter code: 294065

### COMIC RELIEF

Comic relief is the use of comedy by an author to break up a dramatic or tragic scene and infuse it with a bit of **lightheartedness**. In William Shakespeare's *Hamlet*, two gravediggers digging the grave for Ophelia share a joke while they work. The death and burial of Ophelia are tragic moments that directly follow each other.

Shakespeare uses an instance of comedy to break up the tragedy and give his audience a bit of a break from the tragic drama. Authors sometimes use comic relief so that their work will be less depressing; other times they use it to create irony or contrast between the darkness of the situation and the lightness of the joke. Often, authors will use comedy to parallel what is happening in the tragic scenes.

> **Review Video: Comic Relief**
> Visit mometrix.com/academy and enter code: 779604

### FORESHADOWING

**Foreshadowing** is a device authors use to give readers **hints** about events that will take place later in a story. Foreshadowing most often takes place through a character's dialogue or actions. Sometimes the character will know what is going to happen and will purposefully allude to future events. For example, consider a protagonist who is about to embark on a journey through the woods. Just before the protagonist begins the trip, another character says, "Be careful, you never know what could be out in those woods!" This alerts the reader that the woods may be dangerous and prompts the reader to expect something to attack the protagonist in the woods. This is an example of foreshadowing through warning. Alternatively, a character may unknowingly foreshadow later events. For example, consider a story where a brother and sister run through their house and knock over a vase and break it. The brother says, "Don't worry, we'll clean it up! Mom will never know!" However, the reader knows that their mother will most likely find out what they have done, so the reader expects the siblings to later get in trouble for running, breaking the vase, and hiding it from their mother.

### SYMBOLISM

**Symbolism** describes an author's use of a **symbol**, an element of the story that **represents** something else. Symbols can impact stories in many ways, including deepening the meaning of a story or its elements, comparing a story to another work, or foreshadowing later events in a story. Symbols can be objects, characters, colors, numbers, or anything else the author establishes as a symbol. Symbols can be clearly established through direct comparison or repetition, but they can also be established subtly or gradually over a large portion of the story. Another form of symbolism is **allusion**, which is when something in a story is used to prompt the reader to think about another work. Many well-known works use **Biblical allusions**, which are allusions to events or details in the Bible that inform a work or an element within it.

# Rhetoric

## CRITICAL READING SKILLS
### OPINIONS, FACTS, AND FALLACIES

Critical thinking skills are mastered through understanding various types of writing and the different purposes authors can have for writing different passages. Every author writes for a purpose. When you understand their purpose and how they accomplish their goal, you will be able to analyze their writing and determine whether or not you agree with their conclusions.

Readers must always be aware of the difference between fact and opinion. A **fact** can be subjected to analysis and proven to be true. An **opinion**, on the other hand, is the author's personal thoughts or feelings and may not be altered by research or evidence. If the author writes that the distance from New York City to Boston is about two hundred miles, then he or she is stating a fact. If the author writes that New York City is too crowded, then he or she is giving an opinion because there is no objective standard for overpopulation. Opinions are often supported by facts. For instance, an author might use a comparison between the population density of New York City and that of other major American cities as evidence of an overcrowded population. An opinion supported by facts tends to be more convincing. On the other hand, when authors support their opinions with other opinions, readers should employ critical thinking and approach the argument with skepticism.

> **Review Video: Distinguishing Fact and Opinion**
> Visit mometrix.com/academy and enter code: 870899

## RELIABLE SOURCES

When you read an argumentative passage, you need to be sure that facts are presented to the reader from **reliable sources**. An opinion is what the author thinks about a given topic. An opinion is not common knowledge or proven by expert sources, instead the information is the personal beliefs and thoughts of the author. To distinguish between fact and opinion, a reader needs to consider the type of source that is presenting information, the information that backs-up a claim, and the author's motivation to have a certain point-of-view on a given topic. For example, if a panel of scientists has conducted multiple studies on the effectiveness of taking a certain vitamin, then the results are more likely to be factual than those of a company that is selling a vitamin and simply claims that taking the vitamin can produce positive effects. The company is motivated to sell their product, and the scientists are using the scientific method to prove a theory. Remember, if you find sentences that contain phrases such as "I think…", then the statement is an opinion.

## BIASES

In their attempts to persuade, writers often make mistakes in their thought processes and writing choices. These processes and choices are important to understand so you can make an informed decision about the author's credibility. Every author has a point of view, but authors demonstrate a **bias** when they ignore reasonable counterarguments or distort opposing viewpoints. A bias is evident whenever the author's claims are presented in a way that is unfair or inaccurate. Bias can be intentional or unintentional, but readers should be skeptical of the author's argument in either case. Remember that a biased author may still be correct. However, the author will be correct in spite of, not because of, his or her bias.

A **stereotype** is a bias applied specifically to a group of people or a place. Stereotyping is considered to be particularly abhorrent because it promotes negative, misleading generalizations about people. Readers should be very cautious of authors who use stereotypes in their writing. These faulty assumptions typically reveal the author's ignorance and lack of curiosity.

> **Review Video: Bias and Stereotype**
> Visit mometrix.com/academy and enter code: 644829

## PERSUASION AND RHETORIC

### PERSUASIVE TECHNIQUES

To **appeal using reason**, writers present logical arguments, such as using "If… then… because" statements. To **appeal to emotions**, authors may ask readers how they would feel about something or to put themselves in another's place, present their argument as one that will make the audience feel good, or tell readers how they should feel. To **appeal to character**, **morality**, or **ethics**, authors present their points to readers as the right or most moral choices. Authors cite expert opinions to show readers that someone very knowledgeable about the subject or viewpoint agrees with the author's claims. **Testimonials**, usually via anecdotes or quotations regarding the author's subject, help build the audience's trust in an author's message through positive support from ordinary people. **Bandwagon appeals** claim that everybody else agrees with the author's argument and persuade readers to conform and agree, also. Authors **appeal to greed** by presenting their choice as cheaper, free, or more valuable for less cost. They **appeal to laziness** by presenting their views as more convenient, easy, or relaxing. Authors also anticipate potential objections and argue against them before audiences think of them, thereby depicting those objections as weak.

Authors can use **comparisons** like analogies, similes, and metaphors to persuade audiences. For example, a writer might represent excessive expenses as "hemorrhaging" money, which the author's recommended solution will stop. Authors can use negative word connotations to make some choices unappealing to readers, and positive word connotations to make others more appealing. Using **humor** can relax readers and garner their agreement. However, writers must take care: ridiculing opponents can be a successful strategy for appealing to readers who already agree with the author, but can backfire by angering other readers. **Rhetorical questions** need no answer, but create effect that can force agreement, such as asking the question, "Wouldn't you rather be paid more than less?" **Generalizations** persuade readers by being impossible to disagree with. Writers can easily make generalizations that appear to support their viewpoints, like saying, "We all want peace, not war" regarding more specific political arguments. **Transfer** and **association** persuade by example: if advertisements show attractive actors enjoying their products, audiences imagine they will experience the same. **Repetition** can also sometimes effectively persuade audiences.

> **Review Video: Using Rhetorical Strategies for Persuasion**
> Visit mometrix.com/academy and enter code: 302658

## CLASSICAL AUTHOR APPEALS

In his *On Rhetoric,* ancient Greek philosopher Aristotle defined three basic types of appeal used in writing, which he called *pathos, ethos,* and *logos.* **Pathos** means suffering or experience and refers to appeals to the emotions (the English word *pathetic* comes from this root). Writing that is meant to entertain audiences, by making them either happy, as with comedy, or sad, as with tragedy, uses *pathos*. Aristotle's *Poetics* states that evoking the emotions of terror and pity is one of the criteria for writing tragedy. **Ethos** means character and connotes ideology (the English word *ethics* comes from this root). Writing that appeals to credibility, based on academic, professional, or personal merit, uses *ethos*. **Logos** means "I say" and refers to a plea, opinion, expectation, word or speech, account, opinion, or reason (the English word *logic* comes from this root.) Aristotle used it to mean persuasion that appeals to the audience through reasoning and logic to influence their opinions.

## RHETORICAL DEVICES

- An **anecdote** is a brief story authors may relate to their argument, which can illustrate their points in a more real and relatable way.
- **Aphorisms** concisely state common beliefs and may rhyme. For example, Benjamin Franklin's "Early to bed and early to rise / Makes a man healthy, wealthy, and wise" is an aphorism.
- **Allusions** refer to literary or historical figures to impart symbolism to a thing or person and to create reader resonance. In John Steinbeck's *Of Mice and Men,* protagonist George's last name is Milton. This alludes to John Milton, who wrote *Paradise Lost*, and symbolizes George's eventual loss of his dream.
- **Satire** exaggerates, ridicules, or pokes fun at human flaws or ideas, as in the works of Jonathan Swift and Mark Twain.
- A **parody** is a form of satire that imitates another work to ridicule its topic or style.
- A **paradox** is a statement that is true despite appearing contradictory.
- **Hyperbole** is overstatement using exaggerated language.
- An **oxymoron** combines seeming contradictions, such as "deafening silence."
- **Analogies** compare two things that share common elements.
- **Similes** (stated comparisons using the words *like* or *as*) and **metaphors** (stated comparisons that do not use *like* or *as*) are considered forms of analogy.
- When using logic to reason with audiences, **syllogism** refers either to deductive reasoning or a deceptive, very sophisticated, or subtle argument.
- **Deductive reasoning** moves from general to specific, **inductive reasoning** from specific to general.
- **Diction** is author word choice that establishes tone and effect.
- **Understatement** achieves effects like contrast or irony by downplaying or describing something more subtly than warranted.

- **Chiasmus** uses parallel clauses, the second reversing the order of the first. Examples include T. S. Eliot's "Has the Church failed mankind, or has mankind failed the Church?" and John F. Kennedy's "Ask not what your country can do for you; ask what you can do for your country."
- **Anaphora** regularly repeats a word or phrase at the beginnings of consecutive clauses or phrases to add emphasis to an idea. A classic example of anaphora was Winston Churchill's emphasis of determination: "[W]e shall fight on the beaches, we shall fight on the landing grounds, we shall fight in the fields and in the streets, we shall fight in the hills; we shall never surrender…"

## READING ARGUMENTATIVE WRITING

### AUTHOR'S ARGUMENT IN ARGUMENTATIVE WRITING

In argumentative writing, the argument is a belief, position, or opinion that the author wants to convince readers to believe as well. For the first step, readers should identify the **issue**. Some issues are controversial, meaning people disagree about them. Gun control, foreign policy, and the death penalty are all controversial issues. The next step is to determine the **author's position** on the issue. That position or viewpoint constitutes the author's argument. Readers should then identify the **author's assumptions**: things he or she accepts, believes, or takes for granted without needing proof. Inaccurate or illogical assumptions produce flawed arguments and can mislead readers. Readers should identify what kinds of **supporting evidence** the author offers, such as research results, personal observations or experiences, case studies, facts, examples, expert testimony and opinions, and comparisons. Readers should decide how relevant this support is to the argument.

> **Review Video: Argumentative Writing**
> Visit mometrix.com/academy and enter code: 561544

### EVALUATING AN AUTHOR'S ARGUMENT

The first three reader steps to **evaluate an author's argument** are to identify the **author's assumptions**, identify the **supporting evidence**, and decide **whether the evidence is relevant**. For example, if an author is not an expert on a particular topic, then that author's personal experience or opinion might not be relevant. The fourth step is to assess the **author's objectivity**. For example, consider whether the author introduces clear, understandable supporting evidence and facts to support the argument. The fifth step is evaluating whether the author's **argument is complete**. When authors give sufficient support for their arguments and also anticipate and respond effectively to opposing arguments or objections to their points, their arguments are complete. However, some authors omit information that could detract from their arguments. If instead they stated this information and refuted it, it would strengthen their arguments. The sixth step in evaluating an author's argumentative writing is to assess whether the **argument is valid**. Providing clear, logical reasoning makes an author's argument valid. Readers should ask themselves whether the author's points follow a sequence that makes sense, and whether each point leads to the next. The seventh step is to determine whether the author's **argument is credible**, meaning that it is convincing and believable. Arguments that are not valid are not credible, so step seven depends on step six. Readers should be mindful of their own biases as they evaluate and should not expect authors to conclusively prove their arguments, but rather to provide effective support and reason.

### EVALUATING AN AUTHOR'S METHOD OF APPEAL

To evaluate the effectiveness of an appeal, it is important to consider the author's purpose for writing. Any appeals an author uses in their argument must be relevant to the argument's goal. For example, a writer that argues for the reclassification of Pluto, but primarily uses appeals to emotion, will not have an effective argument. This writer should focus on using appeals to logic and support their argument with provable facts. While most arguments should include appeals to logic, emotion, and credibility, some arguments only call for one or two of these types of appeal. Evidence can support an appeal, but the evidence must be relevant to truly strengthen the appeal's effectiveness. If the writer arguing for Pluto's reclassification uses the reasons for Jupiter's classification as evidence, their argument would be weak. This information may seem relevant because it is related to the classification of planets. However, this classification is highly dependent on the size of the celestial object, and Jupiter is significantly bigger than Pluto. This use of evidence is illogical and does not support the appeal. Even when appropriate evidence and appeals are used, appeals and arguments lose their effectiveness when they create logical fallacies.

## EVIDENCE

The term **text evidence** refers to information that supports a main point or minor points and can help lead the reader to a conclusion about the text's credibility. Information used as text evidence is precise, descriptive, and factual. A main point is often followed by supporting details that provide evidence to back up a claim. For example, a passage may include the claim that winter occurs during opposite months in the Northern and Southern hemispheres. Text evidence for this claim may include examples of countries where winter occurs in opposite months. Stating that the tilt of the Earth as it rotates around the sun causes winter to occur at different times in separate hemispheres is another example of text evidence. Text evidence can come from common knowledge, but it is also valuable to include text evidence from credible, relevant outside sources.

> **Review Video: Textual Evidence**
> Visit mometrix.com/academy and enter code: 486236

Evidence that supports the thesis and additional arguments needs to be provided. Most arguments must be supported by facts or statistics. A fact is something that is known with certainty, has been verified by several independent individuals, and can be proven to be true. In addition to facts, examples and illustrations can support an argument by adding an emotional component. With this component, you persuade readers in ways that facts and statistics cannot. The emotional component is effective when used alongside objective information that can be confirmed.

## CREDIBILITY

The text used to support an argument can be the argument's downfall if the text is not credible. A text is **credible**, or believable, when its author is knowledgeable and objective, or unbiased. The author's motivations for writing the text play a critical role in determining the credibility of the text and must be evaluated when assessing that credibility. Reports written about the ozone layer by an environmental scientist and a hairdresser will have a different level of credibility.

> **Review Video: Author Credibility**
> Visit mometrix.com/academy and enter code: 827257

## APPEAL TO EMOTION

Sometimes, authors will appeal to the reader's emotion in an attempt to persuade or to distract the reader from the weakness of the argument. For instance, the author may try to inspire the pity of the reader by delivering a heart-rending story. An author also might use the bandwagon approach, in which he suggests that his opinion is correct because it is held by the majority. Some authors resort to name-calling, in which insults and harsh words are delivered to the opponent in an attempt to distract. In advertising, a common appeal is the celebrity testimonial, in which a famous person endorses a product. Of course, the fact that a famous person likes something should not really mean anything to the reader. These and other emotional appeals are usually evidence of poor reasoning and a weak argument.

> **Review Video: Emotional Language in Literature**
> Visit mometrix.com/academy and enter code: 759390

## COUNTER ARGUMENTS

When authors give both sides to the argument, they build trust with their readers. As a reader, you should start with an undecided or neutral position. If an author presents only his or her side to the argument, then they are not exhibiting credibility and are weakening their argument.

Building common ground with readers can be effective for persuading neutral, skeptical, or opposed readers. Sharing values with undecided readers can allow people to switch positions without giving up what they feel is important. People who may oppose a position need to feel that they can change their minds without betraying who they are as a person. This appeal to having an open mind can be a powerful tool in arguing a position without antagonizing other views. Objections can be countered on a point-by-point basis or in a summary paragraph. Be mindful of how an author points out flaws in counter arguments. If they are unfair to the other side of the argument, then you should lose trust with the author.

# Synthesis

## COMPARING TWO TEXTS
### SYNTHESIS OF MULTIPLE TEXTS

Synthesizing, i.e., understanding and integrating, information from multiple texts can at times be among the most challenging skills for some students to succeed with on tests and in school, and yet it is also among the most important. Students who read at the highest cognitive levels can select related material from different text sources and construct coherent arguments that account for these varied information sources. Synthesizing ideas and information from multiple texts actually combines other reading skills that students should have mastered previously in reading one text at a time, and applies them in the context of reading more than one text. For example, students are required to read texts closely, including identifying explicit and implicit meanings; use critical thinking and reading; draw inferences; assess author reasoning; analyze supporting evidence; and formulate opinions they can justify, based on more passages than one. When two paired texts represent opposing sides of the same argument, students can find analyzing them easier; but this is not always the case.

### SIMILARITIES IN TEXTS

When students are called upon to compare things two texts share in common, the most obvious commonality might be the same subject matter or specific topic. However, two texts need not be about the same thing to compare them. Some other features texts can share include structural characteristics. For example, they may both be written using a sequential format, such as narrating events or giving instructions in chronological order; listing and/or discussing subtopics by order of importance; or describing a place spatially in sequence from each point to the next. They may both use a comparison-contrast structure, identifying similarities and differences between, among, or within topics. They might both organize information by identifying cause-and-effect relationships. Texts can be similar in type, e.g., description, narration, persuasion, or exposition. They can be similar in using technical vocabulary or using formal or informal language. They may share similar tones and/or styles, e.g., humorous, satirical, serious, etc. They can share similar purposes, e.g., to alarm audiences, incite them to action, reassure them, inspire them, provoke strong emotional responses, etc.

### CONTRASTS IN TEXTS

When analyzing paired or multiple texts, students might observe differences in tone; for example, one text might take a serious approach while another uses a humorous one. Even within approaches or treatments, style can differ: one text may be humorous in a witty, sophisticated, clever way while another may exercise broad, "lowbrow" humor; another may employ mordant sarcasm; another may use satire, couching outrageous suggestions in a "deadpan" logical voice to lampoon social attitudes and behaviors as Jonathan Swift did in *A Modest Proposal*. Serious writing can range from darkly pessimistic to alarmist to objective and unemotional. Texts might have similar information, yet organize it using different structures. One text may support points or ideas using logical arguments, while another may seek to persuade its audience by appealing to their emotions. A very obvious difference in text is genre: for example, the same mythological or traditional stories have been told as oral folk tales, written dramas, written novels, etc.; and/or set in different times and places (e.g., Shakespeare's *Romeo and Juliet* vs. Laurents, Bernstein, and Sondheim's *West Side Story*).

# Vocabulary

## WORD ROOTS AND PREFIXES AND SUFFIXES
### AFFIXES

Affixes in the English language are morphemes that are added to words to create related but different words. Derivational affixes form new words based on and related to the original words. For example, the affix *–ness* added to the end of the adjective *happy* forms the noun *happiness*. Inflectional affixes form different grammatical versions of words. For example, the plural affix *–s* changes the singular noun *book* to the plural noun *books*, and the past tense affix *–ed* changes the present tense verb *look* to the past tense *looked*. Prefixes are affixes placed in front of words. For example, *heat* means to make hot; *preheat* means to heat in advance. Suffixes are affixes placed at the ends of words. The *happiness* example above contains the suffix *–ness*. Circumfixes add parts both before and after words, such as how *light* becomes *enlighten* with the prefix *en-* and the suffix *–en*. Interfixes create compound words via central affixes: *speed* and *meter* become *speedometer* via the interfix *–o–*.

> **Review Video: Affixes**
> Visit mometrix.com/academy and enter code: 782422

### WORD ROOTS, PREFIXES, AND SUFFIXES TO HELP DETERMINE MEANINGS OF WORDS

Many English words were formed from combining multiple sources. For example, the Latin *habēre* means "to have," and the prefixes *in-* and *im-* mean a lack or prevention of something, as in *insufficient* and *imperfect*. Latin combined *in-* with *habēre* to form *inhibēre*, whose past participle was *inhibitus*. This is the origin of the English word *inhibit*, meaning to prevent from having. Hence by knowing the meanings of both the prefix and the root, one can decipher the word meaning. In Greek, the root *enkephalo-* refers to the brain. Many medical terms are based on this root, such as encephalitis and hydrocephalus. Understanding the prefix and suffix meanings (*-itis* means inflammation; *hydro-* means water) allows a person to deduce that encephalitis refers to brain inflammation and hydrocephalus refers to water (or other fluid) in the brain.

> **Review Video: Root Words in English**
> Visit mometrix.com/academy and enter code: 896380
>
> **Review Video: Determining Word Meanings**
> Visit mometrix.com/academy and enter code: 894894

### PREFIXES

Knowing common prefixes is helpful for all readers as they try to determining meanings or definitions of unfamiliar words. For example, a common word used when cooking is *preheat*. Knowing that *pre-* means in advance can also inform them that *presume* means to assume in advance, that *prejudice* means advance judgment, and that this understanding can be applied to many other words beginning with *pre-*. Knowing that the prefix *dis-* indicates opposition informs the meanings of words like *disbar, disagree, disestablish,* and many more. Knowing *dys-* means bad, impaired, abnormal, or difficult informs *dyslogistic, dysfunctional, dysphagia,* and *dysplasia*.

### SUFFIXES

In English, certain suffixes generally indicate both that a word is a noun, and that the noun represents a state of being or quality. For example, *-ness* is commonly used to change an adjective into its noun form, as with *happy* and *happiness, nice* and *niceness,* and so on. The suffix *–tion* is commonly used to transform a verb into its noun form, as with *converse* and *conversation* or *move* and *motion*. Thus, if readers are unfamiliar with the second form of a word, knowing the meaning of the transforming suffix can help them determine meaning.

## PREFIXES FOR NUMBERS

| Prefix | Definition | Examples |
|---|---|---|
| bi- | two | bisect, biennial |
| mono- | one, single | monogamy, monologue |
| poly- | many | polymorphous, polygamous |
| semi- | half, partly | semicircle, semicolon |
| uni- | one | uniform, unity |

## PREFIXES FOR TIME, DIRECTION, AND SPACE

| Prefix | Definition | Examples |
|---|---|---|
| a- | in, on, of, up, to | abed, afoot |
| ab- | from, away, off | abdicate, abjure |
| ad- | to, toward | advance, adventure |
| ante- | before, previous | antecedent, antedate |
| anti- | against, opposing | antipathy, antidote |
| cata- | down, away, thoroughly | catastrophe, cataclysm |
| circum- | around | circumspect, circumference |
| com- | with, together, very | commotion, complicate |
| contra- | against, opposing | contradict, contravene |
| de- | from | depart |
| dia- | through, across, apart | diameter, diagnose |
| dis- | away, off, down, not | dissent, disappear |
| epi- | upon | epilogue |
| ex- | out | extract, excerpt |
| hypo- | under, beneath | hypodermic, hypothesis |
| inter- | among, between | intercede, interrupt |
| intra- | within | intramural, intrastate |
| ob- | against, opposing | objection |
| per- | through | perceive, permit |
| peri- | around | periscope, perimeter |
| post- | after, following | postpone, postscript |
| pre- | before, previous | prevent, preclude |
| pro- | forward, in place of | propel, pronoun |
| retro- | back, backward | retrospect, retrograde |
| sub- | under, beneath | subjugate, substitute |
| super- | above, extra | supersede, supernumerary |
| trans- | across, beyond, over | transact, transport |
| ultra- | beyond, excessively | ultramodern, ultrasonic |

## NEGATIVE PREFIXES

| Prefix | Definition | Examples |
|---|---|---|
| a- | without, lacking | atheist, agnostic |
| in- | not, opposing | incapable, ineligible |
| non- | not | nonentity, nonsense |
| un- | not, reverse of | unhappy, unlock |

## EXTRA PREFIXES

| Prefix | Definition | Examples |
|---|---|---|
| for- | away, off, from | forget, forswear |

| Prefix | Definition | Examples |
|---|---|---|
| fore- | previous | foretell, forefathers |
| homo- | same, equal | homogenized, homonym |
| hyper- | excessive, over | hypercritical, hypertension |
| in- | in, into | intrude, invade |
| mal- | bad, poorly, not | malfunction, malpractice |
| mis- | bad, poorly, not | misspell, misfire |
| neo- | new | Neolithic, neoconservative |
| omni- | all, everywhere | omniscient, omnivore |
| ortho- | right, straight | orthogonal, orthodox |
| over- | above | overbearing, oversight |
| pan- | all, entire | panorama, pandemonium |
| para- | beside, beyond | parallel, paradox |
| re- | backward, again | revoke, recur |
| sym- | with, together | sympathy, symphony |

Below is a list of common suffixes and their meanings:

## ADJECTIVE SUFFIXES

| Suffix | Definition | Examples |
|---|---|---|
| -able (-ible) | capable of being | tolerable, edible |
| -esque | in the style of, like | picturesque, grotesque |
| -ful | filled with, marked by | thankful, zestful |
| -ific | make, cause | terrific, beatific |
| -ish | suggesting, like | churlish, childish |
| -less | lacking, without | hopeless, countless |
| -ous | marked by, given to | religious, riotous |

## NOUN SUFFIXES

| Suffix | Definition | Examples |
|---|---|---|
| -acy | state, condition | accuracy, privacy |
| -ance | act, condition, fact | acceptance, vigilance |
| -ard | one that does excessively | drunkard, sluggard |
| -ation | action, state, result | occupation, starvation |
| -dom | state, rank, condition | serfdom, wisdom |
| -er (-or) | office, action | teacher, elevator, honor |
| -ess | feminine | waitress, duchess |
| -hood | state, condition | manhood, statehood |
| -ion | action, result, state | union, fusion |
| -ism | act, manner, doctrine | barbarism, socialism |
| -ist | worker, follower | monopolist, socialist |
| -ity (-ty) | state, quality, condition | acidity, civility, twenty |
| -ment | result, action | Refreshment |
| -ness | quality, state | greatness, tallness |
| -ship | position | internship, statesmanship |
| -sion (-tion) | state, result | revision, expedition |
| -th | act, state, quality | warmth, width |
| -tude | quality, state, result | magnitude, fortitude |

## Verb Suffixes

| Suffix | Definition | Examples |
|---|---|---|
| -ate | having, showing | separate, desolate |
| -en | cause to be, become | deepen, strengthen |
| -fy | make, cause to have | glorify, fortify |
| -ize | cause to be, treat with | sterilize, mechanize |

## Nuance and Word Meanings

### Synonyms and Antonyms

When you understand how words relate to each other, you will discover more in a passage. This is explained by understanding **synonyms** (e.g., words that mean the same thing) and **antonyms** (e.g., words that mean the opposite of one another). As an example, *dry* and *arid* are synonyms, and *dry* and *wet* are antonyms.

There are many pairs of words in English that can be considered synonyms, despite having slightly different definitions. For instance, the words *friendly* and *collegial* can both be used to describe a warm interpersonal relationship, and one would be correct to call them synonyms. However, *collegial* (kin to *colleague*) is often used in reference to professional or academic relationships, and *friendly* has no such connotation.

If the difference between the two words is too great, then they should not be called synonyms. *Hot* and *warm* are not synonyms because their meanings are too distinct. A good way to determine whether two words are synonyms is to substitute one word for the other word and verify that the meaning of the sentence has not changed. Substituting *warm* for *hot* in a sentence would convey a different meaning. Although warm and hot may seem close in meaning, warm generally means that the temperature is moderate, and hot generally means that the temperature is excessively high.

Antonyms are words with opposite meanings. *Light* and *dark*, *up* and *down*, *right* and *left*, *good* and *bad*: these are all sets of antonyms. Be careful to distinguish between antonyms and pairs of words that are simply different. *Black* and *gray*, for instance, are not antonyms because gray is not the opposite of black. *Black* and *white*, on the other hand, are antonyms.

Not every word has an antonym. For instance, many nouns do not. What would be the antonym of *chair*? During your exam, the questions related to antonyms are more likely to concern adjectives. You will recall that adjectives are words that describe a noun. Some common adjectives include *purple*, *fast*, *skinny*, and *sweet*. From those four adjectives, *purple* is the item that lacks a group of obvious antonyms.

> **Review Video: Synonyms and Antonyms**
> Visit mometrix.com/academy and enter code: 105612

### Denotative vs. Connotative Meaning

The **denotative** meaning of a word is the literal meaning. The **connotative** meaning goes beyond the denotative meaning to include the emotional reaction that a word may invoke. The connotative meaning often takes the denotative meaning a step further due to associations the reader makes with the denotative meaning. Readers can differentiate between the denotative and connotative meanings by first recognizing how authors use each meaning. Most non-fiction, for example, is fact-based and authors do not use flowery, figurative language. The reader can assume that the writer is using the denotative meaning of words. In fiction, the author may use the connotative meaning. Readers can determine whether the author is using the denotative or connotative meaning of a word by implementing context clues.

> **Review Video: Connotation and Denotation**
> Visit mometrix.com/academy and enter code: 310092

## NUANCES OF WORD MEANING

A word's denotation is simply its objective dictionary definition. However, its connotation refers to the subjective associations, often emotional, that specific words evoke in listeners and readers. Two or more words can have the same dictionary meaning, but very different connotations. Writers use diction (word choice) to convey various nuances of thought and emotion by selecting synonyms for other words that best communicate the associations they want to trigger for readers. For example, a car engine is naturally greasy; in this sense, "greasy" is a neutral term. But when a person's smile, appearance, or clothing is described as "greasy," it has a negative connotation. Some words have even gained additional or different meanings over time. For example, *awful* used to be used to describe things that evoked a sense of awe. When *awful* is separated into its root word, awe, and suffix, -ful, it can be understood to mean "full of awe." However, the word is now commonly used to describe things that evoke repulsion, terror, or another intense, negative reaction.

> **Review Video: Word Usage in Sentences**
> Visit mometrix.com/academy and enter code: 197863

## USING CONTEXT TO DETERMINE MEANING

### CONTEXT CLUES

Readers of all levels will encounter words that they have either never seen or have encountered only on a limited basis. The best way to define a word in **context** is to look for nearby words that can assist in revealing the meaning of the word. For instance, unfamiliar nouns are often accompanied by examples that provide a definition. Consider the following sentence: *Dave arrived at the party in hilarious garb: a leopard-print shirt, buckskin trousers, and bright green sneakers.* If a reader was unfamiliar with the meaning of garb, he or she could read the examples (i.e., a leopard-print shirt, buckskin trousers, and bright green sneakers) and quickly determine that the word means *clothing*. Examples will not always be this obvious. Consider this sentence: *Parsley, lemon, and flowers were just a few of the items he used as garnishes.* Here, the word *garnishes* is exemplified by parsley, lemon, and flowers. Readers who have eaten in a variety of restaurants will probably be able to identify a garnish as something used to decorate a plate.

> **Review Video: Reading Comprehension: Using Context Clues**
> Visit mometrix.com/academy and enter code: 613660

### USING CONTRAST IN CONTEXT CLUES

In addition to looking at the context of a passage, readers can use contrast to define an unfamiliar word in context. In many sentences, the author will not describe the unfamiliar word directly; instead, he or she will describe the opposite of the unfamiliar word. Thus, you are provided with some information that will bring you closer to defining the word. Consider the following example: *Despite his intelligence, Hector's low brow and bad posture made him look obtuse.* The author writes that Hector's appearance does not convey intelligence. Therefore, *obtuse* must mean unintelligent. Here is another example: *Despite the horrible weather, we were beatific about our trip to Alaska.* The word *despite* indicates that the speaker's feelings were at odds with the weather. Since the weather is described as *horrible*, then *beatific* must mean something positive.

### SUBSTITUTION TO FIND MEANING

In some cases, there will be very few contextual clues to help a reader define the meaning of an unfamiliar word. When this happens, one strategy that readers may employ is **substitution**. A good reader will brainstorm some possible synonyms for the given word, and he or she will substitute these words into the sentence. If the sentence and the surrounding passage continue to make sense, then the substitution has revealed at least some information about the unfamiliar word. Consider the sentence: *Frank's admonition rang in her ears as she climbed the mountain.* A reader unfamiliar with *admonition* might come up with some substitutions like *vow, promise, advice, complaint,* or *compliment*. All of these words make general sense of the sentence, though their meanings are diverse. However, this process has suggested that an admonition is some

sort of message. The substitution strategy is rarely able to pinpoint a precise definition, but this process can be effective as a last resort.

Occasionally, you will be able to define an unfamiliar word by looking at the descriptive words in the context. Consider the following sentence: *Fred dragged the recalcitrant boy kicking and screaming up the stairs.* The words *dragged*, *kicking*, and *screaming* all suggest that the boy does not want to go up the stairs. The reader may assume that *recalcitrant* means something like unwilling or protesting. In this example, an unfamiliar adjective was identified.

Additionally, using description to define an unfamiliar noun is a common practice compared to unfamiliar adjectives, as in this sentence: *Don's wrinkled frown and constantly shaking fist identified him as a curmudgeon of the first order.* Don is described as having a *wrinkled frown and constantly shaking fist*, suggesting that a *curmudgeon* must be a grumpy person. Contrasts do not always provide detailed information about the unfamiliar word, but they at least give the reader some clues.

## Words with Multiple Meanings

When a word has more than one meaning, readers can have difficulty determining how the word is being used in a given sentence. For instance, the verb *cleave*, can mean either *join* or *separate*. When readers come upon this word, they will have to select the definition that makes the most sense. Consider the following sentence: *Hermione's knife cleaved the bread cleanly*. Since a knife cannot join bread together, the word must indicate separation. A slightly more difficult example would be the sentence: *The birds cleaved to one another as they flew from the oak tree.* Immediately, the presence of the words *to one another* should suggest that in this sentence *cleave* is being used to mean *join*. Discovering the intent of a word with multiple meanings requires the same tricks as defining an unknown word: look for contextual clues and evaluate the substituted words.

## Context Clues to Help Determine Meanings of Words

If readers simply bypass unknown words, they can reach unclear conclusions about what they read. However, looking for the definition of every unfamiliar word in the dictionary can slow their reading progress. Moreover, the dictionary may list multiple definitions for a word, so readers must search the word's context for meaning. Hence context is important to new vocabulary regardless of reader methods. Four types of context clues are examples, definitions, descriptive words, and opposites. Authors may use a certain word, and then follow it with several different examples of what it describes. Sometimes authors actually supply a definition of a word they use, which is especially true in informational and technical texts. Authors may use descriptive words that elaborate upon a vocabulary word they just used. Authors may also use opposites with negation that help define meaning.

## Examples and Definitions

An author may use a word and then give examples that illustrate its meaning. Consider this text: "Teachers who do not know how to use sign language can help students who are deaf or hard of hearing understand certain instructions by using gestures instead, like pointing their fingers to indicate which direction to look or go; holding up a hand, palm outward, to indicate stopping; holding the hands flat, palms up, curling a finger toward oneself in a beckoning motion to indicate 'come here'; or curling all fingers toward oneself repeatedly to indicate 'come on', 'more', or 'continue.'" The author of this text has used the word "gestures" and then followed it with examples, so a reader unfamiliar with the word could deduce from the examples that "gestures" means "hand motions." Readers can find examples by looking for signal words "for example," "for instance," "like," "such as," and "e.g."

While readers sometimes have to look for definitions of unfamiliar words in a dictionary or do some work to determine a word's meaning from its surrounding context, at other times an author may make it easier for readers by defining certain words. For example, an author may write, "The company did not have sufficient capital, that is, available money, to continue operations." The author defined "capital" as "available money," and heralded the definition with the phrase "that is." Another way that authors supply word definitions is with appositives. Rather than being introduced by a signal phrase like "that is," "namely," or "meaning," an appositive comes after the vocabulary word it defines and is enclosed within two commas. For example, an author may write, "The Indians introduced the Pilgrims to pemmican, cakes they made of lean meat dried and mixed with fat, which proved greatly beneficial to keep settlers from starving while trapping." In this example, the appositive phrase following "pemmican" and preceding "which" defines the word "pemmican."

## Descriptions

When readers encounter a word they do not recognize in a text, the author may expand on that word to illustrate it better. While the author may do this to make the prose more picturesque and vivid, the reader can also take advantage of this description to provide context clues to the meaning of the unfamiliar word. For example, an author may write, "The man sitting next to me on the airplane was obese. His shirt stretched across his vast expanse of flesh, strained almost to bursting." The descriptive second sentence elaborates on and helps to define the previous sentence's word "obese" to mean extremely fat. A reader unfamiliar with the word "repugnant" can decipher its meaning through an author's accompanying description: "The way the child grimaced and shuddered as he swallowed the medicine showed that its taste was particularly repugnant."

## Opposites

Text authors sometimes introduce a contrasting or opposing idea before or after a concept they present. They may do this to emphasize or heighten the idea they present by contrasting it with something that is the reverse. However, readers can also use these context clues to understand familiar words. For example, an author may write, "Our conversation was not cheery. We sat and talked very solemnly about his experience and a number of similar events." The reader who is not familiar with the word "solemnly" can deduce by the author's preceding use of "not cheery" that "solemn" means the opposite of cheery or happy, so it must mean serious or sad. Or if someone writes, "Don't condemn his entire project because you couldn't find anything good to say about it," readers unfamiliar with "condemn" can understand from the sentence structure that it means the opposite of saying anything good, so it must mean reject, dismiss, or disapprove. "Entire" adds another context clue, meaning total or complete rejection.

## Syntax to Determine Part of Speech and Meanings of Words

Syntax refers to sentence structure and word order. Suppose that a reader encounters an unfamiliar word when reading a text. To illustrate, consider an invented word like "splunch." If this word is used in a sentence like "Please splunch that ball to me," the reader can assume from syntactic context that "splunch" is a verb. We would not use a noun, adjective, adverb, or preposition with the object "that ball," and the prepositional phrase "to me" further indicates "splunch" represents an action. However, in the sentence, "Please hand that splunch to me," the reader can assume that "splunch" is a noun. Demonstrative adjectives like "that" modify nouns. Also, we hand someone some*thing*—a thing being a noun; we do not hand someone a verb, adjective, or adverb. Some sentences contain further clues. For example, from the sentence, "The princess wore the glittering splunch on her head," the reader can deduce that it is a crown, tiara, or something similar from the syntactic context, without knowing the word.

## Syntax to Indicate Different Meanings of Similar Sentences

The syntax, or structure, of a sentence affords grammatical cues that aid readers in comprehending the meanings of words, phrases, and sentences in the texts that they read. Seemingly minor differences in how the words or phrases in a sentence are ordered can make major differences in meaning. For example, two sentences can use exactly the same words but have different meanings based on the word order:

- "The man with a broken arm sat in a chair."
- "The man sat in a chair with a broken arm."

While both sentences indicate that a man sat in a chair, differing syntax indicates whether the man's or chair's arm was broken.

> **Review Video: Syntax**
> Visit mometrix.com/academy and enter code: 242280

## DETERMINING MEANING OF PHRASES AND PARAGRAPHS

Like unknown words, the meanings of phrases, paragraphs, and entire works can also be difficult to discern. Each of these can be better understood with added context. However, for larger groups of words, more context is needed. Unclear phrases are similar to unclear words, and the same methods can be used to understand their meaning. However, it is also important to consider how the individual words in the phrase work together. Paragraphs are a bit more complicated. Just as words must be compared to other words in a sentence, paragraphs must be compared to other paragraphs in a composition or a section.

## DETERMINING MEANING IN VARIOUS TYPES OF COMPOSITIONS

To understand the meaning of an entire composition, the type of composition must be considered. **Expository writing** is generally organized so that each paragraph focuses on explaining one idea, or part of an idea, and its relevance. **Persuasive writing** uses paragraphs for different purposes to organize the parts of the argument. **Unclear paragraphs** must be read in the context of the paragraphs around them for their meaning to be fully understood. The meaning of full texts can also be unclear at times. The purpose of composition is also important for understanding the meaning of a text. To quickly understand the broad meaning of a text, look to the introductory and concluding paragraphs. Fictional texts are different. Some fictional works have implicit meanings, but some do not. The target audience must be considered for understanding texts that do have an implicit meaning, as most children's fiction will clearly state any lessons or morals. For other fiction, the application of literary theories and criticism may be helpful for understanding the text.

## RESOURCES FOR DETERMINING WORD MEANING AND USAGE

While these strategies are useful for determining the meaning of unknown words and phrases, sometimes additional resources are needed to properly use the terms in different contexts. Some words have multiple definitions, and some words are inappropriate in particular contexts or modes of writing. The following tools are helpful for understanding all meanings and proper uses for words and phrases.

- **Dictionaries** provide the meaning of a multitude of words in a language. Many dictionaries include additional information about each word, such as its etymology, its synonyms, or variations of the word.
- **Glossaries** are similar to dictionaries, as they provide the meanings of a variety of terms. However, while dictionaries typically feature an extensive list of words and comprise an entire publication, glossaries are often included at the end of a text and only include terms and definitions that are relevant to the text they follow.
- **Spell Checkers** are used to detect spelling errors in typed text. Some spell checkers may also detect the misuse of plural or singular nouns, verb tenses, or capitalization. While spell checkers are a helpful tool, they are not always reliable or attuned to the author's intent, so it is important to review the spell checker's suggestions before accepting them.
- **Style Manuals** are guidelines on the preferred punctuation, format, and grammar usage according to different fields or organizations. For example, the Associated Press Stylebook is a style guide often used for media writing. The guidelines within a style guide are not always applicable across different contexts and usages, as the guidelines often cover grammatical or formatting situations that are not objectively correct or incorrect.

## Chapter Quiz

Ready to see how well you retained what you just read? Scan the QR code to go directly to the chapter quiz interface for this study guide. If you're using a computer, simply visit the online resources page at **mometrix.com/resources719/accuplacer-28992** and click the Chapter Quizzes link.

# Writing

Transform passive reading into active learning! After immersing yourself in this chapter, put your comprehension to the test by taking a quiz. The insights you gained will stay with you longer this way. Scan the QR code to go directly to the chapter quiz interface for this study guide. If you're using a computer, simply visit the online resources page at **mometrix.com/resources719/accuplacer-28992** and click the Chapter Quizzes link.

## Development

### THE WRITING PROCESS

#### PREWRITING

The **prewriting stage** is the part of the process in which the writer focuses on **generating ideas** and developing a broad plan for what he or she wants to accomplish. **Brainstorming** is the process of thinking about a topic and writing down every thought that comes to mind. Brainstorming may also take the form of asking questions that need to be answered by the composition. **Free writing** has a similar goal of writing about a topic in a continuous flow for a short span of time (e.g., 2 to 3 minutes). The goal of these exercises is not to produce high-quality, polished thoughts, but to generate leads to follow when the more structured writing happens later in the process. In research writing, the prewriting stage may also include doing a literature review and **collecting information** to use as evidence in arguments later on. When collecting information, it is important to take clear notes of where an idea was originally found so it can be cited later on. Another key aspect of the prewriting process is **planning phase**. This entails deciding on the overall topic, purpose, tone, and general organization for the rest of the composition. The planning process may involve using aids like outlines, Venn diagrams, flowcharts, and other visual models to help collect and organize information. The planning process does not set the whole composition in stone, but it does help structure the ideas to be written in the drafting phase.

#### DRAFTING

The **drafting stage** of the writing process involves taking the plan for the composition and filling out all of the main ideas for the composition. Some writers prefer to start by writing the introduction and write their whole composition from start to finish, while others may prefer writing the main body paragraphs first and then coming back to the introduction and conclusion. In any case, the drafting process is a first attempt at writing the whole composition from start to finish. A writer may succeed in communicating what he or she wants in the first draft, but it often takes writing **several drafts** before the ideas and arguments take their final form. By the end of the drafting stage, the composition should be close to its final organization with its arguments clearly identified, but it will still need organizational, grammatical, and formatting improvements to be called complete.

#### REVISING

The **revision stage** is when the writer reads back through his or her work and looks for big-picture issues that affect **clarity** and **cohesion**. These can include organizational issues or flaws in logical flow. Writers should look back through their work to find any assertions or arguments that may be misplaced or lacking in support. They should look also through their work to find any information that does not contribute to the main idea or goal of the composition. Beginning writers may find it difficult to clearly communicate more than two or three main points in their arguments. If this is the case, these writers should eliminate information that detracts from those main points. In this stage, clarity is often more important than comprehensiveness.

## Editing/Proofreading

The **editing or proofreading stage** is focused specifically on improving the grammar and punctuation of the composition. The writer should read each paragraph closely and slowly to identify and fix any grammatical, spelling, or punctuation errors. Some of the worst offenders include subject-verb agreement in complex sentences, changes in tense throughout the document, and changes in perspective (first, second, or third person) or tone (professional, casual, opinionated, etc.). When writing at home, it is often helpful to have a friend or family member look for errors as well. Finally, this phase involves looking for very small errors, so multiple passes should be taken to catch as many problems as possible. One good rule of thumb is to keep reading through the whole document until a full read-through can be accomplished without finding any more errors.

## Publishing

The **publishing stage** refers to putting the document into its final format and delivering it to the audience. This involves formatting the document for presentation. In research writing, the final document may need to conform to a specific publishing standard, such as MLA or APA. In literal publishing, this would also take the form of presenting the document to the final audience, which may involve physical printing or digital publication. Note that once a composition has been published, it is often difficult to change or retract. Before reaching the publishing stage, the writer should have looped through the drafting, revision, and editing process a few times to ensure the writer says exactly what he or she wants before putting it before the final audience.

## Recursive Writing Process

However you approach writing, you may find comfort in knowing that the revision process can occur in any order. The **recursive writing process** is not as difficult as the phrase may make it seem. Simply put, the recursive writing process means that you may need to revisit steps after completing other steps. It also implies that the steps are not required to take place in any certain order. Indeed, you may find that planning, drafting, and revising can all take place at about the same time. The writing process involves moving back and forth between planning, drafting, and revising, followed by more planning, more drafting, and more revising until the writing is satisfactory.

> **Review Video: Recursive Writing Process**
> Visit mometrix.com/academy and enter code: 951611

## Common Types of Writing

### Autobiographical Narratives

**Autobiographical narratives** are narratives written by an author about an event or period in their life. Autobiographical narratives are written from one person's perspective, in first person, and often include the author's thoughts and feelings alongside their description of the event or period. Structure, style, or theme varies between different autobiographical narratives, since each narrative is personal and specific to its author and his or her experience.

### Reflective Essay

A less common type of essay is the reflective essay. **Reflective essays** allow the author to reflect, or think back, on an experience and analyze what they recall. They should consider what they learned from the experience, what they could have done differently, what would have helped them during the experience, or anything else that they have realized from looking back on the experience. Reflection essays incorporate both objective reflection on one's own actions and subjective explanation of thoughts and feelings. These essays can be written for a number of experiences in a formal or informal context.

### Journals and Diaries

A **journal** is a personal account of events, experiences, feelings, and thoughts. Many people write journals to express their feelings and thoughts or to help them process experiences they have had. Since journals are

**private documents** not meant to be shared with others, writers may not be concerned with grammar, spelling, or other mechanics. However, authors may write journals that they expect or hope to publish someday; in this case, they not only express their thoughts and feelings and process their experiences, but they also attend to their craft in writing them. Some authors compose journals to record a particular time period or a series of related events, such as a cancer diagnosis, treatment, surviving the disease, and how these experiences have changed or affected them. Other experiences someone might include in a journal are recovering from addiction, journeys of spiritual exploration and discovery, time spent in another country, or anything else someone wants to personally document. Journaling can also be therapeutic, as some people use journals to work through feelings of grief over loss or to wrestle with big decisions.

## EXAMPLES OF DIARIES IN LITERATURE

*The Diary of a Young Girl* by Dutch Jew Anne Frank (1947) contains her life-affirming, nonfictional diary entries from 1942-1944 while her family hid in an attic from World War II's genocidal Nazis. *Go Ask Alice* (1971) by Beatrice Sparks is a cautionary, fictional novel in the form of diary entries by Alice, an unhappy, rebellious teen who takes LSD, runs away from home and lives with hippies, and eventually returns home. Frank's writing reveals an intelligent, sensitive, insightful girl, raised by intellectual European parents—a girl who believes in the goodness of human nature despite surrounding atrocities. Alice, influenced by early 1970s counterculture, becomes less optimistic. However, similarities can be found between them: Frank dies in a Nazi concentration camp while the fictitious Alice dies from a drug overdose. Both young women are also unable to escape their surroundings. Additionally, adolescent searches for personal identity are evident in both books.

> **Review Video: Journals, Diaries, Letters, and Blogs**
> Visit mometrix.com/academy and enter code: 432845

## LETTERS

**Letters** are messages written to other people. In addition to letters written between individuals, some writers compose letters to the editors of newspapers, magazines, and other publications, while some write "Open Letters" to be published and read by the general public. Open letters, while intended for everyone to read, may also identify a group of people or a single person whom the letter directly addresses. In everyday use, the most-used forms are business letters and personal or friendly letters. Both kinds share common elements: business or personal letterhead stationery; the writer's return address at the top; the addressee's address next; a salutation, such as "Dear [name]" or some similar opening greeting, followed by a colon in business letters or a comma in personal letters; the body of the letter, with paragraphs as indicated; and a closing, like "Sincerely/Cordially/Best regards/etc." or "Love," in intimate personal letters.

## EARLY LETTERS

The Greek word for "letter" is *epistolē*, which became the English word "epistle." The earliest letters were called epistles, including the New Testament's epistles from the apostles to the Christians. In ancient Egypt, the writing curriculum in scribal schools included the epistolary genre. Epistolary novels frame a story in the form of letters. Examples of noteworthy epistolary novels include:

- *Pamela* (1740), by 18th-century English novelist Samuel Richardson
- *Shamela* (1741), Henry Fielding's satire of *Pamela* that mocked epistolary writing.
- *Lettres persanes* (1721) by French author Montesquieu
- *The Sorrows of Young Werther* (1774) by German author Johann Wolfgang von Goethe
- *The History of Emily Montague* (1769), the first Canadian novel, by Frances Brooke
- *Dracula* (1897) by Bram Stoker
- *Frankenstein* (1818) by Mary Shelley
- *The Color Purple* (1982) by Alice Walker

## Blogs

The word "blog" is derived from "weblog" and refers to writing done exclusively on the internet. Readers of reputable newspapers expect quality content and layouts that enable easy reading. These expectations also apply to blogs. For example, readers can easily move visually from line to line when columns are narrow, while overly wide columns cause readers to lose their places. Blogs must also be posted with layouts enabling online readers to follow them easily. However, because the way people read on computer, tablet, and smartphone screens differs from how they read print on paper, formatting and writing blog content is more complex than writing newspaper articles. Two major principles are the bases for blog-writing rules: The first is while readers of print articles skim to estimate their length, online they must scroll down to scan; therefore, blog layouts need more subheadings, graphics, and other indications of what information follows. The second is onscreen reading can be harder on the eyes than reading printed paper, so legibility is crucial in blogs.

### Rules and Rationales for Writing Blogs

1. Format all posts for smooth page layout and easy scanning.
2. Column width should not be too wide, as larger lines of text can be difficult to read
3. Headings and subheadings separate text visually, enable scanning or skimming, and encourage continued reading.
4. Bullet-pointed or numbered lists enable quick information location and scanning.
5. Punctuation is critical, so beginners should use shorter sentences until confident in their knowledge of punctuation rules.
6. Blog paragraphs should be far shorter—two to six sentences each—than paragraphs written on paper to enable "chunking" because reading onscreen is more difficult.
7. Sans-serif fonts are usually clearer than serif fonts, and larger font sizes are better.
8. Highlight important material and draw attention with **boldface**, but avoid overuse. Avoid hard-to-read *italics* and ALL CAPITALS.
9. Include enough blank spaces: overly busy blogs tire eyes and brains. Images not only break up text but also emphasize and enhance text and can attract initial reader attention.
10. Use background colors judiciously to avoid distracting the eye or making it difficult to read.
11. Be consistent throughout posts, since people read them in different orders.
12. Tell a story with a beginning, middle, and end.

## Specialized Types of Writing

### Editorials

Editorials are articles in newspapers, magazines, and other serial publications. Editorials express an opinion or belief belonging to the majority of the publication's leadership. This opinion or belief generally refers to a specific issue, topic, or event. These articles are authored by a member, or a small number of members, of the publication's leadership and are often written to affect their readers, such as persuading them to adopt a stance or take a particular action.

### Resumes

Resumes are brief, but formal, documents that outline an individual's experience in a certain area. Resumes are most often used for job applications. Such resumes will list the applicant's work experience, certification, and achievements or qualifications related to the position. Resumes should only include the most pertinent information. They should also use strategic formatting to highlight the applicant's most impressive experiences and achievements, to ensure the document can be read quickly and easily, and to eliminate both visual clutter and excessive negative space.

### Reports

Reports summarize the results of research, new methodology, or other developments in an academic or professional context. Reports often include details about methodology and outside influences and factors. However, a report should focus primarily on the results of the research or development. Reports are objective and deliver information efficiently, sacrificing style for clear and effective communication.

## Memoranda

A memorandum, also called a memo, is a formal method of communication used in professional settings. Memoranda are printed documents that include a heading listing the sender and their job title, the recipient and their job title, the date, and a specific subject line. Memoranda often include an introductory section explaining the reason and context for the memorandum. Next, a memorandum includes a section with details relevant to the topic. Finally, the memorandum will conclude with a paragraph that politely and clearly defines the sender's expectations of the recipient.

## Technology in the Writing Process

Modern technology has yielded several tools that can be used to make the writing process more convenient and organized. Word processors and online tools, such as databases and plagiarism detectors, allow much of the writing process to be completed in one place, using one device.

## Technology for Planning and Drafting

For the planning and drafting stages of the writing process, word processors are a helpful tool. These programs also feature formatting tools, allowing users to create their own planning tools or create digital outlines that can be easily converted into sentences, paragraphs, or an entire essay draft. Online databases and references also complement the planning process by providing convenient access to information and sources for research. Word processors also allow users to keep up with their work and update it more easily than if they wrote their work by hand. Online word processors often allow users to collaborate, making group assignments more convenient. These programs also allow users to include illustrations or other supplemental media in their compositions.

## Technology for Revising, Editing, and Proofreading

Word processors also benefit the revising, editing, and proofreading stages of the writing process. Most of these programs indicate errors in spelling and grammar, allowing users to catch minor errors and correct them quickly. There are also websites designed to help writers by analyzing text for deeper errors, such as poor sentence structure, inappropriate complexity, lack of sentence variety, and style issues. These websites can help users fix errors they may not know to look for or may have simply missed. As writers finish these steps, they may benefit from checking their work for any plagiarism. There are several websites and programs that compare text to other documents and publications across the internet and detect any similarities within the text. These websites show the source of the similar information, so users know whether or not they referenced the source and unintentionally plagiarized its contents.

## Technology for Publishing

Technology also makes managing written work more convenient. Digitally storing documents keeps everything in one place and is easy to reference. Digital storage also makes sharing work easier, as documents can be attached to an email or stored online. This also allows writers to publish their work easily, as they can electronically submit it to other publications or freely post it to a personal blog, profile, or website.

# Organization

## Outlining and Organizing Ideas

### Essays

Essays usually focus on one topic, subject, or goal. There are several types of essays, including informative, persuasive, and narrative. An essay's structure and level of formality depend on the type of essay and its goal.

While narrative essays typically do not include outside sources, other types of essays often require some research and the integration of primary and secondary sources.

The basic format of an essay typically has three major parts: the introduction, the body, and the conclusion. The body is further divided into the writer's main points. Short and simple essays may have three main points, while essays covering broader ranges and going into more depth can have almost any number of main points, depending on length.

An essay's introduction should answer three questions:

1. What is the **subject** of the essay?

   If a student writes an essay about a book, the answer would include the title and author of the book and any additional information needed—such as the subject or argument of the book.

2. How does the essay **address** the subject?

   To answer this, the writer identifies the essay's organization by briefly summarizing main points and the evidence supporting them.

3. What will the essay **prove**?

   This is the thesis statement, usually the opening paragraph's last sentence, clearly stating the writer's message.

The body elaborates on all the main points related to the thesis, introducing one main point at a time, and includes supporting evidence with each main point. Each body paragraph should state the point in a topic sentence, which is usually the first sentence in the paragraph. The paragraph should then explain the point's meaning, support it with quotations or other evidence, and then explain how this point and the evidence are related to the thesis. The writer should then repeat this procedure in a new paragraph for each additional main point.

The conclusion reiterates the content of the introduction, including the thesis, to remind the reader of the essay's main argument or subject. The essay writer may also summarize the highlights of the argument or description contained in the body of the essay, following the same sequence originally used in the body. For example, a conclusion might look like: Point 1 + Point 2 + Point 3 = Thesis, or Point 1 → Point 2 → Point 3 → Thesis Proof. Good organization makes essays easier for writers to compose and provides a guide for readers to follow. Well-organized essays hold attention better and are more likely to get readers to accept their theses as valid.

## Main Ideas, Supporting Details, and Outlining a Topic

A writer often begins the first paragraph of a paper by stating the **main idea** or point, also known as the **topic sentence**. The rest of the paragraph supplies particular details that develop and support the main point. One way to visualize the relationship between the main point and supporting information is by considering a table: the tabletop is the main point, and each of the table's legs is a supporting detail or group of details. Both professional authors and students can benefit from planning their writing by first making an outline of the topic. Outlines facilitate quick identification of the main point and supporting details without having to wade through the additional language that will exist in the fully developed essay, article, or paper. Outlining can also help readers to analyze a piece of existing writing for the same reason. The outline first summarizes the main idea in one sentence. Then, below that, it summarizes the supporting details in a numbered list. Writing the paper then consists of filling in the outline with detail, writing a paragraph for each supporting point, and adding an introduction and conclusion.

## Introduction

The purpose of the introduction is to capture the reader's attention and announce the essay's main idea. Normally, the introduction contains 50-80 words, or 3-5 sentences. An introduction can begin with an interesting quote, a question, or a strong opinion—something that will **engage** the reader's interest and prompt them to keep reading. If you are writing your essay to a specific prompt, your introduction should include a **restatement or summarization** of the prompt so that the reader will have some context for your essay. Finally, your introduction should briefly state your **thesis or main idea**: the primary thing you hope to communicate to the reader through your essay. Don't try to include all of the details and nuances of your thesis, or all of your reasons for it, in the introduction. That's what the rest of the essay is for!

> **Review Video: Introduction**
> Visit mometrix.com/academy and enter code: 961328

## THESIS STATEMENT

The thesis is the main idea of the essay. A temporary thesis, or working thesis, should be established early in the writing process because it will serve to keep the writer focused as ideas develop. This temporary thesis is subject to change as you continue to write.

The temporary thesis has two parts: a **topic** (i.e., the focus of your essay based on the prompt) and a **comment**. The comment makes an important point about the topic. A temporary thesis should be interesting and specific. Also, you need to limit the topic to a manageable scope. These three questions are useful tools to measure the effectiveness of any temporary thesis:

- Does the focus of my essay have enough interest to hold an audience?
- Is the focus of my essay specific enough to generate interest?
- Is the focus of my essay manageable for the time limit? Too broad? Too narrow?

The thesis should be a generalization rather than a fact because the thesis prepares readers for facts and details that support the thesis. The process of bringing the thesis into sharp focus may help in outlining major sections of the work. Once the thesis and introduction are complete, you can address the body of the work.

> **Review Video: Thesis Statements**
> Visit mometrix.com/academy and enter code: 691033

## SUPPORTING THE THESIS

Throughout your essay, the thesis should be **explained clearly and supported** adequately by additional arguments. The thesis sentence needs to contain a clear statement of the purpose of your essay and a comment about the thesis. With the thesis statement, you have an opportunity to state what is noteworthy of this particular treatment of the prompt. Each sentence and paragraph should build on and support the thesis.

When you respond to the prompt, use parts of the passage to support your argument or defend your position. Using supporting evidence from the passage strengths your argument because readers can see your attention to the entire passage and your response to the details and facts within the passage. You can use facts, details, statistics, and direct quotations from the passage to uphold your position. Be sure to point out which information comes from the original passage and base your argument around that evidence.

## BODY

In an essay's introduction, the writer establishes the thesis and may indicate how the rest of the piece will be structured. In the body of the piece, the writer **elaborates** upon, **illustrates**, and **explains** the **thesis statement**. How writers arrange supporting details and their choices of paragraph types are development techniques. Writers may give examples of the concept introduced in the thesis statement. If the subject includes a cause-and-effect relationship, the author may explain its causality. A writer will explain or analyze the main idea of the piece throughout the body, often by presenting arguments for the veracity or credibility of the thesis statement. Writers may use development to define or clarify ambiguous terms. Paragraphs within the body may be organized using natural sequences, like space and time. Writers may employ **inductive**

**reasoning**, using multiple details to establish a generalization or causal relationship, or **deductive reasoning**, proving a generalized hypothesis or proposition through a specific example or case.

> **Review Video: Drafting Body Paragraphs**
> Visit mometrix.com/academy and enter code: 724590

## PARAGRAPHS

After the introduction of a passage, a series of body paragraphs will carry a message through to the conclusion. Each paragraph should be **unified around a main point**. Normally, a good topic sentence summarizes the paragraph's main point. A topic sentence is a general sentence that gives an introduction to the paragraph.

The sentences that follow support the topic sentence. However, though it is usually the first sentence, the topic sentence can come as the final sentence to the paragraph if the earlier sentences give a clear explanation of the paragraph's topic. This allows the topic sentence to function as a concluding sentence. Overall, the paragraphs need to stay true to the main point. This means that any unnecessary sentences that do not advance the main point should be removed.

The main point of a paragraph requires adequate development (i.e., a substantial paragraph that covers the main point). A paragraph of two or three sentences does not cover a main point. This is especially true when the main point of the paragraph gives strong support to the argument of the thesis. An occasional short paragraph is fine as a transitional device. However, a well-developed argument will have paragraphs with more than a few sentences.

### METHODS OF DEVELOPING PARAGRAPHS

Common methods of adding substance to paragraphs include examples, illustrations, analogies, and cause and effect.

- **Examples** are supporting details to the main idea of a paragraph or a passage. When authors write about something that their audience may not understand, they can provide an example to show their point. When authors write about something that is not easily accepted, they can give examples to prove their point.
- **Illustrations** are extended examples that require several sentences. Well-selected illustrations can be a great way for authors to develop a point that may not be familiar to their audience.
- **Analogies** make comparisons between items that appear to have nothing in common. Analogies are employed by writers to provoke fresh thoughts about a subject. These comparisons may be used to explain the unfamiliar, to clarify an abstract point, or to argue a point. Although analogies are effective literary devices, they should be used carefully in arguments. Two things may be alike in some respects but completely different in others.
- **Cause and effect** is an excellent device to explain the connection between an action or situation and a particular result. One way that authors can use cause and effect is to state the effect in the topic sentence of a paragraph and add the causes in the body of the paragraph. This method can give an author's paragraphs structure, which always strengthens writing.

### TYPES OF PARAGRAPHS

- A **paragraph of narration** tells a story or a part of a story. Normally, the sentences are arranged in chronological order (i.e., the order that the events happened). However, flashbacks (i.e., an anecdote from an earlier time) can be included.
- A **descriptive paragraph** makes a verbal portrait of a person, place, or thing. When specific details are used that appeal to one or more of the senses (i.e., sight, sound, smell, taste, and touch), authors give readers a sense of being present in the moment.
- A **process paragraph** is related to time order (i.e., First, you open the bottle. Second, you pour the liquid, etc.). Usually, this describes a process or teaches readers how to perform a process.

- **Comparing two things** draws attention to their similarities and indicates a number of differences. When authors contrast, they focus only on differences. Both comparing and contrasting may be done point-by-point, noting both the similarities and differences of each point, or in sequential paragraphs, where you discuss all the similarities and then all the differences, or vice versa.

## BREAKING TEXT INTO PARAGRAPHS

For most forms of writing, you will need to use multiple paragraphs. As such, determining when to start a new paragraph is very important. Reasons for starting a new paragraph include:

- To mark off the introduction and concluding paragraphs
- To signal a shift to a new idea or topic
- To indicate an important shift in time or place
- To explain a point in additional detail
- To highlight a comparison, contrast, or cause and effect relationship

## PARAGRAPH LENGTH

Most readers find that their comfort level for a paragraph is between 100 and 200 words. Shorter paragraphs cause too much starting and stopping and give a choppy effect. Paragraphs that are too long often test the attention span of readers. Two notable exceptions to this rule exist. In scientific or scholarly papers, longer paragraphs suggest seriousness and depth. In journalistic writing, constraints are placed on paragraph size by the narrow columns in a newspaper format.

The first and last paragraphs of a text will usually be the introduction and conclusion. These special-purpose paragraphs are likely to be shorter than paragraphs in the body of the work. Paragraphs in the body of the essay follow the subject's outline (e.g., one paragraph per point in short essays and a group of paragraphs per point in longer works). Some ideas require more development than others, so it is good for a writer to remain flexible. A paragraph of excessive length may be divided, and shorter ones may be combined.

## CONCLUSION

Two important principles to consider when writing a conclusion are strength and closure. A strong conclusion gives the reader a sense that the author's main points are meaningful and important, and that the supporting facts and arguments are convincing, solid, and well developed. When a conclusion achieves closure, it gives the impression that the writer has stated all necessary information and points and completed the work, rather than simply stopping after a specified length. Some things to avoid when writing concluding paragraphs include:

- Introducing a completely new idea
- Beginning with obvious or unoriginal phrases like "In conclusion" or "To summarize"
- Apologizing for one's opinions or writing
- Repeating the thesis word for word rather than rephrasing it
- Believing that the conclusion must always summarize the piece

## COHERENCE IN WRITING
### COHERENT PARAGRAPHS

A smooth flow of sentences and paragraphs without gaps, shifts, or bumps will lead to paragraph **coherence**. Ties between old and new information can be smoothed using several methods:

- **Linking ideas clearly**, from the topic sentence to the body of the paragraph, is essential for a smooth transition. The topic sentence states the main point, and this should be followed by specific details, examples, and illustrations that support the topic sentence. The support may be direct or indirect. In **indirect support**, the illustrations and examples may support a sentence that in turn supports the topic directly.
- The **repetition of key words** adds coherence to a paragraph. To avoid dull language, variations of the key words may be used.
- **Parallel structures** are often used within sentences to emphasize the similarity of ideas and connect sentences giving similar information.
- Maintaining a **consistent verb tense** throughout the paragraph helps. Shifting tenses affects the smooth flow of words and can disrupt the coherence of the paragraph.

> **Review Video: How to Write a Good Paragraph**
> Visit mometrix.com/academy and enter code: 682127

### SEQUENCE WORDS AND PHRASES

When a paragraph opens with the topic sentence, the second sentence may begin with a phrase like *first of all*, introducing the first supporting detail or example. The writer may introduce the second supporting item with words or phrases like *also*, *in addition*, and *besides*. The writer might introduce succeeding pieces of support with wording like, *another thing*, *moreover*, *furthermore*, or *not only that, but*. The writer may introduce the last piece of support with *lastly*, *finally*, or *last but not least*. Writers get off the point by presenting off-target items not supporting the main point. For example, a main point *my dog is not smart* is supported by the statement, *he's six years old and still doesn't answer to his name*. But *he cries when I leave for school* is not supportive, as it does not indicate lack of intelligence. Writers stay on point by presenting only supportive statements that are directly relevant to and illustrative of their main point.

> **Review Video: Sequence**
> Visit mometrix.com/academy and enter code: 489027

### TRANSITIONS

Transitions between sentences and paragraphs guide readers from idea to idea and indicate relationships between sentences and paragraphs. Writers should be judicious in their use of transitions, inserting them sparingly. They should also be selected to fit the author's purpose—transitions can indicate time, comparison, and conclusion, among other purposes. Tone is also important to consider when using transitional phrases, varying the tone for different audiences. For example, in a scholarly essay, *in summary* would be preferable to the more informal *in short*.

When working with transitional words and phrases, writers usually find a natural flow that indicates when a transition is needed. In reading a draft of the text, it should become apparent where the flow is disrupted. At this point, the writer can add transitional elements during the revision process. Revising can also afford an opportunity to delete transitional devices that seem heavy handed or unnecessary.

> **Review Video: Transitions in Writing**
> Visit mometrix.com/academy and enter code: 233246

## TYPES OF TRANSITIONAL WORDS

| | |
|---|---|
| **Time** | afterward, immediately, earlier, meanwhile, recently, lately, now, since, soon, when, then, until, before, etc. |
| **Sequence** | too, first, second, further, moreover, also, again, and, next, still, besides, finally |
| **Comparison** | similarly, in the same way, likewise, also, again, once more |
| **Contrasting** | but, although, despite, however, instead, nevertheless, on the one hand... on the other hand, regardless, yet, in contrast |
| **Cause and Effect** | because, consequently, thus, therefore, then, to this end, since, so, as a result, if... then, accordingly |
| **Examples** | for example, for instance, such as, to illustrate, indeed, in fact, specifically |
| **Place** | near, far, here, there, to the left/right, next to, above, below, beyond, opposite, beside |
| **Concession** | granted that, naturally, of course, it may appear, although it is true that |
| **Repetition, Summary, or Conclusion** | as mentioned earlier, as noted, in other words, in short, on the whole, to summarize, therefore, as a result, to conclude, in conclusion |
| **Addition** | and, also, furthermore, moreover |
| **Generalization** | in broad terms, broadly speaking, in general |

> **Review Video: Transition Words**
> Visit mometrix.com/academy and enter code: 707563
>
> **Review Video: How to Effectively Connect Sentences**
> Visit mometrix.com/academy and enter code: 948325

# Effective Language Use

## WRITING STYLE AND FORM

### WRITING STYLE AND LINGUISTIC FORM

**Linguistic form** encodes the literal meanings of words and sentences. It comes from the phonological, morphological, syntactic, and semantic parts of a language. **Writing style** consists of different ways of encoding the meaning and indicating figurative and stylistic meanings. An author's writing style can also be referred to as his or her **voice**.

Writers' stylistic choices accomplish three basic effects on their audiences:

- They **communicate meanings** beyond linguistically dictated meanings,
- They communicate the **author's attitude**, such as persuasive or argumentative effects accomplished through style, and
- They communicate or **express feelings**.

Within style, component areas include:

- Narrative structure
- Viewpoint
- Focus
- Sound patterns
- Meter and rhythm
- Lexical and syntactic repetition and parallelism
- Writing genre

- Representational, realistic, and mimetic effects
- Representation of thought and speech
- Meta-representation (representing representation)
- Irony
- Metaphor and other indirect meanings
- Representation and use of historical and dialectal variations
- Gender-specific and other group-specific speech styles, both real and fictitious
- Analysis of the processes for inferring meaning from writing

## TONE

Tone may be defined as the writer's **attitude** toward the topic, and to the audience. This attitude is reflected in the language used in the writing. The tone of a work should be **appropriate to the topic** and to the intended audience. While it may be fine to use slang or jargon in some pieces, other texts should not contain such terms. Tone can range from humorous to serious and any level in between. It may be more or less formal, depending on the purpose of the writing and its intended audience. All these nuances in tone can flavor the entire writing and should be kept in mind as the work evolves.

> **Review Video: Style, Tone, and Mood**
> Visit mometrix.com/academy and enter code: 416961

## WORD SELECTION

A writer's choice of words is a signature of their style. Careful thought about the use of words can improve a piece of writing. A passage can be an exciting piece to read when attention is given to the use of vivid or specific nouns rather than general ones.

Example:

> General: His kindness will never be forgotten.

> Specific: His thoughtful gifts and bear hugs will never be forgotten.

## ACTIVE AND PASSIVE LANGUAGE

Attention should also be given to the kind of verbs that are used in sentences. Active verbs (e.g., run, swim) are about an action. Whenever possible, an **active verb should replace a linking verb** to provide clear examples for arguments and to strengthen a passage overall. When using an active verb, one should be sure that the verb is used in the active voice instead of the passive voice. Verbs are in the active voice when the subject is the one doing the action. A verb is in the passive voice when the subject is the recipient of an action.

Example:

> Passive: The winners were called to the stage by the judges.

> Active: The judges called the winners to the stage.

> **Review Video: Word Usage In Sentences**
> Visit mometrix.com/academy and enter code: 197863

## CONCISENESS

**Conciseness** is writing that communicates a message in the fewest words possible. Writing concisely is valuable because short, uncluttered messages allow the reader to understand the author's message more easily and efficiently. Planning is important in writing concise messages. If you have in mind what you need to write beforehand, it will be easier to make a message short and to the point. Do not state the obvious.

Revising is also important. After the message is written, make sure you have effective, pithy sentences that efficiently get your point across. When reviewing the information, imagine a conversation taking place, and concise writing will likely result.

### APPROPRIATE KINDS OF WRITING FOR DIFFERENT TASKS, PURPOSES, AND AUDIENCES

When preparing to write a composition, consider the audience and purpose to choose the best type of writing. Four common types of writing are persuasive, expository, and narrative. **Persuasive**, or argumentative writing, is used to convince the audience to take action or agree with the author's claims. **Expository** writing is meant to inform the audience of the author's observations or research on a topic. **Narrative** writing is used to tell the audience a story and often allows more room for creativity. **Descriptive** writing is when a writer provides a substantial amount of detail to the reader so he or she can visualize the topic. While task, purpose, and audience inform a writer's mode of writing, these factors also impact elements such as tone, vocabulary, and formality.

For example, students who are writing to persuade their parents to grant them some additional privilege, such as permission for a more independent activity, should use more sophisticated vocabulary and diction that sounds more mature and serious to appeal to the parental audience. However, students who are writing for younger children should use simpler vocabulary and sentence structure, as well as choose words that are more vivid and entertaining. They should treat their topics more lightly, and include humor when appropriate. Students who are writing for their classmates may use language that is more informal, as well as age-appropriate.

> **Review Video: Writing Purpose and Audience**
> Visit mometrix.com/academy and enter code: 146627

### FORMALITY IN WRITING
#### LEVEL OF FORMALITY

The relationship between writer and reader is important in choosing a **level of formality** as most writing requires some degree of formality. **Formal writing** is for addressing a superior in a school or work environment. Business letters, textbooks, and newspapers use a moderate to high level of formality. **Informal writing** is appropriate for private letters, personal emails, and business correspondence between close associates.

For your exam, you will want to be aware of informal and formal writing. One way that this can be accomplished is to watch for shifts in point of view in the essay. For example, unless writers are using a personal example, they will rarely refer to themselves (e.g., "*I* think that *my* point is very clear.") to avoid being informal when they need to be formal.

Also, be mindful of an author who addresses his or her audience **directly** in their writing (e.g., "Readers, *like you*, will understand this argument.") as this can be a sign of informal writing. Good writers understand the need to be consistent with their level of formality. Shifts in levels of formality or point of view can confuse readers and cause them to discount the message.

#### CLICHÉS

Clichés are phrases that have been **overused** to the point that the phrase has no importance or has lost the original meaning. These phrases have no originality and add very little to a passage. Therefore, most writers will avoid the use of clichés. Another option is to make changes to a cliché so that it is not predictable and empty of meaning.

Examples:

> When life gives you lemons, make lemonade.

> Every cloud has a silver lining.

## JARGON

Jargon is **specialized vocabulary** that is used among members of a certain trade or profession. Since jargon is understood by only a small audience, writers will use jargon in passages that will only be read by a specialized audience. For example, medical jargon should be used in a medical journal but not in a New York Times article. Jargon includes exaggerated language that tries to impress rather than inform. Sentences filled with jargon are not precise and are difficult to understand.

Examples:

> "He is going to *toenail* these frames for us." (Toenail is construction jargon for nailing at an angle.)

> "They brought in a *kip* of material today." (Kip refers to 1000 pounds in architecture and engineering.)

## SLANG

Slang is an **informal** and sometimes private language that is understood by some individuals. Slang terms have some usefulness, but they can have a small audience. So, most formal writing will not include this kind of language.

Examples:

> "Yes, the event was a blast!" (In this sentence, *blast* means that the event was a great experience.)

> "That attempt was an epic fail." (By *epic fail*, the speaker means that his or her attempt was not a success.)

## COLLOQUIALISM

A colloquialism is a word or phrase that is found in informal writing. Unlike slang, **colloquial language** will be familiar to a greater range of people. However, colloquialisms are still considered inappropriate for formal writing. Colloquial language can include some slang, but these are limited to contractions for the most part.

Examples:

> "Can *y'all* come back another time?" (Y'all is a contraction of "you all.")

> "Will you stop him from building this *castle in the air*?" (A "castle in the air" is an improbable or unlikely event.)

## ACADEMIC LANGUAGE

In educational settings, students are often expected to use academic language in their schoolwork. Academic language is also commonly found in dissertations and theses, texts published by academic journals, and other forms of academic research. Academic language conventions may vary between fields, but general academic language is free of slang, regional terminology, and noticeable grammatical errors. Specific terms may also be used in academic language, and it is important to understand their proper usage. A writer's command of academic language impacts their ability to communicate in an academic or professional context. While it is acceptable to use colloquialisms, slang, improper grammar, or other forms of informal speech in social settings or at home, it is inappropriate to practice non-academic language in academic contexts.

# Sentence Structure

## AGREEMENT AND SENTENCE STRUCTURE

### SUBJECTS AND PREDICATES

#### SUBJECTS

The **subject** of a sentence names who or what the sentence is about. The subject may be directly stated in a sentence, or the subject may be the implied *you*. The **complete subject** includes the simple subject and all of its modifiers. To find the complete subject, ask *Who* or *What* and insert the verb to complete the question. The answer, including any modifiers (adjectives, prepositional phrases, etc.), is the complete subject. To find the **simple subject**, remove all of the modifiers in the complete subject. Being able to locate the subject of a sentence helps with many problems, such as those involving sentence fragments and subject-verb agreement.

Examples:

The small, red <u>car</u> is the one that he wants for Christmas.
(simple subject: car; complete subject: The small, red car)

The young <u>artist</u> is coming over for dinner.
(simple subject: artist; complete subject: The young artist)

> **Review Video: Subjects in English**
> Visit mometrix.com/academy and enter code: 444771

In **imperative** sentences, the verb's subject is understood (e.g., [You] Run to the store), but is not actually present in the sentence. Normally, the subject comes before the verb. However, the subject comes after the verb in sentences that begin with *There are* or *There was*.

Direct:

| John knows the way to the park. | Who knows the way to the park? | John |
| The cookies need ten more minutes. | What needs ten minutes? | The cookies |
| By five o'clock, Bill will need to leave. | Who needs to leave? | Bill |
| There are five letters on the table for him. | What is on the table? | Five letters |
| There were coffee and doughnuts in the house. | What was in the house? | Coffee and doughnuts |

Implied:

| Go to the post office for me. | Who is going to the post office? | You |
| Come and sit with me, please? | Who needs to come and sit? | You |

#### PREDICATES

In a sentence, you always have a predicate and a subject. The subject tells who or what the sentence is about, and the **predicate** explains or describes the subject. The predicate includes the verb or verb phrase and any direct or indirect objects of the verb, as well as any words or phrases modifying these.

Think about the sentence *He sings*. In this sentence, we have a subject (He) and a predicate (sings). This is all that is needed for a sentence to be complete. Most sentences contain more information, but if this is all the information that you are given, then you have a complete sentence.

Now, let's look at another sentence: *John and Jane sing on Tuesday nights at the dance hall.*

> subject: John and Jane
> predicate: sing on Tuesday nights at the dance hall.

> **Review Video: Complete Predicate**
> Visit mometrix.com/academy and enter code: 293942

## SUBJECT-VERB AGREEMENT

Verbs must **agree** with their subjects in number and in person. To agree in number, singular subjects need singular verbs and plural subjects need plural verbs. A **singular** noun refers to **one** person, place, or thing. A **plural** noun refers to **more than one** person, place, or thing. To agree in person, the correct verb form must be chosen to match the first, second, or third person subject. The present tense ending -*s* or -*es* is used on a verb if its subject is third person singular; otherwise, the verb's ending is not modified.

> **Review Video: Subject-Verb Agreement**
> Visit mometrix.com/academy and enter code: 479190

### NUMBER AGREEMENT EXAMPLES:

Single Subject and Verb: Dan (singular subject) calls (singular verb) home.

Dan is one person. So, the singular verb *calls* is needed.

Plural Subject and Verb: Dan and Bob (plural subject) call (plural verb) home.

More than one person needs the plural verb *call*.

### PERSON AGREEMENT EXAMPLES:

First Person: I *am* walking.

Second Person: You *are* walking.

Third Person: He *is* walking.

## COMPLICATIONS WITH SUBJECT-VERB AGREEMENT
### WORDS BETWEEN SUBJECT AND VERB

Words that come between the simple subject and the verb have no bearing on subject-verb agreement.

Examples:

The joy (singular subject) of my life returns (singular verb) home tonight.

The phrase *of my life* does not influence the verb *returns*.

The question *(singular subject)* that still remains unanswered is *(singular verb)* "Who are you?"

Don't let the phrase *"that still remains..."* trouble you. The subject *question* goes with *is*.

## COMPOUND SUBJECTS

A compound subject is formed when two or more nouns joined by *and*, *or*, or *nor* jointly act as the subject of the sentence.

### JOINED BY AND

When a compound subject is joined by *and*, it is treated as a plural subject and requires a plural verb.

Examples:

You and Jon *(plural subject)* are *(plural verb)* invited to come to my house.

The pencil and paper *(plural subject)* belong *(plural verb)* to me.

### JOINED BY OR/NOR

For a compound subject joined by *or* or *nor*, the verb must agree in number with the part of the subject that is closest to the verb (italicized in the examples below).

Examples:

Today or *tomorrow* *(subject)* is *(verb)* the day.

Stan or *Phil* *(subject)* wants *(verb)* to read the book.

Neither the pen nor *the book* *(subject)* is *(verb)* on the desk.

Either the blanket or *pillows* *(subject)* arrive *(verb)* this afternoon.

## INDEFINITE PRONOUNS AS SUBJECT

An indefinite pronoun is a pronoun that does not refer to a specific noun. Some indefinite pronouns function as only singular, some function as only plural, and some can function as either singular or plural depending on how they are used.

### ALWAYS SINGULAR

Pronouns such as *each*, *either*, *everybody*, *anybody*, *somebody*, and *nobody* are always singular.

Examples:

Each *(singular subject)* of the runners has *(singular verb)* a different bib number.

Is *(singular verb)* either *(singular subject)* of you ready for the game?

Note: The words *each* and *either* can also be used as adjectives (e.g., *each* person is unique). When one of these adjectives modifies the subject of a sentence, it is always a singular subject.

*Everybody* (singular subject) *grows* (singular verb) a day older every day.

*Anybody* (singular subject) *is* (singular verb) welcome to bring a tent.

## ALWAYS PLURAL

Pronouns such as *both*, *several*, and *many* are always plural.

Examples:

*Both* (plural subject) of the siblings *were* (plural verb) too tired to argue.

*Many* (plural subject) *have tried* (plural verb), but none have succeeded.

## DEPEND ON CONTEXT

Pronouns such as *some*, *any*, *all*, *none*, *more*, and *most* can be either singular or plural depending on what they are representing in the context of the sentence.

Examples:

*All* (singular subject) of my dog's food *was* (singular verb) still there in his bowl.

By the end of the night, *all* (plural subject) of my guests *were* (plural verb) already excited about coming to my next party.

## OTHER CASES INVOLVING PLURAL OR IRREGULAR FORM

Some nouns are **singular in meaning but plural in form**: news, mathematics, physics, and economics.

The *news is* coming on now.

*Mathematics is* my favorite class.

Some nouns are plural in form and meaning, and have **no singular equivalent**: scissors and pants.

Do these *pants come* with a shirt?

The *scissors are* for my project.

Mathematical operations are **irregular** in their construction, but are normally considered to be **singular in meaning**.

*One plus one is* two.

*Three times three is* nine.

Note: Look to your **dictionary** for help when you aren't sure whether a noun with a plural form has a singular or plural meaning.

## COMPLEMENTS

A complement is a noun, pronoun, or adjective that is used to give more information about the subject or object in the sentence.

### DIRECT OBJECTS

A direct object is a noun or pronoun that tells who or what **receives** the action of the verb. A sentence will only include a direct object if the verb is a transitive verb. If the verb is an intransitive verb or a linking verb, there will be no direct object. When you are looking for a direct object, find the verb and ask *who* or *what*.

Examples:

> I took *the blanket*.
>
> Jane read *books*.

### INDIRECT OBJECTS

An indirect object is a noun or pronoun that indicates what or whom the action had an **influence** on. If there is an indirect object in a sentence, then there will also be a direct object. When you are looking for the indirect object, find the verb and ask *to/for whom or what*.

Examples:

> We taught the old dog (indirect object) a new trick (direct object).
>
> I gave them (indirect object) a math lesson (direct object).

> **Review Video: Direct and Indirect Objects**
> Visit mometrix.com/academy and enter code: 817385

### PREDICATE NOMINATIVES AND PREDICATE ADJECTIVES

As we looked at previously, verbs may be classified as either action verbs or linking verbs. A linking verb is so named because it links the subject to words in the predicate that describe or define the subject. These words are called predicate nominatives (if nouns or pronouns) or predicate adjectives (if adjectives).

Examples:

> My father (subject) is a lawyer (predicate nominative).
>
> Your mother (subject) is patient (predicate adjective).

## PRONOUN USAGE

The **antecedent** is the noun that has been replaced by a pronoun. A pronoun and its antecedent **agree** when they have the same number (singular or plural) and gender (male, female, or neutral).

Examples:

    **Singular agreement**: <u>John</u> (antecedent) came into town, and <u>he</u> (pronoun) played for us.

    **Plural agreement**: <u>John and Rick</u> (antecedent) came into town, and <u>they</u> (pronoun) played for us.

To determine which is the correct pronoun to use in a compound subject or object, try each pronoun **alone** in place of the compound in the sentence. Your knowledge of pronouns will tell you which one is correct.

Example:

    Bob and (I, me) will be going.

    Test: (1) *I will be going* or (2) *Me will be going*. The second choice cannot be correct because *me* cannot be used as the subject of a sentence. Instead, *me* is used as an object.

    **Answer**: Bob and I will be going.

When a pronoun is used with a noun immediately following (as in "we boys"), try the sentence **without the added noun**.

Example:

    (We/Us) boys played football last year.

    Test: (1) *We played football last year* or (2) *Us played football last year*. Again, the second choice cannot be correct because *us* cannot be used as a subject of a sentence. Instead, *us* is used as an object.

    **Answer**: We boys played football last year.

> **Review Video: Pronoun Usage**
> Visit mometrix.com/academy and enter code: 666500
>
> **Review Video: Pronoun-Antecedent Agreement**
> Visit mometrix.com/academy and enter code: 919704

A pronoun should point clearly to the **antecedent**. Here is how a pronoun reference can be unhelpful if it is puzzling or not directly stated.

    **Unhelpful**: <u>Ron and Jim</u> (antecedent) went to the store, and <u>he</u> (pronoun) bought soda.

    Who bought soda? Ron or Jim?

    **Helpful**: <u>Jim</u> (antecedent) went to the store, and <u>he</u> (pronoun) bought soda.

    The sentence is clear. Jim bought the soda.

Some pronouns change their form by their placement in a sentence. A pronoun that is a **subject** in a sentence comes in the **subjective case**. Pronouns that serve as **objects** appear in the **objective case**. Finally, the pronouns that are used as **possessives** appear in the **possessive case**.

Examples:

> **Subjective case**: *He* is coming to the show.
>
> The pronoun *He* is the subject of the sentence.
>
> **Objective case**: Josh drove *him* to the airport.
>
> The pronoun *him* is the object of the sentence.
>
> **Possessive case**: The flowers are *mine*.
>
> The pronoun *mine* shows ownership of the flowers.

The word *who* is a subjective-case pronoun that can be used as a **subject**. The word *whom* is an objective-case pronoun that can be used as an **object**. The words *who* and *whom* are common in subordinate clauses or in questions.

Examples:

He knows *who* (subject) *wants* (verb) to come.

He knows the man *whom* (object) we *want* (verb) at the party.

## CLAUSES

A clause is a group of words that contains both a subject and a predicate (verb). There are two types of clauses: independent and dependent. An **independent clause** contains a complete thought, while a **dependent (or subordinate) clause** does not. A dependent clause includes a subject and a verb, and may also contain objects or complements, but it cannot stand as a complete thought without being joined to an independent clause. Dependent clauses function within sentences as adjectives, adverbs, or nouns.

Example:

*I am running* (independent clause) *because I want to stay in shape* (dependent clause).

The clause *I am running* is an independent clause: it has a subject and a verb, and it gives a complete thought. The clause *because I want to stay in shape* is a dependent clause: it has a subject and a verb, but it does not express a complete thought. It adds detail to the independent clause to which it is attached.

> **Review Video: Clauses**
> Visit mometrix.com/academy and enter code: 940170
>
> **Review Video: Independent and Dependent Clauses**
> Visit mometrix.com/academy and enter code: 556903

### TYPES OF DEPENDENT CLAUSES
#### ADJECTIVE CLAUSES

An **adjective clause** is a dependent clause that modifies a noun or a pronoun. Adjective clauses begin with a relative pronoun (*who, whose, whom, which,* and *that*) or a relative adverb (*where, when,* and *why*).

Also, adjective clauses usually come immediately after the noun that the clause needs to explain or rename. This is done to ensure that it is clear which noun or pronoun the clause is modifying.

Examples:

I learned the reason [independent clause] why I won the award. [adjective clause]

This is the place [independent clause] where I started my first job. [adjective clause]

An adjective clause can be an essential or nonessential clause. An essential clause is very important to the sentence. **Essential clauses** explain or define a person or thing. **Nonessential clauses** give more information about a person or thing but are not necessary to define them. Nonessential clauses are set off with commas while essential clauses are not.

Examples:

A person who works hard at first [essential clause] can often rest later in life.

Neil Armstrong, who walked on the moon, [nonessential clause] is my hero.

> **Review Video: Adjective Clauses and Phrases**
> Visit mometrix.com/academy and enter code: 520888

## ADVERB CLAUSES

An **adverb clause** is a dependent clause that modifies a verb, adjective, or adverb. In sentences with multiple dependent clauses, adverb clauses are usually placed immediately before or after the independent clause. An adverb clause is introduced with words such as *after, although, as, before, because, if, since, so, unless, when, where,* and *while*.

Examples:

When you walked outside, [adverb clause] I called the manager.

I will go with you unless you want to stay. [adverb clause]

## NOUN CLAUSES

A **noun clause** is a dependent clause that can be used as a subject, object, or complement. Noun clauses begin with words such as *how, that, what, whether, which, who,* and *why*. These words can also come with an adjective clause. Unless the noun clause is being used as the subject of the sentence, it should come after the verb of the independent clause.

Examples:

The real mystery is {how you avoided serious injury}[noun clause].

{What you learn from each other}[noun clause] depends on your honesty with others.

## SUBORDINATION

When two related ideas are not of equal importance, the ideal way to combine them is to make the more important idea an independent clause and the less important idea a dependent or subordinate clause. This is called **subordination**.

Example:

> **Separate ideas**: The team had a perfect regular season. The team lost the championship.
>
> **Subordinated**: Despite having a perfect regular season, *the team lost the championship.*

## PHRASES

A phrase is a group of words that functions as a single part of speech, usually a noun, adjective, or adverb. A **phrase** is not a complete thought and does not contain a subject and predicate, but it adds detail or explanation to a sentence, or renames something within the sentence.

## PREPOSITIONAL PHRASES

One of the most common types of phrases is the prepositional phrase. A **prepositional phrase** begins with a preposition and ends with a noun or pronoun that is the object of the preposition. Normally, the prepositional phrase functions as an **adjective** or an **adverb** within the sentence.

Examples:

The picnic is {on the blanket}[prepositional phrase].

I am sick {with a fever}[prepositional phrase] today.

{Among the many flowers}[prepositional phrase], John found a four-leaf clover.

## VERBAL PHRASES

A **verbal** is a word or phrase that is formed from a verb but does not function as a verb. Depending on its particular form, it may be used as a noun, adjective, or adverb. A verbal does **not** replace a verb in a sentence.

Examples:

Correct: {Walk}[verb] a mile daily.

This is a complete sentence with the implied subject *you*.

Incorrect: To walk a mile. *(verbal: To walk)*

This is not a sentence since there is no functional verb.

There are three types of verbal: **participles**, **gerunds**, and **infinitives**. Each type of verbal has a corresponding **phrase** that consists of the verbal itself along with any complements or modifiers.

## PARTICIPLES

A **participle** is a type of verbal that always functions as an adjective. The present participle always ends with -*ing*. Past participles end with -*d, -ed, -n,* or -*t*. Participles are combined with helping verbs to form certain verb tenses, but a participle by itself cannot function as a verb.

Examples: dance (verb) | dancing (present participle) | danced (past participle)

**Participial phrases** most often come right before or right after the noun or pronoun that they modify.

Examples:

*Shipwrecked on an island*, the boys started to fish for food. *(participial phrase)*

*Having been seated for five hours*, we got out of the car to stretch our legs. *(participial phrase)*

*Praised for their work*, the group accepted the first-place trophy. *(participial phrase)*

## GERUNDS

A **gerund** is a type of verbal that always functions as a **noun**. Like present participles, gerunds always end with -*ing*, but they can be easily distinguished from participles by the part of speech they represent (participles always function as adjectives). Since a gerund or gerund phrase always functions as a noun, it can be used as the subject of a sentence, the predicate nominative, or the object of a verb or preposition.

Examples:

We want to be known for *teaching* the poor. *(gerund; object of preposition)*

*Coaching* this team is the best job of my life. *(gerund; subject)*

We like *practicing* our songs in the basement. *(gerund; object of verb)*

## INFINITIVES

An **infinitive** is a type of verbal that can function as a noun, an adjective, or an adverb. An infinitive is made of the word *to* and the basic form of the verb. As with all other types of verbal phrases, an infinitive phrase includes the verbal itself and all of its complements or modifiers.

Examples:

    *To join* the team is my goal in life. (infinitive, noun)

    The animals have enough food *to eat* for the night. (infinitive, adjective)

    People lift weights *to exercise* their muscles. (infinitive, adverb)

> **Review Video: Verbals**
> Visit mometrix.com/academy and enter code: 915480

## APPOSITIVE PHRASES

An **appositive** is a word or phrase that is used to explain or rename nouns or pronouns. Noun phrases, gerund phrases, and infinitive phrases can all be used as appositives.

Examples:

    Terriers, *hunters at heart*, have been dressed up to look like lap dogs. (appositive)

    The noun phrase *hunters at heart* renames the noun *terriers*.

    His plan, *to save and invest his money*, was proven as a safe approach. (appositive)

    The infinitive phrase explains what the plan is.

Appositive phrases can be **essential** or **nonessential**. An appositive phrase is essential if the person, place, or thing being described or renamed is too general for its meaning to be understood without the appositive.

Examples:

    Two of America's Founding Fathers, *George Washington and Thomas Jefferson*, served as presidents. (essential)

    George Washington and Thomas Jefferson, *two Founding Fathers*, served as presidents. (nonessential)

## ABSOLUTE PHRASES

An absolute phrase is a phrase that consists of **a noun followed by a participle**. An absolute phrase provides **context** to what is being described in the sentence, but it does not modify or explain any particular word; it is essentially independent.

Examples:

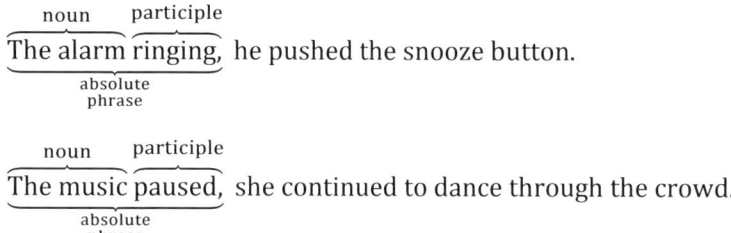

The alarm ringing, he pushed the snooze button.

The music paused, she continued to dance through the crowd.

## PARALLELISM

When multiple items or ideas are presented in a sentence in series, such as in a list, the items or ideas must be stated in grammatically equivalent ways. For example, if two ideas are listed in parallel and the first is stated in gerund form, the second cannot be stated in infinitive form. (e.g., *I enjoy reading and to study*. [incorrect]) An infinitive and a gerund are not grammatically equivalent. Instead, you should write *I enjoy reading and studying* OR *I like to read and to study*. In lists of more than two, all items must be parallel.

Example:

**Incorrect**: He stopped at the office, grocery store, and the pharmacy before heading home.

The first and third items in the list of places include the article *the*, so the second item needs it as well.

**Correct**: He stopped at the office, *the* grocery store, and the pharmacy before heading home.

Example:

**Incorrect**: While vacationing in Europe, she went biking, skiing, and climbed mountains.

The first and second items in the list are gerunds, so the third item must be as well.

**Correct**: While vacationing in Europe, she went biking, skiing, and *mountain climbing*.

> **Review Video: Parallel Sentence Construction**
> Visit mometrix.com/academy and enter code: 831988

## SENTENCE PURPOSE

There are four types of sentences: declarative, imperative, interrogative, and exclamatory.

A **declarative** sentence states a fact and ends with a period.

*The football game starts at seven o'clock.*

An **imperative** sentence tells someone to do something and generally ends with a period. An urgent command might end with an exclamation point instead.

*Don't forget to buy your ticket.*

An **interrogative** sentence asks a question and ends with a question mark.

*Are you going to the game on Friday?*

An **exclamatory** sentence shows strong emotion and ends with an exclamation point.

*I can't believe we won the game!*

## SENTENCE STRUCTURE

Sentences are classified by structure based on the type and number of clauses present. The four classifications of sentence structure are the following:

**Simple**: A simple sentence has one independent clause with no dependent clauses. A simple sentence may have **compound elements** (i.e., compound subject or verb).

Examples:

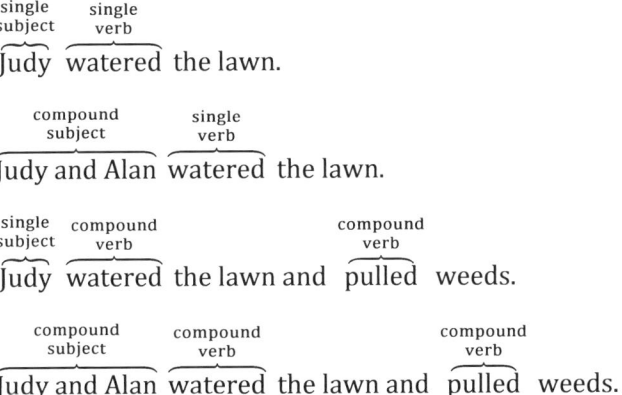

**Compound**: A compound sentence has two or more independent clauses with no dependent clauses. Usually, the independent clauses are joined with a comma and a coordinating conjunction or with a semicolon.

Examples:

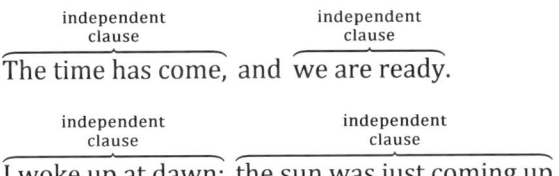

**Complex**: A complex sentence has one independent clause and at least one dependent clause.

Examples:

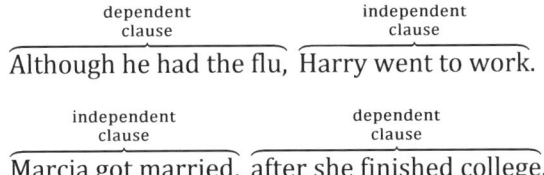

**Compound-Complex**: A compound-complex sentence has at least two independent clauses and at least one dependent clause.

Examples:

John is my friend [independent clause] who went to India, [dependent clause] and he brought back souvenirs. [independent clause]

You may not realize this, [independent clause] but we heard the music [independent clause] that you played last night. [dependent clause]

> **Review Video: Sentence Structure**
> Visit mometrix.com/academy and enter code: 700478

**Sentence variety** is important to consider when writing an essay or speech. A variety of sentence lengths and types creates rhythm, makes a passage more engaging, and gives writers an opportunity to demonstrate their writing style. Writing that uses the same length or type of sentence without variation can be boring or difficult to read. To evaluate a passage for effective sentence variety, it is helpful to note whether the passage contains diverse sentence structures and lengths. It is also important to pay attention to the way each sentence starts and avoid beginning with the same words or phrases.

## SENTENCE FRAGMENTS

Recall that a group of words must contain at least one **independent clause** in order to be considered a sentence. If it doesn't contain even one independent clause, it is called a **sentence fragment**.

The appropriate process for **repairing** a sentence fragment depends on what type of fragment it is. If the fragment is a dependent clause, it can sometimes be as simple as removing a subordinating word (e.g., when, because, if) from the beginning of the fragment. Alternatively, a dependent clause can be incorporated into a closely related neighboring sentence. If the fragment is missing some required part, like a subject or a verb, the fix might be as simple as adding the missing part.

Examples:

> **Fragment**: Because he wanted to sail the Mediterranean.
>
> **Removed subordinating word**: He wanted to sail the Mediterranean.
>
> **Combined with another sentence**: Because he wanted to sail the Mediterranean, he booked a Greek island cruise.

## RUN-ON SENTENCES

Run-on sentences consist of multiple independent clauses that have not been joined together properly. Run-on sentences can be corrected in several different ways:

**Join clauses properly**: This can be done with a comma and coordinating conjunction, with a semicolon, or with a colon or dash if the second clause is explaining something in the first.

Example:

> **Incorrect**: I went on the trip, we visited lots of castles.
>
> **Corrected**: I went on the trip, and we visited lots of castles.

**Split into separate sentences**: This correction is most effective when the independent clauses are very long or when they are not closely related.

Example:

> **Incorrect**: The drive to New York takes ten hours, my uncle lives in Boston.
>
> **Corrected**: The drive to New York takes ten hours. My uncle lives in Boston.

**Make one clause dependent**: This is the easiest way to make the sentence correct and more interesting at the same time. It's often as simple as adding a subordinating word between the two clauses or before the first clause.

Example:

> **Incorrect**: I finally made it to the store and I bought some eggs.
>
> **Corrected**: When I finally made it to the store, I bought some eggs.

**Reduce to one clause with a compound verb**: If both clauses have the same subject, remove the subject from the second clause, and you now have just one clause with a compound verb.

Example:

> **Incorrect**: The drive to New York takes ten hours, it makes me very tired.
>
> **Corrected**: The drive to New York takes ten hours and makes me very tired.

Note: While these are the simplest ways to correct a run-on sentence, often the best way is to completely reorganize the thoughts in the sentence and rewrite it.

> **Review Video: Fragments and Run-on Sentences**
> Visit mometrix.com/academy and enter code: 541989

## DANGLING AND MISPLACED MODIFIERS
### DANGLING MODIFIERS

A dangling modifier is a dependent clause or verbal phrase that does not have a clear logical connection to a word in the sentence.

Example:

> **Incorrect**: <u>Reading each magazine article</u>, the stories caught my attention.
> *(dangling modifier)*
>
> The word *stories* cannot be modified by *Reading each magazine article*. People can read, but stories cannot read. Therefore, the subject of the sentence must be a person.
>
> **Corrected**: <u>Reading each magazine article</u>, I was entertained by the stories.
> *(gerund phrase)*

Example:

**Incorrect**: Ever since childhood, my grandparents have visited me for Christmas. *(dangling modifier: "Ever since childhood")*

The speaker in this sentence can't have been visited by her grandparents when *they* were children, since she wouldn't have been born yet. Either the modifier should be clarified or the sentence should be rearranged to specify whose childhood is being referenced.

**Clarified**: Ever since I was a child, my grandparents have visited for Christmas. *(dependent clause: "Ever since I was a child")*

**Rearranged**: Ever since childhood, I have enjoyed my grandparents visiting for Christmas. *(adverb phrase: "Ever since childhood")*

## MISPLACED MODIFIERS

Because modifiers are grammatically versatile, they can be put in many different places within the structure of a sentence. The danger of this versatility is that a modifier can accidentally be placed where it is modifying the wrong word or where it is not clear which word it is modifying.

Example:

**Incorrect**: She read the book to a crowd that was filled with beautiful pictures. *(modifier: "that was filled with beautiful pictures")*

The book was filled with beautiful pictures, not the crowd.

**Corrected**: She read the book that was filled with beautiful pictures to a crowd. *(modifier: "that was filled with beautiful pictures")*

Example:

**Ambiguous**: Derek saw a bus nearly hit a man on his way to work. *(modifier: "on his way to work")*

Was Derek on his way to work or was the other man?

**Derek**: On his way to work, Derek saw a bus nearly hit a man. *(modifier: "On his way to work")*

**The other man**: Derek saw a bus nearly hit a man who was on his way to work. *(modifier: "who was on his way to work")*

## SPLIT INFINITIVES

A split infinitive occurs when a modifying word comes between the word *to* and the verb that pairs with *to*.

Example: To *clearly* explain vs. To explain clearly | To *softly* sing vs. To sing softly

Though considered improper by some, split infinitives may provide better clarity and simplicity in some cases than the alternatives. As such, avoiding them should not be considered a universal rule.

## DOUBLE NEGATIVES

Standard English allows **two negatives** only when a **positive** meaning is intended. (e.g., The team was *not displeased* with their performance.) Double negatives to emphasize negation are not used in standard English.

**Negative modifiers** (e.g., never, no, and not) should not be paired with other negative modifiers or negative words (e.g., none, nobody, nothing, or neither). The modifiers *hardly, barely*, and *scarcely* are also considered negatives in standard English, so they should not be used with other negatives.

# Conventions of Usage

## PARTS OF SPEECH

### NOUNS

A noun is a person, place, thing, or idea. The two main types of nouns are **common** and **proper** nouns. Nouns can also be categorized as abstract (i.e., general) or concrete (i.e., specific).

### COMMON NOUNS

**Common nouns** are generic names for people, places, and things. Common nouns are not usually capitalized.

Examples of common nouns:

*People*: boy, girl, worker, manager

*Places*: school, bank, library, home

*Things*: dog, cat, truck, car

> **Review Video: Nouns**
> Visit mometrix.com/academy and enter code: 344028

### PROPER NOUNS

**Proper nouns** name specific people, places, or things. All proper nouns are capitalized.

Examples of proper nouns:

*People*: Abraham Lincoln, George Washington, Martin Luther King, Jr.

*Places*: Los Angeles, California; New York; Asia

*Things*: Statue of Liberty, Earth, Lincoln Memorial

Note: Some nouns can be either common or proper depending on their use. For example, when referring to the planet that we live on, *Earth* is a proper noun and is capitalized. When referring to the dirt, rocks, or land on our planet, *earth* is a common noun and is not capitalized.

## GENERAL AND SPECIFIC NOUNS

**General nouns** are the names of conditions or ideas. **Specific nouns** name people, places, and things that are understood by using your senses.

General nouns:

*Condition*: beauty, strength

*Idea*: truth, peace

Specific nouns:

*People*: baby, friend, father

*Places*: town, park, city hall

*Things*: rainbow, cough, apple, silk, gasoline

## COLLECTIVE NOUNS

**Collective nouns** are the names for a group of people, places, or things that may act as a whole. The following are examples of collective nouns: *class, company, dozen, group, herd, team,* and *public*. Collective nouns usually require an article, which denotes the noun as being a single unit. For instance, a choir is a group of singers. Even though there are many singers in a choir, the word choir is grammatically treated as a single unit. If we refer to the members of the group, and not the group itself, it is no longer a collective noun.

Incorrect: The *choir are* going to compete nationally this year.

Correct: The *choir is* going to compete nationally this year.

Incorrect: The *members* of the choir *is* competing nationally this year.

Correct: The *members* of the choir *are* competing nationally this year.

## PRONOUNS

Pronouns are words that are used to stand in for nouns. A pronoun may be classified as personal, intensive, relative, interrogative, demonstrative, indefinite, and reciprocal.

**Personal**: *Nominative* is the case for nouns and pronouns that are the subject of a sentence. *Objective* is the case for nouns and pronouns that are an object in a sentence. *Possessive* is the case for nouns and pronouns that show possession or ownership.

*Singular*

|  | Nominative | Objective | Possessive |
|---|---|---|---|
| **First Person** | I | me | my, mine |
| **Second Person** | you | you | your, yours |
| **Third Person** | he, she, it | him, her, it | his, her, hers, its |

*Plural*

|  | Nominative | Objective | Possessive |
|---|---|---|---|
| **First Person** | we | us | our, ours |
| **Second Person** | you | you | your, yours |
| **Third Person** | they | them | their, theirs |

**Intensive**: I myself, you yourself, he himself, she herself, the (thing) itself, we ourselves, you yourselves, they themselves

**Relative**: which, who, whom, whose

**Interrogative**: what, which, who, whom, whose

**Demonstrative**: this, that, these, those

**Indefinite**: all, any, each, everyone, either/neither, one, some, several

**Reciprocal**: each other, one another

> **Review Video: Nouns and Pronouns**
> Visit mometrix.com/academy and enter code: 312073

## VERBS

A verb is a word or group of words that indicates action or being. In other words, the verb shows something's action or state of being or the action that has been done to something. If you want to write a sentence, then you need a verb. Without a verb, you have no sentence.

### TRANSITIVE AND INTRANSITIVE VERBS

A **transitive verb** is a verb whose action indicates a receiver. **Intransitive verbs** do not indicate a receiver of an action. In other words, the action of the verb does not point to an object.

**Transitive**: He drives a car. | She feeds the dog.

**Intransitive**: He runs every day. | She voted in the last election.

A dictionary will tell you whether a verb is transitive or intransitive. Some verbs can be transitive or intransitive.

### ACTION VERBS AND LINKING VERBS

**Action verbs** show what the subject is doing. In other words, an action verb shows action. Unlike most types of words, a single action verb, in the right context, can be an entire sentence. **Linking verbs** link the subject of a sentence to a noun or pronoun, or they link a subject with an adjective. You always need a verb if you want a complete sentence. However, linking verbs on their own cannot be a complete sentence.

Common linking verbs include *appear, be, become, feel, grow, look, seem, smell, sound,* and *taste*. However, any verb that shows a condition and connects to a noun, pronoun, or adjective that describes the subject of a sentence is a linking verb.

**Action**: He sings. | Run! | Go! | I talk with him every day. | She reads.

**Linking**:

Incorrect: I am.

Correct: I am John. | The roses smell lovely. | I feel tired.

Note: Some verbs are followed by words that look like prepositions, but they are a part of the verb and a part of the verb's meaning. These are known as phrasal verbs, and examples include *call off, look up,* and *drop off*.

> **Review Video: Action Verbs and Linking Verbs**
> Visit mometrix.com/academy and enter code: 743142

## VOICE

Transitive verbs may be in active voice or passive voice. The difference between active voice and passive voice is whether the subject is acting or being acted upon. When the subject of the sentence is doing the action, the verb is in **active voice**. When the subject is being acted upon, the verb is in **passive voice**.

**Active**: Jon drew the picture. (The subject *Jon* is doing the action of *drawing a picture*.)

**Passive**: The picture is drawn by Jon. (The subject *picture* is receiving the action from Jon.)

## VERB TENSES

Verb **tense** is a property of a verb that indicates when the action being described takes place (past, present, or future) and whether or not the action is completed (simple or perfect). Describing an action taking place in the present (*I talk*) requires a different verb tense than describing an action that took place in the past (*I talked*). Some verb tenses require an auxiliary (helping) verb. These helping verbs include *am, are, is | have, has, had | was, were, will* (or *shall*).

| Present: I talk | Present perfect: I have talked |
|---|---|
| Past: I talked | Past perfect: I had talked |
| Future: I will talk | Future perfect: I will have talked |

**Present**: The action is happening at the current time.

Example: He *walks* to the store every morning.

To show that something is happening right now, use the progressive present tense: I *am walking*.

**Past**: The action happened in the past.

Example: She *walked* to the store an hour ago.

**Future**: The action will happen later.

Example: I *will walk* to the store tomorrow.

**Present perfect**: The action started in the past and continues into the present or took place previously at an unspecified time.

Example: I *have walked* to the store three times today.

**Past perfect**: The action was completed at some point in the past. This tense is usually used to describe an action that was completed before some other reference time or event.

Example: I *had eaten* already before they arrived.

**Future perfect**: The action will be completed before some point in the future. This tense may be used to describe an action that has already begun or has yet to begin.

Example: The project *will have been completed* by the deadline.

> **Review Video: Present Perfect, Past Perfect, and Future Perfect Verb Tenses**
> Visit mometrix.com/academy and enter code: 269472

## CONJUGATING VERBS

When you need to change the form of a verb, you are **conjugating** a verb. The key forms of a verb are present tense (sing/sings), past tense (sang), present participle (singing), and past participle (sung). By combining these forms with helping verbs, you can make almost any verb tense. The following table demonstrate some of the different ways to conjugate a verb:

| Tense | First Person | Second Person | Third Person Singular | Third Person Plural |
|---|---|---|---|---|
| Simple Present | I sing | You sing | He, she, it sings | They sing |
| Simple Past | I sang | You sang | He, she, it sang | They sang |
| Simple Future | I will sing | You will sing | He, she, it will sing | They will sing |
| Present Progressive | I am singing | You are singing | He, she, it is singing | They are singing |
| Past Progressive | I was singing | You were singing | He, she, it was singing | They were singing |
| Present Perfect | I have sung | You have sung | He, she, it has sung | They have sung |
| Past Perfect | I had sung | You had sung | He, she, it had sung | They had sung |

## MOOD

There are three **moods** in English: the indicative, the imperative, and the subjunctive.

The **indicative mood** is used for facts, opinions, and questions.

>Fact: You can do this.

>Opinion: I think that you can do this.

>Question: Do you know that you can do this?

The **imperative** is used for orders or requests.

>Order: You are going to do this!

>Request: Will you do this for me?

The **subjunctive mood** is for wishes and statements that go against fact.

>Wish: I wish that I were famous.

>Statement against fact: If I were you, I would do this. (This goes against fact because I am not you. You have the chance to do this, and I do not have the chance.)

## ADJECTIVES

An **adjective** is a word that is used to modify a noun or pronoun. An adjective answers a question: *Which one? What kind?* or *How many?* Usually, adjectives come before the words that they modify, but they may also come after a linking verb.

Which one? The *third* suit is my favorite.

What kind? This suit is *navy blue*.

How many? I am going to buy *four* pairs of socks to match the suit.

> **Review Video: Descriptive Text**
> Visit mometrix.com/academy and enter code: 174903

## ARTICLES

**Articles** are adjectives that are used to distinguish nouns as definite or indefinite. *A*, *an*, and *the* are the only articles. **Definite** nouns are preceded by *the* and indicate a specific person, place, thing, or idea. **Indefinite** nouns are preceded by *a* or *an* and do not indicate a specific person, place, thing, or idea.

Note: *An* comes before words that start with a vowel sound. For example, "Are you going to get an **u**mbrella?"

**Definite**: I lost *the* bottle that belongs to me.

**Indefinite**: Does anyone have *a* bottle to share?

> **Review Video: Function of Articles in a Sentence**
> Visit mometrix.com/academy and enter code: 449383

## COMPARISON WITH ADJECTIVES

Some adjectives are relative and other adjectives are absolute. Adjectives that are **relative** can show the comparison between things. **Absolute** adjectives can also show comparison, but they do so in a different way. Let's say that you are reading two books. You think that one book is perfect, and the other book is not exactly perfect. It is not possible for one book to be more perfect than the other. Either you think that the book is perfect, or you think that the book is imperfect. In this case, perfect and imperfect are absolute adjectives.

Relative adjectives will show the different **degrees** of something or someone to something else or someone else. The three degrees of adjectives include positive, comparative, and superlative.

The **positive** degree is the normal form of an adjective.

Example: This work is *difficult*. | She is *smart*.

The **comparative** degree compares one person or thing to another person or thing.

Example: This work is *more difficult* than your work. | She is *smarter* than me.

The **superlative** degree compares more than two people or things.

Example: This is the *most difficult* work of my life. | She is the *smartest* lady in school.

> **Review Video: Adjectives**
> Visit mometrix.com/academy and enter code: 470154

## ADVERBS

An **adverb** is a word that is used to **modify** a verb, an adjective, or another adverb. Usually, adverbs answer one of these questions: *When? Where? How?* and *Why?* The negatives *not* and *never* are considered adverbs. Adverbs that modify adjectives or other adverbs **strengthen** or **weaken** the words that they modify.

Examples:

He walks *quickly* through the crowd.

The water flows *smoothly* on the rocks.

Note: Adverbs are usually indicated by the morpheme *-ly*, which has been added to the root word. For instance, *quick* can be made into an adverb by adding *-ly* to construct *quickly*. Some words that end in *-ly* do not follow this rule and can behave as other parts of speech. Examples of adjectives ending in *-ly* include: *early, friendly, holy, lonely, silly*, and *ugly*. To know if a word that ends in *-ly* is an adjective or adverb, check your dictionary. Also, while many adverbs end in *-ly*, you need to remember that not all adverbs end in *-ly*.

Examples:

He is *never* angry.

You are *too* irresponsible to travel alone.

> **Review Video: Adverbs**
> Visit mometrix.com/academy and enter code: 713951
>
> **Review Video: Adverbs that Modify Adjectives**
> Visit mometrix.com/academy and enter code: 122570

## COMPARISON WITH ADVERBS

The rules for comparing adverbs are the same as the rules for adjectives.

The **positive** degree is the standard form of an adverb.

Example: He arrives *soon*. | She speaks *softly* to her friends.

The **comparative** degree compares one person or thing to another person or thing.

Example: He arrives *sooner* than Sarah. | She speaks *more softly* than him.

The **superlative** degree compares more than two people or things.

Example: He arrives *soonest* of the group. | She speaks the *most softly* of any of her friends.

## PREPOSITIONS

A **preposition** is a word placed before a noun or pronoun that shows the relationship between that noun or pronoun and another word in the sentence.

*Common prepositions*:

| | | | | |
|---|---|---|---|---|
| about | before | during | on | under |
| after | beneath | for | over | until |
| against | between | from | past | up |
| among | beyond | in | through | with |
| around | by | of | to | within |
| at | down | off | toward | without |

Examples:

    The napkin is *in* the drawer.

    The Earth rotates *around* the Sun.

    The needle is *beneath* the haystack.

    Can you find "me" *among* the words?

> **Review Video: Prepositions**
> Visit mometrix.com/academy and enter code: 946763

## CONJUNCTIONS

**Conjunctions** join words, phrases, or clauses and they show the connection between the joined pieces. **Coordinating conjunctions** connect equal parts of sentences. **Correlative conjunctions** show the connection between pairs. **Subordinating conjunctions** join subordinate (i.e., dependent) clauses with independent clauses.

### COORDINATING CONJUNCTIONS

The **coordinating conjunctions** include: *and, but, yet, or, nor, for,* and *so*

Examples:

    The rock was small, *but* it was heavy.

    She drove in the night, *and* he drove in the day.

## CORRELATIVE CONJUNCTIONS

The **correlative conjunctions** are: *either...or* | *neither...nor* | *not only...but also*

Examples:

*Either* you are coming *or* you are staying.

He *not only* ran three miles *but also* swam 200 yards.

> **Review Video: Coordinating and Correlative Conjunctions**
> Visit mometrix.com/academy and enter code: 390329
>
> **Review Video: Adverb Equal Comparisons**
> Visit mometrix.com/academy and enter code: 231291

## SUBORDINATING CONJUNCTIONS

Common **subordinating conjunctions** include:

| | | |
|---|---|---|
| after | since | whenever |
| although | so that | where |
| because | unless | wherever |
| before | until | whether |
| in order that | when | while |

Examples:

I am hungry *because* I did not eat breakfast.

He went home *when* everyone left.

> **Review Video: Subordinating Conjunctions**
> Visit mometrix.com/academy and enter code: 958913

## INTERJECTIONS

**Interjections** are words of exclamation (i.e., audible expression of great feeling) that are used alone or as a part of a sentence. Often, they are used at the beginning of a sentence for an introduction. Sometimes, they can be used in the middle of a sentence to show a change in thought or attitude.

Common Interjections: Hey! | Oh, | Ouch! | Please! | Wow!

## Common Usage Mistakes
### Commonly Confused Words
#### Which, That, and Who
The words *which*, *that*, and *who* can act as **relative pronouns** to help clarify or describe a noun.

*Which* is used for things only.

>Example: Andrew's car, *which is old and rusty*, broke down last week.

*That* is used for people or things. *That* is usually informal when used to describe people.

>Example: Is this the only book *that Louis L'Amour wrote?*

>Example: Is Louis L'Amour the author *that wrote Western novels?*

*Who* is used for people or for animals that have an identity or personality.

>Example: Mozart was the composer *who wrote those operas.*

>Example: John's dog, *who is called Max*, is large and fierce.

#### Then and Than
*Then* is an adverb that indicates sequence or order:

>Example: I'm going to run to the library and then come home.

*Than* is special-purpose word used only for comparisons:

>Example: Susie likes chips more than candy.

#### Saw and Seen
*Saw* is the past-tense form of *see*.

>Example: I saw a turtle on my walk this morning.

*Seen* is the past participle of *see*.

>Example: I have seen this movie before.

#### Affect and Effect
There are two main reasons that *affect* and *effect* are so often confused: 1) both words can be used as either a noun or a verb, and 2) unlike most homophones, their usage and meanings are closely related to each other. Here is a quick rundown of the four usage options:

**Affect (n)**: feeling, emotion, or mood that is displayed

>Example: The patient had a flat *affect*. (i.e., his face showed little or no emotion)

**Affect (v)**: to alter, to change, to influence

>Example: The sunshine *affects* the plant's growth.

**Effect (n)**: a result, a consequence

>Example: What *effect* will this weather have on our schedule?

**Effect (v)**: to bring about, to cause to be

>Example: These new rules will *effect* order in the office.

The noun form of *affect* is rarely used outside of technical medical descriptions, so if a noun form is needed on the test, you can safely select *effect*. The verb form of *effect* is not as rare as the noun form of *affect*, but it's still not all that likely to show up on your test. If you need a verb and you can't decide which to use based on the definitions, choosing *affect* is your best bet.

## HOMOPHONES

**Homophones** are words that sound alike (or similar) but have different **spellings** and **definitions**. A homophone is a type of **homonym**, which is a pair or group of words that are pronounced or spelled the same, but do not mean the same thing.

### TO, TOO, AND TWO

*To* can be an adverb or a preposition for showing direction, purpose, and relationship. See your dictionary for the many other ways to use *to* in a sentence.

>Examples: I went to the store. | I want to go with you.

*Too* is an adverb that means *also, as well, very,* or *in excess*.

>Examples: I can walk a mile too. | You have eaten too much.

*Two* is a number.

>Example: You have two minutes left.

### THERE, THEIR, AND THEY'RE

*There* can be an adjective, adverb, or pronoun. Often, *there* is used to show a place or to start a sentence.

>Examples: I went there yesterday. | There is something in his pocket.

*Their* is a pronoun that is used to show ownership.

>Examples: He is their father. | This is their fourth apology this week.

*They're* is a contraction of *they are*.

>Example: Did you know that they're in town?

### KNEW AND NEW

*Knew* is the past tense of *know*.

>Example: I knew the answer.

*New* is an adjective that means something is current, has not been used, or is modern.

>Example: This is my new phone.

### ITS AND IT'S

*Its* is a pronoun that shows ownership.

>Example: The guitar is in its case.

*It's* is a contraction of *it is*.

> Example: It's an honor and a privilege to meet you.

Note: The *h* in honor is silent, so *honor* starts with the vowel sound *o*, which must have the article *an*.

## YOUR AND YOU'RE

*Your* is a pronoun that shows ownership.

> Example: This is your moment to shine.

*You're* is a contraction of *you are*.

> Example: Yes, you're correct.

## HOMOGRAPHS

**Homographs** are words that share the same spelling, but have different meanings and sometimes different pronunciations. To figure out which meaning is being used, you should be looking for context clues. The context clues give hints to the meaning of the word. For example, the word *spot* has many meanings. It can mean "a place" or "a stain or blot." In the sentence "After my lunch, I saw a spot on my shirt," the word *spot* means "a stain or blot." The context clues of "After my lunch" and "on my shirt" guide you to this decision. A homograph is another type of homonym.

### BANK

> (noun): an establishment where money is held for savings or lending

> (verb): to collect or pile up

### CONTENT

> (noun): the topics that will be addressed within a book

> (adjective): pleased or satisfied

> (verb): to make someone pleased or satisfied

### FINE

> (noun): an amount of money that acts a penalty for an offense

> (adjective): very small or thin

> (adverb): in an acceptable way

> (verb): to make someone pay money as a punishment

### INCENSE

> (noun): a material that is burned in religious settings and makes a pleasant aroma

> (verb): to frustrate or anger

## Lead
(noun): the first or highest position

(noun): a heavy metallic element

(verb): to direct a person or group of followers

(adjective): containing lead

## Object
(noun): a lifeless item that can be held and observed

(verb): to disagree

## Produce
(noun): fruits and vegetables

(verb): to make or create something

## Refuse
(noun): garbage or debris that has been thrown away

(verb): to not allow

## Subject
(noun): an area of study

(verb): to force or subdue

## Tear
(noun): a fluid secreted by the eyes

(verb): to separate or pull apart

### *Commonly Misused Words and Phrases*
## A Lot
The phrase *a lot* should always be written as two words; never as *alot*.

**Correct**: That's a lot of chocolate!

**Incorrect**: He does that alot.

## Can
The word *can* is used to describe things that are possible occurrences; the word *may* is used to described things that are allowed to happen.

**Correct**: May I have another piece of pie?

**Correct**: I can lift three of these bags of mulch at a time.

**Incorrect**: Mom said we can stay up thirty minutes later tonight.

## COULD HAVE

The phrase *could of* is often incorrectly substituted for the phrase *could have*. Similarly, *could of*, *may of*, and *might of* are sometimes used in place of the correct phrases *could have*, *may have*, and *might have*.

**Correct**: If I had known, I would have helped out.

**Incorrect**: Well, that could of gone much worse than it did.

## MYSELF

The word *myself* is a reflexive pronoun, often incorrectly used in place of *I* or *me*.

**Correct**: He let me do it myself.

**Incorrect**: The job was given to Dave and myself.

## OFF

The phrase *off of* is a redundant expression that should be avoided. In most cases, it can be corrected simply by removing *of*.

**Correct**: My dog chased the squirrel off its perch on the fence.

**Incorrect**: He finally moved his plate off of the table.

## SUPPOSED TO

The phrase *suppose to* is sometimes used incorrectly in place of the phrase *supposed to*.

**Correct**: I was supposed to go to the store this afternoon.

**Incorrect**: When are we suppose to get our grades?

## TRY TO

The phrase *try and* is often used in informal writing and conversation to replace the correct phrase *try to*.

**Correct**: It's a good policy to try to satisfy every customer who walks in the door.

**Incorrect**: Don't try and do too much.

# Conventions of Punctuation

## PUNCTUATION
### END PUNCTUATION
#### PERIODS

Use a period to end all sentences except direct questions and exclamations. Periods are also used for abbreviations.

Examples: 3 p.m. | 2 a.m. | Mr. Jones | Mrs. Stevens | Dr. Smith | Bill, Jr. | Pennsylvania Ave.

Note: An abbreviation is a shortened form of a word or phrase.

## QUESTION MARKS

Question marks should be used following a **direct question**. A polite request can be followed by a period instead of a question mark.

**Direct Question**: What is for lunch today? | How are you? | Why is that the answer?

**Polite Requests**: Can you please send me the item tomorrow. | Will you please walk with me on the track.

> **Review Video: Question Marks**
> Visit mometrix.com/academy and enter code: 118471

## EXCLAMATION MARKS

Exclamation marks are used after a word group or sentence that shows much feeling or has special importance. Exclamation marks should not be overused. They are saved for proper **exclamatory interjections**.

Example: We're going to the finals! | You have a beautiful car! | "That's crazy!" she yelled.

> **Review Video: Exclamation Points**
> Visit mometrix.com/academy and enter code: 199367

## COMMAS

The comma is a punctuation mark that can help you understand connections in a sentence. Not every sentence needs a comma. However, if a sentence needs a comma, you need to put it in the right place. A comma in the wrong place (or an absent comma) will make a sentence's meaning unclear.

These are some of the rules for commas:

| Use Case | Example |
| --- | --- |
| Before a **coordinating conjunction** joining independent clauses | Bob caught three fish, and I caught two fish. |
| After an **introductory phrase** | After the final out, we went to a restaurant to celebrate. |
| After an **adverbial clause** | Studying the stars, I was awed by the beauty of the sky. |
| Between **items in a series** | I will bring the turkey, the pie, and the coffee. |
| For **interjections** | Wow, you know how to play this game. |
| After *yes* and *no* responses | No, I cannot come tomorrow. |
| Separate **nonessential modifiers** | John Frank, who coaches the team, was promoted today. |
| Separate **nonessential appositives** | Thomas Edison, an American inventor, was born in Ohio. |
| Separate **nouns of direct address** | You, John, are my only hope in this moment. |
| Separate **interrogative tags** | This is the last time, correct? |
| Separate **contrasts** | You are my friend, not my enemy. |
| Writing **dates** | July 4, 1776, is an important date to remember. |
| Writing **addresses** | He is meeting me at 456 Delaware Avenue, Washington, D.C., tomorrow morning. |
| Writing **geographical names** | Paris, France, is my favorite city. |
| Writing **titles** | John Smith, PhD, will be visiting your class today. |
| Separate **expressions like** *he said* | "You can start," she said, "with an apology." |

A comma is also used **between coordinate adjectives** not joined with *and*. However, not all adjectives are coordinate (i.e., equal or parallel). To determine if your adjectives are coordinate, try connecting them with *and* or reversing their order. If it still sounds right, they are coordinate.

**Incorrect**: The kind, brown dog followed me home.

**Correct**: The kind, loyal dog followed me home.

> **Review Video: When to Use a Comma**
> Visit mometrix.com/academy and enter code: 786797

## SEMICOLONS

The semicolon is used to join closely related independent clauses without the need for a coordinating conjunction. Semicolons are also used in place of commas to separate list elements that have internal commas. Some rules for semicolons include:

| Use Case | Example |
| --- | --- |
| Between closely connected independent clauses **not connected with a coordinating conjunction** | You are right; we should go with your plan. |
| Between independent clauses **linked with a transitional word** | I think that we can agree on this; however, I am not sure about my friends. |
| Between items in a **series that has internal punctuation** | I have visited New York, New York; Augusta, Maine; and Baltimore, Maryland. |

> **Review Video: How to Use Semicolons**
> Visit mometrix.com/academy and enter code: 370605

## COLONS

The colon is used to call attention to the words that follow it. When used in a sentence, a colon should only come at the **end** of a **complete sentence**. The rules for colons are as follows:

| Use Case | Example |
| --- | --- |
| After an independent clause to **make a list** | I want to learn many languages: Spanish, German, and Italian. |
| For **explanations** | There is one thing that stands out on your resume: responsibility. |
| To give a **quote** | He started with an idea: "We are able to do more than we imagine." |
| After the **greeting in a formal letter** | To Whom It May Concern: |
| Show **hours and minutes** | It is 3:14 p.m. |
| Separate a **title and subtitle** | The essay is titled "America: A Short Introduction to a Modern Country." |

> **Review Video: Using Colons**
> Visit mometrix.com/academy and enter code: 868673

## PARENTHESES

Parentheses are used for additional information. Also, they can be used to put labels for letters or numbers in a series. Parentheses should be not be used very often. If they are overused, parentheses can be a distraction instead of a help.

Examples:

**Extra Information**: The rattlesnake (see Image 2) is a dangerous snake of North and South America.

**Series**: Include in the email (1) your name, (2) your address, and (3) your question for the author.

> **Review Video: Parentheses**
> Visit mometrix.com/academy and enter code: 947743

## QUOTATION MARKS

Use quotation marks to close off **direct quotations** of a person's spoken or written words. Do not use quotation marks around indirect quotations. An indirect quotation gives someone's message without using the person's exact words. Use **single quotation marks** to close off a quotation inside a quotation.

**Direct Quote**: Nancy said, "I am waiting for Henry to arrive."

**Indirect Quote**: Henry said that he is going to be late to the meeting.

**Quote inside a Quote**: The teacher asked, "Has everyone read 'The Gift of the Magi'?"

Quotation marks should be used around the titles of **short works**: newspaper and magazine articles, poems, short stories, songs, television episodes, radio programs, and subdivisions of books or websites.

Examples:

"Rip Van Winkle" (short story by Washington Irving)

"O Captain! My Captain!" (poem by Walt Whitman)

Although it is not standard usage, quotation marks are sometimes used to highlight **irony** or the use of words to mean something other than their dictionary definition. This type of usage should be employed sparingly, if at all.

Examples:

| | |
|---|---|
| The boss warned Frank that he was walking on "thin ice." | Frank is not walking on real ice. Instead, he is being warned to avoid mistakes. |
| The teacher thanked the young man for his "honesty." | The quotation marks around *honesty* show that the teacher does not believe the young man's explanation. |

> **Review Video: Quotation Marks**
> Visit mometrix.com/academy and enter code: 884918

Periods and commas are put **inside** quotation marks. Colons and semicolons are put **outside** the quotation marks. Question marks and exclamation points are placed inside quotation marks when they are part of a quote. When the question or exclamation mark goes with the whole sentence, the mark is left outside of the quotation marks.

Examples:

| Period and comma | We read "The Gift of the Magi," "The Skylight Room," and "The Cactus." |
|---|---|
| Semicolon | They watched "The Nutcracker"; then, they went home. |
| Exclamation mark that is a part of a quote | The crowd cheered, "Victory!" |
| Question mark that goes with the whole sentence | Is your favorite short story "The Tell-Tale Heart"? |

## APOSTROPHES

An apostrophe is used to show **possession** or the **deletion of letters in contractions**. An apostrophe is not needed with the possessive pronouns *his, hers, its, ours, theirs, whose*, and *yours*.

**Singular Nouns**: David's car | a book's theme | my brother's board game

**Plural Nouns that end with -s**: the scissors' handle | boys' basketball

**Plural Nouns that end without -s**: Men's department | the people's adventure

> **Review Video: When to Use an Apostrophe**
> Visit mometrix.com/academy and enter code: 213068
>
> **Review Video: Punctuation Errors in Possessive Pronouns**
> Visit mometrix.com/academy and enter code: 221438

## HYPHENS

Hyphens are used to **separate compound words**. Use hyphens in the following cases:

| Use Case | Example |
|---|---|
| **Compound numbers** from 21 to 99 when written out in words | This team needs twenty-five points to win the game. |
| **Written-out fractions** that are used as adjectives | The recipe says that we need a three-fourths cup of butter. |
| **Compound adjectives** that come before a noun | The well-fed dog took a nap. |
| **Unusual compound words** that would be hard to read or easily confused with other words | This is the best anti-itch cream on the market. |

Note: This is not a complete set of the rules for hyphens. A dictionary is the best tool for knowing if a compound word needs a hyphen.

> **Review Video: Hyphens**
> Visit mometrix.com/academy and enter code: 981632

## DASHES

Dashes are used to show a **break** or a **change in thought** in a sentence or to act as parentheses in a sentence. When typing, use two hyphens to make a dash. Do not put a space before or after the dash. The following are the functions of dashes:

| Use Case | Example |
| --- | --- |
| Set off parenthetical statements or an **appositive with internal punctuation** | The three trees—oak, pine, and magnolia—are coming on a truck tomorrow. |
| Show a **break or change in tone or thought** | The first question—how silly of me—does not have a correct answer. |

## ELLIPSIS MARKS

The ellipsis mark has **three** periods (...) to show when **words have been removed** from a quotation. If a **full sentence or more** is removed from a quoted passage, you need to use **four** periods to show the removed text and the end punctuation mark. The ellipsis mark should not be used at the beginning of a quotation. The ellipsis mark should also not be used at the end of a quotation unless some words have been deleted from the end of the final quoted sentence.

Example:

"Then he picked up the groceries...paid for them...later he went home."

## BRACKETS

There are two main reasons to use brackets:

| Use Case | Example |
| --- | --- |
| Placing **parentheses inside of parentheses** | The hero of this story, Paul Revere (a silversmith and industrialist [see Ch. 4]), rode through towns of Massachusetts to warn of advancing British troops. |
| Adding **clarification or detail to a quotation** that is not part of the quotation | The father explained, "My children are planning to attend my alma mater [State University]." |

**Review Video: Brackets**
Visit mometrix.com/academy and enter code: 727546

## Chapter Quiz

Ready to see how well you retained what you just read? Scan the QR code to go directly to the chapter quiz interface for this study guide. If you're using a computer, simply visit the online resources page at mometrix.com/resources719/accuplacer-28992 and click the Chapter Quizzes link.

# Arithmetic

Transform passive reading into active learning! After immersing yourself in this chapter, put your comprehension to the test by taking a quiz. The insights you gained will stay with you longer this way. Scan the QR code to go directly to the chapter quiz interface for this study guide. If you're using a computer, simply visit the online resources page at **mometrix.com/resources719/accuplacer-28992** and click the Chapter Quizzes link.

## Rounding and Estimation

**Rounding** is reducing the digits in a number while still trying to keep the value similar. The result will be less accurate but in a simpler form and easier to use. Whole numbers can be rounded to the nearest ten, hundred, or thousand, for instance.

To round a number, we make it a little smaller (rounding down) or a little larger (rounding up) to get a number that ends in zeros. We specify the number of zeros by naming the last place that we will not "zero out." For example, to round 8,327 to the nearest hundred, we round down to 8,300, zeroing out every digit to the right of the hundreds place. To round 4,728 to the nearest thousand, we round up to 5,000, increasing the thousands digit by one (to make the number larger) and zeroing out every digit to the right of the thousands place.

We decide whether to round down or up by looking at the first digit we are going to zero out. If it is less than 5 (namely, 0, 1, 2, 3, or 4) we round down. If it is greater than or equal to 5 (namely, 5, 6, 7, 8, or 9) we round up by adding 1 to the place we are rounding to. So, rounding 8,327 to the nearest hundred, we round down to 8,300 because the tens digit, 2, is less than 5. And rounding 4,728 to the nearest thousand, we round up to 5,000, increasing the thousands digit by 1, because the hundreds digit, 7, is greater than or equal to 5.

This even works with decimals. For example, rounding 39.7426 to the nearest tenth, we round down to 39.7000 (or simply 39.7) because the hundredths digit, 4, is less than 5. And rounding 0.019823 to the nearest thousandth, we round up to 0.020000 (or simply 0.02) by increasing the thousandths digit by 1, because the ten-thousandths digit, 8, is greater than or equal to 5.

When you are asked to estimate the solution to a problem, you will need to provide only an approximate figure or **estimation** for your answer. In this situation, you will need to round each number in the calculation to the level indicated (nearest hundred, nearest thousand, etc.) or to a level that makes sense for the numbers involved. When estimating a sum **all numbers must be rounded to the same level**. You cannot round one number to the nearest thousand while rounding another to the nearest hundred.

For instance, suppose you are considering buying four pieces of equipment for your home office. Their prices are $485, $1,217, $750, and $643. To estimate their total cost, you might round each price to the nearest hundred and add the rounded figures, getting an estimate of $500 + $1,200 + $800 + $600 = $3,100. By estimating instead of making an exact calculation, you give up a little accuracy to get a simpler calculation.

> **Review Video: Rounding and Estimation**
> Visit mometrix.com/academy and enter code: 126243

## Operations

An **operation** is simply a mathematical process that takes some value(s) as input(s) and produces an output. Elementary operations are often written in the following form: *value operation value*. For instance, in the expression 1 + 2 the values are 1 and 2 and the operation is addition. Performing the operation gives the output of 3. In this way we can say that 1 + 2 and 3 are equal, or 1 + 2 = 3.

## ADDITION

**Addition** increases the value of one quantity by the value of another quantity (both called **addends**). Example: 2 + 4 = 6 or 8 + 9 = 17. The result is called the **sum**. With addition, the order does not matter, 4 + 2 = 2 + 4.

When adding signed numbers, if the signs are the same simply add the absolute values of the addends and apply the original sign to the sum. For example, (+4) + (+8) = +12 and (−4) + (−8) = −12. When the original signs are different, take the absolute values of the addends and subtract the smaller value from the larger value, then apply the original sign of the larger value to the difference. Example: (+4) + (−8) = −4 and (−4) + (+8) = +4.

## SUBTRACTION

**Subtraction** is the opposite operation to addition; it decreases the value of one quantity (the **minuend**) by the value of another quantity (the **subtrahend**). For example, 6 − 4 = 2 or 17 − 8 = 9. The result is called the **difference**. Note that with subtraction, the order does matter, 6 − 4 ≠ 4 − 6.

For subtracting signed numbers, change the sign of the subtrahend and then follow the same rules used for addition. Example: (+4) − (+8) = (+4) + (−8) = −4

## MULTIPLICATION

**Multiplication** can be thought of as repeated addition. One number (the **multiplier**) indicates how many times to add the other number (the **multiplicand**) to itself. Example: 3 × 2 = 2 + 2 + 2 = 6. With multiplication, the order does not matter, 2 × 3 = 3 × 2 or 3 + 3 = 2 + 2 + 2, either way the result (the **product**) is the same.

If the signs are the same, the product is positive when multiplying signed numbers. Example: (+4) × (+8) = +32 and (−4) × (−8) = +32. If the signs are opposite, the product is negative. Example: (+4) × (−8) = −32 and (−4) × (+8) = −32. When more than two factors are multiplied together, the sign of the product is determined by how many negative factors are present. If there are an odd number of negative factors then the product is negative, whereas an even number of negative factors indicates a positive product. Example: (+4) × (−8) × (−2) = +64 and (−4) × (−8) × (−2) = −64.

## DIVISION

**Division** is the opposite operation to multiplication; one number (the **divisor**) tells us how many parts to divide the other number (the **dividend**) into. The result of division is called the **quotient**. Example: 20 ÷ 4 = 5. If 20 is split into 4 equal parts, each part is 5. With division, the order of the numbers does matter, 20 ÷ 4 ≠ 4 ÷ 20.

The rules for dividing signed numbers are similar to multiplying signed numbers. If the dividend and divisor have the same sign, the quotient is positive. If the dividend and divisor have opposite signs, the quotient is negative. Example: (−4) ÷ (+8) = −0.5.

> **Review Video: Mathematical Operations**
> Visit mometrix.com/academy and enter code: 208095

## PARENTHESES

**Parentheses** are used to designate which operations should be done first when there are multiple operations. Example: $4 - (2 + 1) = 1$; the parentheses tell us that we must add 2 and 1, and then subtract the sum from 4, rather than subtracting 2 from 4 and then adding 1 (this would give us an answer of 3).

> **Review Video: Mathematical Parentheses**
> Visit mometrix.com/academy and enter code: 978600

## EXPONENTS

An **exponent** is a superscript number placed next to another number at the top right. It indicates how many times the base number is to be multiplied by itself. Exponents provide a shorthand way to write what would be a longer mathematical expression, Example: $2^4 = 2 \times 2 \times 2 \times 2$. A number with an exponent of 2 is said to be "squared," while a number with an exponent of 3 is said to be "cubed." The value of a number raised to an exponent is called its power. So $8^4$ is read as "8 to the 4th power," or "8 raised to the power of 4."

> **Review Video: Exponents**
> Visit mometrix.com/academy and enter code: 600998

## ROOTS

A **root**, such as a square root, is another way of writing a fractional exponent. Instead of using a superscript, roots use the radical symbol ($\sqrt{\phantom{x}}$) to indicate the operation. A radical will have a number underneath the bar, and may sometimes have a number in the upper left: $\sqrt[n]{a}$, read as "the $n^{\text{th}}$ root of $a$." The relationship between radical notation and exponent notation can be described by this equation:

$$\sqrt[n]{a} = a^{\frac{1}{n}}$$

The two special cases of $n = 2$ and $n = 3$ are called square roots and cube roots. If there is no number to the upper left, the radical is understood to be a square root ($n = 2$). Nearly all of the roots you encounter will be square roots. A square root is the same as a number raised to the one-half power. When we say that $a$ is the square root of $b$ ($a = \sqrt{b}$), we mean that $a$ multiplied by itself equals $b$: ($a \times a = b$).

A **perfect square** is a number that has an integer for its square root. There are 10 perfect squares from 1 to 100: 1, 4, 9, 16, 25, 36, 49, 64, 81, 100 (the squares of integers 1 through 10).

> **Review Video: Roots**
> Visit mometrix.com/academy and enter code: 795655
>
> **Review Video: Perfect Squares and Square Roots**
> Visit mometrix.com/academy and enter code: 648063

## Word Problems and Mathematical Symbols

When working on word problems, you must be able to translate verbal expressions or "math words" into math symbols. This chart contains several "math words" and their appropriate symbols:

| Phrase | Symbol |
|---|---|
| equal, is, was, will be, has, costs, gets to, is the same as, becomes | = |
| times, of, multiplied by, product of, twice, doubles, halves, triples | × |
| divided by, per, ratio of/to, out of | ÷ |
| plus, added to, sum, combined, and, more than, totals of | + |
| subtracted from, less than, decreased by, minus, difference between | − |
| what, how much, original value, how many, a number, a variable | $x, n$, etc. |

**Review Video: Understanding Word Problems**
Visit mometrix.com/academy and enter code: 499199

### Examples of Translated Mathematical Phrases

- The phrase four more than twice a number can be written algebraically as $2x + 4$.
- The phrase half a number decreased by six can be written algebraically as $\frac{1}{2}x - 6$.
- The phrase the sum of a number and the product of five and that number can be written algebraically as $x + 5x$.
- You may see a test question that says, "Olivia is constructing a bookcase from seven boards. Two of them are for vertical supports and five are for shelves. The height of the bookcase is twice the width of the bookcase. If the seven boards total 36 feet in length, what will be the height of Olivia's bookcase?" You would need to make a sketch and then create the equation to determine the width of the shelves. The height can be represented as double the width. (If $x$ represents the width of the shelves in feet, then the height of the bookcase is $2x$. Since the seven boards total 36 feet, $2x + 2x + x + x + x + x + x = 36$ or $9x = 36$; $x = 4$. The height is twice the width, or 8 feet.)

## Subtraction with Regrouping

A great way to make use of some of the features built into the decimal system would be regrouping when attempting longform subtraction operations. When subtracting within a place value, sometimes the minuend is smaller than the subtrahend, **regrouping** enables you to 'borrow' a unit from a place value to the left in order to get a positive difference. For example, consider subtracting 189 from 525 with regrouping.

First, set up the subtraction problem in vertical form:

```
   525
-  189
```

Notice that the numbers in the ones and tens columns of 525 are smaller than the numbers in the ones and tens columns of 189. This means you will need to use regrouping to perform subtraction:

```
   5  2  5
-  1  8  9
```

To subtract 9 from 5 in the ones column you will need to borrow from the 2 in the tens columns:

```
   5  1  15
-  1  8   9
            6
```

Next, to subtract 8 from 1 in the tens column you will need to borrow from the 5 in the hundreds column:

```
  4  11  15
- 1   8   9
      3   6
```

Last, subtract the 1 from the 4 in the hundreds column:

```
  4  11  15
- 1   8   9
  3   3   6
```

> **Review Video: Subtracting Large Numbers**
> Visit mometrix.com/academy and enter code: 603350

## Order of Operations

The **order of operations** is a set of rules that dictates the order in which we must perform each operation in an expression so that we will evaluate it accurately. If we have an expression that includes multiple different operations, the order of operations tells us which operations to do first. The most common mnemonic for the order of operations is **PEMDAS**, or "Please Excuse My Dear Aunt Sally." PEMDAS stands for parentheses, exponents, multiplication, division, addition, and subtraction. It is important to understand that multiplication and division have equal precedence, as do addition and subtraction, so those pairs of operations are simply worked from left to right in order.

For example, evaluating the expression $5 + 20 \div 4 \times (2 + 3)^2 - 6$ using the correct order of operations would be done like this:

- **P:** Perform the operations inside the parentheses: $(2 + 3) = 5$
- **E:** Simplify the exponents: $(5)^2 = 5 \times 5 = 25$
  - The expression now looks like this: $5 + 20 \div 4 \times 25 - 6$
- **MD:** Perform multiplication and division from left to right: $20 \div 4 = 5$; then $5 \times 25 = 125$
  - The expression now looks like this: $5 + 125 - 6$
- **AS:** Perform addition and subtraction from left to right: $5 + 125 = 130$; then $130 - 6 = 124$

> **Review Video: Order of Operations**
> Visit mometrix.com/academy and enter code: 259675

## Properties of Operations

### THE COMMUTATIVE PROPERTY

The commutative property applies to addition and multiplication and states that these operations can be completed in any order. The **commutative property of addition** states that numbers and terms can be added together in any order to still get the same value. For example, $3 + 4 = 7$ and $4 + 3 = 7$. Also, we can use the commutative property of addition to show that $3x + 4 + 2^2$ is equivalent to $4 + 3x + 2^2$ and $2^2 + 4 + 3x$. When adding terms, you can add in any order and get the same value.

The **commutative property of multiplication** states that numbers and terms can be multiplied in any order to get the same value. For example, $12 \times 3$ is equivalent to $3 \times 12$. Additionally, we can use the commutative property of multiplication to assume that $(5 + 3) \times (36 - 6)$ is equivalent to $(36 - 6) \times (5 + 3)$. You can multiply terms in any order and still get the same value.

## THE ASSOCIATIVE PROPERTY

The **associative property of addition** states that if three or more terms are being added together, the value is the same regardless of the groupings.

For example, given the expression $3 + 4 + 6$, these terms can be grouped and added in any form. $3 + 4 + 6$ is equivalent to $(3 + 4) + 6$ and is also equivalent to $3 + (4 + 6)$. This can be applied to write equivalent expressions in a variety of ways.

For example, suppose we are given the expression $5 + (y + 2) + 4$. We can generate equivalent expressions knowing the associative property. Knowing that when three or more terms are added, the grouping is irrelevant, we can say that this expression is equivalent to $5 + y + (2 + 4)$, and it is equivalent to $(5 + y) + (2 + 4)$. It is even equivalent to $5 + y + 2 + 4$.

The **associative property of multiplication** states that if three or more terms are being multiplied together, the value is the same regardless of the grouping. We can use this property to identify and generate equivalent expressions.

For example, given the expression $2 \times 7 \times 3$, these terms can be grouped in any way and still get the same value. $2 \times 7 \times 3$ is equivalent to $(2 \times 7) \times 3$ or $2 \times (7 \times 3)$.

## THE IDENTITY PROPERTY

The **identity property of multiplication** states that when a number is multiplied by 1, you get the same number. That is, anything multiplied by 1 is itself. For example, $2 \times 1 = 2$, or $1 \times -36 = -36$. Using the identity property of multiplication, we can identify and generate equivalent expressions. Let's say that we are given the expression $15 - (3 \times 4)$. We can generate equivalent expressions using the identity property. One equivalent expression example would be $(15 \times 1) - (3 \times 4)$. Another example would be $15 - (1 \times 3 \times 4)$. We can say these expressions are equivalent because the identity property of multiplication states that we can multiply any portion of an expression by 1 to get the same value.

The **identity property of addition** states that when 0 is added to a number, you get the same number. For example, $2 + 0 = 2$, or $0 + -3 = -3$. We can also use this property to identify and generate equivalent expressions. For example, if we are given the expression $2 \times (1 + 2)$, we could write the equivalent expressions $2 \times (0 + 1 + 2)$ or $(2 + 0) \times (1 + 2)$.

## THE INVERSE PROPERTY

The **inverse property of addition** states that the sum of a number and its opposite is always equal to 0. Remember, the opposite of a number is a number that is opposite on the number line from zero, or the same number with the opposite sign. For example, $-4$ is opposite to 4, and 1,726.9 is opposite to $-1,726.9$. So, the inverse property of addition states that if you add opposite numbers, their sum is zero. For example, $5 + (-5) = 0$ and $-5 + 5 = 0$.

The **inverse property of multiplication** states that a number multiplied by its reciprocal is always equal to 1. The **reciprocal** of a number is its "flipped" fraction. For example, the reciprocal of 5 is $\frac{1}{5}$, or the reciprocal of $\frac{2}{3}$ is $\frac{3}{2}$. The inverse property of multiplication can be applied for these values, $5 \times \frac{1}{5} = 1$ and $\frac{2}{3} \times \frac{3}{2} = 1$. This is because when you multiply across, you get a fraction that is equal to 1.

$$\frac{2}{3} \times \frac{3}{2} = \frac{6}{6} = 1$$

## THE DISTRIBUTIVE PROPERTY

The **distributive property** explains how multiplication and addition interact. It says that when multiplying one number by the sum of two other numbers, the same result can also be obtained by multiplying the one

number by each of the numbers individually and then adding the products. For example, to multiply 2 by the sum of 7 and 3, the direct approach says, "the sum of 7 and 3 is 10, and 2 times 10 is 20." This would be expressed as $2 \times (7 + 3) = 2 \times 10 = 20$. On the other hand, the distributive property states that the same answer can be achieved by multiplying each number inside the parentheses and adding the products. That is, "the product of 2 and 7 is 14, the product of 2 and 3 is 6, and the sum of 14 and 6 is 20." This would be expressed as $2 \times (7 + 3) = 2 \times 7 + 2 \times 3 = 14 + 6 = 20$, and it is demonstrated below.

$$2 \times (7 + 3) = 2 \times 7 + 2 \times 3$$

This same concept can be used when multiplying a number by the difference of two numbers. For example, $5 \times (10 - 4) = 5 \times 10 - 5 \times 4$. Since $5 \times 10 = 50$ and $5 \times 4 = 20$, the result is $50 - 20 = 30$. This answer can be checked by subtracting inside the parentheses first and then multiplying: $5 \times (10 - 4) = 5 \times 6 = 30$.

> **Review Video: Commutative, Associative, and Distributive Properties**
> Visit mometrix.com/academy and enter code: 483176

# Fractions

A **fraction** is a number that is expressed as one integer written above another integer, with a dividing line between them $\left(\frac{x}{y}\right)$. It represents the **quotient** of the two numbers "$x$ divided by $y$." It can also be thought of as $x$ out of $y$ equal parts.

The top number of a fraction is called the **numerator**, and it represents the number of parts under consideration. The 1 in $\frac{1}{4}$ means that 1 part out of the whole is being considered in the calculation. The bottom number of a fraction is called the **denominator**, and it represents the total number of equal parts. The 4 in $\frac{1}{4}$ means that the whole consists of 4 equal parts. A fraction cannot have a denominator of zero; this is referred to as "undefined."

Fractions can be manipulated, without changing the value of the fraction, by multiplying or dividing (but not adding or subtracting) both the numerator and denominator by the same number. If you divide both numbers by a common factor, you are **reducing** or simplifying the fraction. Two fractions that have the same value but are expressed differently are known as **equivalent fractions**. For example, $\frac{2}{10}, \frac{3}{15}, \frac{4}{20}$, and $\frac{5}{25}$ are all equivalent fractions. They can also all be reduced or simplified to $\frac{1}{5}$.

When two fractions are manipulated so that they have the same denominator, this is known as finding a **common denominator**. The number chosen to be that common denominator should be the least common multiple of the two original denominators. Example: $\frac{3}{4}$ and $\frac{5}{6}$; the least common multiple of 4 and 6 is 12. Manipulating to achieve the common denominator: $\frac{3}{4} = \frac{9}{12}$; $\frac{5}{6} = \frac{10}{12}$.

> **Review Video: Overview of Fractions**
> Visit mometrix.com/academy and enter code: 262335

## PROPER FRACTIONS AND MIXED NUMBERS

A fraction whose denominator is greater than its numerator is known as a **proper fraction**, while a fraction whose numerator is greater than its denominator is known as an **improper fraction**. Proper fractions have values *less than one* and improper fractions have values *greater than one*.

A **mixed number** is a number that contains both an integer and a fraction. Any improper fraction can be rewritten as a mixed number. Example: $\frac{8}{3} = \frac{6}{3} + \frac{2}{3} = 2 + \frac{2}{3} = 2\frac{2}{3}$. Similarly, any mixed number can be rewritten as an improper fraction. Example: $1\frac{3}{5} = 1 + \frac{3}{5} = \frac{5}{5} + \frac{3}{5} = \frac{8}{5}$.

> **Review Video: Proper and Improper Fractions and Mixed Numbers**
> Visit mometrix.com/academy and enter code: 211077

## ADDING AND SUBTRACTING FRACTIONS

If two fractions have a common denominator, they can be added or subtracted simply by adding or subtracting the two numerators and retaining the same denominator. If the two fractions do not already have the same denominator, one or both of them must be manipulated to achieve a common denominator before they can be added or subtracted. Example: $\frac{1}{2} + \frac{1}{4} = \frac{2}{4} + \frac{1}{4} = \frac{3}{4}$.

> **Review Video: Adding and Subtracting Fractions**
> Visit mometrix.com/academy and enter code: 378080

## MULTIPLYING FRACTIONS

Two fractions can be multiplied by multiplying the two numerators to find the new numerator and the two denominators to find the new denominator. Example: $\frac{1}{3} \times \frac{2}{3} = \frac{1 \times 2}{3 \times 3} = \frac{2}{9}$.

## DIVIDING FRACTIONS

Two fractions can be divided by flipping the numerator and denominator of the second fraction and then proceeding as though it were a multiplication problem. Example: $\frac{2}{3} \div \frac{3}{4} = \frac{2}{3} \times \frac{4}{3} = \frac{8}{9}$.

> **Review Video: Multiplying and Dividing Fractions**
> Visit mometrix.com/academy and enter code: 473632

## MULTIPLYING A MIXED NUMBER BY A WHOLE NUMBER OR A DECIMAL

When multiplying a mixed number by something, it is usually best to convert it to an improper fraction first. Additionally, if the multiplicand is a decimal, it is most often simplest to convert it to a fraction. For instance, to multiply $4\frac{3}{8}$ by 3.5, begin by rewriting each quantity as a whole number plus a proper fraction. Remember, a mixed number is a fraction added to a whole number and a decimal is a representation of the sum of fractions, specifically tenths, hundredths, thousandths, and so on:

$$4\frac{3}{8} \times 3.5 = \left(4 + \frac{3}{8}\right) \times \left(3 + \frac{1}{2}\right)$$

Next, the quantities being added need to be expressed with the same denominator. This is achieved by multiplying and dividing the whole number by the denominator of the fraction. Recall that a whole number is equivalent to that number divided by 1:

$$= \left(\frac{4}{1} \times \frac{8}{8} + \frac{3}{8}\right) \times \left(\frac{3}{1} \times \frac{2}{2} + \frac{1}{2}\right)$$

When multiplying fractions, remember to multiply the numerators and denominators separately:

$$= \left(\frac{4 \times 8}{1 \times 8} + \frac{3}{8}\right) \times \left(\frac{3 \times 2}{1 \times 2} + \frac{1}{2}\right)$$
$$= \left(\frac{32}{8} + \frac{3}{8}\right) \times \left(\frac{6}{2} + \frac{1}{2}\right)$$

Now that the fractions have the same denominators, they can be added:

$$= \frac{35}{8} \times \frac{7}{2}$$

Finally, perform the last multiplication and then simplify:

$$= \frac{35 \times 7}{8 \times 2} = \frac{245}{16} = \frac{240}{16} + \frac{5}{16} = 15\frac{5}{16}$$

## COMPARING FRACTIONS

It is important to master the ability to compare and order fractions. This skill is relevant to many real-world scenarios. For example, carpenters often compare fractional construction nail lengths when preparing for a project, and bakers often compare fractional measurements to have the correct ratio of ingredients. There are three commonly used strategies when comparing fractions. These strategies are referred to as the common denominator approach, the decimal approach, and the cross-multiplication approach.

### USING A COMMON DENOMINATOR TO COMPARE FRACTIONS

The fractions $\frac{2}{3}$ and $\frac{4}{7}$ have different denominators. $\frac{2}{3}$ has a denominator of 3, and $\frac{4}{7}$ has a denominator of 7. In order to precisely compare these two fractions, it is necessary to use a common denominator. A common denominator is a common multiple that is shared by both denominators. In this case, the denominators 3 and 7 share a multiple of 21. In general, it is most efficient to select the least common multiple for the two denominators.

Rewrite each fraction with the common denominator of 21. Then, calculate the new numerators as illustrated below.

$$\frac{2}{3} = \frac{14}{21} \qquad \frac{4}{7} = \frac{12}{21}$$

(×7 to both numerator and denominator for the first; ×3 for the second)

For $\frac{2}{3}$, multiply the numerator and denominator by 7. The result is $\frac{14}{21}$.

For $\frac{4}{7}$, multiply the numerator and denominator by 3. The result is $\frac{12}{21}$.

Now that both fractions have a denominator of 21, the fractions can accurately be compared by comparing the numerators. Since 14 is greater than 12, the fraction $\frac{14}{21}$ is greater than $\frac{12}{21}$. This means that $\frac{2}{3}$ is greater than $\frac{4}{7}$.

## USING DECIMALS TO COMPARE FRACTIONS

Sometimes decimal values are easier to compare than fraction values. For example, $\frac{5}{8}$ is equivalent to 0.625 and $\frac{3}{5}$ is equivalent to 0.6. This means that the comparison of $\frac{5}{8}$ and $\frac{3}{5}$ can be determined by comparing the decimals 0.625 and 0.6. When both decimal values are extended to the thousandths place, they become 0.625 and 0.600, respectively. It becomes clear that 0.625 is greater than 0.600 because 625 thousandths is greater than 600 thousandths. In other words, $\frac{5}{8}$ is greater than $\frac{3}{5}$ because 0.625 is greater than 0.6.

## USING CROSS-MULTIPLICATION TO COMPARE FRACTIONS

Cross-multiplication is an efficient strategy for comparing fractions. This is a shortcut for the common denominator strategy. Start by writing each fraction next to one another. Multiply the numerator of the fraction on the left by the denominator of the fraction on the right. Write down the result next to the fraction on the left. Now multiply the numerator of the fraction on the right by the denominator of the fraction on the left. Write down the result next to the fraction on the right. Compare both products. The fraction with the larger result is the larger fraction.

Consider the fractions $\frac{4}{7}$ and $\frac{5}{9}$.

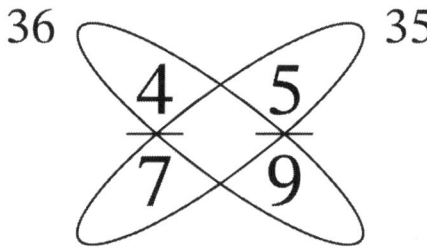

36 is greater than 35. Therefore, $\frac{4}{7}$ is greater than $\frac{5}{9}$.

# Decimals

Decimals are one way to represent parts of a whole. Using the place value system, each digit to the right of a decimal point denotes the number of units of a corresponding *negative* power of ten. For example, consider the decimal 0.24. We can use a model to represent the decimal. Since a dime is worth one-tenth of a dollar and a penny is worth one-hundredth of a dollar, one possible model to represent this fraction is to have 2 dimes representing the 2 in the tenths place and 4 pennies representing the 4 in the hundredths place:

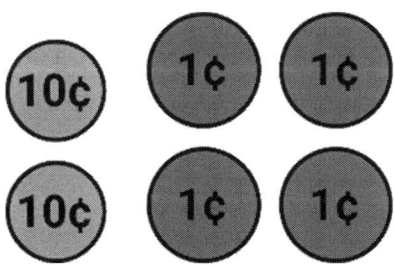

To write the decimal as a fraction, put the decimal in the numerator with 1 in the denominator. Multiply the numerator and denominator by tens until there are no more decimal places. Then simplify the fraction to lowest terms. For example, converting 0.24 to a fraction:

$$0.24 = \frac{0.24}{1} = \frac{0.24 \times 100}{1 \times 100} = \frac{24}{100} = \frac{6}{25}$$

> **Review Video: Decimals**
> Visit mometrix.com/academy and enter code: 837268

## OPERATIONS WITH DECIMALS
### ADDING AND SUBTRACTING DECIMALS

When adding and subtracting decimals, the decimal points must always be aligned. Adding decimals is just like adding regular whole numbers. Example: $4.5 + 2.0 = 6.5$.

If the problem-solver does not properly align the decimal points, an incorrect answer of 4.7 may result. An easy way to add decimals is to align all of the decimal points in a vertical column visually. This will allow you to see exactly where the decimal should be placed in the final answer. Begin adding from right to left. Add each column in turn, making sure to carry the number to the left if a column adds up to more than 9. The same rules apply to the subtraction of decimals.

> **Review Video: Adding and Subtracting Decimals**
> Visit mometrix.com/academy and enter code: 381101

### MULTIPLYING DECIMALS

A simple multiplication problem has two components: a **multiplicand** and a **multiplier**. When multiplying decimals, work as though the numbers were whole rather than decimals. Once the final product is calculated, count the number of places to the right of the decimal in both the multiplicand and the multiplier. Then, count that number of places from the right of the product and place the decimal in that position.

For example, $12.3 \times 2.56$ has a total of three places to the right of the respective decimals. Multiply $123 \times 256$ to get 31,488. Now, beginning on the right, count three places to the left and insert the decimal. The final product will be 31.488.

> **Review Video: How to Multiply Decimals**
> Visit mometrix.com/academy and enter code: 731574

### DIVIDING DECIMALS

Every division problem has a **divisor** and a **dividend**. The dividend is the number that is being divided. In the problem $14 \div 7$, 14 is the dividend and 7 is the divisor. In a division problem with decimals, the divisor must be converted into a whole number. Begin by moving the decimal in the divisor to the right until a whole number is created. Next, move the decimal in the dividend the same number of spaces to the right. For example, 4.9 into 24.5 would become 49 into 245. The decimal was moved one space to the right to create a whole number in the divisor, and then the same was done for the dividend. Once the whole numbers are created, the problem is carried out normally: $245 \div 49 = 5$.

> **Review Video: Dividing Decimals**
> Visit mometrix.com/academy and enter code: 560690
>
> **Review Video: Dividing Decimals by Whole Numbers**
> Visit mometrix.com/academy and enter code: 535669

## Percentages

**Percentages** can be thought of as fractions that are based on a whole of 100; that is, one whole is equal to 100%. The word **percent** means "per hundred." Percentage problems are often presented in three main ways:

- Find what percentage of some number another number is.
  - Example: What percentage of 40 is 8?
- Find what number is some percentage of a given number.
  - Example: What number is 20% of 40?
- Find what number another number is a given percentage of.
  - Example: What number is 8 20% of?

There are three components in each of these cases: a **whole** ($W$), a **part** ($P$), and a **percentage** (%). These are related by the equation: $P = W \times \%$. This can easily be rearranged into other forms that may suit different questions better: $\% = \frac{P}{W}$ and $W = \frac{P}{\%}$. Percentage problems are often also word problems. As such, a large part of solving them is figuring out which quantities are what. For example, consider the following word problem:

*In a school cafeteria, 7 students choose pizza, 9 choose hamburgers, and 4 choose tacos. What percentage of student choose tacos?*

To find the whole, you must first add all of the parts: $7 + 9 + 4 = 20$. The percentage can then be found by dividing the part by the whole $\left(\% = \frac{P}{W}\right)$: $\frac{4}{20} = \frac{20}{100} = 20\%$.

> **Review Video: Computation with Percentages**
> Visit mometrix.com/academy and enter code: 693099

### CALCULATING PERCENT CHANGE

Suppose a quantity has a particular value (the *old value*) and then we add something (the *change*) to it to get another value (the *new value*). We can describe this process by the simple equation (old value) + change = (new value). If we know the old and new values, we can rearrange this equation to find the change, getting change = (new value) − (old value). For instance, if a store's price for a box of computer paper goes from $20 last week to $25 this week, this is a change of (new value) − (old value) = $25 − $20 = $5. Or, if the size of the freshman class at a college goes from 500 students one year to 440 students the next year, this is a change of (new value) − (old value) = 440 − 500 = −60 students. So, we see that change can be positive or negative.

Instead of the word *change*, we sometimes use the words *increase* or *decrease* to specify whether the value goes up or down, respectively. In the examples above, the price of computer paper increases by $5 and the freshman class decreases by 60 students. Note that the decrease is 60 students and not –60 because the word *decrease* already means that the value goes down. So, *increase* is the same as positive change and *decrease* is the opposite or negative change.

If the changing quantity represents an amount (how much of something there is), we can also calculate the **percent change**. This is the change expressed as a percentage of the old amount. To calculate this, we divide the change by the old amount and express the quotient as a percent. That is, we use the formula percent change = $\frac{\text{change}}{\text{old value}}$, converting the resulting decimal answer to a percent. In the examples above, the price of a box of computer paper has a percent change of $\frac{\text{change in price}}{\text{old price}} = \frac{\$5}{\$20} = 0.25 = 25\%$, and the size of the freshman class at the college has a percent change of $\frac{\text{change in enrollment}}{\text{old enrollment}} = \frac{-60}{500} = -0.12 = -12\%$. We can also use the terms *percent increase* and *percent decrease*, saying that the price of computer paper increases by 25%

and the size of the freshman class decreases by 12%. Note that the denominator is always the old amount, never the new amount.

Example: Your landlord raises your rent from $1,500 to $1,700 per month. To find the percent change in your rent (rounded to the nearest tenth of a percent), you calculate as follows.

$$\text{percent change in rent} = \frac{\text{change in rent}}{\text{old rent}} = \frac{(\text{new rent}) - (\text{old rent})}{\text{old rent}}$$
$$= \frac{\$1,700 - \$1,500}{\$1,500} = \frac{\$200}{\$1,500} = 0.1333\ldots \approx 13.3\%$$

Therefore, the percent change in your rent is approximately 13.3%.

> **Review Video: Percent Change**
> Visit mometrix.com/academy and enter code: 907890

## Converting Between Percentages, Fractions, and Decimals

Converting decimals to percentages and percentages to decimals is as simple as moving the decimal point. To *convert from a decimal to a percentage*, move the decimal point **two places to the right**. To *convert from a percentage to a decimal*, move it **two places to the left**. It may be helpful to remember that the percentage number will always be larger than the equivalent decimal number. Example:

$$0.23 = 23\% \quad 5.34 = 534\% \quad 0.007 = 0.7\%$$
$$700\% = 7.00 \quad 86\% = 0.86 \quad 0.15\% = 0.0015$$

To convert a fraction to a decimal, simply divide the numerator by the denominator in the fraction. To convert a decimal to a fraction, put the decimal in the numerator with 1 in the denominator. Multiply the numerator and denominator by tens until there are no more decimal places. Then simplify the fraction to lowest terms. For example, converting 0.24 to a fraction:

$$0.24 = \frac{0.24}{1} = \frac{0.24 \times 100}{1 \times 100} = \frac{24}{100} = \frac{6}{25}$$

Fractions can be converted to a percentage by finding equivalent fractions with a denominator of 100. Example:

$$\frac{7}{10} = \frac{70}{100} = 70\% \quad \frac{1}{4} = \frac{25}{100} = 25\%$$

To convert a percentage to a fraction, divide the percentage number by 100 and reduce the fraction to its simplest possible terms. Example:

$$60\% = \frac{60}{100} = \frac{3}{5} \quad 96\% = \frac{96}{100} = \frac{24}{25}$$

**Review Video: Converting Fractions to Percentages and Decimals**
Visit mometrix.com/academy and enter code: 306233

**Review Video: Converting Percentages to Decimals and Fractions**
Visit mometrix.com/academy and enter code: 287297

**Review Video: Converting Decimals to Fractions and Percentages**
Visit mometrix.com/academy and enter code: 986765

**Review Video: Converting Decimals, Improper Fractions, and Mixed Numbers**
Visit mometrix.com/academy and enter code: 696924

## Number Lines

A number line is a graph to see the distance between numbers. Basically, this graph shows the relationship between numbers. So a number line may have a point for zero and may show negative numbers on the left side of the line. Any positive numbers are placed on the right side of the line. For example, consider the points labeled on the following number line:

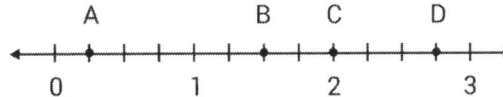

We can use the dashed lines on the number line to identify each point. Each dashed line between two whole numbers is $\frac{1}{4}$. The line halfway between two numbers is $\frac{1}{2}$.

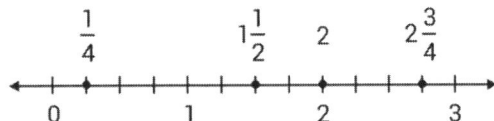

**Review Video: The Number Line**
Visit mometrix.com/academy and enter code: 816439

# Comparing Numbers

## INEQUALITY NOTATION

The symbols < and > mean "is less than" and "is greater than," respectively. For instance, 3 < 5 means "3 is less than 5," and 7 > 4 means "7 is greater than 4." Statements like 3 < 5 and 7 > 4 are **inequalities**, and the symbols < and > are **inequality symbols**.

## WHOLE NUMBERS AND DECIMAL NUMBERS

To compare whole or decimal numbers, we look at the most significant place (the leftmost digit) at which they differ. The number with the larger digit in that place is larger. For instance, 0.3874 and 0.39 differ in the hundredths place (underlined). Since 8 is smaller than 9, we see 0.3874 < 0.39. This is clearer if we make the decimals equal in length by writing extra zeroes: 0.3874 < 0.3900. Similarly, 23.984 < 25.112 because 3 is smaller than 5, or 23 is smaller than 25.

## FRACTIONS

If fractions have the same denominator, the fraction with the larger numerator is larger. For instance, $\frac{2}{7} < \frac{5}{7}$ since 2 < 5. We compare fractions with different denominators by finding a common denominator. When comparing the fractions with a common denominator we only compare the numerator, so as a shortcut, we can multiply each numerator by the denominator of the other fraction. The numerator that produces the larger product belongs to the larger fraction. For example, to compare $\frac{7}{8}$ and $\frac{5}{6}$, we note that $7 \cdot 6 = 42$ is larger than $5 \cdot 8 = 40$. Since the numerator 7 produces the larger product, we see $\frac{7}{8} > \frac{5}{6}$. We can also compare fractions by converting them to decimals. For instance, since $\frac{3}{4} = 0.75$ and $\frac{4}{5} = 0.8$ and $0.75 < 0.8$, we conclude $\frac{3}{4} < \frac{4}{5}$.

## MIXED NUMBERS

To compare mixed numbers we compare their whole number parts. If those are equal, then we compare their fractional parts. For instance, $5\frac{3}{8} > 4\frac{7}{8}$ because 5 > 4, but $3\frac{5}{9} < 3\frac{8}{9}$ because $\frac{5}{9} < \frac{8}{9}$.

## SQUARE ROOTS

To compare square roots, we convert it to a decimal, usually with a calculator. To compare two square roots, we compare their radicands. For instance, $\sqrt{11} < \sqrt{14}$ because 11 < 14.

## NEGATIVE NUMBERS

A negative number is always less than a positive number. Two negative numbers compare in the reverse order of their opposites. For instance, $-6 < -2$ (that is, -6 is smaller, more negative, than -2) because 6 > 2.

# Chapter Quiz

Ready to see how well you retained what you just read? Scan the QR code to go directly to the chapter quiz interface for this study guide. If you're using a computer, simply visit the online resources page at mometrix.com/resources719/accuplacer-28992 and click the Chapter Quizzes link.

# Quantitative Reasoning, Algebra, and Statistics

Transform passive reading into active learning! After immersing yourself in this chapter, put your comprehension to the test by taking a quiz. The insights you gained will stay with you longer this way. Scan the QR code to go directly to the chapter quiz interface for this study guide. If you're using a computer, simply visit the online resources page at **mometrix.com/resources719/accuplacer-28992** and click the Chapter Quizzes link.

## Absolute Value

A precursor to working with negative numbers is understanding what **absolute values** are. A number's absolute value is simply the distance away from zero a number is on the number line. The absolute value of a number is always positive and is written $|x|$. For example, the absolute value of 3, written as $|3|$, is 3 because the distance between 0 and 3 on a number line is three units. Likewise, the absolute value of −3, written as $|-3|$, is 3 because the distance between 0 and −3 on a number line is three units. So $|3| = |-3|$.

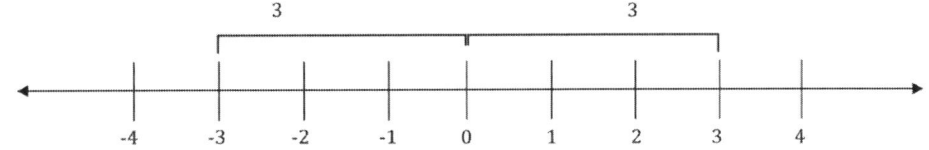

> **Review Video: Absolute Value**
> Visit mometrix.com/academy and enter code: 314669

## Rational and Irrational Numbers

The term **rational** means that the number can be expressed as a ratio or fraction. That is, a number, $r$, is rational if and only if it can be represented by a fraction $\frac{a}{b}$ where $a$ and $b$ are integers and $b$ does not equal 0. The set of rational numbers includes integers and decimals. If there is no finite way to represent a value with a fraction of integers, then the number is **irrational**. Common irrational numbers are $\pi$ and the square roots of whole numbers that are not perfect squares (e.g., $\sqrt{5}$ or $\sqrt{21}$). The sum or product of an integer and an irrational number is always irrational (e.g., $3\pi$ or $7 + \sqrt{6}$).

> **Review Video: Rational and Irrational Numbers**
> Visit mometrix.com/academy and enter code: 280645
>
> **Review Video: Ordering Rational Numbers**
> Visit mometrix.com/academy and enter code: 419578
>
> **Review Video: Irrational Numbers on a Number Line**
> Visit mometrix.com/academy and enter code: 433866

# Proportions and Ratios

## PROPORTIONS

There is a **proportion** between two variable quantities if there is a constant relationship between their products or quotients, a relationship that does not change as the quantities themselves change.

Given variable quantities $x$ and $y$, we say that they are **directly proportional** (or that $y$ **varies directly with** $x$) if their quotient or *ratio* is constant—that is, if there is a constant $k$ such that $\frac{y}{x} = k$ is always true. Another way of saying this is that $y$ is a constant multiple of $x$, so that $y = kx$ is always true. We call the number $k$ the **constant of proportionality**. For example, if you drive at a constant 50 miles per hour, then the distance, $y$, that you travel in miles is 50 times the number of hours, $x$, that you drive. In symbols, $y = 50x$ miles (or $\frac{y}{x} = 50$ mph). So, the distance you travel, $y$, is directly proportional to (or varies directly with) the time you travel, $x$, with constant of proportionality $k = 50$ mph.

The quantities $x$ and $y$ are **inversely proportional** (or $y$ varies inversely with $x$) if their product is constant—that is, if there is a constant $k$ such that $xy = k$ is always true. Another way of saying this is to say that $y$ is a constant multiple of the reciprocal of $x$ so that $y = \frac{k}{x}$ is always true. For instance, suppose you drive at speed (rate) $y$ mph for $x$ hours, going a total of 120 miles. Since rate × time = distance, we get $xy = 120$ miles (or $y = \frac{120}{x}$ miles per hour). Thus, your driving speed, $y$, is inversely proportional to (or varies inversely with) your drive time, $x$, with constant of proportionality $k = 120$ miles.

> **Review Video: Proportions**
> Visit mometrix.com/academy and enter code: 505355

## RATIOS

A **ratio** expresses the sizes of two quantities relative to each other. For instance, suppose we have 3 copies of sheet music to share among 6 singers. We can divide the singers into groups of 2 and give each group 1 copy of the music. Thus, there is 1 copy of the music for every 2 singers, and we say that the **ratio** of sheet music to singers is 1 to 2, which we write either as a fraction $\frac{1}{2}$ or using a colon 1 : 2. Of course, it is also true there are 3 copies for every 6 singers so that the ratio of sheet music to singers is also 3 to 6, which we write as $\frac{3}{6}$ or 3 : 6. So, the ratios $\frac{1}{2}$ and $\frac{3}{6}$ express the same relative quantities of music and singers. We say that these ratios are equal or **equivalent**, and we note that ratios are equal precisely when their fractions are equal (so, in this case, $\frac{1}{2} = \frac{3}{6}$ as fractions). We can also express the quantities in the other order and say that the ratio of singers to music is $\frac{2}{1}$ or 2 : 1 (or $\frac{6}{3}$ or 6 : 3).

> **Review Video: Ratios**
> Visit mometrix.com/academy and enter code: 996914

## CONSTANT OF PROPORTIONALITY

If variable quantities $x$ and $y$ are proportional and we know a pair of corresponding values for them, then we can find their constant of proportionality. If they are directly proportional, we use the formula $\frac{y}{x} = k$. If they are inversely proportional, we use the formula $xy = k$

Example: The cost in dollars, $y$, of buying fence posts is directly proportional to the number, $x$, that you buy. If it costs $51 to buy 17 fence posts, what is the constant of proportionality? Because of direct proportionality, we know that $\frac{y}{x} = k$. Since this works for every pair of corresponding $x$- and $y$-values, it also works for $x = 17$

and $y = 51$. This gives us $\frac{51}{17} = k$, which simplifies to $k = 3$. Note also that this is the unit price, namely $3 per fence post.

## WORK/UNIT RATE

**Unit rate** expresses a quantity of one thing in terms of one unit of another. For example, if you travel 30 miles every two hours, a unit rate expresses this comparison in terms of one hour: in one hour you travel 15 miles, so your unit rate is 15 miles per hour. Other examples are how much one ounce of food costs (price per ounce) or figuring out how much one egg costs out of the dozen (price per 1 egg, instead of price per 12 eggs). The denominator of a unit rate is always 1. Unit rates are used to compare different situations to solve problems. For example, to make sure you get the best deal when deciding which kind of soda to buy, you can find the unit rate of each. If soda #1 costs $1.50 for a 1-liter bottle, and soda #2 costs $2.75 for a 2-liter bottle, it would be a better deal to buy soda #2, because its unit rate is only $1.375 per 1-liter, which is cheaper than soda #1. Unit rates can also help determine the length of time a given event will take. For example, if you can paint 2 rooms in 4.5 hours, you can determine how long it will take you to paint 5 rooms by solving for the unit rate per room and then multiplying that by 5.

> **Review Video: Rates and Unit Rates**
> Visit mometrix.com/academy and enter code: 185363

# Cross Multiplication

## FINDING AN UNKNOWN IN EQUIVALENT EXPRESSIONS

It is often necessary to apply information given about a rate or proportion to a new scenario. For example, if you know that Jedha can run a marathon (26.2 miles) in 3 hours, how long would it take her to run 10 miles at the same pace? Start by setting up equivalent expressions:

$$\frac{26.2 \text{ mi}}{3 \text{ hr}} = \frac{10 \text{ mi}}{x \text{ hr}}$$

Now, cross multiply and solve for $x$:

$$26.2x = 30$$
$$x = \frac{30}{26.2} = \frac{15}{13.1}$$
$$x \approx 1.15 \text{ hrs } or \text{ 1 hr 9 min}$$

So, at this pace, Jedha could run 10 miles in about 1.15 hours or about 1 hour and 9 minutes.

> **Review Video: Cross Multiplying Fractions**
> Visit mometrix.com/academy and enter code: 893904

# Slope

## FINDING SLOPE GIVEN GRAPH OR TABLE

On a graph with two points, $(x_1, y_1)$ and $(x_2, y_2)$, the **slope** is found with the formula $m = \frac{y_2 - y_1}{x_2 - x_1}$; where $x_1 \neq x_2$ and $m$ stands for slope. If the value of the slope is **positive**, the line has an *upward direction* from left to right. If the value of the slope is **negative**, the line has a *downward direction* from left to right. Consider the following example:

131

A new book goes on sale in bookstores and online stores. In the first month, 5,000 copies of the book are sold. Over time, the book continues to grow in popularity. The data for the number of copies sold is in the table below.

| # of Months on Sale | 1 | 2 | 3 | 4 | 5 |
|---|---|---|---|---|---|
| # of Copies Sold (In Thousands) | 5 | 10 | 15 | 20 | 25 |

So, the number of copies that are sold and the time that the book is on sale is a proportional relationship. In this example, an equation can be used to show the data: $y = 5x$, where $x$ is the number of months that the book is on sale. Also, $y$ is the number of copies sold. So, the slope of the corresponding line is $\frac{\text{rise}}{\text{run}} = \frac{5}{1} = 5$.

## FINDING SLOPE GIVEN AN EQUATION

When given an equation of a line, it is necessary to solve for $y$ to determine the slope of the line. Given the equation $6x + 2y = 8$, find the slope. First, subtract $6x$ from both sides of the equation, resulting in $2y = -6x + 8$. Then divide both sides of the equation by 2, resulting in $y = -3x + 4$. This then allows us to conclude that the slope of the line is $m = -3$, the coefficient of $x$. Once an equation is in the form $y = mx + b$, the slope and y-intercept can easily be determined. For this reason, we refer to the equation $y = mx + b$ as "slope-intercept form" of the equation of a line.

> **Review Video: Finding the Slope of a Line**
> Visit mometrix.com/academy and enter code: 766664

# Metric and Customary Measurements

## METRIC MEASUREMENT PREFIXES

| Giga- | One billion | 1 *giga*watt is one billion watts |
| Mega- | One million | 1 *mega*hertz is one million hertz |
| Kilo- | One thousand | 1 *kilo*gram is one thousand grams |
| Deci- | One-tenth | 1 *deci*meter is one-tenth of a meter |
| Centi- | One-hundredth | 1 *centi*meter is one-hundredth of a meter |
| Milli- | One-thousandth | 1 *milli*liter is one-thousandth of a liter |
| Micro- | One-millionth | 1 *micro*gram is one-millionth of a gram |

> **Review Video: How the Metric System Works**
> Visit mometrix.com/academy and enter code: 163709

## MEASUREMENT CONVERSION

When converting between units, the goal is to maintain the same meaning but change the way it is displayed. In order to go from a larger unit to a smaller unit, multiply the number of the known amount by the equivalent amount. When going from a smaller unit to a larger unit, divide the number of the known amount by the equivalent amount.

For complicated conversions, it may be helpful to set up conversion fractions. In these fractions, one fraction is the **conversion factor**. The other fraction has the unknown amount in the numerator. So, the known value is placed in the denominator. Sometimes, the second fraction has the known value from the problem in the numerator and the unknown in the denominator. Multiply the two fractions to get the converted measurement. Note that since the numerator and the denominator of the factor are equivalent, the value of the fraction is 1. That is why we can say that the result in the new units is equal to the result in the old units even though they have different numbers.

It can often be necessary to chain known conversion factors together. As an example, consider converting 512 square inches to square meters. We know that there are 2.54 centimeters in an inch and 100 centimeters in a meter, and we know we will need to square each of these factors to achieve the conversion we are looking for.

$$\frac{512 \text{ in}^2}{1} \times \left(\frac{2.54 \text{ cm}}{1 \text{ in}}\right)^2 \times \left(\frac{1 \text{ m}}{100 \text{ cm}}\right)^2 = \frac{512 \text{ in}^2}{1} \times \left(\frac{6.4516 \text{ cm}^2}{1 \text{ in}^2}\right) \times \left(\frac{1 \text{ m}^2}{10,000 \text{ cm}^2}\right) = 0.330 \text{ m}^2$$

> **Review Video: Measurement Conversions**
> Visit mometrix.com/academy and enter code: 316703
>
> **Review Video: Converting Kilograms to Pounds**
> Visit mometrix.com/academy and enter code: 241463

## COMMON UNITS AND EQUIVALENTS

### METRIC EQUIVALENTS

| | |
|---|---|
| 1000 μg (microgram) | 1 mg |
| 1000 mg (milligram) | 1 g |
| 1000 g (gram) | 1 kg |
| 1000 kg (kilogram) | 1 metric ton |
| 1000 mL (milliliter) | 1 L |
| 1000 μm (micrometer) | 1 mm |
| 1000 mm (millimeter) | 1 m |
| 100 cm (centimeter) | 1 m |
| 1000 m (meter) | 1 km |

### DISTANCE AND AREA MEASUREMENT

| Unit | Abbreviation | US equivalent | Metric equivalent |
|---|---|---|---|
| Inch | in | 1 inch | 2.54 centimeters |
| Foot | ft | 12 inches | 0.305 meters |
| Yard | yd | 3 feet | 0.914 meters |
| Mile | mi | 5280 feet | 1.609 kilometers |
| Acre | ac | 4840 square yards | 0.405 hectares |
| Square Mile | sq. mi. or mi.² | 640 acres | 2.590 square kilometers |

### CAPACITY MEASUREMENTS

| Unit | Abbreviation | US equivalent | Metric equivalent |
|---|---|---|---|
| Fluid Ounce | fl oz | 8 fluid drams | 29.573 milliliters |
| Cup | c | 8 fluid ounces | 0.237 liter |
| Pint | pt. | 16 fluid ounces | 0.473 liter |
| Quart | qt. | 2 pints | 0.946 liter |
| Gallon | gal. | 4 quarts | 3.785 liters |
| Teaspoon | t or tsp. | 1 fluid dram | 5 milliliters |
| Tablespoon | T or tbsp. | 4 fluid drams | 15 or 16 milliliters |
| Cubic Centimeter | cc or cm³ | 0.271 drams | 1 milliliter |

### WEIGHT MEASUREMENTS

| Unit | Abbreviation | US equivalent | Metric equivalent |
|---|---|---|---|
| Ounce | oz | 16 drams | 28.35 grams |
| Pound | lb | 16 ounces | 453.6 grams |
| Ton | tn. | 2,000 pounds | 907.2 kilograms |

## Volume and Weight Measurement Clarifications

Always be careful when using ounces and fluid ounces. They are not equivalent.

| 1 pint = 16 fluid ounces | 1 fluid ounce ≠ 1 ounce |
| 1 pound = 16 ounces | 1 pint ≠ 1 pound |

Having one pint of something does not mean you have one pound of it. In the same way, just because something weighs one pound does not mean that its volume is one pint.

In the United States, the word "ton" by itself refers to a short ton or a net ton. Do not confuse this with a long ton (also called a gross ton) or a metric ton (also spelled *tonne*), which have different measurement equivalents.

$$1 \text{ US ton} = 2000 \text{ pounds} \quad \neq \quad 1 \text{ metric ton} = 1000 \text{ kilograms}$$

# Properties of Exponents

The properties of exponents are as follows:

| Property | Description |
| --- | --- |
| $a^1 = a$ | Any number to the power of 1 is equal to itself |
| $1^n = 1$ | The number 1 raised to any power is equal to 1 |
| $a^0 = 1$ | Any number raised to the power of 0 is equal to 1 |
| $a^n \times a^m = a^{n+m}$ | Add exponents to multiply powers of the same base number |
| $a^n \div a^m = a^{n-m}$ | Subtract exponents to divide powers of the same base number |
| $(a^n)^m = a^{n \times m}$ | When a power is raised to a power, the exponents are multiplied |
| $(a \times b)^n = a^n \times b^n$ | Multiplication and division operations inside parentheses can be raised to a |
| $(a \div b)^n = a^n \div b^n$ | power. This is the same as each term being raised to that power. |
| $a^{-n} = \dfrac{1}{a^n}$ | A negative exponent is the same as the reciprocal of a positive exponent |

Note that exponents do not have to be integers. Fractional or decimal exponents follow all the rules above as well. Example: $5^{\frac{1}{4}} \times 5^{\frac{3}{4}} = 5^{\frac{1}{4}+\frac{3}{4}} = 5^1 = 5$.

> **Review Video: Properties of Exponents**
> Visit mometrix.com/academy and enter code: 532558

# Scientific Notation

Scientific notation is a way of writing large numbers in a shorter form. The form $a \times 10^n$ is used in scientific notation, where $a$ is greater than or equal to 1 but less than 10, and $n$ is the number of places the decimal must move to get from the original number to $a$. Example: The number 230,400,000 is cumbersome to write. To write the value in scientific notation, place a decimal point between the first and second numbers, and include all digits through the last non-zero digit ($a = 2.304$). To find the appropriate power of 10, count the number of places the decimal point had to move ($n = 8$). The number is positive if the decimal moved to the left, and negative if it moved to the right. We can then write 230,400,000 as $2.304 \times 10^8$. If we look instead at the number 0.00002304, we have the same value for $a$, but this time the decimal moved 5 places to the right ($n = -5$). Thus, 0.00002304 can be written as $2.304 \times 10^{-5}$. Using this notation makes it simple to compare very large or very small numbers. By comparing exponents, it is easy to see that $3.28 \times 10^4$ is smaller than $1.51 \times 10^5$, because 4 is less than 5.

> **Review Video: Scientific Notation**
> Visit mometrix.com/academy and enter code: 976454

## Linear Expressions

### TERMS AND COEFFICIENTS

**Mathematical expressions** consist of a combination of one or more values arranged in terms that are added together. As such, an expression could be just a single number, including zero. A **variable term** is the product of a real number, also called a **coefficient**, and one or more variables, each of which may be raised to an exponent. Expressions may also include numbers without a variable, called **constants** or **constant terms**. The expression $6s^2$, for example, is a single term where the coefficient is the real number 6 and the variable term is $s^2$. Note that if a term is written as simply a variable to some exponent, like $t^2$, then the coefficient is 1, because $t^2 = 1t^2$.

### LINEAR EXPRESSIONS

A **single variable linear expression** is the sum of a single variable term, where the variable has no exponent, and a constant, which may be zero. For instance, the expression $2w + 7$ has $2w$ as the variable term and 7 as the constant term. It is important to realize that terms are separated by addition or subtraction. Since an expression is a sum of terms, expressions such as $5x - 3$ can be written as $5x + (-3)$ to emphasize that the constant term is negative. A real-world example of a single variable linear expression is the perimeter of a square, four times the side length, often expressed: $4s$.

In general, a **linear expression** is the sum of any number of variable terms so long as none of the variables have an exponent and none of the terms have two variables multiplied together. For example, $3m + 8n - \frac{1}{4}p + 5.5q - 1$ is a linear expression, but $3y^3$ and $5xy$ are not. In the same way, the expression for the perimeter of a general triangle $(a + b + c)$ is linear, but the expression for the area of a square $(s^2)$ is not.

## Solving Equations

### MANIPULATING EQUATIONS

#### LIKE TERMS

Like terms are terms in an equation that have the same variable, regardless of whether they also have the same coefficient. This includes terms that *lack* a variable; all constants (i.e., numbers without variables) are considered like terms. If the equation involves terms with a variable raised to different powers, the like terms are those that have the variable raised to the same power.

For example, consider the equation $x^2 + 3x + 2 = 2x^2 + x - 7 + 2x$. In this equation, 2 and –7 are like terms; they are both constants. The terms $3x$, $x$, and $2x$ are like terms, they all include the variable $x$ raised to the first power. The terms $x^2$ and $2x^2$ are like terms, they both include the variable $x$, raised to the second power. The terms $2x$ and $2x^2$ are not like terms; although they both involve the variable $x$, the variable is not raised to the same power in both terms. The fact that they have the same coefficient, 2, is not relevant.

> **Review Video: Rules for Manipulating Equations**
> Visit mometrix.com/academy and enter code: 838871

## Carrying Out the Same Operation on Both Sides of an Equation

When solving an equation, the general procedure is to carry out a series of operations on both sides of an equation, choosing operations that simplify the equation when doing so. The reason why the same operation must be carried out on both sides of the equation is because that leaves the meaning of the equation unchanged, and yields a result that is equivalent to the original equation. This would not be the case if we carried out an operation on one side of an equation and not the other. Consider what an equation means: it is a statement that two values or expressions are equal. If we carry out the same operation on both sides of the equation—add 3 to both sides, for example—then the two sides of the equation are changed in the same way, and so remain equal. If we do that to only one side of the equation—add 3 to one side but not the other—then that wouldn't be true; if we change one side of the equation but not the other then the two sides are no longer equal.

## Combining Like Terms

Combining like terms refers to adding or subtracting like terms—terms with the same variable—and therefore reducing sets of like terms to a single term. The main advantage of doing this is that it simplifies the equation. Often, combining like terms can be done as the first step in solving an equation, though it can also be done later, such as after distributing terms in a product.

For example, consider the equation $2(x + 3) + 3(2 + x + 3) = -4$. The 2 and the 3 in the second set of parentheses are like terms, and we can combine them, yielding $2(x + 3) + 3(x + 5) = -4$. Now we can carry out the multiplications implied by the parentheses, distributing the outer 2 and 3 accordingly: $2x + 6 + 3x + 15 = -4$. The $2x$ and the $3x$ are like terms, and we can add them together: $5x + 6 + 15 = -4$. Now, the constants 6, 15, and –4 are also like terms, and we can combine them as well: subtracting 6 and 15 from both sides of the equation, we get $5x = -4 - 6 - 15$, or $5x = -25$, which simplifies further to $x = -5$.

> **Review Video: Solving Equations by Combining Like Terms**
> Visit mometrix.com/academy and enter code: 668506

## Canceling Terms on Opposite Sides of an Equation

Two terms on opposite sides of an equation can be canceled if and only if they *exactly* match each other. They must have the same variable raised to the same power and the same coefficient. For example, in the equation $3x + 2x^2 + 6 = 2x^2 - 6$, $2x^2$ appears on both sides of the equation and can be canceled, leaving $3x + 6 = -6$. The 6 on each side of the equation *cannot* be canceled, because it is added on one side of the equation and subtracted on the other. While they cannot be canceled, however, the 6 and –6 are like terms and can be combined, yielding $3x = -12$, which simplifies further to $x = -4$.

It's also important to note that the terms to be canceled must be independent terms and cannot be part of a larger term. For example, consider the equation $2(x + 6) = 3(x + 4) + 1$. We cannot cancel the $x$'s, because even though they match each other they are part of the larger terms $2(x + 6)$ and $3(x + 4)$. We must first distribute the 2 and 3, yielding $2x + 12 = 3x + 12 + 1$. Now we see that the terms with the $x$'s do not match, but the 12s do, and can be canceled, leaving $2x = 3x + 1$, which simplifies to $x = -1$.

## Isolating Variables

To isolate a variable means to manipulate the equation so that the variable appears by itself on one side of the equation, and does not appear at all on the other side. Generally, an equation or inequality is considered to be solved once the variable is isolated and the other side of the equation or inequality is simplified as much as possible. In the case of a two-variable equation or inequality, only one variable needs to be isolated; it will not usually be possible to simultaneously isolate both variables.

For a linear equation—an equation in which the variable only appears raised to the first power—isolating a variable can be done by first moving all the terms with the variable to one side of the equation and all other terms to the other side. (*Moving* a term really means adding the inverse of the term to both sides; when a term is *moved* to the other side of the equation its sign is flipped.) Then combine like terms on each side. Finally, divide both sides by the coefficient of the variable, if applicable. The steps need not necessarily be done in this order, but this order will always work.

> **Review Video: Solving Equations for Specific Variables**
> Visit mometrix.com/academy and enter code: 130695
>
> **Review Video: Solving Equations Involving Algebraic Fractions**
> Visit mometrix.com/academy and enter code: 237770
>
> **Review Video: Solving One-Step Equations**
> Visit mometrix.com/academy and enter code: 777004

## SOLVING ONE-VARIABLE LINEAR EQUATIONS

### EQUATIONS WITH ONE SOLUTION (THE USUAL CASE)

To solve a one-variable linear equation, we use the techniques above to isolate the variable.

1. If any coefficients or constants are fractions, it is often helpful first to multiply both sides of the equation by the least common denominator (of all fractions) to clear the fractions.
2. Simplify both sides of the equation by combining any like terms.
3. Put all terms with the variable on one side of the equation and all constant terms on the other side, by adding or subtracting the same terms on both sides of the equation.
4. Divide both sides by the coefficient of the variable (or multiply both sides by its reciprocal).
5. When we have a value for the variable, we can check it by substituting the value into the original equation to make sure it produces a true result.

Consider the following example for solving the equation $\frac{2}{3}x + 8 = 14$:

| | |
|---|---|
| $3 \cdot \left(\frac{2}{3}x + 8\right) = 3 \cdot 14$ | Clear fractions by multiplying both sides by 3. |
| $2x + 24 = 42$ | Simplify, remembering to apply the distributive property. |
| $2x + 24 - 24 = 42 - 24$ | Subtract 24 from both sides to isolate $2x$. |
| $2x = 18$ | Simplify by combining like terms. |
| $\frac{2x}{2} = \frac{18}{2}$ | Divide both sides by 2 to isolate $x$. |
| $x = 9$ | Simplify |

Finally, we check this answer by substituting $x = 9$ into the original equation to make sure we get a true result.

$$\frac{2}{3}x + 8 = \frac{2}{3}(9) + 8 = 6 + 8 = 14$$

This is correct, so the value of $x$ is 9.

> **Review Video: Solving Equations Using the Distributive Property**
> Visit mometrix.com/academy and enter code: 765499

### EQUATIONS WITH MORE THAN ONE SOLUTION

Some types of non-linear equations, such as equations involving squares of variables, may have more than one solution. For example, the equation $x^2 = 4$ has two solutions: 2 and –2. Equations with absolute values can also have multiple solutions: $|x| = 1$ has the solutions $x = 1$ and $x = -1$.

It is possible for a linear equation to have more than one solution but only if the equation is true regardless of the value of the variable. We call such an equation an **identity**. In this case, the equation has infinitely many solutions, because every possible value of the variable is a solution. We discover that a linear equation is an identity when our attempts to isolate the variable cause the variable to disappear, leaving a *true* equation involving only constants. For example, consider the equation $2(3x + 5) = x + 5(x + 2)$. Distributing, we get $6x + 10 = x + 5x + 10$; combining like terms gives $6x + 10 = 6x + 10$, and the $6x$-terms cancel to leave $10 = 10$. This is clearly true, so the original equation is an identity. We could also cancel the 10's leaving $0 = 0$, which is also is clearly true—in general if both sides of the equation can be reduced to match one another exactly, the original equation is an identity.

## EQUATIONS WITH NO SOLUTION

Some types of non-linear equations, such as equations involving squares of variables, may have no solution. For example, the equation $x^2 = -2$ has no solutions in the real numbers because the square of a real number must be positive. Similarly, $|x| = -1$ has no solution because the absolute value of a number is always positive.

It is also possible for a linear equation to have no solution. We call such an equation a **contradiction**. We discover that a linear equation is a contradiction when our attempts to isolate the variable cause the variable to disappear, leaving a *false* equation involving only constants. For example, the equation $2(x + 3) + x = 3x$ has no solution. We can see this by trying to solve it: first we distribute, leaving $2x + 6 + x = 3x$. Combining like terms gives us $3x + 6 = 3x$, and cancelling the term $3x$ on both sides leaves us with $6 = 0$. This is clearly false, so the original equation is a contradiction, having no solutions.

## FEATURES OF EQUATIONS THAT REQUIRE SPECIAL TREATMENT

A linear equation is an equation in which variables only appear by themselves: not multiplied together, not with exponents other than one, and not inside absolute value signs or any other functions. For example, the equation $x + 1 - 3x = 5 - x$ is a linear equation; while $x$ appears multiple times, it never appears with an exponent other than one, or inside any function. The two-variable equation $2x - 3y = 5 + 2x$ is also a linear equation. In contrast, the equation $x^2 - 5 = 3x$ is *not* a linear equation, because it involves the term $x^2$. The equation $\sqrt{x} = 5$ is not linear, because it involves a square root. The equation $(x - 1)^2 = 4$ is not linear because even though there's no exponent on the $x$ directly, it appears as part of an expression that is squared. The two-variable equation $x + xy - y = 5$ is not linear because it includes the term $xy$, where two variables are multiplied together.

As we see above, linear equations can always be solved (or shown to have no solution) by combining like terms and performing simple operations on both sides of the equation. Some non-linear equations can be solved by similar methods, but others may require more advanced methods of solution, if they can be solved analytically at all.

## SOLVING EQUATIONS INVOLVING ROOTS

In an equation involving roots, the first step is to isolate the term with the root, if possible, and then raise both sides of the equation to the appropriate power to eliminate it. Consider an example equation, $2\sqrt{x + 1} - 1 = 3$. In this case, begin by adding 1 to both sides, yielding $2\sqrt{x + 1} = 4$, and then dividing both sides by 2, yielding $\sqrt{x + 1} = 2$. Now square both sides, yielding $x + 1 = 4$. Finally, subtracting 1 from both sides yields $x = 3$.

Squaring both sides of an equation (or raising both sides to any *even* power) may, however, yield a spurious solution—a solution to the squared equation that is *not* a solution of the original equation. It's therefore necessary to plug the solution back into the original equation to make sure it works. In this case, it does: $2\sqrt{3 + 1} - 1 = 2\sqrt{4} - 1 = 2(2) - 1 = 4 - 1 = 3$.

The same procedure applies for other roots as well. For example, given the equation $3 + \sqrt[3]{2x} = 5$, we can first subtract 3 from both sides, yielding $\sqrt[3]{2x} = 2$ and isolating the root. Raising both sides to the third power yields $2x = 2^3$; i.e., $2x = 8$. We can now divide both sides by 2 to get $x = 4$.

> **Review Video: Solving Equations Involving Roots**
> Visit mometrix.com/academy and enter code: 297670

## SOLVING EQUATIONS WITH EXPONENTS

In solving an equation with powers of a variable, sometimes it is possible to eliminate all but one term involving the variable. In that case, we can isolate the power of the variable and then take the appropriate root of both sides to eliminate the exponent. For instance, for the equation $2x^3 + 17 = 5x^3 - 7$, we can subtract $5x^3$ from both sides to get $-3x^3 + 17 = -7$, and then subtract 17 from both sides to get $-3x^3 = -24$. Finally, we can divide both sides by $-3$ to get $x^3 = 8$. Since this isolates the cube of the variable, we can take the cube root of both sides to get $x = \sqrt[3]{8} = 2$.

One important but often overlooked point is that equations with an exponent greater than 1 may have more than one answer. The solution to $x^2 = 9$ isn't simply $x = 3$; it's $x = \pm 3$ (that is, $x = 3$ or $x = -3$). For a slightly more complicated example, consider the equation $(x - 1)^2 - 1 = 3$. Adding 1 to both sides yields $(x - 1)^2 = 4$; taking the square root of both sides yields $x - 1 = 2$. We can then add 1 to both sides to get $x = 3$. However, there's a second solution. We also have the possibility that $x - 1 = -2$, in which case $x = -1$. Both $x = 3$ and $x = -1$ are valid solutions, as can be verified by substituting them both into the original equation.

> **Review Video: Solving Equations with Exponents**
> Visit mometrix.com/academy and enter code: 514557
>
> **Review Video: Adding and Subtracting with Exponents**
> Visit mometrix.com/academy and enter code: 875756

## SOLVING EQUATIONS WITH ABSOLUTE VALUES

When solving an equation with an absolute value, the first step is to isolate the absolute value term. We then consider two possibilities: when the expression inside the absolute value is positive or when it is negative. In the former case, the expression in the absolute value equals the expression on the other side of the equation; in the latter, it equals the additive inverse of that expression—the expression times negative one. We consider each case separately and finally check for spurious solutions.

For instance, consider solving $|2x - 1| + x = 5$ for $x$. We can first isolate the absolute value by moving the $x$ to the other side: $|2x - 1| = -x + 5$. Now, we have two possibilities. First, that $2x - 1$ is positive, and hence $2x - 1 = -x + 5$. Rearranging and combining like terms yields $3x = 6$, and hence $x = 2$. The other possibility is that $2x - 1$ is negative, and hence $2x - 1 = -(-x + 5) = x - 5$. In this case, rearranging and combining like terms yields $x = -4$. Substituting $x = 2$ and $x = -4$ back into the original equation, we see that they are both valid solutions.

Note that the absolute value of a sum or difference applies to the sum or difference as a whole, not to the individual terms; in general, $|2x - 1|$ is not equal to $|2x + 1|$ or to $|2x| - 1$.

> **Review Video: Solving Absolute Value Equations**
> Visit mometrix.com/academy and enter code: 501208

## EXTRANEOUS SOLUTIONS

An **extraneous solution** may arise when we square both sides of an equation (or raise both sides to an even power) as a step in solving it or under certain other operations on the equation. It is a solution to the squared or otherwise modified equation that is *not* a solution of the original equation. To identify an extraneous solution, it's useful when you solve an equation involving roots or absolute values to plug the solution back into the original equation to make sure it's valid.

## Two-Variable Equations

Similar to methods for a one-variable equation, solving a two-variable equation involves isolating a variable: manipulating the equation so that a variable appears by itself on one side of the equation, and not at all on the other side. However, in a two-variable equation, you will usually only be able to isolate one of the variables; the other variable may appear on the other side along with constant terms, or with exponents or other functions. If an equation has multiple variables, the problem should tell you which variable to isolate.

> **Review Video: Solving Equations with Variables on Both Sides**
> Visit mometrix.com/academy and enter code: 402497

# Linear Equations

Equations like $5x = 100$ and $8x - 120 = 200$ and $6x + 4y = 240$ are **linear equations**. Linear equations are named based off the number of distinct variables they include. For example, the equation $3x + 30 = 8x$ is a **one-variable linear equation** because it involves only the single variable $x$. It does not matter that $x$ appears more than once. Any equations that can be written as $ax + b = 0$, where $a \neq 0$, falls into this category. Furthermore, the equation $3x - 5y = 14 + 9y$ is a **two-variable linear equation** because it involves the two variables $x$ and $y$. The equation $7x + 8y - 12z + 14w = 56$ is a linear equation in four variables.

## Satisfying the Equation

When given a one-variable linear equation, the goal is typically to solve it. This means that we want to find the number that makes the equation true if we substitute it for the variable. That number is the **solution,** or root, of the equation. For instance, the equation $5x = 10$ has the solution $x = 2$. This is true because when 2 is substituted for x, the result is $5 \cdot 2 = 10$, which is true. On the other hand, $x = 6$ can not be a solution because $5 \cdot 6 \neq 10$, so it is false. Two equations with the same solution are **equivalent equations**. For example, the equations $5x = 10$ and $5x + 3 = 13$ are equivalent because both have the same solution of $x = 2$.

## Determining a Solution Set

The **solution set** is the set of all solutions of an equation. In the previous example, the solution set would be 2. Solutions to a linear equation in two variables consist of pairs of numbers. For instance, the equation $6x + 4y = 240$ has the solution $x = 20$ and $y = 30$ since $6 \cdot 20 + 4 \cdot 30 = 240$ is true. We can write this solution as the ordered pair (20,30) and plot it as a point on the coordinate plane. Such equations usually have infinitely many solutions; and if we plot the points for all these solutions we get a line, which is a picture of all the solutions. We call this **graphing the equation**. When an equation has no true solutions, it is referred to as an **empty set**.

## Linear Equation Forms

Linear equations can be written many ways. Below is a list of some forms linear equations can take:

- **Standard Form**: $Ax + By = C$; the slope is $\frac{-A}{B}$ and the $y$-intercept is $\frac{C}{B}$
- **Slope Intercept Form**: $y = mx + b$, where $m$ is the slope and $b$ is the $y$-intercept
- **Point-Slope Form**: $y - y_1 = m(x - x_1)$, where $m$ is the slope and $(x_1, y_1)$ is a point on the line

- **Two-Point Form**: $\frac{y-y_1}{x-x_1} = \frac{y_2-y_1}{x_2-x_1}$, where $(x_1, y_1)$ and $(x_2, y_2)$ are two points on the given line
- **Intercept Form**: $\frac{x}{x_1} + \frac{y}{y_1} = 1$, where $(x_1, 0)$ is the point at which a line intersects the $x$-axis, and $(0, y_1)$ is the point at which the same line intersects the $y$-axis

> **Review Video: Slope-Intercept and Point-Slope Forms**
> Visit mometrix.com/academy and enter code: 113216
>
> **Review Video: Converting Between Standard and Slope-Intercept Forms**
> Visit mometrix.com/academy and enter code: 982828
>
> **Review Video: Linear Equations Basics**
> Visit mometrix.com/academy and enter code: 793005

# Inequalities

Commonly in algebra and other upper-level fields of math you find yourself working with mathematical expressions that do not equal each other. The statement comparing such expressions with symbols such as < (less than) or > (greater than) is called an *inequality*. An example of an inequality is $7x > 5$. To solve for $x$, simply divide both sides by 7 and the solution is shown to be $x > \frac{5}{7}$. Graphs of the solution set of inequalities are represented on a number line. Open circles are used to show that an expression approaches a number but is never quite equal to that number.

> **Review Video: Solving One-Step Inequalities**
> Visit mometrix.com/academy and enter code: 229684
>
> **Review Video: Solving Multi-Step Inequalities**
> Visit mometrix.com/academy and enter code: 347842
>
> **Review Video: Solving Inequalities Using All 4 Basic Operations**
> Visit mometrix.com/academy and enter code: 401111

## TYPES OF INEQUALITIES

**Conditional inequalities** are those with certain values for the variable that will make the condition true and other values for the variable where the condition will be false. **Absolute inequalities** can have any real number as the value for the variable to make the condition true, while there is no real number value for the variable that will make the condition false. Solving inequalities is done by following the same rules for solving equations with the exception that when multiplying or dividing by a negative number the direction of the inequality sign must be flipped or reversed. **Double inequalities** are situations where two inequality statements apply to the same variable expression. Example: $-c < ax + b < c$.

> **Review Video: Conditional and Absolute Inequalities**
> Visit mometrix.com/academy and enter code: 980164

# Solving Inequalities

## DETERMINING SOLUTIONS TO INEQUALITIES

To determine whether a coordinate is a solution of an inequality, you can substitute the values of the coordinate into the inequality, simplify, and check whether the resulting statement holds true. For instance, to determine whether $(-2, 4)$ is a solution of the inequality $y \geq -2x + 3$, substitute the values into the inequality,

$4 \geq -2(-2) + 3$. Simplify the right side of the inequality and the result is $4 \geq 7$, which is a false statement. Therefore, the coordinate is not a solution of the inequality. You can also use this method to determine which part of the graph of an inequality is shaded. The graph of $y \geq -2x + 3$ includes the solid line $y = -2x + 3$ and, since it excludes the point $(-2, 4)$ to the left of the line, it is shaded to the right of the line.

> **Review Video: Graphing Linear Inequalities**
> Visit mometrix.com/academy and enter code: 439421
>
> **Review Video: Graphing Solutions to Inequalities**
> Visit mometrix.com/academy and enter code: 391281

## FLIPPING INEQUALITY SIGNS

When given an inequality, we can always turn the entire inequality around, swapping the two sides of the inequality and changing the inequality sign. For instance, $x + 2 > 2x - 3$ is equivalent to $2x - 3 < x + 2$. Aside from that, normally the inequality does not change if we carry out the same operation on both sides of the inequality. There is, however, one principal exception: if we *multiply* or *divide* both sides of the inequality by a *negative number*, the inequality is flipped. For example, if we take the inequality $-2x < 6$ and divide both sides by $-2$, the inequality flips and we are left with $x > -3$. This *only* applies to multiplication and division, and only with negative numbers. Multiplying or dividing both sides by a positive number, or adding or subtracting any number regardless of sign, does not flip the inequality. Another special case that flips the inequality sign is when reciprocals are used. For instance, $3 > 2$ but the relation of the reciprocals is $\frac{1}{3} < \frac{1}{2}$.

## COMPOUND INEQUALITIES

A **compound inequality** is an equality that consists of two inequalities combined with *and* or *or*. The two components of a proper compound inequality must be of opposite type: that is, one must be greater than (or greater than or equal to), the other less than (or less than or equal to). For instance, "$x + 1 < 2$ or $x + 1 > 3$" is a compound inequality, as is "$2x \geq 4$ and $2x \leq 6$." An *and* inequality can be written more compactly by having one inequality on each side of the common part: "$2x \geq 1$ and $2x \leq 6$," can also be written as $1 \leq 2x \leq 6$.

In order for the compound inequality to be meaningful, the two parts of an *and* inequality must overlap; otherwise, no numbers satisfy the inequality. On the other hand, if the two parts of an *or* inequality overlap, then *all* numbers satisfy the inequality and as such the inequality is usually not meaningful.

Solving a compound inequality requires solving each part separately. For example, given the compound inequality "$x + 1 < 2$ or $x + 1 > 3$," the first inequality, $x + 1 < 2$, reduces to $x < 1$, and the second part, $x + 1 > 3$, reduces to $x > 2$, so the whole compound inequality can be written as "$x < 1$ or $x > 2$." Similarly, $1 \leq 2x \leq 6$ can be solved by dividing each term by 2, yielding $\frac{1}{2} \leq x \leq 3$.

> **Review Video: Compound Inequalities**
> Visit mometrix.com/academy and enter code: 786318

## SOLVING INEQUALITIES INVOLVING ABSOLUTE VALUES

To solve an inequality involving an absolute value, first isolate the term with the absolute value. Then proceed to treat the two cases separately as with an absolute value equation, but flipping the inequality in the case where the expression in the absolute value is negative (since that essentially involves multiplying both sides by $-1$.) The two cases are then combined into a compound inequality; if the absolute value is on the greater side of the inequality, then it is an *or* compound inequality, if on the lesser side, then it's an *and*.

Consider the inequality $2 + |x - 1| \geq 3$. We can isolate the absolute value term by subtracting 2 from both sides: $|x - 1| \geq 1$. Now, we're left with the two cases $x - 1 \geq 1$ or $x - 1 \leq -1$: note that in the latter, negative case, the inequality is flipped. $x - 1 \geq 1$ reduces to $x \geq 2$, and $x - 1 \leq -1$ reduces to $x \leq 0$. Since in the inequality $|x-1| \geq 1$ the absolute value is on the greater side, the two cases combine into an *or* compound inequality, so the final, solved inequality is "$x \leq 0$ or $x \geq 2$."

> **Review Video: Solving Absolute Value Inequalities**
> Visit mometrix.com/academy and enter code: 997008

## SOLVING INEQUALITIES INVOLVING SQUARE ROOTS

Solving an inequality with a square root involves two parts. First, we solve the inequality as if it were an equation, isolating the square root and then squaring both sides of the equation. Second, we restrict the solution to the set of values of $x$ for which the value inside the square root sign is non-negative.

For example, in the inequality, $\sqrt{x-2}+1 < 5$, we can isolate the square root by subtracting 1 from both sides, yielding $\sqrt{x-2} < 4$. Squaring both sides of the inequality yields $x - 2 < 16$, so $x < 18$. Since we can't take the square root of a negative number, we also require the part inside the square root to be non-negative. In this case, that means $x - 2 \geq 0$. Adding 2 to both sides of the inequality yields $x \geq 2$. Our final answer is a compound inequality combining the two simple inequalities: $x \geq 2$ and $x < 18$, or $2 \leq x < 18$.

Note that we only get a compound inequality if the two simple inequalities are in opposite directions; otherwise, we take the one that is more restrictive.

The same technique can be used for other even roots, such as fourth roots. It is *not*, however, used for cube roots or other odd roots—negative numbers *do* have cube roots, so the condition that the quantity inside the root sign cannot be negative does not apply.

> **Review Video: Solving Inequalities Involving Square Roots**
> Visit mometrix.com/academy and enter code: 800288

## SPECIAL CIRCUMSTANCES

Sometimes an inequality involving an absolute value or an even exponent is true for all values of $x$, and we don't need to do any further work to solve it. This is true if the inequality, once the absolute value or exponent term is isolated, says that term is greater than a negative number (or greater than or equal to zero). Since an absolute value or a number raised to an even exponent is *always* non-negative, this inequality is always true.

# Graphing Inequalities

## GRAPHING SIMPLE INEQUALITIES

To graph a simple inequality, we first mark on the number line the value that signifies the end point of the inequality. If the inequality is strict (involves a less than or greater than), we use a hollow circle; if it is not strict (less than or equal to or greater than or equal to), we use a solid circle. We then fill in the part of the number line that satisfies the inequality: to the left of the marked point for less than (or less than or equal to), to the right for greater than (or greater than or equal to).

For example, we would graph the inequality $x < 5$ by putting a hollow circle at 5 and filling in the part of the line to the left:

## GRAPHING COMPOUND INEQUALITIES

To graph a compound inequality, we fill in both parts of the inequality for an *or* inequality, or the overlap between them for an *and* inequality. More specifically, we start by plotting the endpoints of each inequality on the number line. For an *or* inequality, we then fill in the appropriate side of the line for each inequality. Typically, the two component inequalities do not overlap, which means the shaded part is *outside* the two points. For an *and* inequality, we instead fill in the part of the line that meets both inequalities.

For the inequality "$x \leq -3$ or $x > 4$," we first put a solid circle at –3 and a hollow circle at 4. We then fill the parts of the line *outside* these circles:

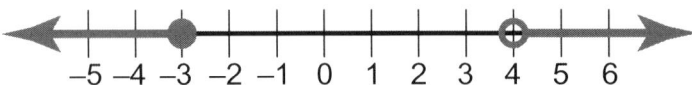

## GRAPHING INEQUALITIES INCLUDING ABSOLUTE VALUES

An inequality with an absolute value can be converted to a compound inequality. To graph the inequality, first convert it to a compound inequality, and then graph that normally. If the absolute value is on the greater side of the inequality, we end up with an *or* inequality; we plot the endpoints of the inequality on the number line and fill in the part of the line *outside* those points. If the absolute value is on the smaller side of the inequality, we end up with an *and* inequality; we plot the endpoints of the inequality on the number line and fill in the part of the line *between* those points.

For example, the inequality $|x + 1| \geq 4$ can be rewritten as $x \geq 3$ or $x \leq -5$. We place solid circles at the points 3 and –5 and fill in the part of the line *outside* them:

## GRAPHING INEQUALITIES IN TWO VARIABLES

To graph an inequality in two variables, we first graph the border of the inequality. This means graphing the equation that we get if we replace the inequality sign with an equals sign. If the inequality is strict ($>$ or $<$), we graph the border with a dashed or dotted line; if it is not strict ($\geq$ or $\leq$), we use a solid line. We can then test any point not on the border to see if it satisfies the inequality. If it does, we shade in that side of the border; if not, we shade in the other side. As an example, consider $y > 2x + 2$. To graph this inequality, we first graph the border, $y = 2x + 2$. Since it is a strict inequality, we use a dashed line. Then, we choose a test point. This can be any point not on the border; in this case, we will choose the origin, (0,0). (This makes the calculation easy and is generally a good choice unless the border passes through the origin.) Putting this into the original inequality, we get $0 > 2(0) + 2$, i.e., $0 > 2$. This is *not* true, so we shade in the side of the border that does *not* include the point (0,0):

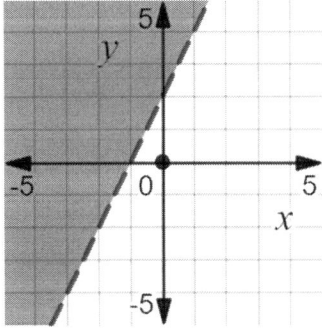

## GRAPHING COMPOUND INEQUALITIES IN TWO VARIABLES

One way to graph a compound inequality in two variables is to first graph each of the component inequalities. For an *and* inequality, we then shade in only the parts where the two graphs overlap; for an *or* inequality, we shade in any region that pertains to either of the individual inequalities.

Consider the graph of "$y \geq x - 1$ and $y \leq -x$":

We first shade in the individual inequalities:

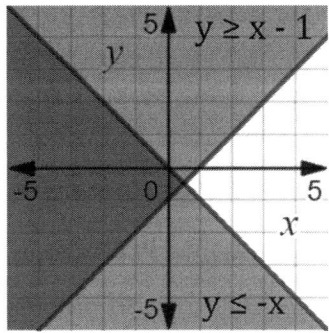

Now, since the compound inequality has an *and*, we only leave shaded the overlap—the part that pertains to *both* inequalities:

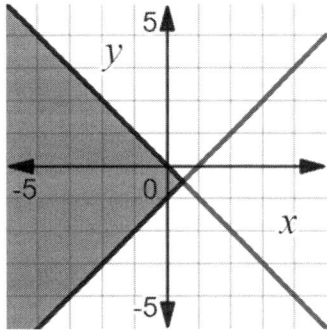

If instead the inequality had been "$y \geq x - 1$ or $y \leq -x$," our final graph would involve the *total* shaded area:

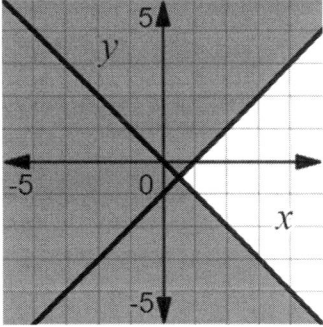

**Review Video: Graphing Solutions to Inequalities**
Visit mometrix.com/academy and enter code: 391281

# Systems of Equations

## SOLVING SYSTEMS OF EQUATIONS

A **system of equations** is a set of simultaneous equations that all use the same variables. A solution to a system of equations must be true for each equation in the system. **Consistent systems** are those with at least one solution. **Inconsistent systems** are systems of equations that have no solution.

> **Review Video: Solving Systems of Linear Equations**
> Visit mometrix.com/academy and enter code: 746745

### SUBSTITUTION

To solve a system of linear equations by **substitution**, start with the easier equation and solve for one of the variables. Express this variable in terms of the other variable. Substitute this expression in the other equation and solve for the other variable. The solution should be expressed in the form $(x, y)$. Substitute the values into both of the original equations to check your answer. Consider the following system of equations:

$$x + 6y = 15$$
$$3x - 12y = 18$$

Solving the first equation for $x$: $x = 15 - 6y$

Substitute this value in place of $x$ in the second equation, and solve for $y$:

$$3(15 - 6y) - 12y = 18$$
$$45 - 18y - 12y = 18$$
$$30y = 27$$
$$y = \frac{27}{30} = \frac{9}{10} = 0.9$$

Plug this value for $y$ back into the first equation to solve for $x$:

$$x = 15 - 6(0.9) = 15 - 5.4 = 9.6$$

Check both equations if you have time:

$$9.6 + 6(0.9) = 15 \qquad 3(9.6) - 12(0.9) = 18$$
$$9.6 + 5.4 = 15 \qquad 28.8 - 10.8 = 18$$
$$15 = 15 \qquad 18 = 18$$

Therefore, the solution is (9.6, 0.9).

> **Review Video: The Substitution Method**
> Visit mometrix.com/academy and enter code: 565151
>
> **Review Video: Substitution and Elimination**
> Visit mometrix.com/academy and enter code: 958611

### ELIMINATION

To solve a system of equations using **elimination**, begin by rewriting both equations in standard form $Ax + By = C$. Check to see if the coefficients of one pair of like variables add to zero. If not, multiply one or both of the equations by a non-zero number to make one set of like variables add to zero. Add the two equations to solve for one of the variables. Substitute this value into one of the original equations to solve for the other variable. Check your work by substituting into the other equation. Now, let's look at solving the following system using the elimination method:

$$5x + 6y = 4$$
$$x + 2y = 4$$

If we multiply the second equation by $-3$, we can eliminate the $y$-terms:

$$5x + 6y = 4$$
$$-3x - 6y = -12$$

Add the equations together and solve for $x$:

$$2x = -8$$
$$x = \frac{-8}{2} = -4$$

Plug the value for $x$ back in to either of the original equations and solve for $y$:

$$-4 + 2y = 4$$
$$y = \frac{4+4}{2} = 4$$

Check both equations if you have time:

$$\begin{aligned}5(-4) + 6(4) &= 4\\ -20 + 24 &= 4\\ 4 &= 4\end{aligned} \qquad \begin{aligned}-4 + 2(4) &= 4\\ -4 + 8 &= 4\\ 4 &= 4\end{aligned}$$

Therefore, the solution is $(-4, 4)$.

> **Review Video: The Elimination Method**
> Visit mometrix.com/academy and enter code: 449121

## GRAPHICALLY

To solve a system of linear equations **graphically**, plot both equations on the same graph. The solution of the equations is the point where both lines cross. If the lines do not cross (are parallel), then there is **no solution**.

For example, consider the following system of equations:

$$y = 2x + 7$$
$$y = -x + 1$$

Since these equations are given in slope-intercept form, they are easy to graph; the $y$-intercepts of the lines are $(0,7)$ and $(0,1)$. The respective slopes are 2 and $-1$, thus the graphs look like this:

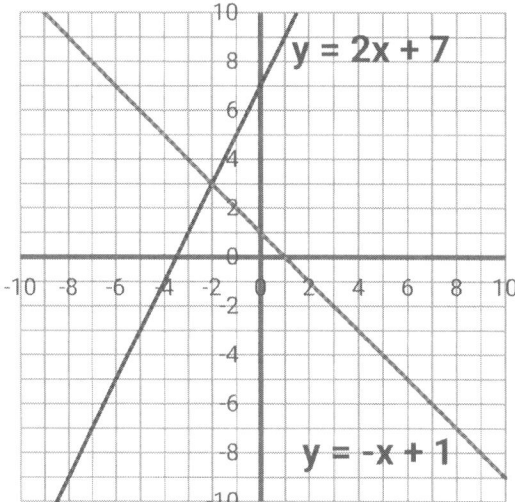

The two lines intersect at the point $(-2,3)$, thus this is the solution to the system of equations.

Solving a system graphically is generally only practical if both coordinates of the solution are integers; otherwise the intersection will lie between gridlines on the graph and the coordinates will be difficult or impossible to determine exactly. It also helps if, as in this example, the equations are in slope-intercept form or some other form that makes them easy to graph. Otherwise, another method of solution (by substitution or elimination) is likely to be more useful.

> **Review Video: Solving Systems by Graphing**
> Visit mometrix.com/academy and enter code: 634812

## SOLVING SYSTEMS OF EQUATIONS USING THE TRACE FEATURE

Using the trace feature on a calculator requires that you rewrite each equation, isolating the $y$-variable on one side of the equal sign. Enter both equations in the graphing calculator and plot the graphs simultaneously. Use the trace cursor to find where the two lines cross. Use the zoom feature if necessary to obtain more accurate results. Always check your answer by substituting into the original equations. The trace method is likely to be less accurate than other methods due to the resolution of graphing calculators but is a useful tool to provide an approximate answer.

# Graphing Equations

## GRAPHICAL SOLUTIONS TO EQUATIONS

When equations are shown graphically, they are usually shown on a **Cartesian coordinate plane**. The Cartesian coordinate plane consists of two number lines placed perpendicular to each other and intersecting at the zero point, also known as the origin. The horizontal number line is known as the $x$-axis, with positive values to the right of the origin, and negative values to the left of the origin. The vertical number line is known as the $y$-axis, with positive values above the origin, and negative values below the origin. Any point on the plane can be identified by an ordered pair in the form $(x, y)$, called coordinates. The $x$-value of the coordinate is called the abscissa, and the $y$-value of the coordinate is called the ordinate. The two number lines divide the plane into **four quadrants**: I, II, III, and IV.

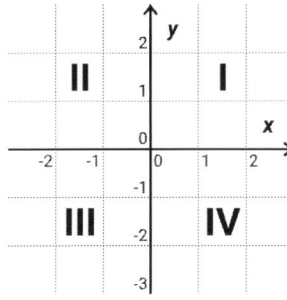

Note that in quadrant I $x > 0$ and $y > 0$, in quadrant II $x < 0$ and $y > 0$, in quadrant III $x < 0$ and $y < 0$, and in quadrant IV $x > 0$ and $y < 0$.

Recall that if the value of the slope of a line is positive, the line slopes upward from left to right. If the value of the slope is negative, the line slopes downward from left to right. If the $y$-coordinates are the same for two points on a line, the slope is 0 and the line is a **horizontal line**. If the $x$-coordinates are the same for two points on a line, there is no slope and the line is a **vertical line**. Two or more lines that have equivalent slopes are **parallel lines**. **Perpendicular lines** have slopes that are negative reciprocals of each other, such as $\frac{a}{b}$ and $\frac{-b}{a}$.

> **Review Video: Cartesian Coordinate Plane and Graphing**
> Visit mometrix.com/academy and enter code: 115173

## GRAPHING EQUATIONS IN TWO VARIABLES

One way of graphing an equation in two variables is to plot enough points to get an idea for its shape and then draw the appropriate curve through those points. A point can be plotted by substituting in a value for one variable and solving for the other. If the equation is linear, we only need two points and can then draw a straight line between them.

For example, consider the equation $y = 2x - 1$. This is a linear equation—both variables only appear raised to the first power—so we only need two points. When $x = 0$, $y = 2(0) - 1 = -1$. When $x = 2$, $y = 2(2) - 1 = 3$. We can therefore choose the points $(0, -1)$ and $(2, 3)$, and draw a line between them:

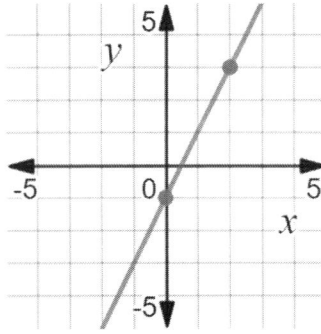

# Probability

**Probability** is the likelihood of a certain outcome occurring for a given event. An **event** is any situation that produces a result. It could be something as simple as flipping a coin or as complex as launching a rocket. Determining the probability of an outcome for an event can be equally simple or complex. As such, there are specific terms used in the study of probability that need to be understood:

- **Compound event**—an event that involves two or more independent events (rolling a pair of dice and taking the sum)
- **Desired outcome** (or success)—an outcome that meets a particular set of criteria (a roll of 1 or 2 if we are looking for numbers less than 3)
- **Independent events**—two or more events whose outcomes do not affect one another (two coins tossed at the same time)
- **Dependent events**—two or more events whose outcomes affect one another (two cards drawn consecutively from the same deck)
- **Certain outcome**—probability of outcome is 100% or 1
- **Impossible outcome**—probability of outcome is 0% or 0
- **Mutually exclusive outcomes**—two or more outcomes whose criteria cannot all be satisfied in a single event (a coin coming up heads and tails on the same toss)
- **Random variable**—refers to all possible outcomes of a single event which may be discrete or continuous.

> **Review Video: Intro to Probability**
> Visit mometrix.com/academy and enter code: 212374

## SAMPLE SPACE

The total set of all possible results of a test or experiment is called a **sample space**, or sometimes a universal sample space. The sample space, represented by one of the variables $S$, $\Omega$, or $U$ (for universal sample space) has individual elements called outcomes. Other terms for outcome that may be used interchangeably include elementary outcome, simple event, or sample point. The number of outcomes in a given sample space could be infinite or finite, and some tests may yield multiple unique sample sets. For example, tests conducted by drawing playing cards from a standard deck would have one sample space of the card values, another sample space of the card suits, and a third sample space of suit-denomination combinations. For most tests, the sample spaces considered will be finite.

An **event**, represented by the variable $E$, is a portion of a sample space. It may be one outcome or a group of outcomes from the same sample space. If an event occurs, then the test or experiment will generate an outcome that satisfies the requirement of that event. For example, given a standard deck of 52 playing cards as the sample space, and defining the event as the collection of face cards, then the event will occur if the card drawn is a $J$, $Q$, or $K$. If any other card is drawn, the event is said to have not occurred.

For every sample space, each possible outcome has a specific likelihood, or probability, that it will occur. The probability measure, also called the **distribution**, is a function that assigns a real number probability, from zero to one, to each outcome. For a probability measure to be accurate, every outcome must have a real number probability measure that is greater than or equal to zero and less than or equal to one. Also, the probability measure of the sample space must equal one, and the probability measure of the union of multiple outcomes must equal the sum of the individual probability measures.

Probabilities of events are expressed as real numbers from zero to one. They give a numerical value to the chance that a particular event will occur. The probability of an event occurring is the sum of the probabilities of the individual elements of that event. For example, in a standard deck of 52 playing cards as the sample space and the collection of face cards as the event, the probability of drawing a specific face card is $\frac{1}{52} = 0.019$, but the probability of drawing any one of the twelve face cards is $12(0.019) = 0.228$. Note that rounding of numbers can generate different results. If you multiplied 12 by the fraction $\frac{1}{52}$ before converting to a decimal, you would get the answer $\frac{12}{52} = 0.231$.

## THEORETICAL AND EXPERIMENTAL PROBABILITY

**Theoretical probability** can usually be determined without actually performing the event. The likelihood of an outcome occurring, or the probability of an outcome occurring, is given by the formula:

$$P(A) = \frac{\text{Number of acceptable outcomes}}{\text{Number of possible outcomes}}$$

Note that $P(A)$ is the probability of an outcome $A$ occurring, and each outcome is just as likely to occur as any other outcome. If each outcome has the same probability of occurring as every other possible outcome, the outcomes are said to be equally likely to occur. The total number of acceptable outcomes must be less than or equal to the total number of possible outcomes. If the two are equal, then the outcome is certain to occur and the probability is 1. If the number of acceptable outcomes is zero, then the outcome is impossible and the probability is 0. For example, if there are 20 marbles in a bag and 5 are red, then the theoretical probability of randomly selecting a red marble is 5 out of 20, $\left(\frac{5}{20} = \frac{1}{4}, 0.25, \text{or } 25\%\right)$.

If the theoretical probability is unknown or too complicated to calculate, it can be estimated by an experimental probability. **Experimental probability**, also called empirical probability, is an estimate of the likelihood of a certain outcome based on repeated experiments or collected data. In other words, while theoretical probability is based on what *should* happen, experimental probability is based on what *has* happened. Experimental probability is calculated in the same way as theoretical probability, except that actual outcomes are used instead of possible outcomes. The more experiments performed or datapoints gathered, the better the estimate should be.

Theoretical and experimental probability do not always line up with one another. Theoretical probability says that out of 20 coin-tosses, 10 should be heads. However, if we were actually to toss 20 coins, we might record just 5 heads. This doesn't mean that our theoretical probability is incorrect; it just means that this particular experiment had results that were different from what was predicted. A practical application of empirical probability is the insurance industry. There are no set functions that define lifespan, health, or safety. Insurance companies look at factors from hundreds of thousands of individuals to find patterns that they then use to set the formulas for insurance premiums.

> **Review Video: Empirical Probability**
> Visit mometrix.com/academy and enter code: 513468

### OBJECTIVE AND SUBJECTIVE PROBABILITY

**Objective probability** is based on mathematical formulas and documented evidence. Examples of objective probability include raffles or lottery drawings where there is a pre-determined number of possible outcomes and a predetermined number of outcomes that correspond to an event. Other cases of objective probability include probabilities of rolling dice, flipping coins, or drawing cards. Most gambling games are based on objective probability.

In contrast, **subjective probability** is based on personal or professional feelings and judgments. Often, there is a lot of guesswork following extensive research. Areas where subjective probability is applicable include sales trends and business expenses. Attractions set admission prices based on subjective probabilities of attendance based on varying admission rates in an effort to maximize their profit.

## COMPLEMENT OF AN EVENT

Sometimes it may be easier to calculate the possibility of something not happening, or the **complement of an event**. Represented by the symbol $\bar{A}$, the complement of $A$ is the probability that event $A$ does not happen. When you know the probability of event $A$ occurring, you can use the formula $P(\bar{A}) = 1 - P(A)$, where $P(\bar{A})$ is the probability of event $A$ not occurring, and $P(A)$ is the probability of event $A$ occurring.

## ADDITION RULE

The **addition rule** for probability is used for finding the probability of a compound event. Use the formula $P(A \cup B) = P(A) + P(B) - P(A \cap B)$, where $P(A \cap B)$ is the probability of both events occurring to find the probability of a compound event. The probability of both events occurring at the same time must be subtracted to eliminate any overlap in the first two probabilities.

## CONDITIONAL PROBABILITY

Given two events $A$ and $B$, the **conditional probability** $P(A|B)$ is the probability that event $A$ will occur, given that event $B$ has occurred. The conditional probability cannot be calculated simply from $P(A)$ and $P(B)$; these probabilities alone do not give sufficient information to determine the conditional probability. It can, however, be determined if you are also given the probability of the intersection of events $A$ and $B$, $P(A \cap B)$, the probability that events $A$ and $B$ both occur. Specifically, $P(A|B) = \frac{P(A \cap B)}{P(B)}$. For instance, suppose you have a jar containing two red marbles and two blue marbles, and you draw two marbles at random. Consider event $A$ being the event that the first marble drawn is red, and event $B$ being the event that the second marble drawn is blue. If we want to find the probability that $B$ occurs given that $A$ occurred, $P(B|A)$, then we can compute it using the fact that $P(A)$ is $\frac{1}{2}$, and $P(A \cap B)$ is $\frac{1}{3}$. (The latter may not be obvious, but may be determined by finding the product of $\frac{1}{2}$ and $\frac{2}{3}$). Therefore $P(B|A) = \frac{P(A \cap B)}{P(A)} = \frac{1/3}{1/2} = \frac{2}{3}$.

### CONDITIONAL PROBABILITY IN EVERYDAY SITUATIONS

Conditional probability often arises in everyday situations in, for example, estimating the risk or benefit of certain activities. The conditional probability of having a heart attack given that you exercise daily may be smaller than the overall probability of having a heart attack. The conditional probability of having lung cancer given that you are a smoker is larger than the overall probability of having lung cancer. Note that changing the order of the conditional probability changes the meaning: the conditional probability of having lung cancer given that you are a smoker is a very different thing from the probability of being a smoker given that you have lung cancer. In an extreme case, suppose that a certain rare disease is caused only by eating a certain food, but even then, it is unlikely. Then the conditional probability of having that disease given that you eat the dangerous food is nonzero but low, but the conditional probability of having eaten that food given that you have the disease is 100%!

> **Review Video: Conditional Probability**
> Visit mometrix.com/academy and enter code: 397924

## INDEPENDENCE

The conditional probability $P(A|B)$ is the probability that event $A$ will occur given that event $B$ occurs. If the two events are independent, we do not expect that whether or not event $B$ occurs should have any effect on whether or not event $A$ occurs. In other words, we expect $P(A|B) = P(A)$.

This can be proven using the usual equations for conditional probability and the joint probability of independent events. The conditional probability $P(A|B) = \frac{P(A \cap B)}{P(B)}$. If $A$ and $B$ are independent, then $P(A \cap B) = P(A)P(B)$. So $P(A|B) = \frac{P(A)P(B)}{P(B)} = P(A)$. By similar reasoning, if $A$ and $B$ are independent then $P(B|A) = P(B)$.

## MULTIPLICATION RULE

The **multiplication rule** can be used to find the probability of two independent events occurring using the formula $P(A \cap B) = P(A) \times P(B)$, where $P(A \cap B)$ is the probability of two independent events occurring, $P(A)$ is the probability of the first event occurring, and $P(B)$ is the probability of the second event occurring.

The multiplication rule can also be used to find the probability of two dependent events occurring using the formula $P(A \cap B) = P(A) \times P(B|A)$, where $P(A \cap B)$ is the probability of two dependent events occurring and $P(B|A)$ is the probability of the second event occurring after the first event has already occurred.

Use a **combination of the multiplication** rule and the rule of complements to find the probability that at least one outcome of the element will occur. This is given by the general formula $P(\text{at least one event occurring}) = 1 - P(\text{no outcomes occurring})$. For example, to find the probability that at least one even number will show when a pair of dice is rolled, find the probability that two odd numbers will be rolled (no even numbers) and subtract from one. You can always use a tree diagram or make a chart to list the possible outcomes when the sample space is small, such as in the dice-rolling example, but in most cases it will be much faster to use the multiplication and complement formulas.

> **Review Video: Multiplication Rule**
> Visit mometrix.com/academy and enter code: 782598

## UNION AND INTERSECTION OF TWO SETS OF OUTCOMES

If $A$ and $B$ are each a set of elements or outcomes from an experiment, then the **union** (symbol ∪) of the two sets is the set of elements found in set $A$ or set $B$. For example, if $A = \{2, 3, 4\}$ and $B = \{3, 4, 5\}$, $A \cup B = \{2, 3, 4, 5\}$. Note that the outcomes 3 and 4 appear only once in the union. For statistical events, the union is equivalent to "or"; $P(A \cup B)$ is the same thing as $P(A \text{ or } B)$. The **intersection** (symbol ∩) of two sets is the set of outcomes common to both sets. For the above sets $A$ and $B$, $A \cap B = \{3, 4\}$. For statistical events, the intersection is equivalent to "and"; $P(A \cap B)$ is the same thing as $P(A \text{ and } B)$. It is important to note that union and intersection operations commute. That is:

$$A \cup B = B \cup A \text{ and } A \cap B = B \cap A$$

# Two-Way Frequency Tables

If we have a two-way frequency table, it is generally a straightforward matter to read off the probabilities of any two events $A$ and $B$, as well as the joint probability of both events occurring, $P(A \cap B)$. We can then find the conditional probability $P(A|B)$ by calculating $P(A|B) = \frac{P(A \cap B)}{P(B)}$. We could also check whether or not events are independent by verifying whether $P(A)P(B) = P(A \cap B)$.

For example, a certain store's recent T-shirt sales:

|  | Small | Medium | Large | Total |
|---|---|---|---|---|
| Blue | 25 | 40 | 35 | 100 |
| White | 27 | 25 | 22 | 74 |
| Black | 8 | 23 | 15 | 46 |
| Total | 60 | 88 | 72 | 220 |

Suppose we want to find the conditional probability that a customer buys a black shirt (event $A$), given that the shirt he buys is size small (event $B$). From the table, the probability $P(B)$ that a customer buys a small shirt is $\frac{60}{220} = \frac{3}{11}$. The probability $P(A \cap B)$ that he buys a small, black shirt is $\frac{8}{220} = \frac{2}{55}$. The conditional probability $P(A|B)$ that he buys a black shirt, given that he buys a small shirt, is therefore $P(A|B) = \frac{2/55}{3/11} = \frac{2}{15}$.

Similarly, if we want to check whether the event a customer buys a blue shirt, $A$, is independent of the event that a customer buys a medium shirt, $B$. From the table, $P(A) = \frac{100}{220} = \frac{5}{11}$ and $P(B) = \frac{88}{220} = \frac{4}{10}$. Also, $P(A \cap B) = \frac{40}{220} = \frac{2}{11}$. Since $\left(\frac{5}{11}\right)\left(\frac{4}{10}\right) = \frac{20}{110} = \frac{2}{11}$, $P(A)P(B) = P(A \cap B)$ and these two events are indeed independent.

## Data Analysis

### DISPERSION

A **measure of dispersion** is a single value that helps to "interpret" the measure of central tendency by providing more information about how the data values in the set are distributed about the measure of central tendency. The measure of dispersion helps to eliminate or reduce the disadvantages of using the mean, median, or mode as a single measure of central tendency, and give a more accurate picture of the dataset as a whole. To have a measure of dispersion, you must know or calculate the range, standard deviation, or variance of the data set.

### RANGE

The **range** of a set of data is the difference between the greatest and lowest values of the data in the set. To calculate the range, you must first make sure the units for all data values are the same, and then identify the greatest and lowest values. If there are multiple data values that are equal for the highest or lowest, just use one of the values in the formula. Write the answer with the same units as the data values you used to do the calculations.

> **Review Video: Statistical Range**
> Visit mometrix.com/academy and enter code: 778541

### SAMPLE STANDARD DEVIATION

Standard deviation is a measure of dispersion that compares all the data values in the set to the mean of the set to give a more accurate picture. To find the **standard deviation of a sample**, use the formula

$$s = \sqrt{\frac{\sum_{i=1}^{n}(x_i - \bar{x})^2}{n-1}}$$

Note that $s$ is the standard deviation of a sample, $x_i$ represents the individual values in the data set, $\bar{x}$ is the mean of the data values in the set, and $n$ is the number of data values in the set. The higher the value of the standard deviation is, the greater the variance of the data values from the mean. The units associated with the standard deviation are the same as the units of the data values.

> **Review Video: Standard Deviation**
> Visit mometrix.com/academy and enter code: 419469

### SAMPLE VARIANCE

The **variance of a sample** is the square of the sample standard deviation (denoted $s^2$). While the mean of a set of data gives the average of the set and gives information about where a specific data value lies in relation to the average, the variance of the sample gives information about the degree to which the data values are spread out and tells you how close an individual value is to the average compared to the other values. The units associated with variance are the same as the units of the data values squared.

## PERCENTILE

Percentiles and quartiles are other methods of describing data within a set. **Percentiles** tell what percentage of the data in the set fall below a specific point. For example, achievement test scores are often given in percentiles. A score at the 80th percentile is one which is equal to or higher than 80 percent of the scores in the set. In other words, 80 percent of the scores were lower than that score.

**Quartiles** are percentile groups that make up quarter sections of the data set. The first quartile is the 25th percentile. The second quartile is the 50th percentile; this is also the median of the dataset. The third quartile is the 75th percentile.

## SKEWNESS

**Skewness** is a way to describe the symmetry or asymmetry of the distribution of values in a dataset. If the distribution of values is symmetrical, there is no skew. In general the closer the mean of a data set is to the median of the data set, the less skew there is. Generally, if the mean is to the right of the median, the data set is *positively skewed*, or right-skewed, and if the mean is to the left of the median, the data set is *negatively skewed*, or left-skewed. However, this rule of thumb is not infallible. When the data values are graphed on a curve, a set with no skew will be a perfect bell curve.

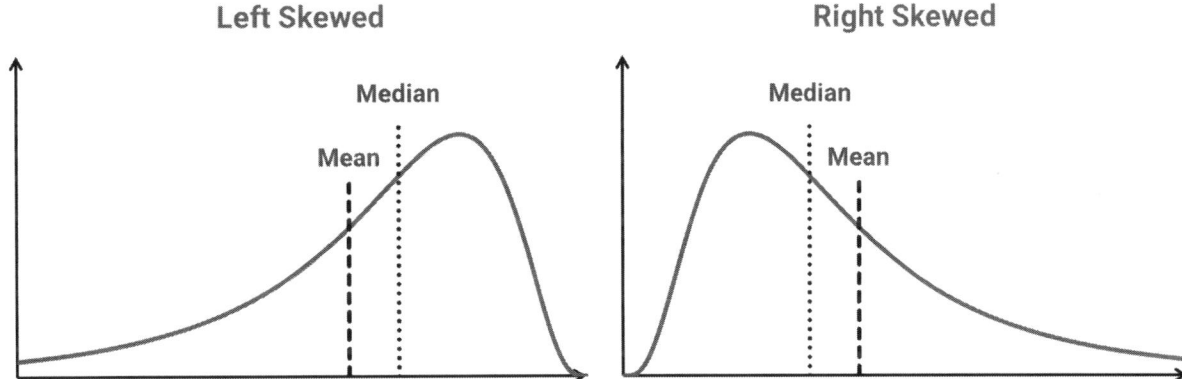

To estimate skew, use the formula:

$$\text{skew} = \frac{\sqrt{n(n-1)}}{n-2} \left( \frac{\frac{1}{n}\sum_{i=1}^{n}(x_i - \bar{x})^3}{\left(\frac{1}{n}\sum_{i=1}^{n}(x_i - \bar{x})^2\right)^{\frac{3}{2}}} \right)$$

Note that $n$ is the datapoints in the set, $x_i$ is the $i^{th}$ value in the set, and $\bar{x}$ is the mean of the set.

> **Review Video: Skew**
> Visit mometrix.com/academy and enter code: 661486

## UNIMODAL VS. BIMODAL

If a distribution has a single peak, it would be considered **unimodal**. If it has two discernible peaks it would be considered **bimodal**. Bimodal distributions may be an indication that the set of data being considered is actually the combination of two sets of data with significant differences. A **uniform distribution** is a distribution in which there is *no distinct peak or variation* in the data. No values or ranges are particularly more common than any other values or ranges.

## OUTLIER

An outlier is an extremely high or extremely low value in the data set. It may be the result of measurement error, in which case, the outlier is not a valid member of the data set. However, it may also be a valid member of the distribution. Unless a measurement error is identified, the experimenter cannot know for certain if an outlier is or is not a member of the distribution. There are arbitrary methods that can be employed to designate an extreme value as an outlier. One method designates an outlier (or possible outlier) to be any value less than $Q_1 - 1.5(IQR)$ or any value greater than $Q_3 + 1.5(IQR)$.

## DATA ANALYSIS
### SIMPLE REGRESSION

In statistics, **simple regression** is using an equation to represent a relation between independent and dependent variables. The independent variable is also referred to as the explanatory variable or the predictor and is generally represented by the variable $x$ in the equation. The dependent variable, usually represented by the variable $y$, is also referred to as the response variable. The equation may be any type of function – linear, quadratic, exponential, etc. The best way to handle this task is to use the regression feature of your graphing calculator. This will easily give you the curve of best fit and provide you with the coefficients and other information you need to derive an equation.

### LINE OF BEST FIT

In a scatter plot, the **line of best fit** is the line that best shows the trends of the data. The line of best fit is given by the equation $\hat{y} = ax + b$, where $a$ and $b$ are the regression coefficients. The regression coefficient $a$ is also the slope of the line of best fit, and $b$ is also the $y$-coordinate of the point at which the line of best fit crosses the $y$-axis. Not every point on the scatter plot will be on the line of best fit. The differences between the $y$-values of the points in the scatter plot and the corresponding $y$-values according to the equation of the line of best fit are the residuals. The line of best fit is also called the least-squares regression line because it is also the line that has the lowest sum of the squares of the residuals.

### CORRELATION COEFFICIENT

The **correlation coefficient** is the numerical value that indicates how strong the relationship is between the two variables of a linear regression equation. A correlation coefficient of –1 is a perfect negative correlation. A correlation coefficient of +1 is a perfect positive correlation. Correlation coefficients close to –1 or +1 are very strong correlations. A correlation coefficient equal to zero indicates there is no correlation between the two variables. This test is a good indicator of whether or not the equation for the line of best fit is accurate. The formula for the correlation coefficient is

$$r = \frac{\sum_{i=1}^{n}(x_i - \bar{x})(y_i - \bar{y})}{\sqrt{\sum_{i=1}^{n}(x_i - \bar{x})^2}\sqrt{\sum_{i=1}^{n}(y_i - \bar{y})^2}}$$

where $r$ is the correlation coefficient, $n$ is the number of data values in the set, $(x_i, y_i)$ is a point in the set, and $\bar{x}$ and $\bar{y}$ are the means.

### Z-SCORE

A **z-score** is an indication of how many standard deviations a given value falls from the sample mean. To calculate a z-score, use the formula:

$$\frac{x - \bar{x}}{\sigma}$$

In this formula $x$ is the data value, $\bar{x}$ is the mean of the sample data, and $\sigma$ is the standard deviation of the population. If the z-score is positive, the data value lies above the mean. If the z-score is negative, the data value falls below the mean. These scores are useful in interpreting data such as standardized test scores, where every piece of data in the set has been counted, rather than just a small random sample. In cases where standard deviations are calculated from a random sample of the set, the z-scores will not be as accurate.

## CENTRAL LIMIT THEOREM

According to the **central limit theorem**, regardless of what the original distribution of a sample is, the distribution of the means tends to get closer and closer to a normal distribution as the sample size gets larger and larger (this is necessary because the sample is becoming more all-encompassing of the elements of the population). As the sample size gets larger, the distribution of the sample mean will approach a normal distribution with a mean of the population mean and a variance of the population variance divided by the sample size.

# Measures of Central Tendency

A **measure of central tendency** is a statistical value that gives a reasonable estimate for the center of a group of data. There are several different ways of describing the measure of central tendency. Each one has a unique way it is calculated, and each one gives a slightly different perspective on the data set. Whenever you give a measure of central tendency, always make sure the units are the same. If the data has different units, such as hours, minutes, and seconds, convert all the data to the same unit, and use the same unit in the measure of central tendency. If no units are given in the data, do not give units for the measure of central tendency.

## MEAN

The **statistical mean** of a group of data is the same as the arithmetic average of that group. To find the mean of a set of data, first convert each value to the same units, if necessary. Then find the sum of all the values, and count the total number of data values, making sure you take into consideration each individual value. If a value appears more than once, count it more than once. Divide the sum of the values by the total number of values and apply the units, if any. Note that the mean does not have to be one of the data values in the set, and may not divide evenly.

$$\text{mean} = \frac{\text{sum of the data values}}{\text{quantity of data values}}$$

For instance, the mean of the data set {88, 72, 61, 90, 97, 68, 88, 79, 86, 93, 97, 71, 80, 84, 89} would be the sum of the fifteen numbers divided by 15:

$$\frac{88 + 72 + 61 + 90 + 97 + 68 + 88 + 79 + 86 + 93 + 97 + 71 + 80 + 84 + 89}{15} = \frac{1242}{15} = 82.8$$

While the mean is relatively easy to calculate and averages are understood by most people, the mean can be very misleading if it is used as the sole measure of central tendency. If the data set has outliers (data values that are unusually high or unusually low compared to the rest of the data values), the mean can be very distorted, especially if the data set has a small number of values. If unusually high values are countered with unusually low values, the mean is not affected as much. For example, if five of twenty students in a class get a 100 on a test, but the other 15 students have an average of 60 on the same test, the class average would appear as 70. Whenever the mean is skewed by outliers, it is always a good idea to include the median as an alternate measure of central tendency.

A **weighted mean**, or weighted average, is a mean that uses "weighted" values. The formula is weighted mean $= \frac{w_1 x_1 + w_2 x_2 + w_3 x_3 \ldots + w_n x_n}{w_1 + w_2 + w_3 + \cdots + w_n}$. Weighted values, such as $w_1, w_2, w_3, \ldots w_n$ are assigned to each member of the set $x_1, x_2, x_3, \ldots x_n$. When calculating the weighted mean, make sure a weight value for each member of the set is used.

> **Review Video: All About Averages**
> Visit mometrix.com/academy and enter code: 176521

## MEDIAN

The **statistical median** is the value in the middle of the set of data. To find the median, list all data values in order from smallest to largest or from largest to smallest. Any value that is repeated in the set must be listed the number of times it appears. If there are an odd number of data values, the median is the value in the middle of the list. If there is an even number of data values, the median is the arithmetic mean of the two middle values.

For example, the median of the data set {88, 72, 61, 90, 97, 68, 88, 79, 86, 93, 97, 71, 80, 84, 88} is 86 since the ordered set is {61, 68, 71, 72, 79, 80, 84, **86**, 88, 88, 88, 90, 93, 97, 97}.

The big disadvantage of using the median as a measure of central tendency is that is relies solely on a value's relative size as compared to the other values in the set. When the individual values in a set of data are evenly dispersed, the median can be an accurate tool. However, if there is a group of rather large values or a group of rather small values that are not offset by a different group of values, the information that can be inferred from the median may not be accurate because the distribution of values is skewed.

## MODE

The **statistical mode** is the data value that occurs the greatest number of times in the data set. It is possible to have exactly one mode, more than one mode, or no mode. To find the mode of a set of data, arrange the data like you do to find the median (all values in order, listing all multiples of data values). Count the number of times each value appears in the data set. If all values appear an equal number of times, there is no mode. If one value appears more than any other value, that value is the mode. If two or more values appear the same number of times, but there are other values that appear fewer times and no values that appear more times, all of those values are the modes.

For example, the mode of the data set {**88**, 72, 61, 90, 97, 68, **88**, 79, 86, 93, 97, 71, 80, 84, **88**} is 88.

The main disadvantage of the mode is that the values of the other data in the set have no bearing on the mode. The mode may be the largest value, the smallest value, or a value anywhere in between in the set. The mode only tells which value or values, if any, occurred the greatest number of times. It does not give any suggestions about the remaining values in the set.

> **Review Video: Mean, Median, and Mode**
> Visit mometrix.com/academy and enter code: 286207

# Displaying Information

## FREQUENCY TABLES

**Frequency tables** show how frequently each unique value appears in a set. A **relative frequency table** is one that shows the proportions of each unique value compared to the entire set. Relative frequencies are given as percentages; however, the total percent for a relative frequency table will not necessarily equal 100 percent due to rounding. An example of a frequency table with relative frequencies is below.

| Favorite Color | Frequency | Relative Frequency |
|---|---|---|
| Blue | 4 | 13% |
| Red | 7 | 22% |
| Green | 3 | 9% |
| Purple | 6 | 19% |
| Cyan | 12 | 38% |

> **Review Video: Data Interpretation of Graphs**
> Visit mometrix.com/academy and enter code: 200439

## CIRCLE GRAPHS

**Circle graphs**, also known as *pie charts*, provide a visual depiction of the relationship of each type of data compared to the whole set of data. The circle graph is divided into sections by drawing radii to create central angles whose percentage of the circle is equal to the individual data's percentage of the whole set. Each 1% of data is equal to 3.6° in the circle graph. Therefore, data represented by a 90° section of the circle graph makes up 25% of the whole. When complete, a circle graph often looks like a pie cut into uneven wedges. The pie chart below shows the data from the frequency table referenced earlier where people were asked their favorite color.

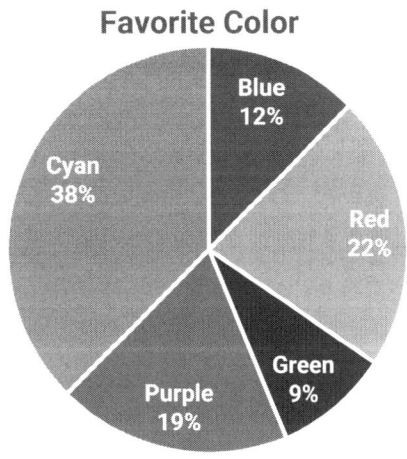

## PICTOGRAPHS

A **pictograph** is a graph, generally in the horizontal orientation, that uses pictures or symbols to represent the data. Each pictograph must have a key that defines the picture or symbol and gives the quantity each picture or symbol represents. Pictures or symbols on a pictograph are not always shown as whole elements. In this case, the fraction of the picture or symbol shown represents the same fraction of the quantity a whole picture or symbol stands for. For example, a row with $3\frac{1}{2}$ ears of corn, where each ear of corn represents 100 stalks of corn in a field, would equal $3\frac{1}{2} \times 100 = 350$ stalks of corn in the field.

| Name | Number of ears of corn eaten | Field | Number of stalks of corn |
|---|---|---|---|
| Michael | 🌽🌽🌽🌽 | Field 1 | 🌽🌽🌽🌽🌽 |
| Tara | 🌽🌽 | Field 2 | 🌽🌽🌽 (partial) |
| John | 🌽🌽🌽 | Field 3 | 🌽🌽🌽🌽 |
| Sara | 🌽 | Field 4 | 🌽 |
| Jacob | 🌽🌽🌽 | Field 5 | 🌽🌽🌽 (partial) |

Each 🌽 represents 1 ear of corn eaten.   Each 🌽 represents 100 stalks of corn.

> **Review Video: Pictographs**
> Visit mometrix.com/academy and enter code: 147860

## LINE GRAPHS

**Line graphs** have one or more lines of varying styles (solid or broken) to show the different values for a set of data. The individual data are represented as ordered pairs, much like on a Cartesian plane. In this case, the $x$- and $y$-axes are defined in terms of their units, such as dollars or time. The individual plotted points are joined by line segments to show whether the value of the data is increasing (line sloping upward), decreasing (line sloping downward), or staying the same (horizontal line). Multiple sets of data can be graphed on the same line graph to give an easy visual comparison. An example of this would be graphing achievement test scores for different groups of students over the same time period to see which group had the greatest increase or decrease in performance from year to year (as shown below).

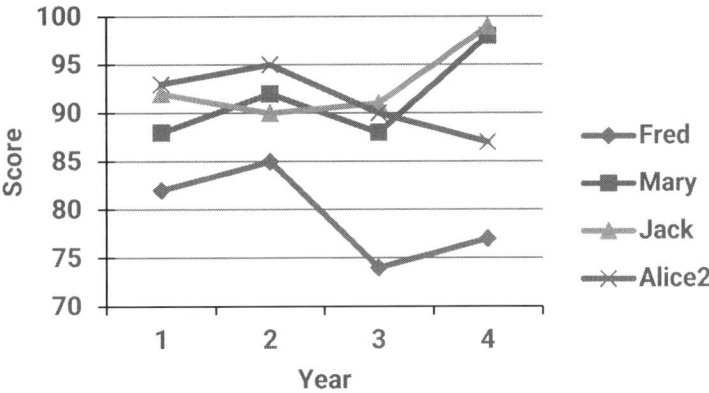

| Review Video: **How to Create a Line Graph** |
| --- |
| Visit mometrix.com/academy and enter code: 480147 |

## LINE PLOTS

A **line plot**, also known as a *dot plot*, has plotted points that are not connected by line segments. In this graph, the horizontal axis lists the different possible values for the data, and the vertical axis lists the number of times the individual value occurs. A single dot is graphed for each value to show the number of times it occurs. This graph is more closely related to a bar graph than a line graph. Do not connect the dots in a line plot or it will misrepresent the data.

| Review Video: **Line Plot** |
| --- |
| Visit mometrix.com/academy and enter code: 754610 |

## STEM AND LEAF PLOTS

A **stem and leaf plot** is useful for depicting groups of data that fall into a range of values. Each piece of data is separated into two parts: the first, or left, part is called the stem; the second, or right, part is called the leaf. Each stem is listed in a column from smallest to largest. Each leaf that has the common stem is listed in that stem's row from smallest to largest. For example, in a set of two-digit numbers, the digit in the tens place is the stem, and the digit in the ones place is the leaf. With a stem and leaf plot, you can easily see which subset of numbers (10s, 20s, 30s, etc.) is the largest. This information is also readily available by looking at a histogram, but a stem and leaf plot also allows you to look closer and see exactly which values fall in that range. Using a sample set of test scores (82, 88, 92, 93, 85, 90, 92, 95, 74, 88, 90, 91, 78, 87, 98, 99), we can assemble a stem and leaf plot like the one below.

**Test Scores**

| | |
|---|---|
| 7 | 4 8 |
| 8 | 2 5 7 8 8 |
| 9 | 0 0 1 2 2 3 5 8 9 |

| Review Video: **Stem and Leaf Plots** |
| --- |
| Visit mometrix.com/academy and enter code: 302339 |

## BAR GRAPHS

A **bar graph** is one of the few graphs that can be drawn correctly in two different configurations – both horizontally and vertically. A bar graph is similar to a line plot in the way the data is organized on the graph. Both axes must have their categories defined for the graph to be useful. Rather than placing a single dot to mark the point of the data's value, a bar, or thick line, is drawn from zero to the exact value of the data, whether it is a number, percentage, or other numerical value. Longer bar lengths correspond to greater data values. To read a bar graph, read the labels for the axes to find the units being reported. Then, look where the bars end in relation to the scale given on the corresponding axis and determine the associated value.

The bar chart below represents the responses from our favorite-color survey.

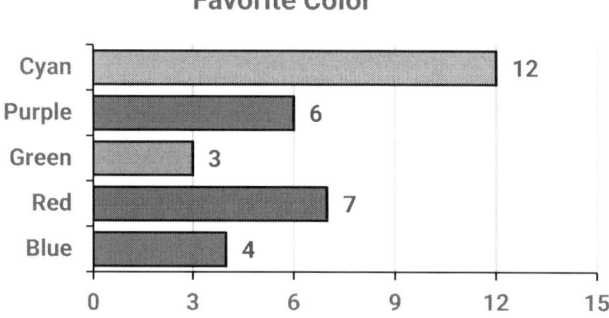

## HISTOGRAMS

At first glance, a **histogram** looks like a vertical bar graph. The difference is that a bar graph has a separate bar for each piece of data and a histogram has one continuous bar for each *range* of data. For example, a histogram may have one bar for the range 0–9, one bar for 10–19, etc. While a bar graph has numerical values on one axis, a histogram has numerical values on both axes. Each range is of equal size, and they are ordered left to right from lowest to highest. The height of each column on a histogram represents the number of data values within that range. Like a stem and leaf plot, a histogram makes it easy to glance at the graph and quickly determine which range has the greatest quantity of values. A simple example of a histogram is below.

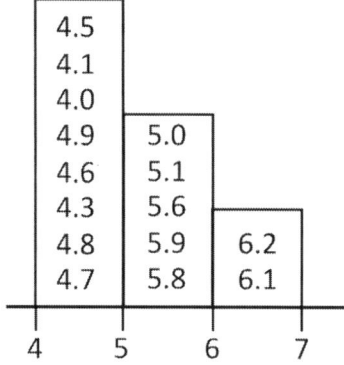

## 5-NUMBER SUMMARY

The **5-number summary** of a set of data gives a very informative picture of the set. The five numbers in the summary include the minimum value, maximum value, and the three quartiles. This information gives the reader the range and median of the set, as well as an indication of how the data is spread about the median.

## BOX AND WHISKER PLOTS

A **box-and-whiskers plot** is a graphical representation of the 5-number summary. To draw a box-and-whiskers plot, plot the points of the 5-number summary on a number line. Draw a box whose ends are through the points for the first and third quartiles. Draw a vertical line in the box through the median to divide the box in half. Draw a line segment from the first quartile point to the minimum value, and from the third quartile point to the maximum value.

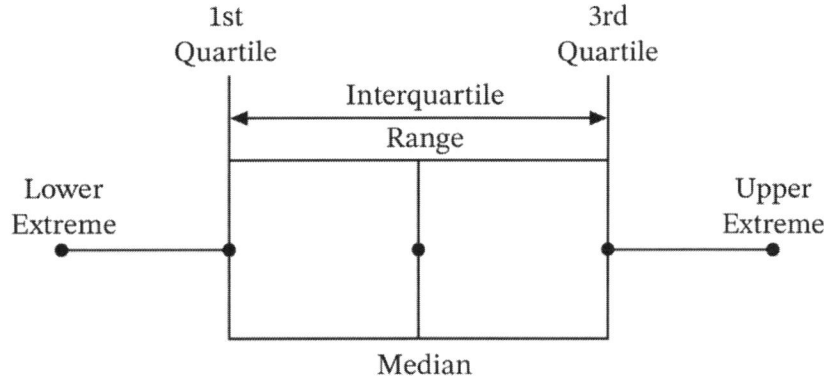

**Review Video: Box and Whisker Plots**
Visit mometrix.com/academy and enter code: 810817

### EXAMPLE

Given the following data (32, 28, 29, 26, 35, 27, 30, 31, 27, 32), we first sort it into numerical order: 26, 27, 27, 28, 29, 30, 31, 32, 32, 35. We can then find the median. Since there are ten values, we take the average of the 5th and 6th values to get 29.5. We find the lower quartile by taking the median of the data smaller than the median. Since there are five values, we take the 3rd value, which is 27. We find the upper quartile by taking the median of the data larger than the overall median, which is 32. Finally, we note our minimum and maximum, which are simply the smallest and largest values in the set: 26 and 35, respectively. Now we can create our box plot:

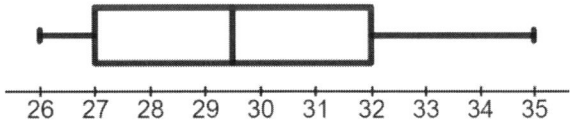

This plot is fairly "long" on the right whisker, showing one or more unusually high values (but not quite outliers). The other quartiles are similar in length, showing a fairly even distribution of data.

## INTERQUARTILE RANGE

The **interquartile range, or IQR**, is the difference between the upper and lower quartiles. It measures how the data is dispersed: a high IQR means that the data is more spread out, while a low IQR means that the data is clustered more tightly around the median. To find the IQR, subtract the lower quartile value ($Q_1$) from the upper quartile value ($Q_3$).

### EXAMPLE

To find the upper and lower quartiles, we first find the median and then take the median of all values above it and all values below it. In the following data set (16, 18, 13, 24, 16, 51, 32, 21, 27, 39), we first rearrange the values in numerical order: 13, 16, 16, 18, 21, 24, 27, 32, 39, 51. There are 10 values, so the median is the average of the 5th and 6th: $\frac{21+24}{2} = \frac{45}{2} = 22.5$. We do not actually need this value to find the upper and lower quartiles. We look at the set of numbers below the median: 13, 16, 16, 18, 21. There are five values, so the 3rd is the median (16), or the value of the lower quartile ($Q_1$). Then we look at the numbers above the median: 24, 27, 32, 39, 51. Again there are five values, so the 3rd is the median (32), or the value of the upper quartile ($Q_3$). We find the IQR by subtracting $Q_1$ from $Q_3$: $32 - 16 = 16$.

## 68-95-99.7 RULE

The **68–95–99.7 rule** describes how a normal distribution of data should appear when compared to the mean. This is also a description of a normal bell curve. According to this rule, 68 percent of the data values in a normally distributed set should fall within one standard deviation of the mean (34 percent above and 34 percent below the mean), 95 percent of the data values should fall within two standard deviations of the mean (47.5 percent above and 47.5 percent below the mean), and 99.7 percent of the data values should fall within three standard deviations of the mean, again, equally distributed on either side of the mean. This means that only 0.3 percent of all data values should fall more than three standard deviations from the mean. On the graph below, the normal curve is centered on the $y$-axis. The $x$-axis labels are how many standard deviations away from the center you are. Therefore, it is easy to see how the 68-95-99.7 rule can apply.

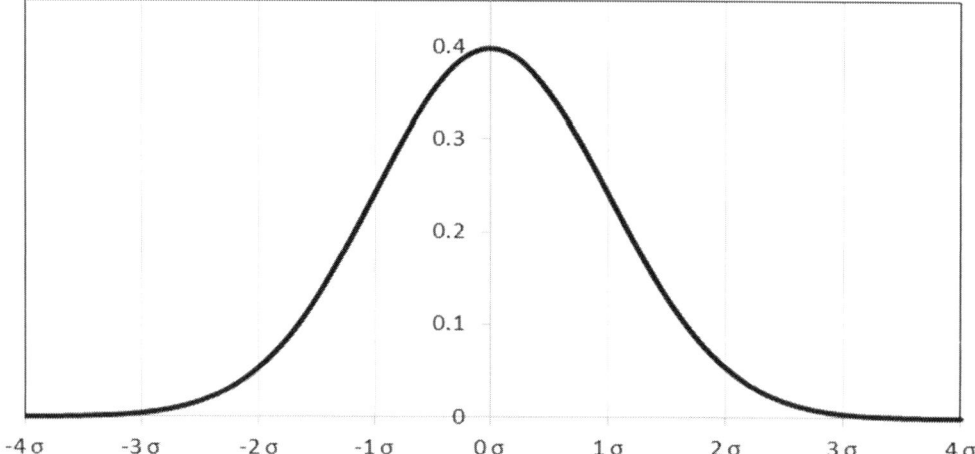

# Scatter Plots

## BIVARIATE DATA

**Bivariate data** is simply data from two different variables. (The prefix *bi-* means *two*.) In a *scatter plot*, each value in the set of data is plotted on a grid similar to a Cartesian plane, where each axis represents one of the two variables. By looking at the pattern formed by the points on the grid, you can often determine whether or not there is a relationship between the two variables, and what that relationship is, if it exists. The variables may be directly proportionate, inversely proportionate, or show no proportion at all. It may also be possible to determine if the data is linear, and if so, to find an equation to relate the two variables. The following scatter plot shows the relationship between preference for brand "A" and the age of the consumers surveyed.

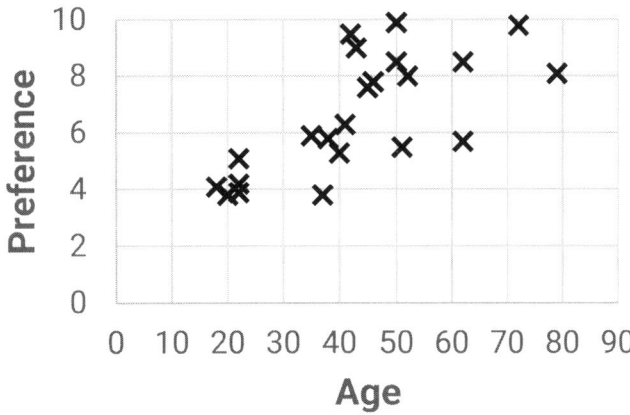

## SCATTER PLOTS

**Scatter plots** are also useful in determining the type of function represented by the data and finding the simple regression. Linear scatter plots may be positive or negative. Nonlinear scatter plots are generally exponential or quadratic. Below are some common types of scatter plots:

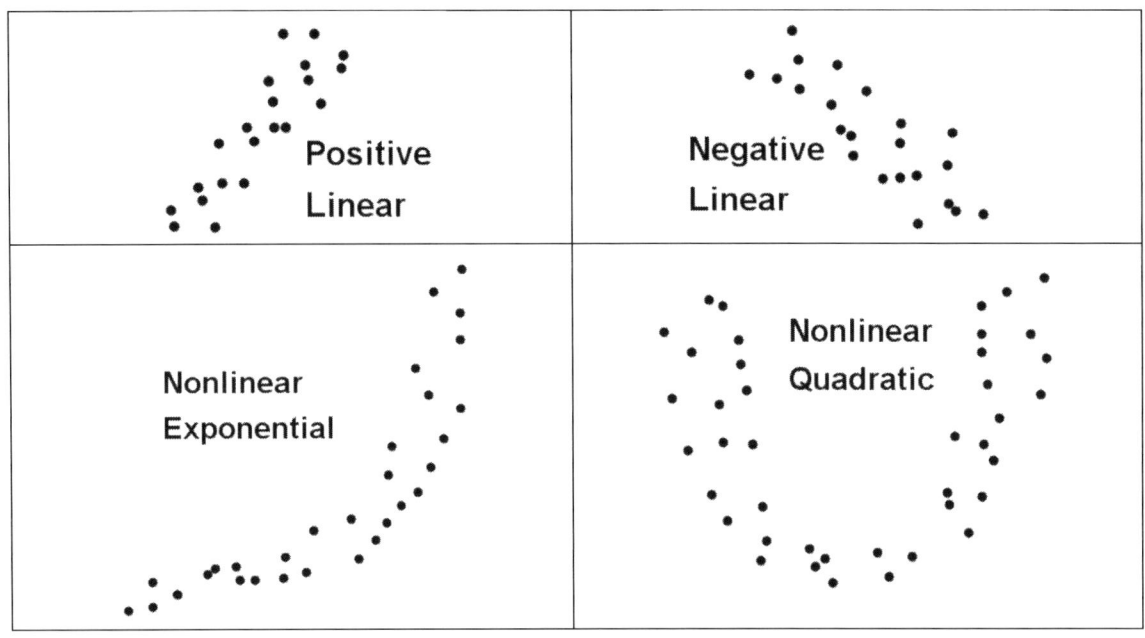

**Review Video: Scatter Plot**
Visit mometrix.com/academy and enter code: 596526

# Triangles

A triangle is a three-sided figure with the sum of its interior angles being 180°. The **perimeter of any triangle** is found by summing the three side lengths; $P = a + b + c$. For an equilateral triangle, this is the same as $P = 3a$, where $a$ is any side length, since all three sides are the same length.

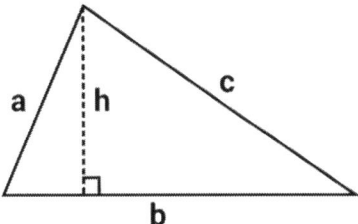

**Review Video: Proof that a Triangle is 180 Degrees**
Visit mometrix.com/academy and enter code: 687591

**Review Video: Area and Perimeter of a Triangle**
Visit mometrix.com/academy and enter code: 853779

The **area of any triangle** can be found by taking half the product of one side length referred to as the base, often given the variable $b$ and the perpendicular distance from that side to the opposite vertex called the altitude or height and given the variable $h$. In equation form that is $A = \frac{1}{2}bh$. Another formula that works for any triangle is $A = \sqrt{s(s-a)(s-b)(s-c)}$, where $s$ is the semiperimeter: $\frac{a+b+c}{2}$, and $a$, $b$, and $c$ are the lengths of the three sides. Special cases include isosceles triangles, $A = \frac{1}{2}b\sqrt{a^2 - \frac{b^2}{4}}$, where $b$ is the unique side and $a$ is the length of one of the two congruent sides, and equilateral triangles, $A = \frac{\sqrt{3}}{4}a^2$, where $a$ is the length of a side.

> **Review Video: Area of Any Triangle**
> Visit mometrix.com/academy and enter code: 138510

## PARTS OF A TRIANGLE

An **altitude** of a triangle is a line segment drawn from one vertex perpendicular to the opposite side. In the diagram that follows, $\overline{BE}$, $\overline{AD}$, and $\overline{CF}$ are altitudes. The length of an altitude is also called the height of the triangle. The three altitudes in a triangle are always concurrent. The point of concurrency of the altitudes of a triangle, $O$, is called the **orthocenter**. Note that in an obtuse triangle, the orthocenter will be outside the triangle, and in a right triangle, the orthocenter is the vertex of the right angle.

A **median** of a triangle is a line segment drawn from one vertex to the midpoint of the opposite side. In the diagram that follows, $\overline{BH}$, $\overline{AG}$, and $\overline{CI}$ are medians. This is not the same as the altitude, except the altitude to the base of an isosceles triangle and all three altitudes of an equilateral triangle. The point of concurrency of the medians of a triangle, $T$, is called the **centroid**. This is the same point as the orthocenter only in an equilateral triangle. Unlike the orthocenter, the centroid is always inside the triangle. The centroid can also be considered the exact center of the triangle. Any shape triangle can be perfectly balanced on a tip placed at the centroid. The centroid is also the point that is two-thirds the distance from the vertex to the opposite side.

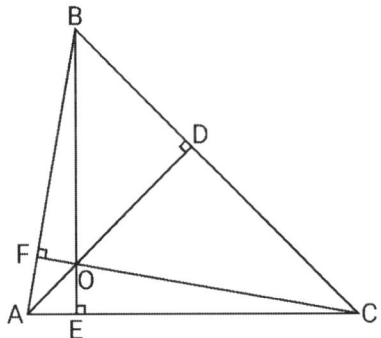 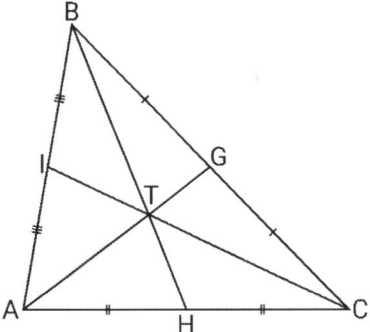

> **Review Video: Centroid, Incenter, Circumcenter, and Orthocenter**
> Visit mometrix.com/academy and enter code: 598260

# Quadrilaterals

A **quadrilateral** is a closed two-dimensional geometric figure that has four straight sides. The sum of the interior angles of any quadrilateral is 360°.

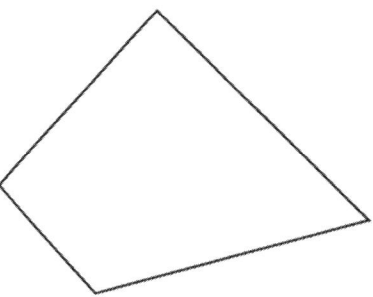

**Review Video: Diagonals of Parallelograms, Rectangles, and Rhombi**
Visit mometrix.com/academy and enter code: 320040

## KITE

A **kite** is a quadrilateral with two pairs of adjacent sides that are congruent. A result of this is perpendicular diagonals. A kite can be concave or convex and has one line of symmetry.

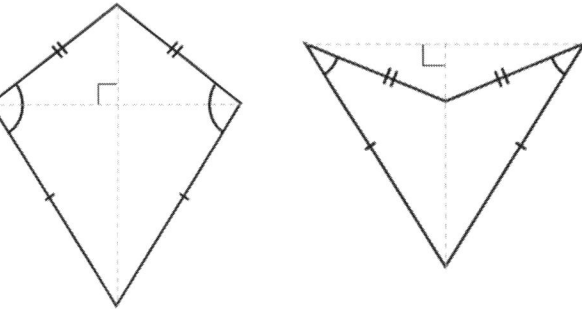

## TRAPEZOID

**Trapezoid**: A trapezoid is defined as a quadrilateral that has at least one pair of parallel sides. There are no rules for the second pair of sides. So, there are no rules for the diagonals and no lines of symmetry for a trapezoid.

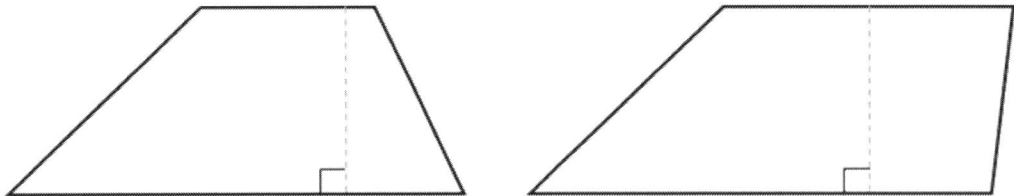

The **area of a trapezoid** is found by the formula $A = \frac{1}{2}h(b_1 + b_2)$, where $h$ is the height (segment joining and perpendicular to the parallel bases), and $b_1$ and $b_2$ are the two parallel sides (bases). Do not use one of the other two sides as the height unless that side is also perpendicular to the parallel bases.

The **perimeter of a trapezoid** is found by the formula $P = a + b_1 + c + b_2$, where $a, b_1, c,$ and $b_2$ are the four sides of the trapezoid.

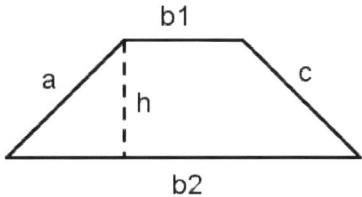

**Review Video: Area and Perimeter of a Trapezoid**
Visit mometrix.com/academy and enter code: 587523

**Isosceles trapezoid**: A trapezoid with equal base angles. This gives rise to other properties including: the two nonparallel sides have the same length, the two non-base angles are also equal, and there is one line of symmetry through the midpoints of the parallel sides.

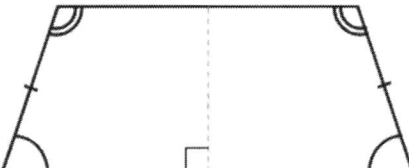

## PARALLELOGRAM

A **parallelogram** is a quadrilateral that has two pairs of opposite parallel sides. As such it is a special type of trapezoid. The sides that are parallel are also congruent. The opposite interior angles are always congruent, and the consecutive interior angles are supplementary. The diagonals of a parallelogram divide each other. Each diagonal divides the parallelogram into two congruent triangles. A parallelogram has no line of symmetry, but does have 180-degree rotational symmetry about the midpoint.

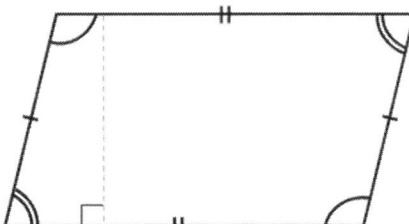

The **area of a parallelogram** is found by the formula $A = bh$, where $b$ is the length of the base, and $h$ is the height. Note that the base and height correspond to the length and width in a rectangle, so this formula would apply to rectangles as well. Do not confuse the height of a parallelogram with the length of the second side. The two are only the same measure in the case of a rectangle.

The **perimeter of a parallelogram** is found by the formula $P = 2a + 2b$ or $P = 2(a + b)$, where $a$ and $b$ are the lengths of the two sides.

**Review Video: Area and Perimeter of a Parallelogram**
Visit mometrix.com/academy and enter code: 718313

## RECTANGLE

A **rectangle** is a quadrilateral with four right angles. All rectangles are parallelograms and trapezoids, but not all parallelograms or trapezoids are rectangles. The diagonals of a rectangle are congruent. Rectangles have two lines of symmetry (through each pair of opposing midpoints) and 180-degree rotational symmetry about the midpoint.

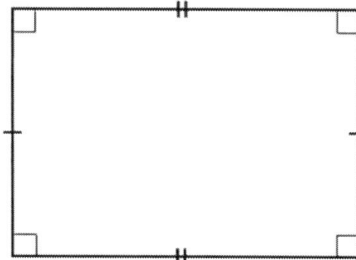

The **area of a rectangle** is found by the formula $A = lw$, where $A$ is the area of the rectangle, $l$ is the length (usually considered to be the longer side) and $w$ is the width (usually considered to be the shorter side). The numbers for $l$ and $w$ are interchangeable.

The **perimeter of a rectangle** is found by the formula $P = 2l + 2w$ or $P = 2(l + w)$, where $l$ is the length, and $w$ is the width. It may be easier to add the length and width first and then double the result, as in the second formula.

## Rhombus

A **rhombus** is a quadrilateral with four congruent sides. All rhombuses are parallelograms and kites; thus, they inherit all the properties of both types of quadrilaterals. The diagonals of a rhombus are perpendicular to each other. Rhombi have two lines of symmetry (along each of the diagonals) and 180° rotational symmetry. The **area of a rhombus** is half the product of the diagonals: $A = \frac{d_1 d_2}{2}$ and the perimeter of a rhombus is: $P = 2\sqrt{(d_1)^2 + (d_2)^2}$.

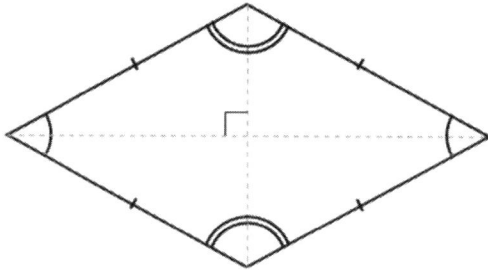

## Square

A **square** is a quadrilateral with four right angles and four congruent sides. Squares satisfy the criteria of all other types of quadrilaterals. The diagonals of a square are congruent and perpendicular to each other. Squares have four lines of symmetry (through each pair of opposing midpoints and along each of the diagonals) as well as 90° rotational symmetry about the midpoint.

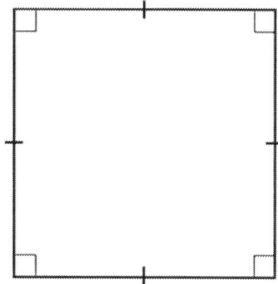

The **area of a square** is found by using the formula $A = s^2$, where $s$ is the length of one side. The **perimeter of a square** is found by using the formula $P = 4s$, where $s$ is the length of one side. Because all four sides are equal in a square, it is faster to multiply the length of one side by 4 than to add the same number four times. You could use the formulas for rectangles and get the same answer.

> **Review Video: Area and Perimeter of Rectangles and Squares**
> Visit mometrix.com/academy and enter code: 428109

## HIERARCHY OF QUADRILATERALS

The hierarchy of quadrilaterals is as follows:

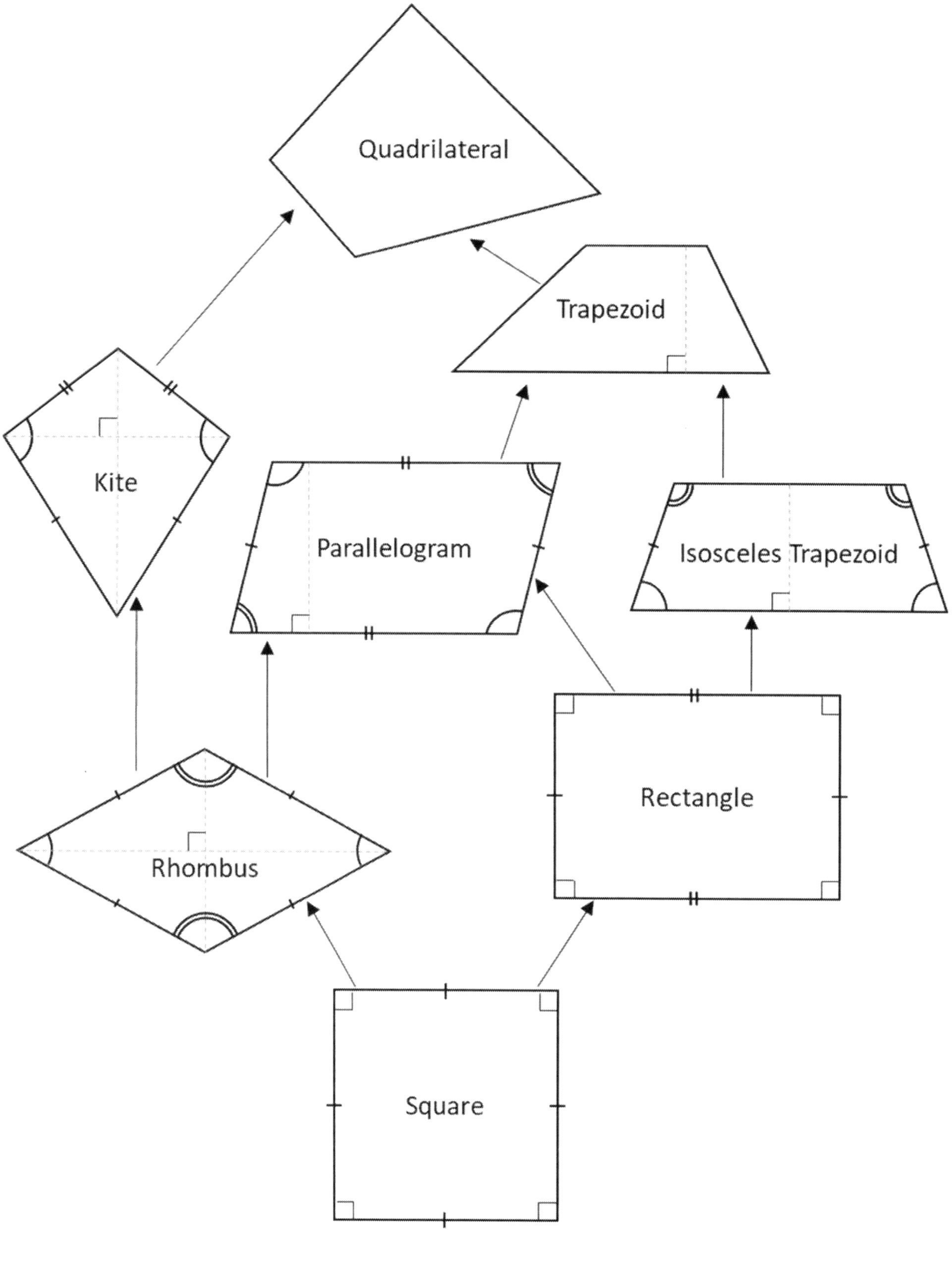

# Circles

The **center** of a circle is the single point from which every point on the circle is **equidistant**. The **radius** is a line segment that joins the center of the circle and any one point on the circle. All radii of a circle are equal. Circles that have the same center but not the same length of radii are **concentric**. The **diameter** is a line segment that passes through the center of the circle and has both endpoints on the circle. The length of the diameter is exactly twice the length of the radius. Point $O$ in the diagram below is the center of the circle, segments $\overline{OX}, \overline{OY}$, and $\overline{OZ}$ are radii; and segment $\overline{XZ}$ is a diameter.

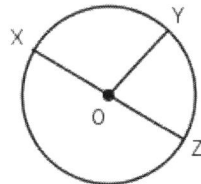

> **Review Video: Points of a Circle**
> Visit mometrix.com/academy and enter code: 420746
>
> **Review Video: Diameter, Radius, and Circumference**
> Visit mometrix.com/academy and enter code: 448988

The **area of a circle** is found by the formula $A = \pi r^2$, where $r$ is the length of the radius. If the diameter of the circle is given, remember to divide it in half to get the length of the radius before proceeding.

The **circumference** of a circle is found by the formula $C = 2\pi r$, where $r$ is the radius. Again, remember to convert the diameter if you are given that measure rather than the radius.

> **Review Video: Area and Circumference of a Circle**
> Visit mometrix.com/academy and enter code: 243015

## INSCRIBED AND CIRCUMSCRIBED FIGURES

These terms can both be used to describe a given arrangement of figures, depending on perspective. If each of the vertices of figure A lie on figure B, then it can be said that figure A is **inscribed** in figure B, but it can also be said that figure B is **circumscribed** about figure A. The following table and examples help to illustrate the concept. Note that the figures cannot both be circles, as they would be completely overlapping and neither would be inscribed or circumscribed.

| Given | Description | Equivalent Description | Figures |
|---|---|---|---|
| Each of the sides of a pentagon is tangent to a circle | The circle is inscribed in the pentagon | The pentagon is circumscribed about the circle | |
| Each of the vertices of a pentagon lie on a circle | The pentagon is inscribed in the circle | The circle is circumscribed about the pentagon | |

# 3D Shapes

## SOLIDS

The **surface area of a solid object** is the area of all sides or exterior surfaces. For objects such as prisms and pyramids, a further distinction is made between base surface area ($B$) and lateral surface area ($LA$). For a prism, the total surface area ($SA$) is $SA = LA + 2B$. For a pyramid or cone, the total surface area is $SA = LA + B$.

The **surface area of a sphere** can be found by the formula $A = 4\pi r^2$, where $r$ is the radius. The volume is given by the formula $V = \frac{4}{3}\pi r^3$, where $r$ is the radius. Both quantities are generally given in terms of $\pi$.

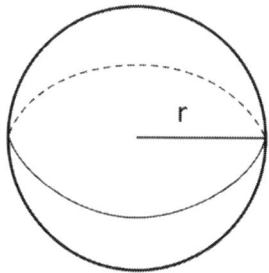

**Review Video: Volume and Surface Area of a Sphere**
Visit mometrix.com/academy and enter code: 786928

**Review Video: How to Calculate the Volume of 3D Objects**
Visit mometrix.com/academy and enter code: 163343

The **volume of any prism** is found by the formula $V = Bh$, where $B$ is the area of the base, and $h$ is the height (perpendicular distance between the bases). The surface area of any prism is the sum of the areas of both bases and all sides. It can be calculated as $SA = 2B + Ph$, where $P$ is the perimeter of the base.

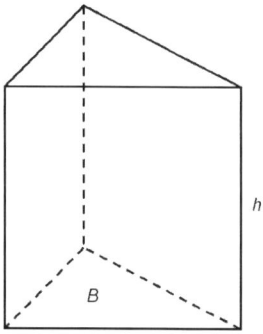

**Review Video: Volume and Surface Area of a Prism**
Visit mometrix.com/academy and enter code: 420158

For a **rectangular prism**, the volume can be found by the formula $V = lwh$, where $V$ is the volume, $l$ is the length, $w$ is the width, and $h$ is the height. The surface area can be calculated as $SA = 2lw + 2hl + 2wh$ or $SA = 2(lw + hl + wh)$.

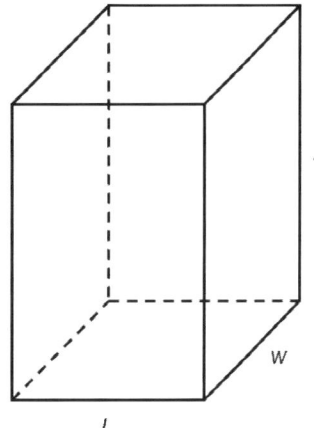

**Review Video: Volume and Surface Area of a Rectangular Prism**
Visit mometrix.com/academy and enter code: 282814

The **volume of a cube** can be found by the formula $V = s^3$, where $s$ is the length of a side. The surface area of a cube is calculated as $SA = 6s^2$, where $SA$ is the total surface area and $s$ is the length of a side. These formulas are the same as the ones used for the volume and surface area of a rectangular prism, but simplified since all three quantities (length, width, and height) are the same.

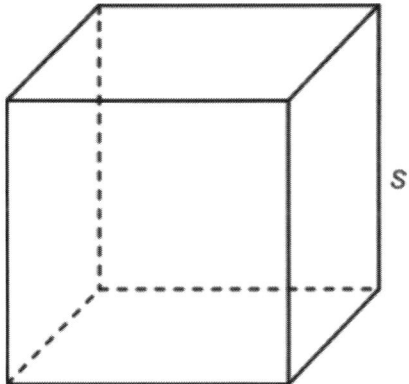

**Review Video: Volume and Surface Area of a Cube**
Visit mometrix.com/academy and enter code: 664455

The **volume of a cylinder** can be calculated by the formula $V = \pi r^2 h$, where $r$ is the radius, and $h$ is the height. The surface area of a cylinder can be found by the formula $SA = 2\pi r^2 + 2\pi rh$. The first term is the base area multiplied by two, and the second term is the perimeter of the base multiplied by the height.

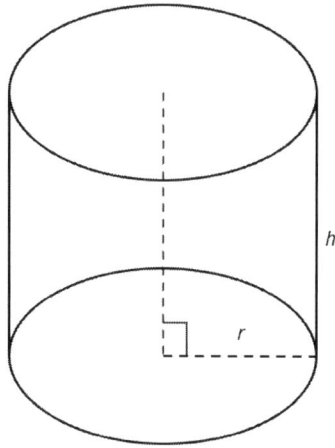

**Review Video: Volume and Surface Area of a Right Circular Cylinder**
Visit mometrix.com/academy and enter code: 226463

The **volume of a pyramid** is found by the formula $V = \frac{1}{3}Bh$, where $B$ is the area of the base, and $h$ is the height (perpendicular distance from the vertex to the base). Notice this formula is the same as $\frac{1}{3}$ times the volume of a prism. Like a prism, the base of a pyramid can be any shape.

Finding the **surface area of a pyramid** is not as simple as the other shapes we've looked at thus far. If the pyramid is a right pyramid, meaning the base is a regular polygon and the vertex is directly over the center of that polygon, the surface area can be calculated as $SA = B + \frac{1}{2}Ph_s$, where $P$ is the perimeter of the base, and $h_s$ is the slant height (distance from the vertex to the midpoint of one side of the base). If the pyramid is irregular, the area of each triangle side must be calculated individually and then summed, along with the base.

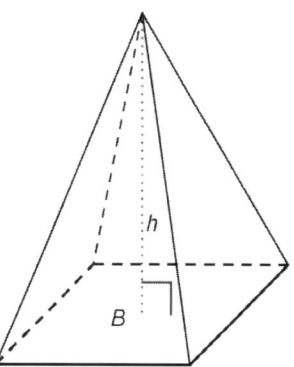

**Review Video: Volume and Surface Area of a Pyramid**
Visit mometrix.com/academy and enter code: 621932

The **volume of a cone** is found by the formula $V = \frac{1}{3}\pi r^2 h$, where $r$ is the radius, and $h$ is the height. Notice this is the same as $\frac{1}{3}$ times the volume of a cylinder. The surface area can be calculated as $SA = \pi r^2 + \pi rs$, where $s$

is the slant height. The slant height can be calculated using the Pythagorean theorem to be $\sqrt{r^2 + h^2}$, so the surface area formula can also be written as $SA = \pi r^2 + \pi r\sqrt{r^2 + h^2}$.

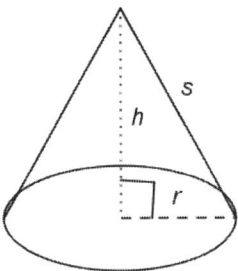

Review Video: **Volume and Surface Area of a Right Circular Cone**
Visit mometrix.com/academy and enter code: 573574

## Midpoint and Distance Formulas

If you know the coordinates of the endpoints of a line segment, you can calculate the midpoint and length of the line segment. Conveniently, the length of the line segment is also the distance between the two endpoints.

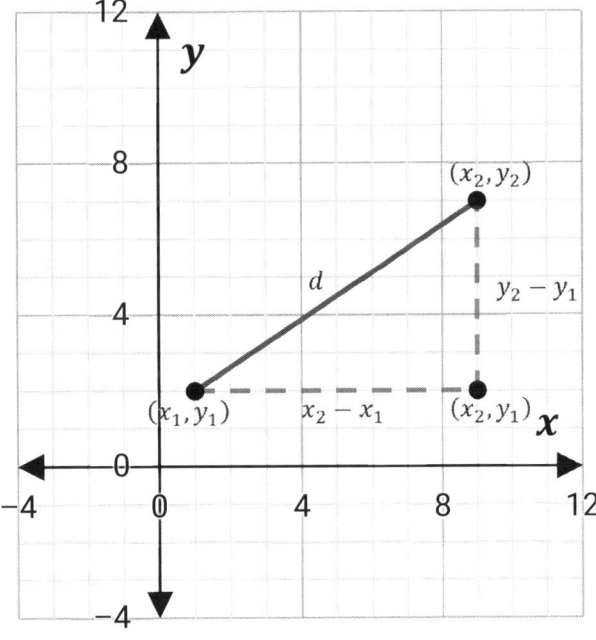

To find the **midpoint** of the line segment with endpoints $(x_1, y_1)$ and $(x_2, y_2)$, average the $x$-coordinates to get the $x$-coordinate of the midpoint, and average the $y$-coordinates to get the $y$-coordinate of the midpoint. Thus, the **midpoint formula** is:

$$\left(\frac{x_1 + x_2}{2}, \frac{y_1 + y_2}{2}\right)$$

The **distance** between points $(x_1, y_1)$ and $(x_2, y_2)$ is the same as the length of the hypotenuse of a right triangle with the two given points as endpoints, and the two sides of the right triangle parallel to the $x$-axis and $y$-axis, respectively. The length of the segment parallel to the $x$-axis is the difference between the $x$-coordinates of the two points. The length of the segment parallel to the $y$-axis is the difference between the $y$-coordinates of the two points. Use the Pythagorean theorem $a^2 + b^2 = c^2$ or $c = \sqrt{a^2 + b^2}$ to find the distance. Thus, the **distance formula** is:

$$d = \sqrt{(x_2 - x_1)^2 + (y_2 - y_1)^2}$$

> **Review Video: Calculations Using Points on a Graph**
> Visit mometrix.com/academy and enter code: 883228

## Transformations

### ROTATION

A **rotation** is a transformation that turns a figure around a point called the **center of rotation**, which can lie anywhere in the plane. If a line is drawn from a point on a figure to the center of rotation, and another line is drawn from the center to the rotated image of that point, the angle between the two lines is the **angle of rotation**. The vertex of the angle of rotation is the center of rotation.

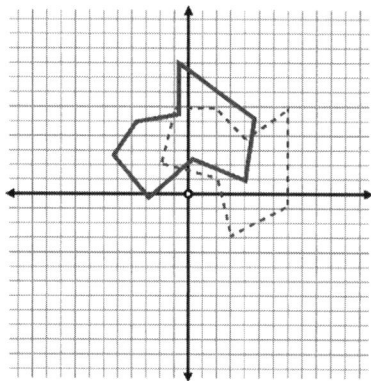

> **Review Video: Rotation**
> Visit mometrix.com/academy and enter code: 602600

### TRANSLATION AND DILATION

A **translation** is a transformation which slides a figure from one position in the plane to another position in the plane. The original figure and the translated figure have the same size, shape, and orientation. A **dilation** is a transformation which proportionally stretches or shrinks a figure by a **scale factor**. The dilated image is the same shape and orientation as the original image but a different size. A polygon and its dilated image are similar.

Translation

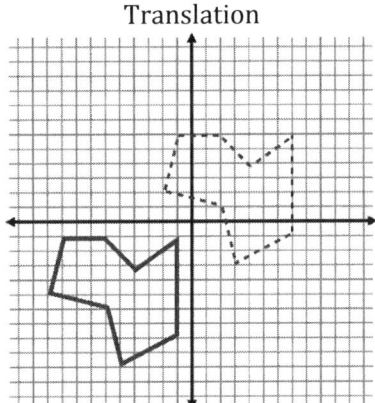

Dilation

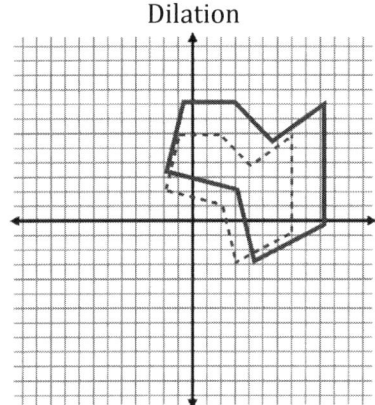

> **Review Video: Translation**
> Visit mometrix.com/academy and enter code: 718628
>
> **Review Video: Dilation**
> Visit mometrix.com/academy and enter code: 471630

A **reflection of a figure over a line** (a "flip") creates a congruent image that is the same distance from the line as the original figure but on the opposite side. The **line of reflection** is the perpendicular bisector of any line segment drawn from a point on the original figure to its reflected image (unless the point and its reflected image happen to be the same point, which happens when a figure is reflected over one of its own sides). A **reflection of a figure over a point** (an inversion) in two dimensions is the same as the rotation of the figure 180° about that point. The image of the figure is congruent to the original figure. The **point of reflection** is the midpoint of a line segment which connects a point in the figure to its image (unless the point and its reflected image happen to be the same point, which happens when a figure is reflected in one of its own points).

Reflection of a figure over a line

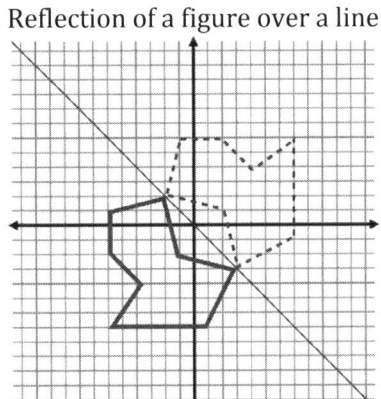

Reflection of a figure over a point

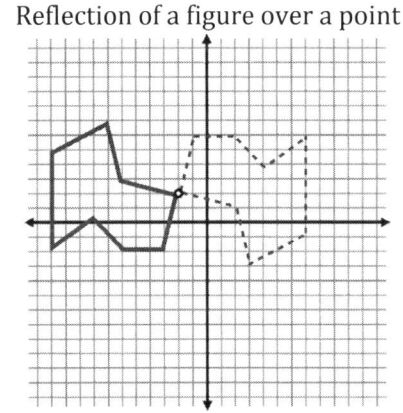

> **Review Video: Reflection**
> Visit mometrix.com/academy and enter code: 955068

## Pythagorean Theorem

The side of a triangle opposite the right angle is called the **hypotenuse**. The other two sides are called the legs. The Pythagorean theorem states a relationship among the legs and hypotenuse of a right triangle: $(a^2 + b^2 = c^2)$, where $a$ and $b$ are the lengths of the legs of a right triangle, and $c$ is the length of the hypotenuse. Note that this formula will only work with right triangles.

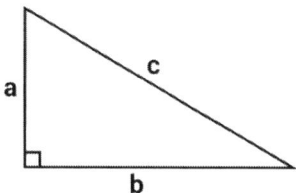

**Review Video: Pythagorean Theorem**
Visit mometrix.com/academy and enter code: 906576

## Chapter Quiz

Ready to see how well you retained what you just read? Scan the QR code to go directly to the chapter quiz interface for this study guide. If you're using a computer, simply visit the online resources page at mometrix.com/resources719/accuplacer-28992 and click the Chapter Quizzes link.

# Advanced Algebra and Functions

Transform passive reading into active learning! After immersing yourself in this chapter, put your comprehension to the test by taking a quiz. The insights you gained will stay with you longer this way. Scan the QR code to go directly to the chapter quiz interface for this study guide. If you're using a computer, simply visit the online resources page at **mometrix.com/resources719/accuplacer-28992** and click the Chapter Quizzes link.

## Quadratics

### SOLVING QUADRATIC EQUATIONS

A quadratic equation is an equation that can be written (possibly after simplification) in the form $ax^2 + bx + c = 0$. Thus, the **solutions** of this equation are precisely the **zeros** of the quadratic polynomial $P(x) = ax^2 + bx + c$. On the graph of this polynomial the zeros, if any, appear as $x$-intercepts. There are several ways to find these solutions including the quadratic formula, factoring, completing the square, and graphing the function.

> **Review Video: Quadratic Equations Overview**
> Visit mometrix.com/academy and enter code: 476276
>
> **Review Video: Solutions of a Quadratic Equation on a Graph**
> Visit mometrix.com/academy and enter code: 328231

### QUADRATIC FORMULA

The **quadratic formula** gives the zeros of a quadratic polynomial. It always works, but it is sometimes a little harder to use than other methods. To use it to solve a quadratic equation, rewrite the equation in the form $ax^2 + bx + c = 0$, where $a$, $b$, and $c$ are coefficients. Now, as explained above, the solutions of the equation are the zeros of the quadratic polynomial $P(x) = ax^2 + bx + c$. To find them, substitute the values of $a$, $b$, and $c$ into the Quadratic Formula:

$$x = \frac{-b \pm \sqrt{b^2 - 4ac}}{2a}$$

After simplification this formula produces two, one, or zero real solutions, depending on whether the **discriminant** (the number $b^2 - 4ac$ under the radical) is positive, zero, or negative. It is a good practice to check each solution by substituting it into the original equation. Incidentally, if the discriminant is negative, then the equation does have two complex solutions, but you often ignore these as meaningless in real-world settings.

> **Review Video: Using the Quadratic Formula**
> Visit mometrix.com/academy and enter code: 163102

### FACTORING

To solve a quadratic equation by factoring, begin by rewriting the equation in the standard form, $ax^2 + bx + c = 0$. In the important special case that $a = 1$, the goal of factoring is to find numbers $f$ and $g$ such that $x^2 + bx + c = (x + f)(x + g) = x^2 + (f + g)x + fg$. In other words, you want to choose $f$ and $g$ to make $fg = c$ and $f + g = b$. To do this, find pairs of numbers (factors) whose product is $c$ and look for a pair whose sum is $b$.

For example, suppose you want to find the solutions of the equation $x^2 + 6x - 16 = 0$ by factoring. Here $b = 6$ and $c = -16$. First, you find the pairs of numbers whose product is $-16$. These are $-4$ and 4, $-8$ and 2, $-2$ and 8, $-1$ and 16, and 1 and $-16$. The pair $-2$ and 8 has a sum of 6. This means $f = -2$ and $g = 8$. So, the factorization is $x^2 + 6x - 16 = (x + f)(x + g) = (x - 2)(x + 8)$, allowing you to rewrite the original equation as $(x - 2)(x + 8) = 0$. The only way for a product to equal zero is for one of the factors to equal zero; so, either $x - 2 = 0$ (in which case $x = 2$) or $x + 8 = 0$ (in which case $x = -8$). Thus, the equation has the solution $x = 2$ or $x = -8$.

In the case that $a \neq 1$, you can attempt to factor the quadratic polynomial $ax^2 + bx + c$ in the form $(mx + f)(nx + g)$ by a similar trial-and-error procedure, but the work tends to be much harder.

> **Review Video: Factoring Quadratic Equations**
> Visit mometrix.com/academy and enter code: 336566

## COMPLETING THE SQUARE

The technique of completing the square comes from a simple observation: Suppose you have the expression $x^2 + bx$. If you take half the linear coefficient, $b$, square it, and add the result to the expression, the result is always a perfect square trinomial:

$$x^2 + bx + \left(\frac{b}{2}\right)^2 = \left(x + \frac{b}{2}\right)^2$$

For example, if you begin with $x^2 + 6x$ and add the square of half of 6 (half of 6 is 3, and $3^2 = 9$), then you get a perfect square trinomial:

$$x^2 + 6x + 9 = (x + 3)^2$$

This also works if $b$ is negative. For instance, if you begin with the expression $x^2 - 10x$ and complete the square by adding 25 (half of $-10$ is $-5$, and $(-5)^2 = 25$), then you get another perfect square trinomial:

$$x^2 - 10x + 25 = (x - 5)^2$$

Now, suppose you want to solve the equation $x^2 + bx + c = 0$. Subtract $c$ from both sides, to get the equation $x^2 + bx = -c$. Complete the square on the left side by adding $(b/2)^2$, but also add this same term to the right side so that the new equation is equivalent to the old one:

$$x^2 + bx + \left(\frac{b}{2}\right)^2 = -c + \left(\frac{b}{2}\right)^2$$
$$\left(x + \frac{b}{2}\right)^2 = -c + \left(\frac{b}{2}\right)^2$$

Take square roots of both sides:

$$x + \frac{b}{2} = \pm\sqrt{-c + \left(\frac{b}{2}\right)^2}$$

Remember to include $\pm$ since every positive number has both a positive and a negative square root. Subtract $b/2$ from both sides to isolate the variable $x$ to finish the problem:

$$x = -\frac{b}{2} \pm \sqrt{-c + \left(\frac{b}{2}\right)^2}$$

This may sound complicated, but in practice it is not hard. For example, suppose you want to solve the equation $x^2 + 6x - 16 = 0$ by completing the square. First, add 16 to both sides:

$$x^2 + 6x = 16$$

Half of 6 is 3 and $3^2 = 9$, so complete the square by adding 9 to both sides of the equation:

$$x^2 + 6x + 9 = 16 + 9$$
$$(x + 3)^2 = 25$$

Now take square root of both sides, remembering to include the $\pm$:

$$\sqrt{(x+3)^2} = \pm\sqrt{25}$$
$$x + 3 = \pm 5$$
$$x = -3 \pm 5$$

So we see that the two solutions to the equation are $x = 2$ and $x = -8$.

> **Review Video: Completing the Square**
> Visit mometrix.com/academy and enter code: 982479

## USING GIVEN SOLUTIONS TO FIND A QUADRATIC EQUATION

To find a quadratic equation with given numbers as solutions, simply find a quadratic polynomial that has those numbers as zeros and set that polynomial equal to zero. This is easy because a polynomial has the number $p$ as a zero precisely when it has the binomial $x - p$ as a factor. Thus, for instance, to find a quadratic polynomial with zeros at $x = 3$ and $x = -5$, construct the polynomial $P(x) = (x - 3)(x - (-5)) = (x - 3)(x + 5) = x^2 + 2x - 15$. Setting this equal to zero produces an equation, $x^2 + 2x - 15 = 0$, whose solutions are $x = 3$ and $x = -5$.

Of course, any constant multiple $P(x) = a(x - 3)(x + 5)$ will also have the same zeros. For instance, if you choose $a = 4$, then you get the polynomial $P(x) = 4(x - 3)(x + 5) = 4x^2 + 8x - 60$, which also has zeros at $x = 3$ and $x = -5$. From this you can get another equation, $4x^2 + 8x - 60 = 0$, with solutions $x = 3$ and $x = -5$.

# Advanced Systems of Equations

## SOLVING A SYSTEM OF EQUATIONS WITH A LINEAR EQUATION AND A QUADRATIC EQUATION
### ALGEBRAICALLY

Generally, the simplest way to solve a system of equations consisting of a linear equation and a quadratic equation algebraically is through the method of substitution. One possible strategy is to solve the linear equation for $y$ and then substitute that expression into the quadratic equation. After expansion and combining like terms, this will result in a new quadratic equation for $x$, which, like all quadratic equations, may have zero, one, or two solutions. Plugging each solution for $x$ back into one of the original equations will then produce the corresponding value of $y$.

For example, consider the following system of equations:

$$x + y = 1$$
$$y = (x + 3)^2 - 2$$

We can solve the linear equation for $y$ to yield $y = -x + 1$. Substituting this expression into the quadratic equation produces $-x + 1 = (x + 3)^2 - 2$. We can simplify this equation:

$$-x + 1 = (x + 3)^2 - 2$$
$$-x + 1 = x^2 + 6x + 9 - 2$$
$$-x + 1 = x^2 + 6x + 7$$
$$0 = x^2 + 7x + 6$$

This quadratic equation can be factored as $(x + 1)(x + 6) = 0$. It therefore has two solutions: $x_1 = -1$ and $x_2 = -6$. Plugging each of these back into the original linear equation yields $y_1 = -x_1 + 1 = -(-1) + 1 = 2$ and $y_2 = -x_2 + 1 = -(-6) + 1 = 7$. Thus, this system of equations has two solutions, $(-1, 2)$ and $(-6, 7)$.

It may help to check your work by putting each $x$- and $y$-value back into the original equations and verifying that they do provide a solution.

## GRAPHICALLY

To solve a system of equations consisting of a linear equation and a quadratic equation graphically, plot both equations on the same graph. The linear equation will, of course, produce a straight line, while the quadratic equation will produce a parabola. These two graphs will intersect at zero, one, or two points; each point of intersection is a solution of the system.

For example, consider the following system of equations:

$$y = -2x + 2$$
$$y = -2x^2 + 4x + 2$$

The linear equation describes a line with a $y$-intercept of $(0, 2)$ and a slope of $-2$.

To graph the quadratic equation, we can first find the vertex of the parabola: the $x$-coordinate of the vertex is $h = -\frac{b}{2a} = -\frac{4}{2(-2)} = 1$, and the $y$-coordinate is $k = -2(1)^2 + 4(1) + 2 = 4$. Thus, the vertex lies at $(1, 4)$. To get a feel for the rest of the parabola, we can plug in a few more values of $x$ to find more points; by putting in $x = 2$ and $x = 3$ in the quadratic equation, we find that the points $(2, 2)$ and $(3, -4)$ lie on the parabola; by symmetry, so must $(0, 2)$ and $(-1, -4)$. We can now plot both equations:

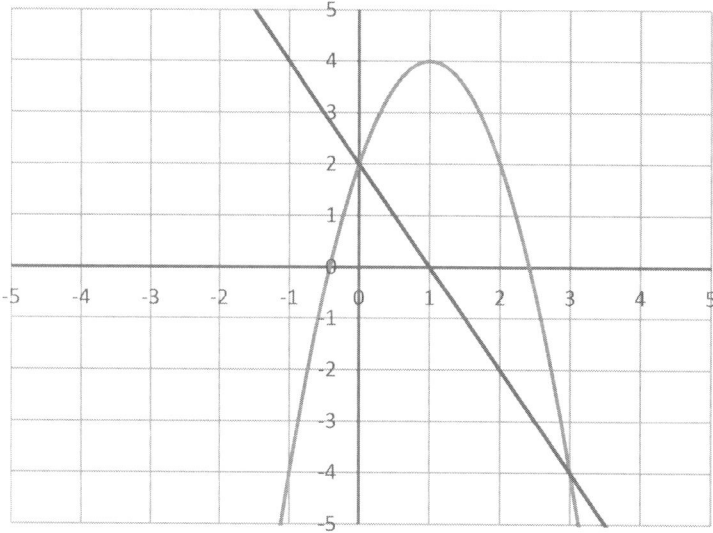

These two curves intersect at the points (0,2) and (3,−4), thus these are the solutions of the equation.

> **Review Video: Parabolas**
> Visit mometrix.com/academy and enter code: 129187
>
> **Review Video: Vertex of a Parabola**
> Visit mometrix.com/academy and enter code: 272300
>
> **Review Video: Solving a System of Linear and Quadratic Equations**
> Visit mometrix.com/academy and enter code: 194870

## Basics of Functions

### DEFINITION OF A FUNCTION

A function is a rule that assigns to every number in a given set (called the **domain**) exactly one corresponding value. For example, if our domain is the set $\{-2,1,2,3\}$, we can define a function by assigning to each number its square. This function assigns to $-2$ the value 4, to 1 the value 1, to 2 the value 4, and to 3 the value 9 (since $(-2)^2 = 4, 1^2 = 1, 2^2 = 4,$ and $3^2 = 9$). The set of all the values assigned by a function is the **range** of the function. The range of the function in our example is the set $\{1, 4, 9\}$. We may think of a function as a kind of machine: we give it a number as an input, and it uses its rule to produce a number as an output. In the squaring function above, the input 3 produces the output 9.

> **Review Video: What is a Function?**
> Visit mometrix.com/academy and enter code: 784611

### FUNCTION NOTATION

We usually name a function by a letter, often the letter $f$ (for *function*—if we need to talk about more than one function, we name the second one $g$, the third one $h$, etc.). To specify the value (the output) corresponding to a particular number in the domain (the input), we write the function letter followed by the input number in parentheses. For instance, in the example above the notation $f(3)$ means the value that the function assigns to the number 3, namely 9—that is, $f(3) = 9$. We read the symbols $f(3)$ as, "$f$ of 3," and we call 3 the **argument** of the function and 9 the **value** of the function (so *argument* means *input* and *value* means *output*).

Using function notation we can define the squaring function above by listing the values the function assigns to each argument in the domain: $f(-2) = 4$, $f(1) = 1$, $f(2) = 4$, and $f(3) = 9$. More efficiently, we can define the function by the single equation $f(x) = x^2$, which says that if $x$ is a number from the domain, then we calculate the value assigned to it by substituting the number $x$ in the formula $x^2$. For instance, we calculate $f(5) = 5^2 = 25$. Similarly, if we define a function $g$ by the equation $g(x) = x^2 - 4x + 7$, then we calculate the value $g(3)$ by substituting 3 for each $x$ in the formula: $g(3) = 3^2 - 4 \cdot 3 + 7 = 9 - 12 + 7 = 4$.

### OTHER WAYS TO DEFINE FUNCTIONS

Instead of denoting the value of the function by $f(x)$, sometimes we simply use another letter, usually $y$. For instance, instead of defining the squaring function by the equation $f(x) = x^2$, we might use the equation $y = x^2$. In this case, we refer to $x$ (the input) as the **independent variable** and $y$ (the output) as the **dependent variable** because the value, $y$, depends on the number we choose for $x$.

A formula (with $y$ or $f(x)$) is the most common way to define a function; but sometimes, if the domain is small enough, we prefer to list explicitly the possible inputs and their corresponding outputs. Some ways of doing this appear above, but a more common approach is to put the input-output pairs in a table. For instance, we can define the squaring function above by the table

| $x$ | $-2$ | 1 | 2 | 3 |
|---|---|---|---|---|
| $y$ | 4 | 1 | 4 | 9 |

We see that the domain of this function is the set of all numbers in the $x$-row and the range is the set of all numbers in the $y$-row. We note that numbers cannot repeat in the $x$-row (because a function assigns exactly one value to each argument in the domain) but they can repeat in the $y$-row (because the function can assign the same value to multiple arguments—for instance, the number 4 appears twice in the $y$-row).

We can also define a function by writing the inputs and corresponding outputs as ordered pairs of $x$- and $y$-values. For instance, we can write the squaring function above as the set of ordered pairs $\{(-2,4), (1,1), (2,4), (3,9)\}$. Further, by treating these ordered pairs as coordinates and plotting the corresponding points on the coordinate plane, we get the **graph** of the function:

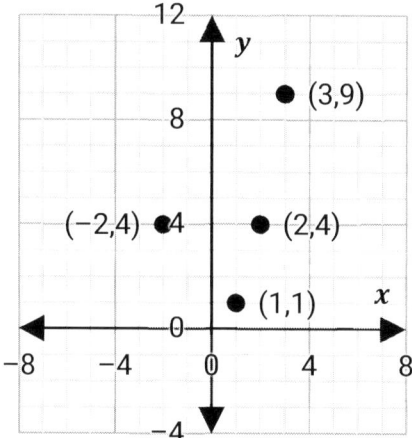

Turning this around, we can potentially use a graph to define a function, namely the function consisting of the coordinate pairs of all the points in the graph. This always works unless the graph has two points with the same $x$-coordinate (because then the function would assign two different $y$-values to the same $x$). It is easy to detect such points: because they have the same $x$-coordinate, a vertical line passes through both of them. Thus, a graph always defines a function unless it is possible to draw a vertical line that intersects the graph in two or more points. We call this condition the **vertical line test**. For example, if our graph is a circle, then by the Vertical Line Test the graph does not define a function because there are vertical lines that will intersect the circle in two different points.

## More on Domains and Ranges

When we define a function by a formula and do not specify the domain, then by default the domain consists of all real numbers for which the formula produces an answer. For instance, suppose we define a function $f$ by the formula $f(x) = 1/x$. If $x = 0$, then $1/x = 1/0$, which is undefined. But if $x$ is any other real number, then we can calculate the value of $1/x$. So, the default domain of this function is all real numbers except zero. Because of this domain convention, the graph of a function defined by a formula usually consists of infinitely many points that "connect to" each other in a way that produces a line or curve (see examples below) rather than the isolated points we see in the squaring function above.

If we have the graph of a function, its domain consists of all numbers on the $x$-axis with corresponding points on the graph and its range consists of all numbers on the $y$-axis with corresponding points on the graph. For example, consider the function $f(x) = x^2 + 3$:

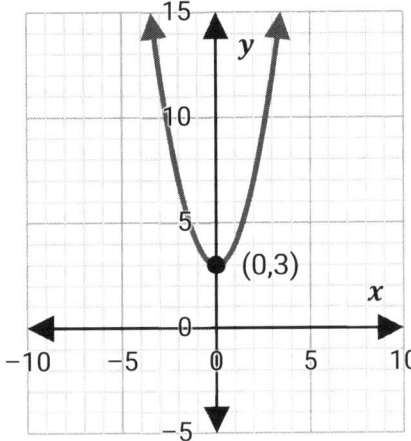

Since the graph continues infinitely to the left and right beyond what we can see, every point on the $x$-axis has a corresponding point on the graph; so, the domain of this function is all real numbers. On the other hand, the lowest point on this graph has a $y$-value of 3, and the graph passes through all higher $y$-values. So, the range of this function is all real numbers greater than or equal to 3, which we can denote algebraically by $y \geq 3$ or, using interval notation, by $[3, \infty)$.

> **Review Video: How to Find Domain and Range**
> Visit mometrix.com/academy and enter code: 778133
>
> **Review Video: Domain and Range of Quadratic Functions**
> Visit mometrix.com/academy and enter code: 331768

## MONOTONIC AND EVEN/ODD FUNCTIONS

A function, $f$, is **increasing** if it always assigns larger values to larger arguments. It is **decreasing** if it always assigns smaller values to larger arguments. That is, $f$ is increasing if $a < b$ always guarantees $f(a) < f(b)$, and it is decreasing if $a < b$ always guarantees $f(a) > f(b)$. The graph of an increasing function consistently rises from left to right, and the graph of a decreasing function consistently falls from left to right. For example, the function $f(x) = 2x$ is an increasing function because doubling a larger number always gives us a larger result than doubling a smaller number. The graph of $f(x) = 2x$ is a line with slope $m = 2$, which, as we expect, rises from left to right. We call a function **monotonic** if it is either increasing or decreasing.

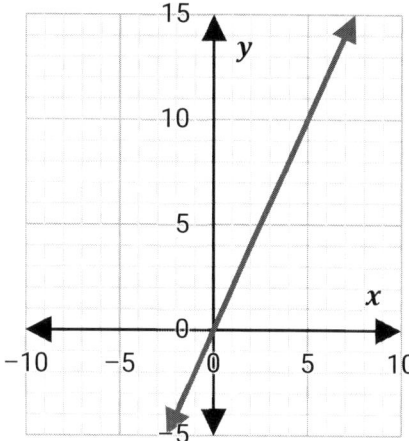

A function, $f$, is **even** if changing the sign of its argument produces the same value. It is **odd** if changing the sign of its argument produces the same value except with the opposite sign. That is, $f$ is even if $f(-x) = f(x)$ and odd if $f(-x) = -f(x)$ for every argument $x$. The function $f(x) = x^2 + 3$ is even because substituting opposite arguments always produces the same value. For instance, $f(5) = 28$ and $f(-5) = 28$ because $5^2 + 3 = 25 + 3 = 28$ and $(-5)^2 + 3 = 25 + 3 = 28$. The function $f(x) = 2x$ is odd because substituting opposite arguments always produces opposite values. For instance, $f(10) = 20$ and $f(-10) = -20$ because $2(10) = 20$ and $2(-10) = -20$. The graph of an even function is always symmetric with respect to the $y$-axis, making the left and right halves of the graph mirror images of each other, as in the graph of the even function $f(x) = x^2 + 3$ above. The graph of an odd function is always symmetric with respect to the origin. This means that if we rotate the graph $180°$ around the origin (think of sticking a pin through the origin on a sheet of graph paper and rotating the paper halfway around) the graph looks the same, as in the graph of the odd function $f(x) = 2x$ above.

It is worth noting that most functions are neither increasing nor decreasing (that is, they are not monotonic) and most functions are neither even nor odd. For example, the function $f(x) = x^2 - x$ is neither increasing nor decreasing and neither even nor odd: its graph neither rises nor falls consistently, and it is symmetric with respect to neither the y-axis nor the origin.

> **Review Video: Even and Odd Functions**
> Visit mometrix.com/academy and enter code: 278985

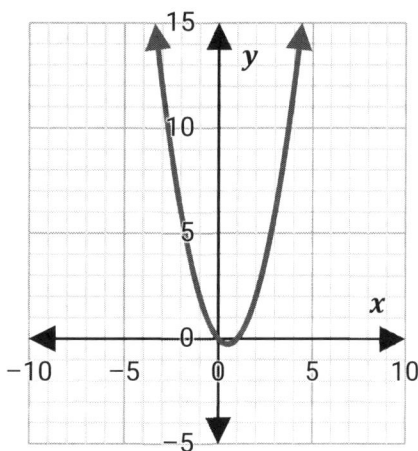

## INVERTIBLE (ONE-TO-ONE) FUNCTIONS

A function, $f$, is one-to-one if it never assigns the same value to different arguments—that is, if $f(a)$ and $f(b)$ are different whenever $a$ and $b$ are different. The graph of a one-to-one function never has two points that lie on the same horizontal line because such points would have different $x$-values but the same $y$-value. Thus, a function is one-to-one if it is impossible to draw a horizontal line that intersects its graph in more than one point. We call this condition the **horizonal line test**. For example, the graph of the function $f(x) = 2x$ above is a line that rises from left to right. Every horizontal line intersects this line in exactly one point, so the function $f(x) = 2x$ is one-to-one. This is also clear without the graph because it is impossible to double two different numbers and get the same answer.

When a function, $f$, is one-to-one, it is possible to define its inverse function, $f^{-1}$, that "undoes" what $f$ does, assigning to each output from $f$ the input that produced it. That is, for each $x$ in the domain of $f$, if $y = f(x)$, then $f^{-1}(y) = x$. For example, the inverse of the function $f(x) = 2x$ above is $f^{-1}(y) = y/2$. So, for instance, $f(5) = 2 \cdot 5 = 10$, and $f^{-1}(10) = 10/2 = 5$ (and similarly for every other value of $x$). Thus, the domain of $f^{-1}$ is the range of $f$ and vice versa. If a function, $f$, has an inverse, we say that $f$ is **invertible**. Since a function has an inverse precisely when it is one-to-one, the terms *invertible* and *one-to-one* are synonyms.

If $f$ is an invertible function defined by a formula, then to find its inverse we simply write the equation $y = f(x)$ and solve it for $x$ (that is, we isolate the $x$). The result will be the equation $f^{-1}(y) = x$. For instance, starting with the function $f(x) = 2x$, we write $y = 2x$ and isolate the $x$ by dividing both sides of the equation by 2. This gives us $y/2 = x$, so we know that $f^{-1}(y) = y/2$. Although this procedure is theoretically simple, in practice the algebra can be difficult.

## Common Functions

Certain functions and certain kinds of functions are particularly useful, coming up frequently in mathematics and its applications. Once we know some basic function terminology and concepts, it is useful to begin developing a mental library of the most common and useful functions.

> **Review Video: Common Functions**
> Visit mometrix.com/academy and enter code: 629798

## CONSTANT FUNCTIONS

A function of the form $f(x) = a$, where $a$ is a real number, is a **constant function**. This function assigns the same value, $a$, to every real argument $x$. For instance, given the constant function $f(x) = 5$, we have $f(2) = 5$, $f(100) = 5$, and $f(-7.1) = 5$.

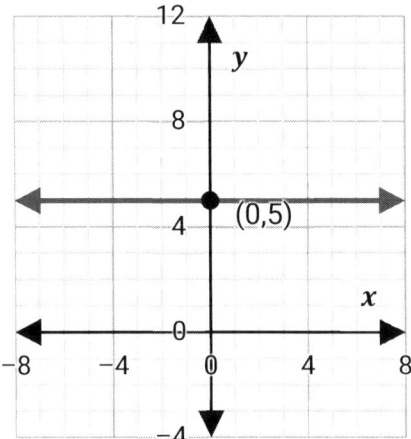

The domain of a constant function is the set of all real numbers, and the range is the set containing the single number $a$. Its graph is a horizontal line passing through the number $y = a$ on the $y$-axis (we call the number at which a function's graph intersects the $y$-axis the **y-intercept** of the function).

## THE IDENTITY FUNCTION

The function $f(x) = x$ is the **identity function**. Its value always equals its argument. Thus, for instance, $f(2) = 2$, $f(100) = 100$, and $f(-7.1) = -7.1$.

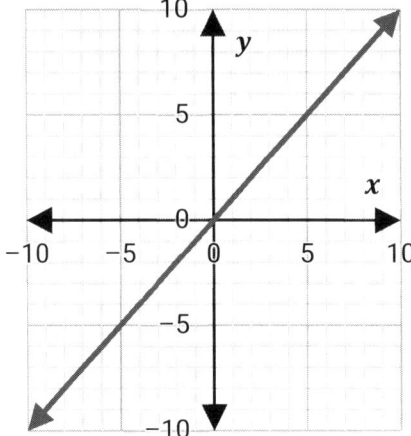

Its domain and range are the set of all real numbers. It is both an increasing function and an odd function. Its graph is a line that passes through the origin and rises from left to right at a 45° angle to the horizontal. Since it passes through the origin, its $y$ intercept is $y = 0$ and it also has an **x-intercept** (a number at which the function's graph intersects the $x$-axis) of $x = 0$.

## LINEAR FUNCTIONS

A function of the form $f(x) = ax + b$, where $a$ and $b$ are real numbers (with $a \neq 0$), is a **linear function** (the identity function is a linear function with $a = 1$ and $b = 0$). Its domain and range are the set of all real numbers. Its graph is a line (the word *linear* contains the root word *line*) with one $x$-intercept (at $x = -b/a$), with a $y$-intercept at $y = b$, and with a direction and steepness that depend on the coefficient $a$, which we call the **slope**. Specifically, the slope $a$ is the amount the $y$-value increases for each increase of 1 in the $x$-value. Thus, for $a > 0$, the line rises from left to right (making $f$ an increasing function), and larger values of $a$ produce steeper ascents. Similarly, for $a < 0$, the line falls from left to right (making $f$ a decreasing function), and smaller (more negative) values of $a$ produce steeper descents. For instance, the graph of the linear function $f(x) = (1/2)x + 3$ is a line that passes through the point $y = 3$ on the $y$-axis and that rises by $1/2$ unit for every unit that $x$ increases.

> **Review Video: Linear Functions**
> Visit mometrix.com/academy and enter code: 200735
>
> **Review Video: Graphing Linear Functions**
> Visit mometrix.com/academy and enter code: 699478

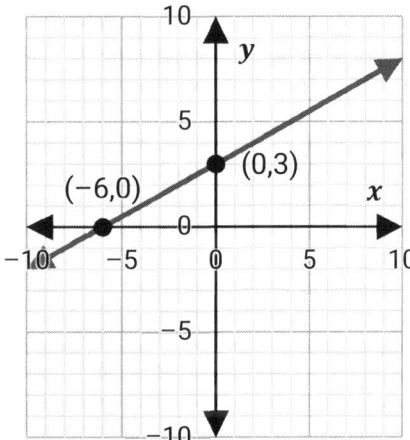

In many contexts it is standard to use the letter $m$ for slope and thus to write the general form of a linear function as $f(x) = mx + b$, known as **slope-intercept form**.

## THE SQUARING FUNCTION

The function $f(x) = x^2$ is the **squaring function**.

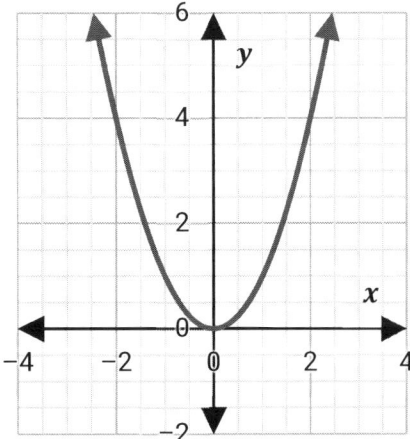

Its graph is U-shaped, opening upward as shown, a shape known as a **parabola**. It has a lowest point, its **vertex**, at the origin, which is also the location of its single $x$-intercept and single $y$-intercept. Thus, its **minimum** is $y = 0$, its domain is the set of all real numbers, and its range is the set of nonnegative real numbers (that is, $y \geq 0$). It is an even function and thus symmetric with respect to the $y$-axis (which we call the **axis of symmetry**), meaning that the left half of the graph is the mirror image of the right half, with the mirror standing on the $y$-axis.

## QUADRATIC FUNCTIONS

A function of the form $f(x) = ax^2 + bx + c$, where $a$, $b$, and $c$ are real numbers (with $a \neq 0$), is a **quadratic function** (the squaring function is a quadratic function with $a = 1$, $b = 0$, and $c = 0$). Its domain is the set of all real numbers, and its graph is a parabola. It is symmetric with respect to its axis of symmetry, the vertical line $x = -b/(2a)$. If $a > 0$, the parabola opens upward, so that its vertex is at its lowest point (its minimum) and its range consists of all real numbers greater than or equal to this minimum $y$-value. If $a < 0$, the parabola opens downward, so that its vertex is at its highest point (its maximum) and its range consists of all real numbers less than or equal to this maximum $y$-value. Its $y$-intercept is $y = c$ since $f(0) = c$, and it may have zero, one, or two $x$-intercepts. For example, the function $f(x) = x^2 - 6x + 5$ has $a = 1$, $b = -6$, and $c = 5$.

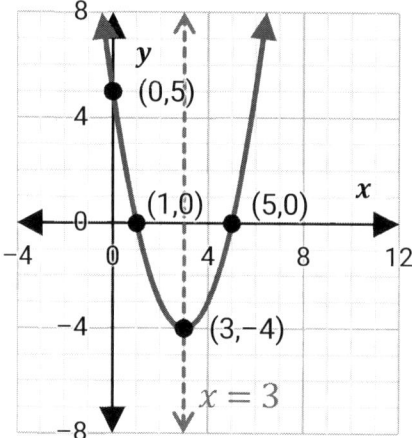

Its graph opens upward (because $a > 0$) and its axis of symmetry is the vertical line $x = 3$ (since $-b/(2a) = -(-6)/(2 \cdot 1) = 3$). Its $y$-intercept is at $y = 5$. It turns out to have its vertex at the point $(3, -4)$, making its minimum value $y = -4$. So, its domain is the set of all real numbers, and its range is $y \geq -4$. It also turns out to have two $x$-intercepts, at $x = 1$ and at $x = 5$ (since $f(1) = 0$ and $f(5) = 0$).

## POLYNOMIAL FUNCTIONS

A function of the form $f(x) = a^n x^n + a^{n-1} x^{n-1} + \cdots + a_2 x^2 + a_1 x + a_0$, where $n$ is a whole number and $a_0, a_1, a_2, \ldots a_{n-1}, a_n$ are real numbers, is a **polynomial function of degree $n$**. Its domain is the set of all real numbers (it is complicated to describe its range in general), and its $y$-intercept is $y = a_0$ (since $f(0) = a_0$). Constant functions, linear functions, and quadratic functions are polynomial functions of degrees 0, 1, and 2, respectively. In general, a polynomial function of degree $n$ has up to $n$ zeros ($x$-intercepts) and up to $n - 1$ "bends." For example, the fourth degree polynomial function $f(x) = x^4 - 11x^3 + 41x^2 - 61x + 30$, whose graph appears here, has four $x$-intercepts (at $x = 1$, $x = 2$, $x = 3$, and $x = 5$) and three "bends," and its $y$-intercept (not visible on the graph) is at $y = 30$.

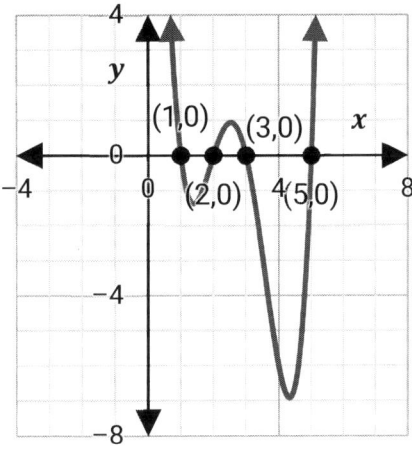

## RATIONAL FUNCTIONS

A function of the form $f(x) = P(x)/Q(x)$, where $P$ and $Q$ are polynomials, is a rational function (we note that the word *rational* includes the root word *ratio*, indicating that a rational function is a ratio of polynomial functions). The domain of a rational function is all real numbers except the zeros of $Q(x)$ since division by zero is undefined (the range can be difficult to describe in general). Its $y$-intercept is $f(0)$, if this is defined; and its $x$-intercepts are the zeros of $P(x)$ that are in the domain of $f$, if there are any. A rational function may also have vertical asymptotes (vertical lines that the graph approaches without crossing) and a horizontal asymptote (a horizontal line that the curve approaches as $x$ becomes very small or very large (toward the left and right edges of the graph). For example, the rational function $f(x) = (2x^2 + x - 1)/(x^2 + x - 2)$ has as its domain the set of all real numbers except $x = -2$ and $x = 1$ (since those numbers make the denominator zero).

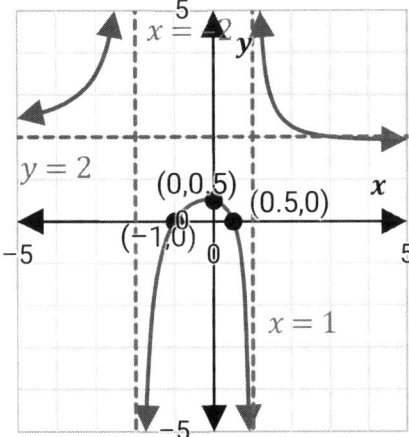

It has a $y$-intercept of $y = 1/2$ since $f(0) = (-1)/(-2) = 1/2$, and it has $x$-intercepts at $x = -1$ and at $x = 1/2$ since those numbers make the numerator zero. It has vertical asymptotes at $x = -2$ and $x = 1$ (not coincidentally, these are the numbers omitted from the domain) and a horizontal asymptote at $y = 2$. It is important to note that vertical asymptotes cannot be crossed in rational functions, but horizontal asymptotes can be crossed if the function tends near the asymptote at infinity and does not go past all possible turning points.

> **Review Video: Simplifying Rational Polynomial Functions**
> Visit mometrix.com/academy and enter code: 351038
>
> **Review Video: Horizontal Asymptotes**
> Visit mometrix.com/academy and enter code: 747796

## THE SQUARE ROOT FUNCTION

The function $f(x) = \sqrt{x}$ is the square root function.

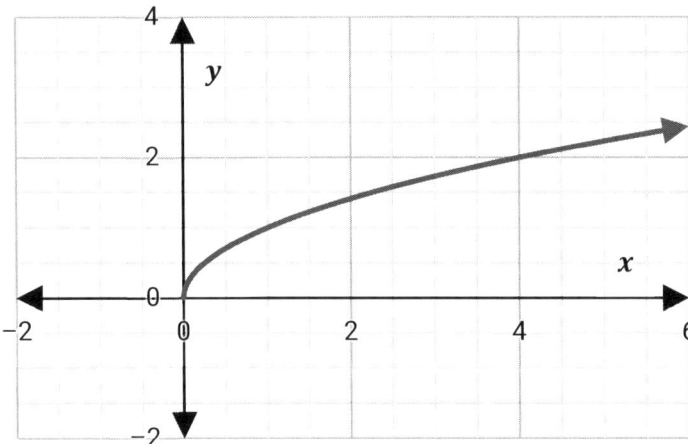

It is an increasing function, and its domain and range are both the set of all nonnegative real numbers. It has one $x$-intercept and one $y$-intercept, both appearing at the origin. Its graph is the upper half of a parabola opening to the right. The square root function is the inverse of the squaring function with domain restricted to the nonnegative real numbers (that is, $f(x) = x^2$ for $x \geq 0$).

## PIECEWISE-DEFINED FUNCTIONS

As the name suggests, a **piecewise-defined function** (or, simply, a **piecewise function**) is a function defined by different rules on different pieces of the domain. We define such a function using the following form:

| Function Name | Rule to Apply | Piece of the Domain on Which the Rule Applies |
|---|---|---|
| $f(x) =$ | $\begin{cases} \text{Rule 1,} \\ \text{Rule 2,} \\ \text{Rule 3,} \\ \text{etc.,} \end{cases}$ | First Piece of the Domain <br> Second Piece of the Domain <br> Third Piece of the Domain <br> etc. |

The pieces of the domain should not overlap, and together they should cover the whole domain. For example, we might craft a piecewise-defined function by

$$f(x) = \begin{cases} x^2, & \text{if } x < 2 \\ 3x - 5, & \text{if } x \geq 2 \end{cases}$$

The two pieces of the domain—namely, $x < 2$ and $x \geq 2$—do not overlap, and together they include all real numbers. To evaluate the function for a particular argument $x$, we determine which piece of the domain includes $x$ and then apply the corresponding rule. For instance, to find $f(4)$, we note that $4 \geq 2$; so, we apply the rule $3x - 5$ to get the value $f(4) = 3 \cdot 4 - 5 = 7$. Similarly, to find $f(-6)$, we note that $-6 < 2$; so, we apply the rule $x^2$ to get the value $f(-6) = (-6)^2 = 36$.

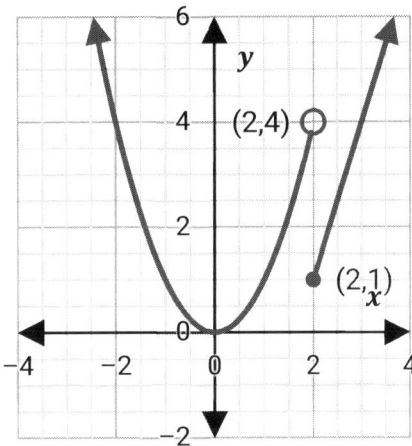

To graph this function, we sketch the graph of the parabola $y = x^2$ on the part of the plane where $x < 2$ and we sketch the line $y = 3x - 5$ on the part of the plane where $x \geq 2$. This produces a graph with a jump at $x = 2$ (a discontinuity—piecewise-defined functions are useful for producing graphs with discontinuities). We plot an open circle at the point (2,4), the end of the left part of the graph, to show that this point is not part of the graph. And we plot a solid dot at the point (2,1), the start of the right part of the graph, to show that this point *is* part of the graph.

> **Review Video: Piecewise Functions**
> Visit mometrix.com/academy and enter code: 707921

## THE ABSOLUTE VALUE FUNCTION

A particularly useful piecewise-defined function is the absolute value function. It is so important that instead of naming it $f(x)$ or $g(x)$, we denote it using the special notation $|x|$. Its definition is

$$|x| = \begin{cases} -x, & \text{if } x < 0 \\ x, & \text{if } x \geq 0 \end{cases}$$

For instance, $|8| = 8$ (since $8 \geq 0$) and $|-5| = -(-5) = 5$, since $-5 < 0$. So, the absolute value function acts like the identity function for nonnegative numbers (it leaves them unchanged), and it gives the opposite of negative numbers (it effectively strips off the minus sign). Thus, we can think of the absolute value of a real number as its distance from zero on the number line, without taking into consideration whether the number is larger than or smaller than zero. For instance, $|-3| = 3$ and $|3| = 3$, showing that both $-3$ and $3$ are three units away from zero. The absolute value function is an even function with a V-shaped graph that looks like the line $y = x$ (the identity function) on the right "half" of the plane (for $x \geq 0$) and the line $y = -x$ on the left "half" of the plane (for $x < 0$).

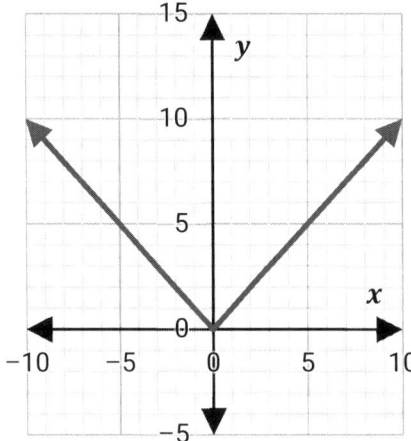

# Rational and Irrational Expressions

## RATIONAL EXPRESSIONS

**Rational expressions** are fractions with polynomials in both the numerator and the denominator; the value of the polynomial in the denominator cannot be equal to zero. Be sure to keep track of values that make the denominator of the original expression zero as the final result inherits the same restrictions. For example, a denominator of $x - 3$ indicates that the expression is not defined when $x = 3$ and, as such, regardless of any operations done to the expression, it remains undefined there.

To **add or subtract** rational expressions, first find the common denominator, then rewrite each fraction as an equivalent fraction with the common denominator. Finally, add or subtract the numerators to get the numerator of the answer, and keep the common denominator as the denominator of the answer.

When **multiplying** rational expressions, factor each polynomial and cancel like factors (a factor which appears in both the numerator and the denominator). Then, multiply all remaining factors in the numerator to get the numerator of the product, and multiply the remaining factors in the denominator to get the denominator of the product. Remember: cancel entire factors, not individual terms.

To **divide** rational expressions, take the reciprocal of the divisor (the rational expression you are dividing by) and multiply by the dividend.

> **Review Video: Rational Expressions**
> Visit mometrix.com/academy and enter code: 415183

## SIMPLIFYING RATIONAL EXPRESSIONS

To simplify a rational expression, factor the numerator and denominator completely. Factors that are the same and appear in the numerator and denominator have a ratio of 1. For example, look at the following expression:

$$\frac{x-1}{1-x^2}$$

The denominator, $(1 - x^2)$, is a difference of squares. It can be factored as $(1 - x)(1 + x)$. The factor $1 - x$ and the numerator $x - 1$ are opposites and have a ratio of –1. Rewrite the numerator as $-1(1 - x)$. So, the rational expression can be simplified as follows:

$$\frac{x-1}{1-x^2} = \frac{-1(1-x)}{(1-x)(1+x)} = \frac{-1}{1+x}$$

Note that since the original expression is only defined for $x \neq \{-1, 1\}$, the simplified expression has the same restrictions.

> **Review Video: Reducing Rational Expressions**
> Visit mometrix.com/academy and enter code: 788868
>
> **Review Video: Simplifying Algebraic Expressions with Parentheses**
> Visit mometrix.com/academy and enter code: 850843

## IRRATIONAL EXPRESSIONS

**Irrational expressions** are mathematical expressions that contain an irrational number and cannot be simplified into a rational form. Usually, this includes expressions that contain radicals or constants such as $\pi$. Most commonly, you will encounter these in the forms of expressions containing roots of non-perfect squares.

## BASIC OPERATIONS ON RADICAL EXPRESSIONS

To add or subtract radical numbers, the numbers within the radicals must match, similar to finding a common denominator in fractions:

$$a\sqrt{x} + b\sqrt{x} = (a+b)\sqrt{x}$$
$$a\sqrt{x} - b\sqrt{x} = (a-b)\sqrt{x}$$

To multiply radicals, the numbers outside the radical are multiplied together and the numbers inside the radical are multiplied together:

$$a\sqrt{x} \times b\sqrt{y} = ab\sqrt{xy}$$

To divide radicals, the radical must be eliminated from the denominator by multiplying both numerator and denominator by a value that will make the denominator a rational number:

$$\frac{a\sqrt{x}}{b\sqrt{y}} = \frac{a\sqrt{x}\sqrt{y}}{b\sqrt{y}\sqrt{y}} = \frac{a\sqrt{xy}}{by}$$

> **Review Video: Adding and Subtracting Radical Expressions**
> Visit mometrix.com/academy and enter code: 752176

## EXAMPLE

To solve $\frac{(3\sqrt{6})(2\sqrt{3})}{4\sqrt{5}}$, we first multiply the numerator, inside the radical and out: $3 \times 2\sqrt{6 \times 3} = 6\sqrt{18} = 18\sqrt{2}$. To divide, we multiply both numerator and denominator by a value that will eliminate the radical:

$$\frac{18\sqrt{2} \times \sqrt{5}}{4\sqrt{5} \times \sqrt{5}} = \frac{18\sqrt{10}}{4 \times 5} = \frac{18\sqrt{10}}{20} = \frac{9\sqrt{10}}{10}$$

# Polynomials

## MONOMIALS AND POLYNOMIALS

A **monomial** is a single constant, variable, or product of constants and variables, such as 7, $x$, $2x$, or $x^3y$. There will never be addition or subtraction symbols in a monomial. Like monomials have like variables, but they may have different coefficients. A **polynomial** is a monomial or the result of combining two or more monomials by sums or differences. In a polynomial we call each monomial a **term**. Two terms make a **binomial** (e.g., $2x + 3y$), three terms make a **trinomial** (e.g., $5x^2 - 4x + 9$). The **degree of a monomial** is the sum of the exponents of the variables. The **degree of a polynomial** is the highest degree of any individual term.

> **Review Video: Polynomials**
> Visit mometrix.com/academy and enter code: 305005

## SIMPLIFYING POLYNOMIALS

Simplifying polynomials requires combining like terms. The like terms in a polynomial expression are those that have the same variables raised to the same powers. It is often helpful to connect the like terms with arrows or lines in order to separate them from the other monomials. Once you have determined the like terms, you can rearrange the polynomial by placing them together. Remember to include the sign that is in front of each term. Once the like terms are placed together, you can apply each operation and simplify. When adding and subtracting polynomials, only add and subtract the **coefficients**, or the number part; the variable and exponent stay the same.

## ADDING POLYNOMIALS

To add polynomials, you need to add like terms. These terms have the same variable part. For example, the terms $4x^2$ and $3x^2$ both include $x^2$ terms. To find the sum of like terms, find the sum of the coefficients. Then, keep the same variable part. You can use the distributive property to distribute the plus sign to each term of the polynomial. For example:

$(4x^2 - 5x + 7) + (3x^2 + 2x + 1) =$
$(4x^2 - 5x + 7) + 3x^2 + 2x + 1 =$
$(4x^2 + 3x^2) + (-5x + 2x) + (7 + 1) =$
$7x^2 - 3x + 8$

## SUBTRACTING POLYNOMIALS

To subtract polynomials, you need to subtract like terms. To find the difference of like terms, find the difference of the coefficients. Then, keep the same variable part. You can use the distributive property to distribute the minus sign to each term of the polynomial. For example:

$(-2x^2 - x + 5) - (3x^2 - 4x + 1) =$
$(-2x^2 - x + 5) - 3x^2 + 4x - 1 =$
$(-2x^2 - 3x^2) + (-x + 4x) + (5 - 1) =$
$-5x^2 + 3x + 4$

> **Review Video: Adding and Subtracting Polynomials**
> Visit mometrix.com/academy and enter code: 124088

## MULTIPLYING POLYNOMIALS

In general, multiplying polynomials is done by multiplying each term in one polynomial by each term in the other and adding the results. In the specific case for multiplying binomials, there is a useful acronym, FOIL, that

can help you make sure to cover each combination of terms. The **FOIL method** for $(Ax + By)(Cx + Dy)$ would be:

| | | | |
|---|---|---|---|
| **F** | Multiply the *first* terms of each binomial | $(\overset{first}{\widetilde{Ax}} + By)(\overset{first}{\widetilde{Cx}} + Dy)$ | $ACx^2$ |
| **O** | Multiply the *outer* terms | $(\overset{outer}{\widetilde{Ax}} + By)(Cx + \overset{outer}{\widetilde{Dy}})$ | $ADxy$ |
| **I** | Multiply the *inner* terms | $(Ax + \overset{inner}{\widetilde{By}})(\overset{inner}{\widetilde{Cx}} + Dy)$ | $BCxy$ |
| **L** | Multiply the *last* terms of each binomial | $(Ax + \overset{last}{\widetilde{By}})(Cx + \overset{last}{\widetilde{Dy}})$ | $BDy^2$ |

Then, add up the result of each and combine like terms: $ACx^2 + (AD + BC)xy + BDy^2$.

For example, using the FOIL method on binomials $(x + 2)$ and $(x - 3)$:

First: $(\boxed{x} + 2)(\boxed{x} + (-3)) \rightarrow (x)(x) = x^2$
Outer: $(\boxed{x} + 2)(x + \boxed{(-3)}) \rightarrow (x)(-3) = -3x$
Inner: $(x + \boxed{2})(\boxed{x} + (-3)) \rightarrow (2)(x) = 2x$
Last: $(x + \boxed{2})(x + \boxed{(-3)}) \rightarrow (2)(-3) = -6$

This results in: $(x^2) + (-3x) + (2x) + (-6)$

Combine like terms: $x^2 + (-3 + 2)x + (-6) = x^2 - x - 6$

> **Review Video: Multiplying Polynomials**
> Visit mometrix.com/academy and enter code: 598293
>
> **Review Video: Multiplying Terms Using the FOIL Method**
> Visit mometrix.com/academy and enter code: 854792

## DIVIDING POLYNOMIALS

Use long division to divide a polynomial by either a monomial or another polynomial of equal or lesser degree.

When **dividing by a monomial**, divide each term of the polynomial by the monomial.

> **Review Video: Dividing Monomials**
> Visit mometrix.com/academy and enter code: 584409

When **dividing by a polynomial**, begin by arranging the terms of each polynomial in order of one variable. You may arrange in ascending or descending order, but be consistent with both polynomials. To get the first term of the quotient, divide the first term of the dividend by the first term of the divisor. Multiply the first term of the quotient by the entire divisor and subtract that product from the dividend. Repeat for the second and successive terms until you either get a remainder of zero or a remainder whose degree is less than the degree of the divisor. If the quotient has a remainder, write the answer as a mixed expression in the form:

$$\text{quotient} + \frac{\text{remainder}}{\text{divisor}}$$

For example, we can evaluate the following expression in the same way as long division:

$$\frac{x^3 - 3x^2 - 2x + 5}{x - 5}$$

$$\begin{array}{r}
x^2 + 2x + 8 \phantom{)} \\
x - 5 \overline{\smash{)} x^3 - 3x^2 - 2x + 5} \\
\underline{-(x^3 - 5x^2)} \phantom{xxxxxxxxx} \\
2x^2 - 2x \phantom{xxxx} \\
\underline{-(2x^2 - 10x)} \phantom{xxx} \\
8x + 5 \\
\underline{-(8x - 40)} \\
45
\end{array}$$

$$\frac{x^3 - 3x^2 - 2x + 5}{x - 5} = x^2 + 2x + 8 + \frac{45}{x - 5}$$

> **Review Video: Dividing Polynomials by Monomials**
> Visit mometrix.com/academy and enter code: 253551
>
> **Review Video: Dividing Trinomials by Binomials**
> Visit mometrix.com/academy and enter code: 651465

When **factoring** a polynomial, first see whether you can factor out a nontrivial greatest common factor (GCF). For example, the trinomial $3x^5 - 18x^4 + 15x^3$ has a GCF of $3x^3$ since the GCF of 3, 18, and 15 is 3 and the GCF of $x^5$, $x^4$, and $x^3$ is $x^3$. Factoring out the GCF simplifies the expression to $3x^3(x^2 - 6x + 5)$.

To factor a quadratic trinomial (this comes up frequently), first check whether it is a perfect square trinomial (see bulleted list below). If not, see if you can factor it by trial and error by making clever choices of values for $a$ and $b$ (or $a$, $b$, $c$, and $d$) in the formulas below (this amounts to trying to use the FOIL mnemonic backwards):

$$x^2 + (a + b)x + ab = (x + a)(x + b)$$
$$(ac)x^2 + (ad + bc)x + bd = (ax + b)(cx + d)$$

For instance, you would try to factor the trinomial $x^2 - 6x + 5$ using the equation $x^2 + (a + b)x + ab = (x + a)(x + b)$. This means that you need to find integers $a$ and $b$ such that $a + b = -6$ and $ab = 5$. Starting with $ab = 5$, you can see that the only ways to write 5 as a product of integers are $(1)(5) = 5$ and $(-1)(-5) = 5$. So, it is easy to see that you want $a = -1$ and $b = -5$ since $a + b = -1 + (-5) = -6$ and $ab = (-1)(-5) = 5$. This tells you that $x^2 - 6x + 5 = (x - 1)(x - 5)$.

For polynomials with four terms (usually a cubic polynomial), sometimes factoring by grouping works: You group the two higher-power terms and the two lower-power terms, factor the GCF out of each group, and then factor out the resulting common binomial factor, if there is one. For example, $x^3 + 5x^2 + 3x + 15 = (x^3 + 5x^2) + (3x + 15) = x^2(x + 5) + 3(x + 5) = (x^2 + 3)(x + 5)$.

Once you have found the factors, write the original polynomial as the product of all the factors. Make sure all of the factors are either monomials, or else linear or irreducible quadratic polynomials (*irreducible* means they have no real zeros, which is easy to check with the quadratic formula). Check your work by multiplying the factors to make sure you get the original polynomial.

> **Review Video: Factoring Out Common Monomial Factors**
> Visit mometrix.com/academy and enter code: 398578
>
> **Review Video: Factoring Trinomials of the Form x^2+bx+c**
> Visit mometrix.com/academy and enter code: 270556

Below are patterns of some special products to remember to help make factoring easier:

- Perfect square trinomials: $x^2 + 2xy + y^2 = (x + y)^2$ or $x^2 - 2xy + y^2 = (x - y)^2$. For example, $x^2 + 10x + 25 = (x + 5)^2$.
- Difference between two squares: $x^2 - y^2 = (x + y)(x - y)$. For example, $x^2 - 9 = (x + 3)(x - 3)$.
- Sum of two cubes: $x^3 + y^3 = (x + y)(x^2 - xy + y^2)$. For example, $x^3 + 27 = (x + 3)(x^2 - 3x + 9)$.
  - Note: the second factor is *not* the same as a perfect square trinomial, so do not try to factor it further.
- Difference between two cubes: $x^3 - y^3 = (x - y)(x^2 + xy + y^2)$. For example, $x^3 - 1000 = (x - 10)(x^2 + 10x + 100)$.
  - Again, the second factor is *not* the same as a perfect square trinomial.
- Perfect cubes: $x^3 + 3x^2y + 3xy^2 + y^3 = (x + y)^3$ and $x^3 - 3x^2y + 3xy^2 - y^3 = (x - y)^3$

> **Review Video: Factoring the Difference of Two Squares**
> Visit mometrix.com/academy and enter code: 128954

## Advanced Functions

### STEP FUNCTIONS

The double brackets indicate a step function. For a step function, the value inside the double brackets is rounded down to the nearest integer. The graph of the function $f_0(x) = [\![x]\!]$ appears on the left graph. In comparison $f(x) = 2 [\![\frac{1}{3}(x - 1)]\!]$ is on the right graph. The coefficient of 2 shows that it's stretched vertically by a factor of 2 (so there's a vertical distance of 2 units between successive "steps"). The coefficient of $\frac{1}{3}$ in front of the $x$ shows that it's stretched horizontally by a factor of 3 (so each "step" is three units long), and the $x - 1$ shows that it's displaced one unit to the right.

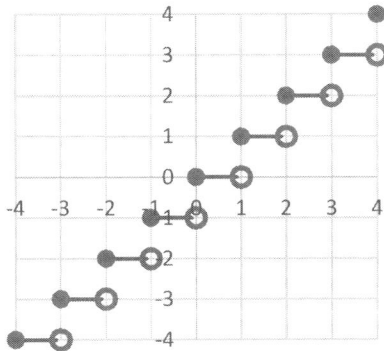
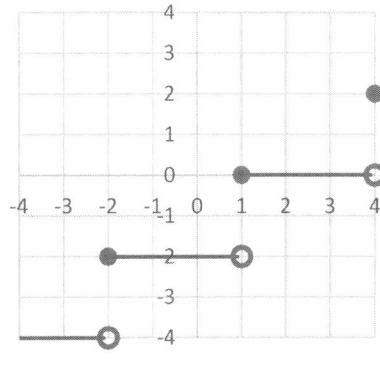

## TRANSCENDENTAL FUNCTIONS

Roughly speaking, algebraic functions are functions defined by formulas involving numbers and variables combined by addition, subtraction, multiplication, division, powers (but not variable powers), and roots. **Transcendental functions** are functions that are not algebraic. A function that includes logarithms, trigonometric functions, or variables as exponents, is transcendental, not algebraic, even if the function also includes polynomials or roots.

## EXPONENTIAL FUNCTIONS

**Exponential functions** are functions that have the form $y = b^x$, where base $b > 0$ and $b \neq 1$. The exponential function can also be written $f(x) = b^x$. The following properties apply to exponential expressions:

| Property | Description |
|---|---|
| $a^x a^y = a^{x+y}$ | The product of exponentials with the same base equals the base raised to the sum of the powers |
| $a^x / a^y = a^{x-y}$ | The quotient of exponentials with the same base equals the base raised to the difference of the powers |
| $(a^x)^y = a^{xy}$ | An exponential raised to a power equals the base raised to the product of the powers |
| $(ab)^x = a^x b^x$ | Exponentiation distributes over multiplication |
| $(a/b)^x = a^x / b^x$ | Exponentiation distributes over division |

The graph of an example exponential function, $f(x) = 2^x$, is below:

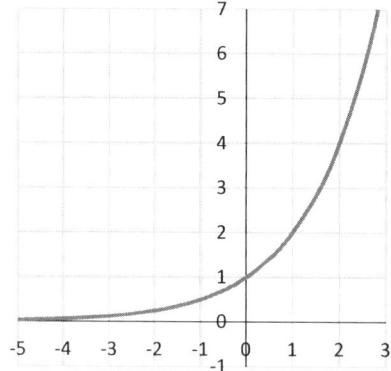

Note in the graph that the $y$-value approaches zero to the left and infinity to the right. One of the key features of an exponential function is that there will be one end that goes off to infinity and another that asymptotically approaches a lower bound. Common forms of exponential functions include the following:

**Geometric sequences**: The terms of a geometric sequence have the form $a_n = a_1 \times r^{n-1}$, where $a_n$ is the value of the $n^{\text{th}}$ term, $a_1$ is the initial term, and $r$ is the common ratio between succesive terms. Note that $a_1 \times r^{1-1} = a_1 \times r^0 = a_1 \times 1 = a_1$

> **Review Video: Geometric Sequences**
> Visit mometrix.com/academy and enter code: 140779

**General exponential growth or decay**: The general exponential growth or decay function is $f(t) = a(1 + r)^t$, where the value of $f(t)$ is the amount (of whatever quantity we are measuring) at time $t$, the constant $a$ is the initial amount (the amount at time $t = 0$), and the constant $r$ is the fixed rate of increase (if $r > 0$) or decrease (if $r < 0$) per unit time. For example, if we invest $1000 at an interest rate of 6% interest compounded annually and we measure time in years, then our investment will grow according to an exponential model with

$a = \$1000$ and $r = 6\% = 0.06$. Thus, after $t$ years the value of our investment will be $f(t) = \$1000(1 + 0.06)^t$. After 5 years, for instance, the investment will grow to $f(5) = \$1000(1 + 0.06)^5 \approx \$1338.23$.

**Compound interest**: We can modify the general exponential growth function above slightly to get a formula for interest compounded $n$ times per year. Replacing the constant $a$ with $P$ (for principal, the initial amount we invest), the total value of our investment after $t$ years is $f(t) = P\left(1 + \frac{r}{n}\right)^{nt}$, where $r$ is the nominal annual interest rate. Thus, if we change our \$1000 investment above by having the interest rate be 6% compounded *semiannually* (two times per year—so $n = 2$), the value of our investment after $t$ years is $f(t) = \$1000\left(1 + \frac{0.06}{2}\right)^{2t} = \$1000(1 + 0.03)^{2t}$. After 5 years, for instance, the investment will grow to $f(5) = \$1000(1 + 0.03)^{10} \approx \$1343.92$. This is slightly higher than the previous investment because the interest compounds twice as often.

> **Review Video: Compound Interest Formula**
> Visit mometrix.com/academy and enter code: 100366
>
> **Review Video: Interest Functions**
> Visit mometrix.com/academy and enter code: 559176

**Population growth and continuously compounded interest**: When a quantity grows (or decays) continuously at a rate that stays constant relative to the size the quantity has already attained, then we can model its size at time $t$ with the function $f(t) = ae^{rt}$, where $a$ is the initial amount, $r$ is the relative growth rate (which we often call simply the **growth rate**), and $e$ is the irrational constant known as Euler's number (approximately 2.718; scientific calculators have a button for finding $e^x$, which is known as the **natural exponential function**). For instance, under some circumstances, if an initial population (of people, plants, or animals, for example) of size $a$ grows at constant relative rate $r$, then the size of the population at time $t$ is $f(t) = ae^{rt}$. Similarly, if we invest principal $P$ (instead of $a$) for $t$ years at nominal annual interest rate $r$ compounded *continuously*, then after $t$ years the value of the investment is $f(t) = Pe^{rt}$.

For example, suppose the initial population of a town is $a = 1{,}200$ people and the relative annual growth rate is $r = 5\% = 0.05$. Then the population of the town after $t$ years is $f(t) = ae^{rt} = 1200e^{0.05t}$. After 10 years, for instance, the town population is $f(10) = 1200e^{0.05 \cdot 10} = 1200e^{0.5} \approx 1978$ people.

> **Review Video: Population Growth**
> Visit mometrix.com/academy and enter code: 109278

## LOGARITHMIC FUNCTIONS

The **logarithmic function base b** is the function $y = \log_b x$ or $f(x) = \log_b x$, where the base $b$ may be any positive number except one. The most common bases for logarithms are base 10 (the **common logarithm**) and base $e$ (the **natural logarithm**). We usually write the common logarithm as $y = \log x$ (that is, $\log x$, with no base listed, means $\log_{10} x$) and the natural logarithm as $y = \ln x$ (that is, $\ln x$ means $\log_e x$).

Exponential functions and logarithmic functions with the same base are inverse functions. That is, if $f(x) = b^x$, then $f^{-1}(x) = \log_b x$. This means that the two equations $y = b^x$ (exponential form) and $x = \log_b y$ (logarithmic form) express the same relationship between the quantities $x$ and $y$. We often solve problems involving logarithms by rewriting them in exponential form, and vice versa. Also, because of this inverse relationship, logarithms and exponentials cancel each other. That is, $\log_b b^x = x$ and $b^{\log_b x} = x$.

The following properties apply to logarithmic expressions:

| Property | Description |
|---|---|
| $\log_b 1 = 0$ | The log of 1 is equal to 0 for any base |
| $\log_b b = 1$ | The log of the base is equal to 1 |
| $\log_b b^p = p$ | The log of the base raised to a power is equal to that power |
| $\log_b MN = \log_b M + \log_b N$ | The log of a product is the sum of the log of each factor |
| $\log_b \frac{M}{N} = \log_b M - \log_b N$ | The log of a quotient is equal to the log of the dividend minus the log of the divisor |
| $\log_b M^p = p \log_b M$ | The log of a value raised to a power is equal to the power times the log of the value |

Logarithms are helpful in solving equations in which the variable appears in an exponent. For instance, consider the example above in which we model the population of a town by the function $f(t) = 1200e^{0.05t}$. Suppose we want to know how long it will take the population of the town to double to 2400 people from its original value of 1200. We find this by solving the equation $1200e^{0.05t} = 2400$. First, we divide both sides of the equation by 1200 to get $e^{0.05t} = 2$. Then we take natural logarithms of both sides to get $\ln e^{0.05t} = \ln 2$, which simplifies (because natural logarithms and natural exponentials are inverse functions) to $0.05t = \ln 2$. Finally, we divide both sides by 0.05 to get $t = (\ln 2)/0.05$, which we evaluate with a calculator to get $t \approx 13.9$ years.

The graph of an example logarithmic function, $f(x) = \log_2(x + 2)$, is below:

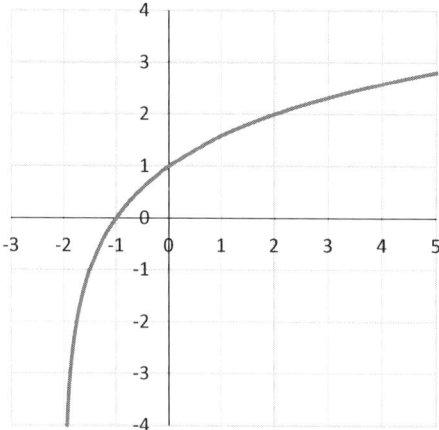

**Review Video: Logarithmic Function**
Visit mometrix.com/academy and enter code: 658985

## Congruence and Similarity

Congruent figures are geometric figures that have the same size and shape. For congruent polygons all corresponding angle measures are equal, and all corresponding side lengths are equal. Congruence is indicated by the symbol ≅. For instance, the expression $ABC \cong DEF$ indicates that the triangles below are congruent.

The order of the letters is important, indicating which parts of the polygons correspond to each other. For example, since the letters A and D both come first, ∠A and ∠D have the same measure.

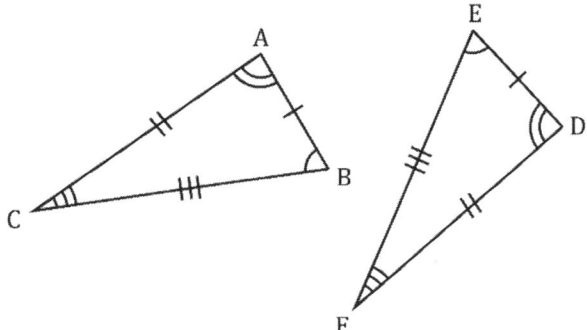

Similar figures are geometric figures that have the same shape, but do not necessarily have the same size. For similar polygons all corresponding angle measures are equal, and all corresponding side lengths are proportional, but they do not have to be equal. It is indicated by the symbol ~. For instance, the expression $ABC \sim DEF$ indicates that the triangles below are similar. Again, the order of the letters indicates which parts of the polygons correspond to each other.

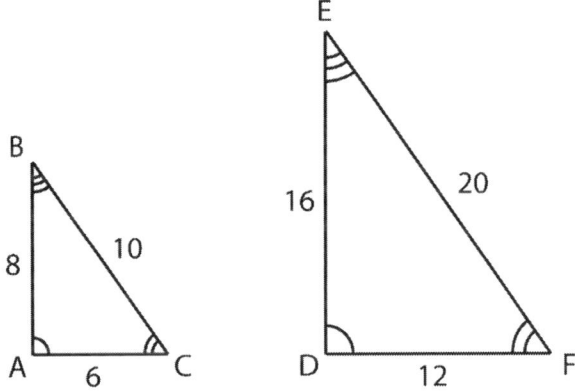

Note that all congruent figures are also similar, but not all similar figures are congruent.

| **Review Video: Congruent Shapes** |
|---|
| Visit mometrix.com/academy and enter code: 492281 |

## Triangle Properties

### CLASSIFICATIONS OF TRIANGLES

A **scalene triangle** is a triangle with no congruent sides. A scalene triangle will also have three angles of different measures. The angle with the largest measure is opposite the longest side, and the angle with the smallest measure is opposite the shortest side. An **acute triangle** is a triangle whose three angles are all less than 90°. If two of the angles are equal, the acute triangle is also an **isosceles triangle**. An isosceles triangle will also have two congruent angles opposite the two congruent sides. If the three angles are all equal, the acute triangle is also an **equilateral triangle**. An equilateral triangle will also have three congruent angles, each 60°. All equilateral triangles are also acute triangles. An **obtuse triangle** is a triangle with exactly one angle greater than 90°. The other two angles may or may not be equal. If the two remaining angles are equal, the obtuse triangle is also an isosceles triangle. A **right triangle** is a triangle with exactly one angle equal to 90°. All right triangles follow the Pythagorean theorem. A right triangle can never be acute or obtuse.

The table below illustrates how each descriptor places a different restriction on the triangle:

| Sides \ Angles | Acute: All angles < 90° | Obtuse: One angle > 90° | Right: One angle = 90° |
|---|---|---|---|
| **Scalene:** No equal side lengths | $90° > \angle a > \angle b > \angle c$ $x > y > z$ | $\angle a > 90° > \angle b > \angle c$ $x > y > z$ | $90° = \angle a > \angle b > \angle c$ $x > y > z$ |
| **Isosceles:** Two equal side lengths | $90° > \angle a, \angle b, \text{or } \angle c$ $\angle b = \angle c, \quad y = z$ | $\angle a > 90° > \angle b = \angle c$ $x > y = z$ | $\angle a = 90°$ $\angle b = \angle c = 45°$ $x > y = z$ |
| **Equilateral:** Three equal side lengths | $60° = \angle a = \angle b = \angle c$ $x = y = z$ | | |

**Review Video: Introduction to Types of Triangles**
Visit mometrix.com/academy and enter code: 511711

## GENERAL RULES FOR TRIANGLES

The **triangle inequality theorem** states that the sum of the measures of any two sides of a triangle is always greater than the measure of the third side. If the sum of the measures of two sides were equal to the third side, a triangle would be impossible because the two sides would lie flat across the third side and there would be no vertex. If the sum of the measures of two of the sides was less than the third side, a closed figure would be impossible because the two shortest sides would never meet. In other words, for a triangle with sides lengths $A$, $B$, and $C$: $A + B > C$, $B + C > A$, and $A + C > B$.

The sum of the measures of the interior angles of a triangle is always 180°. Therefore, a triangle can never have more than one angle greater than or equal to 90°.

In any triangle, the angles opposite congruent sides are congruent, and the sides opposite congruent angles are congruent. The largest angle is always opposite the longest side, and the smallest angle is always opposite the shortest side.

The line segment that joins the midpoints of any two sides of a triangle is always parallel to the third side and exactly half the length of the third side.

> **Review Video: General Rules (Triangle Inequality Theorem)**
> Visit mometrix.com/academy and enter code: 166488

## SIMILARITY AND CONGRUENCE RULES

**Similar triangles** are triangles whose corresponding angles are equal and whose corresponding sides are proportional. Represented by AAA. Similar triangles whose corresponding sides are congruent are also congruent triangles.

Triangles can be shown to be **congruent** in 5 ways:

- **SSS**: Three sides of one triangle are congruent to the three corresponding sides of the second triangle.
- **SAS**: Two sides and the included angle (the angle formed by those two sides) of one triangle are congruent to the corresponding two sides and included angle of the second triangle.
- **ASA**: Two angles and the included side (the side that joins the two angles) of one triangle are congruent to the corresponding two angles and included side of the second triangle.
- **AAS**: Two angles and a non-included side of one triangle are congruent to the corresponding two angles and non-included side of the second triangle.
- **HL**: The hypotenuse and leg of one right triangle are congruent to the corresponding hypotenuse and leg of the second right triangle.

> **Review Video: Similar Triangles**
> Visit mometrix.com/academy and enter code: 398538

# Trigonometric Functions

The basic trigonometric functions are sine (abbreviated 'sin'), cosine (abbreviated 'cos'), and tangent (abbreviated 'tan'). The simplest way to think of them is as describing the ratio of the side lengths of a right triangle in relation to the angles of the triangle.

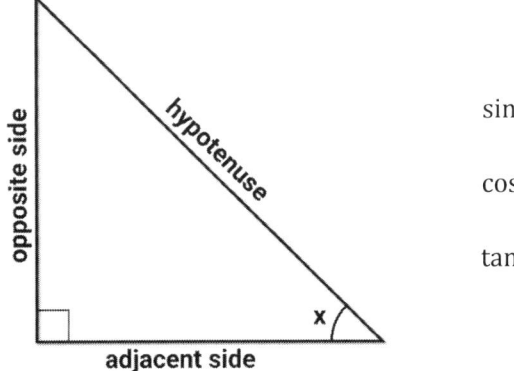

$$\sin x = \frac{\text{opposite side}}{\text{hypotenuse}}$$
$$\cos x = \frac{\text{adjacent side}}{\text{hypotenuse}}$$
$$\tan x = \frac{\text{opposite side}}{\text{adjacent side}}$$

## APPLYING TRIGONOMETRIC FUNCTIONS

Suppose we have a point $(x, y)$ at distance $r$ from the origin such that the line segment between this point and the origin forms an angle of measure $\theta$ with the positive $x$-axis (We allow $\theta$ to be any real number, with the angle measured counterclockwise from the $x$-axis if $\theta > 0$ and clockwise if $\theta < 0$). Then we can define the trigonometric functions sine, cosine, and tangent by the formulas $\sin \theta = y/r$, $\cos \theta = x/r$, and $\tan \theta = y/x$ (and their reciprocal functions cosecant, secant, and cotangent accordingly). These functions are periodic because increasing the angle $\theta$ by $2\pi$ radians (that is, 360°) turns the line segment all the way around the origin so that it ends at the same point $(x, y)$ again.

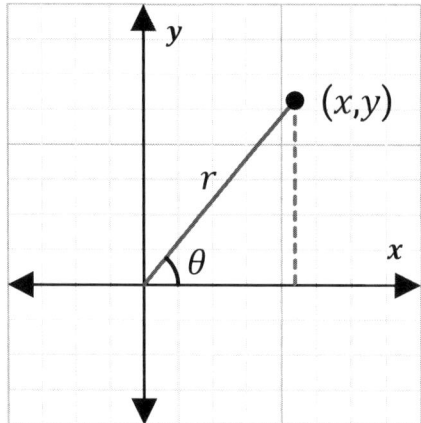

If the angle in the above diagram is acute, we can think of the line segment as the hypotenuse of a right triangle so that we get the familiar formulas $\sin \theta =$ (opposite leg)/hypotenuse, $\cos \theta =$ (adjacent leg)/hypotenuse, and $\tan \theta =$ (opposite leg)/(adjacent leg). In this form, the trigonometric functions are useful for finding missing sides of triangles. For example, suppose that standing 30 feet from the base of a tree, we have to look up at a 58° angle to see the top of the tree (see diagram). If we let $x$ be the height of the tree, then we get the equation $\tan 58° = x/(30 \text{ feet})$. Multiplying both sides of the equation by 30 gives us the height of the tree, namely, $x = 30 \tan 58° \approx 48$ feet.

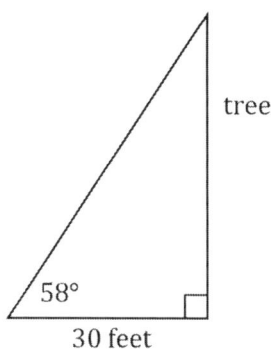

## GRAPHING TRIGONOMETRIC FUNCTIONS
### SINE

To graph the sine function, we let $x$ (rather than $\theta$) be the angle measure (usually in radians) and $y$ be the value of the sine. That is, we graph the equation $y = \sin x$. From the definition of sine above we can show that $\sin 0 = 0$, $\sin(\pi/2) = 1$, $\sin \pi = 0$, $\sin(3\pi/2) = -1$, and $\sin 2\pi = 0$. Thus, the graph of the sine function begins at the origin, peaks at the point $(\pi/2, 1)$, crosses the $x$-axis at $(\pi, 0)$, has its lowest point at $(3\pi/2, -1)$, and returns to the $x$-axis at $(2\pi, 0)$. Because the sine function is periodic with period $2\pi$ radians (or 360°), this curve represents one complete cycle of the graph. The remainder of the graph of $y = \sin x$ consists of infinitely many repetitions of this cycle, producing the familiar "sine wave."

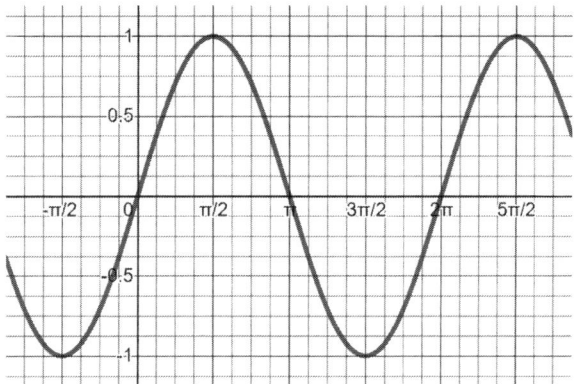

**Review Video: Sine**
Visit mometrix.com/academy and enter code: 193339

By suitable choice of the parameters $A$, $B$, $C$, and $D$, we can construct a "custom" sine function $y = A \sin(Bx + C) + D$ with any desired amplitude (the vertical distance the curve extends above and below its midline), period (distance between successive peaks), phase shift (horizontal shift), and midline (the horizontal line halfway between the peaks and troughs).

## COSINE

Similarly, the graph of the cosine function is the graph of the equation $y = \cos x$. Proceeding as above, we get a graph with the same shape as that of the sine function but shifted by $\pi/2$ to the left.

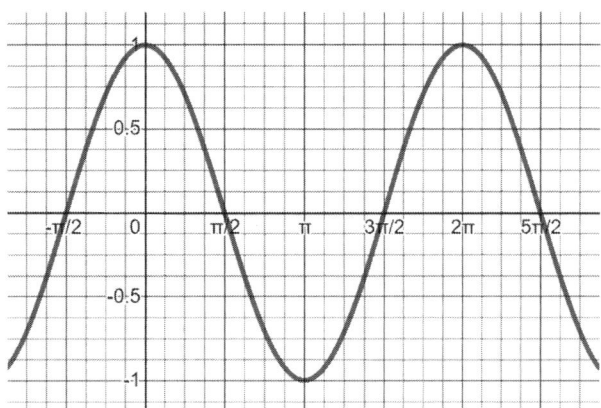

**Review Video: Cosine**
Visit mometrix.com/academy and enter code: 361120

As for the sine function, we can construct custom cosine graphs with desired amplitude, period, phase shift, and midline by choosing suitable values of the parameters in the equation $y = A \cos(Bx + C) + D$.

## TANGENT

The graph of the tangent function (that is, the graph of the equation $y = \tan x$) turns out to be periodic with period $\pi$ radians (or 180°). It consists of an infinite sequence of smooth curves crossing the $x$-axis at every multiple of $\pi$ radians (180°) and having as asymptotes the vertical lines $x = \frac{k\pi}{2}$ radians ($x = k \times 90°$), for every odd integer $k$ (which also means that the domain of the tangent function excludes these $x$-values).

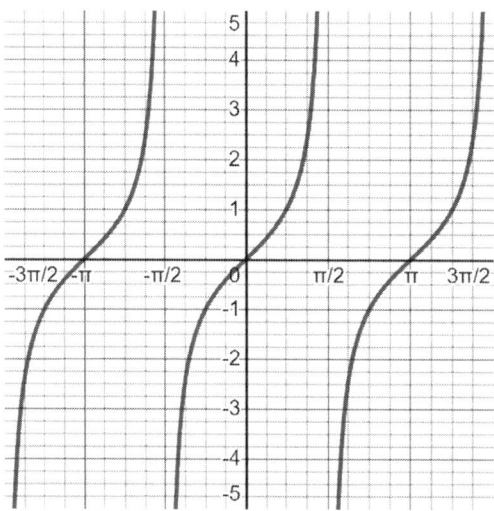

**Review Video: Tangent**
Visit mometrix.com/academy and enter code: 947639

# Circle Properties

## ARCS

An **arc** is a portion of a circle. Specifically, an arc is the set of points between and including two points on a circle. An arc does not contain any points inside the circle. When a segment is drawn from the endpoints of an arc to the center of the circle, a sector is formed. A **minor arc** is an arc that has a measure less than 180°. A **major arc** is an arc that has a measure of at least 180°. Every minor arc has a corresponding major arc that can be found by subtracting the measure of the minor arc from 360°. A **semicircle** is an arc whose endpoints are the endpoints of the diameter of a circle. A semicircle is exactly half of a circle.

**Arc length** is the length of that portion of the circumference between two points on the circle. The formula for arc length is $s = \frac{\pi r \theta}{180°}$, where $s$ is the arc length, $r$ is the length of the radius, and $\theta$ is the angular measure of the arc in degrees, or $s = r\theta$, where $\theta$ is the angular measure of the arc in radians ($2\pi$ radians = 360 degrees).

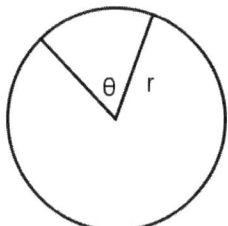

## ANGLES OF CIRCLES

A **central angle** is an angle whose vertex is the center of a circle and whose legs intercept an arc of the circle. The measure of a central angle is equal to the measure of the minor arc it intercepts.

An **inscribed angle** is an angle whose vertex lies on a circle and whose legs contain chords of that circle. The portion of the circle intercepted by the legs of the angle is called the intercepted arc. The measure of the intercepted arc is exactly twice the measure of the inscribed angle. In the following diagram, angle $ABC$ is an inscribed angle. $\widehat{AC} = 2(m\angle ABC)$.

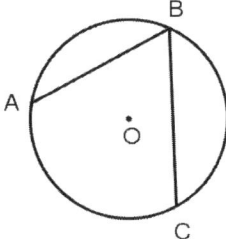

Any angle inscribed in a semicircle is a right angle. The intercepted arc is 180°, making the inscribed angle half that, or 90°. In the diagram below, angle $ABC$ is inscribed in semicircle $ABC$, making angle $ABC$ equal to 90°.

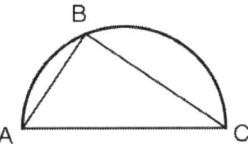

> **Review Video: Arcs and Angles of Circles**
> Visit mometrix.com/academy and enter code: 652838

## SECANTS, CHORDS, AND TANGENTS

A **secant** is a line that intersects a circle in two points. The segment of a secant line that is contained within the circle is called a **chord**. Two secants may intersect inside the circle, on the circle, or outside the circle. When the two secants intersect on the circle, an inscribed angle is formed. When two secants intersect inside a circle, the measure of each of two vertical angles is equal to half the sum of the two intercepted arcs. Consider the following diagram where $m\angle AEB = \frac{1}{2}(\widehat{AB} + \widehat{CD})$ and $m\angle BEC = \frac{1}{2}(\widehat{BC} + \widehat{AD})$.

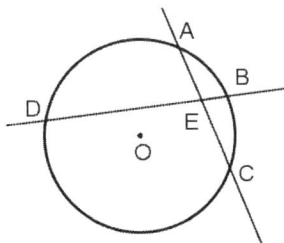

When two secants intersect outside a circle, the measure of the angle formed is equal to half the difference of the two arcs that lie between the two secants. In the diagram below, $m\angle AEB = \frac{1}{2}(\widehat{AB} - \widehat{CD})$.

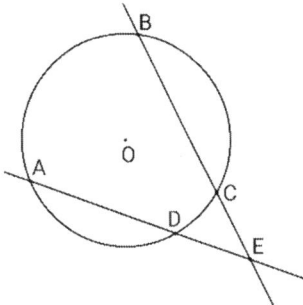

A **tangent** is a line in the same plane as a circle that touches the circle in exactly one point. The point at which a tangent touches a circle is called the **point of tangency**. While a line segment can be tangent to a circle as part of a line that is tangent, it is improper to say a tangent can be simply a line segment that touches the circle in exactly one point.

In the diagram below, $\overleftrightarrow{EB}$ is a secant and contains chord $\overline{EB}$, and $\overleftrightarrow{CD}$ is tangent to circle $A$. Notice that $\overline{FB}$ is not tangent to the circle. $\overline{FB}$ is a line segment that touches the circle in exactly one point, but if the segment were extended, it would touch the circle in a second point. In the diagram below, point $B$ is the point of tangency.

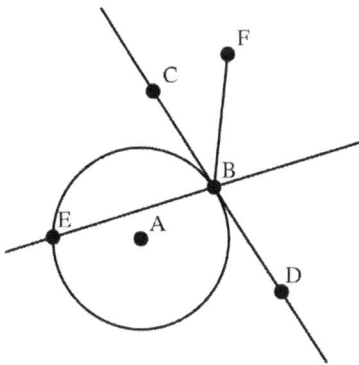

> **Review Video: Secants, Chords, and Tangents**
> Visit mometrix.com/academy and enter code: 258360
>
> **Review Video: Tangent Lines of a Circle**
> Visit mometrix.com/academy and enter code: 780167

## SECTORS

A **sector** is the portion of a circle formed by two radii and their intercepted arc. While the arc length is exclusively the points that are also on the circumference of the circle, the sector is the entire area bounded by the arc and the two radii.

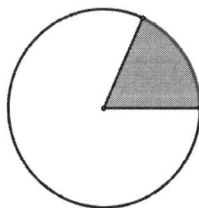

The **area of a sector** of a circle is found by the formula, $A = \frac{\theta r^2}{2}$, where $A$ is the area, $\theta$ is the measure of the central angle in radians, and $r$ is the radius. To find the area with the central angle in degrees, use the formula, $A = \frac{\theta \pi r^2}{360}$, where $\theta$ is the measure of the central angle and $r$ is the radius.

## Trigonometric Formulas

In the diagram below, angle $C$ is the right angle, and side $c$ is the hypotenuse. Side $a$ is the side opposite to angle $A$ and side $b$ is the side opposite to angle $B$. Using ratios of side lengths as a means to calculate the sine, cosine, and tangent of an acute angle only works for right triangles.

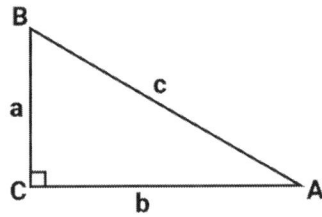

$$\sin A = \frac{\text{opposite side}}{\text{hypotenuse}} = \frac{a}{c} \qquad \csc A = \frac{1}{\sin A} = \frac{\text{hypotenuse}}{\text{opposite side}} = \frac{c}{a}$$

$$\cos A = \frac{\text{adjacent side}}{\text{hypotenuse}} = \frac{b}{c} \qquad \sec A = \frac{1}{\cos A} = \frac{\text{hypotenuse}}{\text{adjacent side}} = \frac{c}{b}$$

$$\tan A = \frac{\text{opposite side}}{\text{adjacent side}} = \frac{a}{b} \qquad \cot A = \frac{1}{\tan A} = \frac{\text{adjacent side}}{\text{opposite side}} = \frac{b}{a}$$

### LAWS OF SINES AND COSINES

The **law of sines** states that $\frac{\sin A}{a} = \frac{\sin B}{b} = \frac{\sin C}{c}$, where $A$, $B$, and $C$ are the angles of a triangle, and $a$, $b$, and $c$ are the sides opposite their respective angles. This formula will work with all triangles, not just right triangles.

The **law of cosines** is given by the formula $c^2 = a^2 + b^2 - 2ab(\cos C)$, where $a$, $b$, and $c$ are the sides of a triangle, and $C$ is the angle opposite side $c$. This is a generalized form of the Pythagorean theorem that can be used on any triangle.

> **Review Video: Law of Sines**
> Visit mometrix.com/academy and enter code: 206844
>
> **Review Video: Law of Cosines**
> Visit mometrix.com/academy and enter code: 158911

## The Unit Circle

### DEGREES, RADIANS, AND THE UNIT CIRCLE

It is important to understand the deep connection between trigonometry and circles. Specifically, the two main units, **degrees** (°) and **radians** (rad), that are used to measure angles are related this way: 360° in one full circle and $2\pi$ radians in one full circle: ($360° = 2\pi$ rad). The conversion factor relating the two is often stated as $\frac{180°}{\pi}$. For example, to convert $\frac{3\pi}{2}$ radians to degrees, multiply by the conversion factor: $\frac{3\pi}{2} \times \frac{180°}{\pi} = 270°$. As another example, to convert 60° to radians, divide by the conversion factor or multiply by the reciprocal: $60° \times \frac{\pi}{180°} = \frac{\pi}{3}$ radians.

Recall that the standard equation for a circle is $(x-h)^2 + (y-k)^2 = r^2$. A **unit circle** is a circle with a radius of 1 ($r = 1$) that has its center at the origin ($h = 0, k = 0$). Thus, the equation for the unit circle simplifies from the standard equation down to $x^2 + y^2 = 1$.

**Standard position** is the position of an angle of measure $\theta$ whose vertex is at the origin, the initial side crosses the unit circle at the point $(1, 0)$, and the terminal side crosses the unit circle at some other point $(a, b)$. In the standard position, $\sin \theta = b$, $\cos \theta = a$, and $\tan \theta = \frac{b}{a}$.

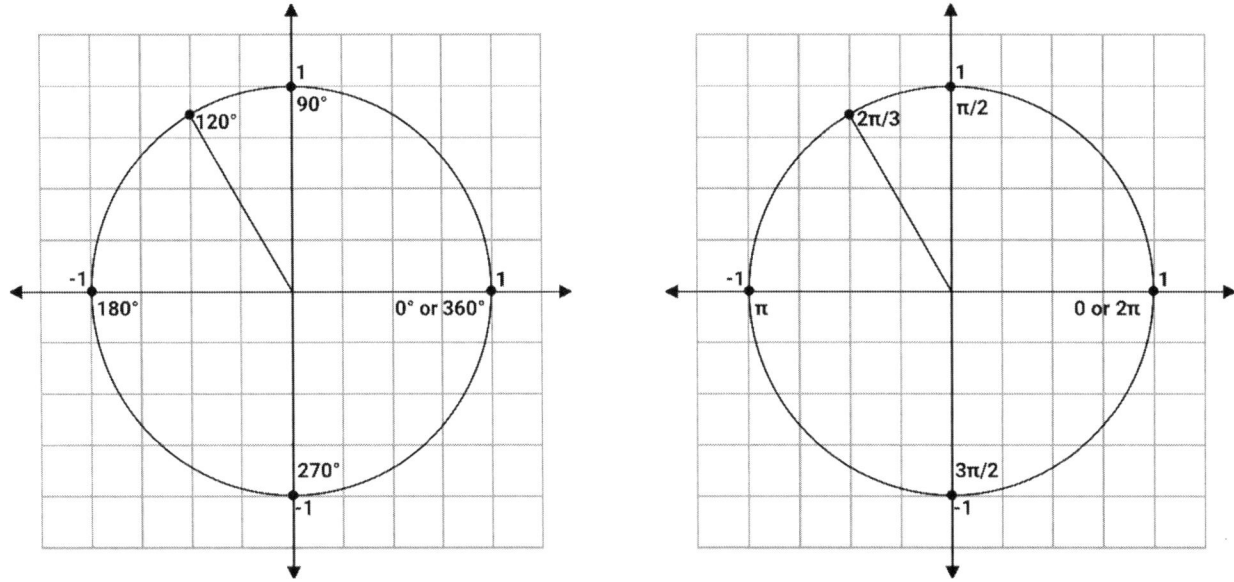

> **Review Video: Unit Circle**
> Visit mometrix.com/academy and enter code: 333922

### TABLE OF COMMONLY ENCOUNTERED ANGLES

$0° = 0$ radians, $30° = \frac{\pi}{6}$ radians, $45° = \frac{\pi}{4}$ radians, $60° = \frac{\pi}{3}$ radians, and $90° = \frac{\pi}{2}$ radians

| | | |
|---|---|---|
| $\sin 0° = 0$ | $\cos 0° = 1$ | $\tan 0° = 0$ |
| $\sin 30° = \frac{1}{2}$ | $\cos 30° = \frac{\sqrt{3}}{2}$ | $\tan 30° = \frac{\sqrt{3}}{3}$ |
| $\sin 45° = \frac{\sqrt{2}}{2}$ | $\cos 45° = \frac{\sqrt{2}}{2}$ | $\tan 45° = 1$ |
| $\sin 60° = \frac{\sqrt{3}}{2}$ | $\cos 60° = \frac{1}{2}$ | $\tan 60° = \sqrt{3}$ |
| $\sin 90° = 1$ | $\cos 90° = 0$ | $\tan 90° = $ undefined |
| $\csc 0° = $ undefined | $\sec 0° = 1$ | $\cot 0° = $ undefined |
| $\csc 30° = 2$ | $\sec 30° = \frac{2\sqrt{3}}{3}$ | $\cot 30° = \sqrt{3}$ |
| $\csc 45° = \sqrt{2}$ | $\sec 45° = \sqrt{2}$ | $\cot 45° = 1$ |
| $\csc 60° = \frac{2\sqrt{3}}{3}$ | $\sec 60° = 2$ | $\cot 60° = \frac{\sqrt{3}}{3}$ |
| $\csc 90° = 1$ | $\sec 90° = $ undefined | $\cot 90° = 0$ |

The values in the upper half of this table are values you should have memorized or be able to find quickly and those in the lower half can easily be determined as the reciprocal of the corresponding function.

# Trigonometric Identities

## SUM AND DIFFERENCE

To find the sine, cosine, or tangent of the sum or difference of two angles, use one of the following formulas where $\alpha$ and $\beta$ are two angles with known sine, cosine, or tangent values as needed:

$$\sin(\alpha \pm \beta) = \sin\alpha \cos\beta \pm \cos\alpha \sin\beta$$
$$\cos(\alpha \pm \beta) = \cos\alpha \cos\beta \mp \sin\alpha \sin\beta$$
$$\tan(\alpha \pm \beta) = \frac{\tan\alpha \pm \tan\beta}{1 \mp \tan\alpha \tan\beta}$$

## HALF ANGLE

To find the sine or cosine of half of a known angle, use the following formulas where $\theta$ is an angle with a known exact cosine value:

$$\sin\left(\frac{\theta}{2}\right) = \pm\sqrt{\frac{(1-\cos\theta)}{2}}$$

$$\cos\left(\frac{\theta}{2}\right) = \pm\sqrt{\frac{(1+\cos\theta)}{2}}$$

To determine the sign of the answer, you must recognize which quadrant the given angle is in and apply the correct sign for the trigonometric function you are using. If you need to find an expression for the exact sine or cosine of an angle that you do not know, such as sine 22.5°, you can rewrite the given angle as a half angle, such as $\sin\left(\frac{45°}{2}\right)$, and use the formula above:

$$\sin\left(\frac{45°}{2}\right) = \pm\sqrt{\frac{(1-\cos(45°))}{2}} = \pm\sqrt{\frac{\left(1-\frac{\sqrt{2}}{2}\right)}{2}} = \pm\sqrt{\frac{(2-\sqrt{2})}{4}} = \pm\frac{1}{2}\sqrt{(2-\sqrt{2})}$$

To find the tangent or cotangent of half of a known angle, use the following formulas where $\theta$ is an angle with known exact sine and cosine values:

$$\tan\frac{\theta}{2} = \frac{\sin\theta}{1+\cos\theta}$$
$$\cot\frac{\theta}{2} = \frac{\sin\theta}{1-\cos\theta}$$

These formulas will work for finding the tangent or cotangent of half of any angle unless the cosine of $\theta$ happens to make the denominator of the identity equal to 0.

The Pythagorean theorem states that $a^2 + b^2 = c^2$ for all right triangles. The trigonometric identity that derives from this principle is stated in this way: $\sin^2\theta + \cos^2\theta = 1$.

Dividing each term by either $\sin^2\theta$ or $\cos^2\theta$ yields two other identities, respectively:

$$1 + \cot^2\theta = \csc^2\theta$$
$$\tan^2\theta + 1 = \sec^2\theta$$

> **Review Video: Sum and Difference Trigonometric Identities**
> Visit mometrix.com/academy and enter code: 468838

## DOUBLE ANGLES

In each case, use one of the double angle formulas. To find the sine or cosine of twice a known angle, use one of the following formulas:

$$\sin(2\theta) = 2\sin\theta\cos\theta$$

$$\cos(2\theta) = \cos^2\theta - \sin^2\theta$$
$$= 2\cos^2\theta - 1$$
$$= 1 - 2\sin^2\theta$$

To find the tangent or cotangent of twice a known angle, use the formulas where $\theta$ is an angle with known exact sine, cosine, tangent, and cotangent values:

$$\tan(2\theta) = \frac{2\tan\theta}{1 - \tan^2\theta}$$
$$\cot(2\theta) = \frac{\cot\theta - \tan\theta}{2}$$

## PRODUCTS

To find the product of the sines and cosines of two different angles, use one of the following formulas where $\alpha$ and $\beta$ are two unique angles:

$$\sin\alpha\sin\beta = \frac{1}{2}[\cos(\alpha - \beta) - \cos(\alpha + \beta)]$$
$$\cos\alpha\cos\beta = \frac{1}{2}[\cos(\alpha + \beta) + \cos(\alpha - \beta)]$$
$$\sin\alpha\cos\beta = \frac{1}{2}[\sin(\alpha + \beta) + \sin(\alpha - \beta)]$$
$$\cos\alpha\sin\beta = \frac{1}{2}[\sin(\alpha + \beta) - \sin(\alpha - \beta)]$$

> **Review Video: Half-Angle, Double Angle, and Product Trig Identities**
> Visit mometrix.com/academy and enter code: 274252

## COMPLEMENTARY

The trigonometric cofunction identities use the trigonometric relationships of complementary angles (angles whose sum is 90°). These are:

$$\cos x = \sin(90° - x)$$
$$\csc x = \sec(90° - x)$$
$$\cot x = \tan(90° - x)$$

## Domain, Range, and Asymptotes in Trigonometry

The domain is the set of all possible real number values of $x$ on the graph of a trigonometric function. Some graphs will impose limits on the values of $x$.

The range is the set of all possible real number values of $y$ on the graph of a trigonometric function. Some graphs will impose limits on the values of $y$.

Asymptotes are lines that the graph of a trigonometric function approaches but never reaches. Asymptotes exist for values of $x$ in the graphs of the tangent, cotangent, secant, and cosecant. The sine and cosine graphs do not have any asymptotes.

### DOMAIN, RANGE, AND ASYMPTOTES OF THE SIX TRIGONOMETRIC FUNCTIONS

The domain, range, and asymptotes for each of the trigonometric functions are as follows:

- In the **sine** function, the domain is all real numbers, the range is $-1 \leq y \leq 1$, and there are no asymptotes.
- In the **cosine** function, the domain is all real numbers, the range is $-1 \leq y \leq 1$, and there are no asymptotes.
- In the **tangent** function, the domain is $x \in \mathbb{R}; x \neq \frac{\pi}{2} + k\pi$, the range is all real numbers, and the asymptotes are the lines $x = \frac{\pi}{2} + k\pi$.
- In the **cosecant** function, the domain is $x \in \mathbb{R}; x \neq k\pi$, the range is $(-\infty, -1]$ and $[1, \infty)$, and the asymptotes are the lines $x = k\pi$.
- In the **secant** function, the domain is $x \in \mathbb{R}; x \neq \frac{\pi}{2} + k\pi$, the range is $(-\infty, 1]$ and $[1, \infty)$, and the asymptotes are the lines $x = \frac{\pi}{2} + k\pi$.
- In the **cotangent** function, the domain is $x \in \mathbb{R}; x \neq k\pi$, the range is all real numbers, and the asymptotes are the lines $x = k\pi$.

In each of the above cases, $k$ represents any integer.

## Chapter Quiz

Ready to see how well you retained what you just read? Scan the QR code to go directly to the chapter quiz interface for this study guide. If you're using a computer, simply visit the online resources page at mometrix.com/resources719/accuplacer-28992 and click the Chapter Quizzes link.

# Practice Test #1

Want to take this practice test in an online interactive format?
Check out the online resources page, which includes interactive practice questions
and much more: **mometrix.com/resources719/accuplacer-28992**

## Reading Placement Test

*Refer to the following for questions 1–4:*

But all this—the mysterious, far-reaching hair-line trail, the absence of sun from the sky, the tremendous cold, and the strangeness and weirdness of it all—made no impression on the man. It was not because he was long used to it. He was a newcomer in the land, a chechaquo, and this was his first winter. The trouble with him was that he was without imagination. He was quick and alert in the things of life, but only in the things, and not in the significances. Fifty degrees below zero meant eighty-odd degrees of frost. Such fact impressed him as being cold and uncomfortable, and that was all. It did not lead him to meditate upon his frailty as a creature of temperature, and upon man's frailty in general, able only to live within certain narrow limits of heat and cold; and from there on it did not lead him to the conjectural field of immortality and man's place in the universe. Fifty degrees below zero stood for a bite of frost that hurt and that must be guarded against by the use of mittens, ear-flaps, warm moccasins, and thick socks. Fifty degrees below zero was to him just precisely fifty degrees below zero. That there should be anything more to it than that was a thought that never entered his head.

. . . .

At the man's heels trotted a dog, a big native husky, the proper wolf-dog, gray-coated and without any visible or temperamental difference from its brother, the wild wolf. The animal was depressed by the tremendous cold. It knew that it was no time for travelling. Its instinct told it a truer tale than was told to the man by the man's judgment. In reality, it was not merely colder than fifty below zero; it was colder than sixty below, than seventy below. It was seventy-five below zero. Since the freezing-point is thirty-two above zero, it meant that one hundred and seven degrees of frost obtained. The dog did not know anything about thermometers. Possibly in its brain there was no sharp consciousness of a condition of very cold such as was in the man's brain. But the brute had its instinct. It experienced a vague but menacing apprehension that subdued it and made it slink along at the man's heels, and that made it question eagerly every unwonted movement of the man as if expecting him to go into camp or to seek shelter somewhere and build a fire. The dog had learned fire, and it wanted fire, or else to burrow under the snow and cuddle its warmth away from the air.

[Adapted from Jack London, "To Build a Fire" (1902)]

**1. What is the point of view used in this passage?**
   a. First person
   b. First person plural
   c. Third person limited
   d. Third person omniscient

## 2. What message does the passage reflect when it mentions immortality and man's place in the universe?

a. Humans are frail.
b. Humans are stronger than nature.
c. Humans will one day attain immortality.
d. Humans are smarter than animals.

## 3. In what way does the narrator say the dog is better off than the man?

a. The dog is better equipped for the cold because of its fur.
b. The dog has a better conscious idea of what the cold means.
c. The dog's instinct guides it, while the man's intellect fails him.
d. The dog understands mankind's place in the universe.

## 4. Which statement best captures the author's meaning in the statement, "The trouble with him was that he was without imagination"?

I. The man was not smart.
II. The man did not need imagination because he was rational.
III. The man did not have the foresight to realize that he was putting himself in danger.

a. I only
b. II only
c. III only
d. I and II

*Refer to the following for questions 5–8:*

### Forest Manager

Salvage logging is removing dead or dying forest stands that are left behind by a fire or disease. This practice has been used for several decades. These dead or dying trees become fuel that feeds future fires. The best way to lower the risk of forest fires is to remove the dead timber from the forest floor. Salvage logging followed by replanting ensures the reestablishment of desirable tree species.

For example, planting conifers accelerates the return of fire-resistant forests. Harvesting timber helps forests by reducing fuel load, thinning the forest stands, and relieving competition between trees. Burned landscapes leave black surfaces and ash layers that have very high soil temperatures. These high soil temperatures can kill many plant species. Logging mixes the soil. So, this lowers surface temperatures to more normal levels. The shade from material that is left behind by logging also helps to lower surface temperatures. After an area has been salvage logged, seedlings in the area start to grow almost immediately. However, this regrowth can take several years in areas that are not managed well.

### Ecology Professor

Salvage logging moves material like small, broken branches to the forest floor. These pieces can become fuel for more fires. The removal of larger, less flammable trees leaves behind small limbs and increases the risk of forest fires. In unmanaged areas, these pieces are found more commonly on the tops of trees where they are unavailable to fires. Logging destroys old forests that are more resistant to wildfires. So, this creates younger forests that are more open to fires. In old forests, branches of bigger trees are higher above the floor where fires may not reach.

Replanting after wildfires creates monoculture plantations where only a single crop is planted. This monoculture allows less biological diversity. Also, it allows plants to be less resistant to disease. So, this increases the chance of fire. Salvage logging also upsets natural forest regrowth by killing most of the seedlings that grow after a wildfire. It breaks up the soil and increases erosion. Also, it removes most of the shade that is needed for young seedlings to grow.

**5. Which of the following is NOT a supporting detail for the forest manager's argument?**
   a. "This practice has been used for decades."
   b. "Logging mixes the soil. So, this lowers surface temperatures to more normal levels."
   c. "After an area has been salvage logged, seedlings in the area start to grow almost immediately."
   d. "Salvage logging is removing dead or dying forest stands that are left behind by a fire or disease."

**6. A study compared two plots of land that were managed differently after a fire. Plot A was salvage logged. Plot B was left unmanaged. After a second fire, they compared two plant groups between Plots A and B. They found that both plant groups burned worse in Plot A than in Plot B. Whose viewpoint do these results support?**
   a. Only the manager
   b. Only the professor
   c. Both the manager and professor
   d. Neither the manager nor the professor

**7. What is the main idea of the forest manager's argument?**
   a. Salvage logging is helpful because it removes dead or dying timber from the forest floor. So, this lowers the risk of future fires.
   b. Salvage logging is helpful because it has been practiced for many decades.
   c. Salvage logging is harmful because it raises soil temperatures above normal levels. So, this threatens the health of plant species.
   d. Salvage logging is helpful because it gives shade for seedlings to grow after a wildfire.

**8. Whose viewpoints would potentially be confirmed by a future study looking at the spreading out and regrowth of seedlings for many years after a wildfire in managed and unmanaged forests?**
   a. Only the manager
   b. Only the professor
   c. Both the manager and professor
   d. Neither the manager nor professor

*Refer to the following for question 9:*

> Alexander the Great died in Babylon at the age of 32 in 323 BC. He had been sick and febrile for two weeks prior to his death. Much speculation exists regarding his cause of death. Poisoning, assassination, and a number of infectious diseases have been posited. An incident mentioned by Plutarch may provide a significant clue. Shortly before his illness, as Alexander entered the city of Babylon, he was met by a flock of ravens. The birds behaved strangely, and many came to die at his feet. The strange behavior of these birds, taken as an ill omen at the time, is similar to the illness and death of birds observed in the United States in the weeks preceding the identification of the first human cases of the West Nile virus. This information suggests that Alexander the Great may have died of encephalitis caused by the West Nile virus.

**9. The main purpose of this passage is to**
   a. describe the symptoms of West Nile virus encephalitis.
   b. describe an incident involving birds and Alexander the Great.
   c. propose a cause for the death of Alexander the Great.
   d. connect Alexander the Great and Plutarch.

*Refer to the following for question 10:*

The loss of barrier islands through erosion poses a serious challenge to many communities along the Atlantic and Gulf Coasts. Along with marshes and wetlands, these islands protect coastal towns from major storms. In the past seventy years, Louisiana alone has lost almost 2,000 square miles of coastal land to hurricanes and flooding. More than 100 square miles of wetlands protecting the city of New Orleans were wiped out by a single storm, Hurricane Katrina. Due to this exposure of coastal communities, recent hurricane seasons have proven the most expensive on record: annual losses since 2005 have been estimated in the hundreds of billions of dollars. This unfortunate trend is likely to continue, since meteorological research shows that the Atlantic basin is in an active storm period that could continue for decades.

**10. The passage describes recent hurricane seasons as the most expensive on record. Which of the following statements gives the implied reason for this increased expense?**
   a. Hurricane Katrina was an extremely violent storm.
   b. Valuable buildings were destroyed in New Orleans.
   c. The Atlantic Basin is entering an active period.
   d. Destruction of barrier islands and coastal wetlands has left the mainland exposed.

**11. The provision of this bill that prevents any nonprofit recipient of a housing grant from conducting voter registration is an outrageous, undemocratic amendment that imposes restrictions on promoting the most fundamental of our civil liberties, the right to vote. This provision forbids any nonprofits from even applying for a grant if they have encouraged voting in the recent past. Restricting the prerogatives of nonprofits in this way is a violation of the First Amendment rights of these organizations. There is absolutely no justification for preventing the efforts of nonprofit organizations to encourage civic activities such as voting.**

**What is the author's tone?**
   a. Entertaining
   b. Angry
   c. Informative
   d. Apologetic

*Refer to the following for question 12:*

The selection of trees for planting in urban areas poses severe challenges due to soil adversities and space restrictions both above and below ground. Restricted spaces, especially in "downtown" areas or in densely built neighborhoods, make selecting, planting, and managing trees in urban areas difficult. Urban sites pose adversities that severely constrain the palette of suitable trees. As a result, an urgent need exists to find tough, small species of trees for urban spaces. Dwarf forms of native species have not been utilized greatly, and some foreign species may prove to be appropriate.

**12. In the last sentence, which of the following statements does the author imply regarding dwarf forms of native species, which have not been greatly utilized?**
   a. that they are too small
   b. that they are ill-suited to urban sites
   c. that they would do better in foreign locations
   d. that they would do well in urban sites

*Refer to the following for question 13:*

Students may take classes in a wide variety of subjects for fun or self-improvement. Some classes provide students with training in useful life skills such as cooking or personal finance. Other classes provide instruction intended for recreational purposes, with topics such as photography, pottery, or painting. Classes may consist of large or small groups, or they may involve one-on-one instruction in subjects like singing or playing a musical instrument. Classes taught by self-enrichment teachers seldom lead to a degree, and attendance in these classes is voluntary. Although often taught in non-academic settings, these classes' topics may include academic subjects such as literature, foreign languages, and history. Despite their informal nature, these courses can provide students with useful work-related skills such as knowledge of computers or foreign languages. These skills make students more attractive to potential employers.

**13. Which of the following statements represents the central idea of this passage?**
   a. Self-improvement classes teach work-related skills.
   b. Attendance is voluntary for self-improvement classes.
   c. Many different kinds of self-improvement classes are available.
   d. Cooking is one type of self-improvement classes.

*Refer to the following for question 14:*

Women have made significant contributions to patent literature in fields as diverse as domestic technology and biomedicine. A woman was involved in the design of the first computer: Lady Ada Lovelace worked with George Babbage to build the "difference engine," a device that could add and subtract. More recently, Gertrude Elion won the 1988 Nobel Prize in Medicine for her invention of a leukemia treatment based on immunosuppressants. She holds numerous medical patents. In addition, women have served as leading members of teams developing surgical methods and all the current AIDS drugs.

**14. The structure of this paragraph is best described as**
   a. Topic sentence and analysis
   b. Topic sentence and consequences
   c. Introductory sentence followed by causes and reasons
   d. Topic sentence followed by examples

15. From what you buy, to what you do, to how much you use, your decisions affect the planet and everyone around you. Now is the time to take action.

When choosing what to buy, look for sustainable products made from renewable or recycled resources. The packaging of the products you buy is just as important as the products themselves. How did the product reach the store? Locally grown food and other products manufactured within your community are the best choices.

You can continue to make a difference for the planet in how you use the resources you have available. Remember the locally grown food you purchased? Food that remains on your plate is a wasted resource, and you can always go back for seconds. You should try to be aware of your consumption of water and energy. Together, we can use less, recycle more, and make the right choices. It may be the only chance we have.

Which organizational pattern did the author use?
   a. Comparison and contrast
   b. Chronological order
   c. Cause and effect
   d. Problem/solution

16. In the American Southwest of the late 1800s, the introduction of barbed wire fencing led to fierce disputes between ranchers and farmers, both eager to protect their rights and their livelihood. The farmers were the clear winners of the two groups, and the barbed wire fences stayed and proliferated. Barbed wire proved to be ideal for use in western conditions; it was cheaper and easier to use than the alternatives of wood fences, stone walls, or hedges. Within a few decades, all the previously open range land became fenced-in private property. This change was so dramatic to the western culture that some consider the introduction of barbed wire fencing to be the event that ended the Old West period of our history.

According to the author, what do some believe the introduction of barbed wire ended?
   a. The disputes between the farmers and the ranchers
   b. The controversy over whether wood fences or stone walls were better
   c. The Old West period of our history
   d. The livelihood of the farmers

17. Geophysicist: Although scientists do not entirely agree on the causes of geomagnetic reversal, they do agree that the process has the potential for significant changes on the earth. A geomagnetic reversal occurs when the magnetic field of the earth adjusts in its orientation, so that the magnetic north becomes the magnetic south, and vice versa. What is more, studies indicate that the magnetic field is gradually losing its strength and that we might expect to see a reversal within the next few millennia. While this might not seem significant, the reversal of the magnetic fields would occur over a long period of time, leaving the earth potentially unprotected from the sun's radiation.

Reviewing the information in the passage above carefully, which of the following represents the geophysicist's primary argument?
   a. While there will be a few effects of a geomagnetic reversal, the negative effects will be limited.
   b. Geomagnetic reversals have occurred within the period of human existence on the earth, and since mankind has survived, there is no reason to fear human eradication from geomagnetic reversal.
   c. Scientists do not fully understand the causes or results of geomagnetic reversal, but there is evidence that the process should not be ignored.
   d. Given the severe possibilities that may arise from a geomagnetic reversal, governments should begin funding studies of this process.

**18. The tourists tried to make the best of things despite the _____ weather.**
   a. ugly
   b. inclement
   c. balmy
   d. insipid

**19. The Ogallala Aquifer, which stretches from Texas to the Dakotas, is one of the major sources of water for the high plains, but it is rapidly being _____ by drought.**
   a. used
   b. contaminated
   c. depleted
   d. undermined

**20. Evan felt that he was always being _____ for things that were not his fault.**
   a. castigated
   b. lauded
   c. interrogated
   d. rescinded

# Writing Placement Test

*Refer to the following for questions 1–5:*

(1) Mrs. Conwer, the Jackson High principal, announced last week that Jackson High is considering a student dress code. (2) She is saying that some of the outfits students are wearing to school are being distracting and inappropriate. (3) For example, she says that some of the boys like to wear their pants too low and that some of the girls like to wear very short skirts. (4) I don't see anything wrong with these. (5) This is only Mrs. Conwer's opinion, and I think there are several reasons why it is important that Jackson High does not have a dress code.

(6) High school students are teenagers. (7) The teen years are a time in life when you are exploring new things and learning about yourself. (8) Many teens also like to express themselves. (9) For example, some people I know keep a blog where they write about things that are important to them. (10) Other people play in a band and can express themselves through music. (11) A lot of teens express themselves through fashion. (12) Since many teens start earning their own money, they can buy their own clothes and choose the fashions that they want. (13) If Jackson High adopts a dress code, the students won't be able to express themselves. (14) Self expression are important and is often taught at Jackson High. (15) Ms. Riley, my dance teacher, tells me to express myself through dance. (16) Mr. Hunter, my English teacher, tells me to express myself through writing. (17) Taking away expression through fashion is hypocritical because it goes against what is taught in many classes.

(18) A dress code at Jackson High will never please everyone. (19) Who gets to decide what is appropriate and what is not? (20) What happens if the students disagree with the code? (21) In school, we learn about respecting different opinions and making compromises. (22) However, if Mrs. Conwer or just a couple of teacher's choose the dress code, they will be ignoring them. (23) Jackson High should stop ignoring the lessons that we learn in our classes every day. (24) Teachers should show us, the students, how people are supposed to dress in the real world when they have jobs, explain why certain choices might be inappropriate, and then let us make our own decisions. (25) That's what we learn in all our classes, and that's how it should be for the dress code.

1. **Consider the following excerpt from the passage:**

    Sentence 2: She is saying that some of the outfits students are wearing to school are being distracting and inappropriate.

   **Select the best version of the sentence.**
    a. NO CHANGE
    b. The outfits are distracting and inappropriate, she says, that students wear to school.
    c. She says some of the outfits that students wear to school are distracting and inappropriate.
    d. She says that it is distracting and inappropriate that students wear outfits to school.

2. **Which is the best way to combine sentences (11) and (12)?**
    a. A lot of teens express themselves through fashion, and since many teens start earning their own money, they can buy their own clothes and choose the fashions that they want.
    b. A lot of teens express themselves through fashion and since many teens start earning their own money, they can buy their own clothes and choose the fashions that they want.
    c. A lot of teens express themselves through fashion, but since many teens start earning their own money, they can buy their own clothes and choose the fashions that they want.
    d. A lot of teens express themselves through fashion but since many teens start earning their own money, they can buy their own clothes and choose the fashions that they want.

3. **What correction should be made to sentence (14)?**
    a. Change *expression* to *expresion*
    b. Insert a comma before *and*
    c. Change *are* to *is*
    d. Insert *the* after *at*

4. **What transition should be added to the beginning of sentence (18)?**
    a. However
    b. Furthermore
    c. First of all
    d. Therefore

5. **What correction should be made to sentence (22)?**
    a. Change *however* to *nevertheless*
    b. Change *a couple* to *several*
    c. Change *teacher's* to *teachers*
    d. Delete the comma after *code*

*Refer to the following for questions 6–10:*

(1) During the 1920s, the U.S. Post Office developed airmail. (2) Before airmail, the post traveled on trains and can take weeks to reach a destination. (3) Flying for the post office was dangerous work. (4) Early pilots didn't have sophistocated instruments and safety equipment on their planes. (5) Many of them had to bail out and use their parachutes when their planes iced up in the cold air or had other trouble.

(6) The most famous pilot of the 1920s, Charles A. Lindbergh, began as a postal pilot. (7) In May 1927, he participated in an air race to fly across the Atlantic Ocean. (8) The prize was $25,000, but the dangers were extensive. (9) Named Nungesser and Coli, two French pilots had recently tried to fly across the Atlantic.

(10) They disappeared.

(11) The newspapers called Charles Lindbergh "the dark horse" to win the race. (12) He had already set a record by making the fastest solo flight between St. Louis, Missouri, and, San Diego, California. (13) Lindbergh's record-setting flight took 23 hours and 15 minutes; today, a flight between St. Louis and San Diego takes about four hours.

(14) After several weather delays, Lindbergh took off in his small plane, The Spirit of St. Louis, on May 20, 1927. (15) He made it across the Atlantic Ocean and arrived in France after 33 hours and 30 minutes of non-stop flight; today, a flight from New York to Paris would take about seven hours.

(16) The flight was taxing. (17) Because Lindbergh flew alone, he had to stay awake for the entire trip. (18) He knew that he couldn't have made it across without a great plane. (19) He said, "I feel that the monoplane was as much a part of the trip as myself."

(20) Lindbergh's trip set off a golden age for aviation. (21) The same people who were nervous about airplanes at the beginning of the 1920s came out by the thousands to cheer Lindbergh. (22) The age of pilots doing odd jobs and dangerous stunt work had ended.

6. What correction should be made to sentence (4)?
    a. Change *pilots* to *pilot's*
    b. Change *sophistocated* to *sophisticated*
    c. Add a comma after *instruments*
    d. Change *their* to *they're*

7. Which is the best version of sentence (9)?
    a. NO CHANGE
    b. Two French pilots Nungesser and Coli had recently tried to fly across the Atlantic.
    c. Recently having tried to fly across the Atlantic, two French pilots were named Nungesser and Coli.
    d. Two French pilots, named Nungesser and Coli, had recently tried to fly across the Atlantic.

8. What correction should be made to sentence (12)?
    a. Delete the comma after *St. Louis*
    b. Delete the comma after *Missouri*
    c. Delete the comma after *and*
    d. Delete the comma after *San Diego*

9. Which is the best way to combine sentences (18) and (19)?
    a. He knew that he couldn't have made it across without a great plane and he said, "I feel that the monoplane was as much a part of the trip as myself."
    b. He knew that he couldn't have made it across without a great plane, he said, "I feel that the monoplane was as much a part of the trip as myself."
    c. He knew that he couldn't have made it across without a great plane and says, "I feel that the monoplane was as much a part of the trip as myself."
    d. He knew that he couldn't have made it across without a great plane and said, "I feel that the monoplane was as much a part of the trip as myself."

10. What transition could be added at the beginning of sentence (20)?
    a. Subsequently
    b. Furthermore
    c. Therefore
    d. Additionally

*Refer to the following for questions 11–15:*

(1) As I stared down at the hitter in the batters box, I remembered what my dad had said to me. (2) "Shut everything out." (3) I focused on the glove in front of me. (4) I looked into the deep, blackened pocket, and sawed my target. (5) The batter tapped his bat against the sides of his cleats and rested the bat on his shoulders. (6) With hard eyes, he stares back at me.

(7) I kicked the front of my cleat into the bright white rubber on the pitching mound and took a deep breath. (8) Shut everything out," he had said. (9) Slowly the noises disappeared. (10) I could no longer hear the shouts from the parents in the stands. (11) In my head, I silenced the cheers from both dugouts. (12) The umpire did not exist. (13) There were no players, no coaches, not even a catcher. (14) There was just me. (15) The ball and the glove.

(16) I took a deep breath and brought my hands together at my chest. (17) I looked over at first base, but there was no runner. (18) In one motion, my feet left the rubber and connected with ground. (19) Dirt flew in the air as my arm rotated forward and released the ball in front of me. (20) I watched as the ball spun and landed into glove with a hard crack. (21) The umpire shot up from his crouched position and pointed his finger to the right and yelled, "Strike Three!"

(22) The noises came back. (23) The crowd cheered in the stands and I could hear stomping feet. (24) My teammate clapped his hand to his glove and ran toward me. (25) My coach raised a first into the air in celebration. (26) I was surrounded by my teammates, and they were patting me on the back. (27) My dad was sitting on a bleacher behind home plate. (28) He raised his thumb to me and smiled as I ran off the field with my teammates.

**11. What correction should be made to sentence (4)?**
   a. Change *blackened* to *blacked*
   b. Change *sawed* to *saw*
   c. Delete the comma after *deep*
   d. Change *into* to *in to*

**12. What correction should be made to sentence (6)?**
   a. NO CHANGE
   b. Change *me* to *I*
   c. Delete the comma after *eyes*
   d. Change *stares* to *stared*

**13. What correction should be made to sentence (8)?**
   a. Change *everything* to *every thing*
   b. Delete the comma after *out*
   c. Change the comma after *out* to a period
   d. Insert quotation marks before *Shut*

**14. Which is the best way to combine sentences (14) and sentence (15)?**
   a. NO CHANGE
   b. There was just me, the ball, and the glove.
   c. There was just me and the ball and the glove.
   d. There was just the ball, the glove, and me.

**15. What is the best transition word that could be added to the beginning of sentence (26)?**
a. However
b. Consequentially
c. Soon
d. Therefore

*Refer to the following for questions 16–20:*

(1) George Washington and all of the other great leaders who fought in the Revolutionary War would be very disappointed in Americans today. (2) The right to choose who will represent us in government has lost its importance. (3) Too many people do not vote in elections and are just throwing away their right our founding fathers fought to give them. (4) Why anyone would do such a thing is beyond me. (5) If people do not stand up and choose their own leaders, someone else will do it for them: and who knows what those leaders will stand for? (6) Many people struggled and died to give us the right to vote, and we should always honor that sacrifice by voting in every election.

(7) The main purpose of the Revolutionary War was to freely break from rulers who did not give their people a say in their own government. (8) British colonists in America lived far away from their leaders in the British Parliament, and could not have a physical presence in government due to the distance between America and England. (9) This led to a denial of the rights that these colonists would have had if they still lived in England. (10) Tired of "taxation without representation," as the popular slogan went during this time in history, the colonists felt so strongly that they should have a say in their government that they took up arms against their own countrymen and fought for their freedom.

(11) Today, Americans take the fact that they have had voting rights for over 200 years for granted. (12) That's why voting isn't as important as it was back in the day. (13) If you look at how other people and countries have all fought for the right to vote, and continue to do so even today, it's plain to see that voting is something that should still be important in our society. (14) I hope that my generation will be the first of many to make voting one of our most important and treasured rights once again.

**16. Which is the best version of sentence (3)?**
a. Too many people do not vote in elections and just throw away their right our founding fathers fought to give them.
b. Too many people do not vote in elections, and, as a result, throw away one of the basic rights our founding fathers fought so hard to ensure for future generations.
c. Too many people today do not value their right to vote as much as our founding fathers.
d. Too many people choose not to vote in elections and throw away our founding fathers' rights.

**17. What correction should be made to sentence (7)?**
a. NO CHANGE
b. change *freely break* to *break free*
c. Add a comma after *rulers*
d. delete *main*

**18. Which sentence, if added after sentence (11), would make Carter's point in the third paragraph more persuasive?**
   a. The fights about voting rights that people in other countries are engaged in even now seem so far removed from life in the U.S.
   b. Americans don't have any memory of having to fight for the right to have a voice in government.
   c. For the most part, our citizens have had the right to vote for their entire lives; it's something that has just always been there.
   d. They should remember that this right was something that had to be fought for, not something that was given to all citizens.

**19. Which of the following is the best way to revise sentence (12) so that the style the writer uses throughout the rest of the essay is maintained?**
   a. Our culture has devalued voting to the point that many simply do not care that an entire war was fought so that they could have that right in the first place.
   b. Voting isn't as important as it was back in the day.
   c. The devaluation of the right to vote by American society has resulted in the overall apathy of our citizenry when it comes to exercising the rights given to them as a result of the Revolutionary War.
   d. People don't think of voting as important anymore.

**20. Which of the following sentences should be removed in order to maintain the focus of the passage?**
   a. Sentence (2)
   b. Sentence (4)
   c. Sentence (9)
   d. Sentence (14)

*Refer to the following for questions 21–25:*

(1) Dear Mrs. Alloway and the Board,

(2) At the school board meeting on January 25, you passed a rule banning soft drinks from the school cafeteria as of the beginning of the next school year. (3) While I agree with your assessment that soft drinks consumed in access can be detrimental to the health of students and adults, I do not agree with the decision to make them unavailable to the student body.

(4) Soft drinks have a significant amount of sugar and can be unhealthy when drunk in large quantities. (5) My classmates and I realize this, but a soft drink is no less unhealthy than many of the food that will continue to be served in the cafeteria. (6) For example, the average 12 ounce soft drink has about 150 calories, no fat, and 39 grams of sugar. (7) The cookies that will continue to be served in the cafeteria (and that were served at the school board meeting) have approximately 190 calories, 9 grams of fat, and 14 grams of sugar. (8) Honestly, it's dumb that soft drinks are being discriminated against. (9) If the school board is serious about promoting healthy eating in the school cafeteria all items served should meet nutritional requirements, not just drinks.

(10) Furthermore, my peers and I are all adolescents and preparing for adulthood. (11) Some of us will be heading off to college in just a year or two and will be living independently. (12) Banning soft drinks in the high school could potentially cause us to drink even more soft drinks when we are not in the high school. (13) Instead, I propose that the school board educate students about making smart choices. (14) By allowing soft drinks in the high school, the school board can ensure that my peers and I learn how to eat and drink responsibly, making us healthier for the rest of our lives.

(15) Instead of banning soft drinks, I propose that the school cafeteria charge higher prices for items that do not meet certain nutritional standards: including those chocolate chip cookies. (16) The extra money brought in can be used to educate students about healthy eating choices. (17) The higher prices may encourage students to

naturally make healthier choices. (18) This method will accomplish the school board's goal of getting students to drink fewer soft drinks, but will still give the students choice and the respect that they deserve.

Sincerely,

Elyse Chan

Student Congress President

**21. Which of the following sentences should be deleted from the second paragraph in order to maintain the focus of the paragraph?**
   a. Sentence (4)
   b. Sentence (5)
   c. Sentence (7)
   d. Sentence (8)

**22. Which word could be deleted from sentence (12) without changing the meaning of the sentence?**
   a. Soft, as it used after *banning*
   b. Potentially
   c. Us
   d. Not

**23. Which sentence could best follow and support sentence (13)?**
   a. Drinking soft drinks is very bad for you.
   b. Education will prepare us for college and for living independently.
   c. I strongly disagree that the school board should ban soft drinks.
   d. It's not fair that no student representatives were invited to the school board meeting.

**24. What correction should be made to sentence (15)?**
   a. Delete the comma after *drinks*
   b. Change *higher* to *high*
   c. Change *nutritional* to *nutrition*
   d. Delete the colon after *standards* and put *including those chocolate chip cookies* in parentheses

**25. What transition word should be added to the beginning of sentence (17)?**
   a. Furthermore
   b. However
   c. Although
   d. In conclusion

## Arithmetic Placement Test

**1. Which of the following inequalities is correct?**
   a. $\frac{1}{3} < \frac{2}{7} < \frac{5}{12}$
   b. $\frac{2}{7} < \frac{1}{3} < \frac{5}{12}$
   c. $\frac{5}{12} < \frac{2}{7} < \frac{1}{3}$
   d. $\frac{5}{12} < \frac{1}{3} < \frac{2}{7}$

2. Simplify the expression: $\frac{2}{3}(3-2) + \frac{1}{2}(2-4)$

   a. $-\frac{1}{3}$
   b. $-\frac{1}{2}$
   c. $\frac{1}{2}$
   d. $\frac{1}{3}$

3. Mrs. Patterson's classroom has sixteen empty chairs. All the chairs are occupied when every student is present. If $\frac{2}{5}$ of the students are absent, how many students make up her entire class?

   a. 16 students
   b. 24 students
   c. 32 students
   d. 40 students

4. 50 is what percent of 40?

   a. 80
   b. 90
   c. 120
   d. 125

5. A dress is marked as 20% off. With the discount, the current price is $40.00. What is the price of the dress without the discount?

   a. $32
   b. $45
   c. $48
   d. $50

6. What is the proper ordering (from greatest to least) of the following numbers?

   I. $\frac{58}{67}$
   II. 0.58%
   III. 58%
   IV. 5.8%

   a. I, III, II, IV
   b. III, IV, II, I
   c. I, III, IV, II
   d. IV, I, III, II

7. What is $\frac{2}{5} \times 2.5$?

   a. 1
   b. 2
   c. 4
   d. 6

8. A cookie recipe calls for $2\frac{1}{4}$ cups of milk. Brian has $1\frac{1}{2}$ cups available. How much more milk does he need in order to make cookies according to the recipe?
   a. $1\frac{1}{2}$ cups
   b. $1\frac{1}{4}$ cups
   c. $\frac{3}{4}$ cup
   d. $\frac{1}{4}$ cup

9. Simplify the expression: $5(80 \div 8) + (7 - 2) - (9 \times 5)$
   a. −150
   b. 10
   c. 100
   d. 230

10. 9.5% of the people in a town voted for a certain proposition in a municipal election. If the town's population is 51,623, about how many people in the town voted for the proposition?
    a. 3,000
    b. 5,000
    c. 7,000
    d. 10,000

11. What is $\frac{7}{8} \times \frac{2}{3} \times \frac{4}{5} \times \frac{3}{7}$?
    a. $\frac{1}{7}$
    b. $\frac{1}{5}$
    c. $\frac{3}{8}$
    d. 1

12. Lauren had $80 in her savings account. When she received her paycheck, she put some money in her savings account. This brought the balance up to $120. By what percentage did the total amount in her account increase by putting this amount in her savings account?
    a. 35%
    b. 40%
    c. 50%
    d. 80%

13. Which of the following is the best estimate for $23.97124 \div 8.023$?
    a. 2
    b. 3
    c. 16
    d. 20

14. What is $\frac{2}{3} + \frac{2}{5}$?
    a. $\frac{1}{4}$
    b. $\frac{1}{2}$
    c. $\frac{8}{15}$
    d. $1\frac{1}{15}$

15. A city in California charges a fine of $49 for each mile per hour a speeder is driving above the speed limit. Tina received an $882 fine for speeding. How many miles per hour above the speed limit was she traveling?
    a. 16 mph
    b. 18 mph
    c. 20 mph
    d. 24 mph

16. What is $2.22 + 0.1 + 0.623$?
    a. 0.855
    b. 2.853
    c. 2.943
    d. 8.46

17. What is $2.2 \times 31.3$?
    a. 6.886
    b. 68.86
    c. 688.6
    d. 6,886.00

18. What is $0.924 - 0.439$?
    a. 0.485
    b. 0.595
    c. 4.850
    d. 5.950

19. Which operation compares $\frac{2}{3}$ to $\frac{5}{6}$?
    a. >
    b. =
    c. <
    d. Impossible to determine

20. Doug drives without backtracking from his apartment to a campsite in another state. His trip requires him to travel at various speeds, and at one point he gets stuck in traffic. After two hours, he is halfway to his destination. After four hours, he is two-thirds of the way there. Which of the following could represent the fraction of his travel distance he has covered after three hours?
    a. $\frac{2}{5}$
    b. $\frac{3}{5}$
    c. $\frac{3}{4}$
    d. $\frac{4}{5}$

## Quantitative Reasoning, Algebra, and Statistics Placement Test

1. A box is 30 cm long, 20 cm wide, and 15 cm high. What is the volume of the box?
    a. 65 cm³
    b. 260 cm³
    c. 1,125 cm³
    d. 9,000 cm³

2. If it takes Alice 12 minutes to make 1 ring, how many rings can she make in 6 hours?
   a. 2 rings
   b. 6 rings
   c. 30 rings
   d. 72 rings

3. A drawer contains eight pairs of socks. If Susan chooses four socks at random from the drawer, what are the chances that she will get two left socks and two right socks?
   a. $\frac{1}{2}$
   b. $\frac{2}{5}$
   c. $\frac{1}{64}$
   d. $\frac{28}{65}$

4. A communications company charges $5.00 for the first 10 minutes of a call and $1.20 for each minute thereafter. Which of the following equations correctly relates the price in dollars, $d$, to the number of minutes, $m$ (when $m \geq 10$)?
   a. $d = 5 + 1.2m$
   b. $d = 5 + 1.2(m - 10)$
   c. $d = 5m + 1.2(m + 10)$
   d. $d = (m + 10)(5 + 1.2)$

5. Put the following numbers in order from the least to greatest: $2^3, 4^2, 6^0, 9, 10^1$.
   a. $2^3, 4^2, 6^0, 9, 10^1$
   b. $6^0, 9, 10^1, 2^3, 4^2$
   c. $10^1, 2^3, 6^0, 9, 4^2$
   d. $6^0, 2^3, 9, 10^1, 4^2$

6. Employees of a small company work in one of three departments and are distributed as shown. Two employees are chosen randomly and independently to attend a conference. What is the probability that the pair chosen includes a woman from Department 1 and a man from Department 2?

|       | Dept. 1 | Dept. 2 | Dept. 3 | Total |
|-------|---------|---------|---------|-------|
| Women | 11      | 27      | 16      | 54    |
| Men   | 19      | 15      | 12      | 46    |
| Total | 30      | 42      | 28      | 100   |

   a. $\frac{1}{30}$
   b. $\frac{1}{40}$
   c. $\frac{1}{50}$
   d. $\frac{1}{60}$

7. A random sample of 90 students at an elementary school were asked these three questions:

*Do you like carrots?*
*Do you like broccoli?*
*Do you like cauliflower?*

**The results of the survey are shown below. If these data are representative of the population of students at the school, which of these is most probable?**

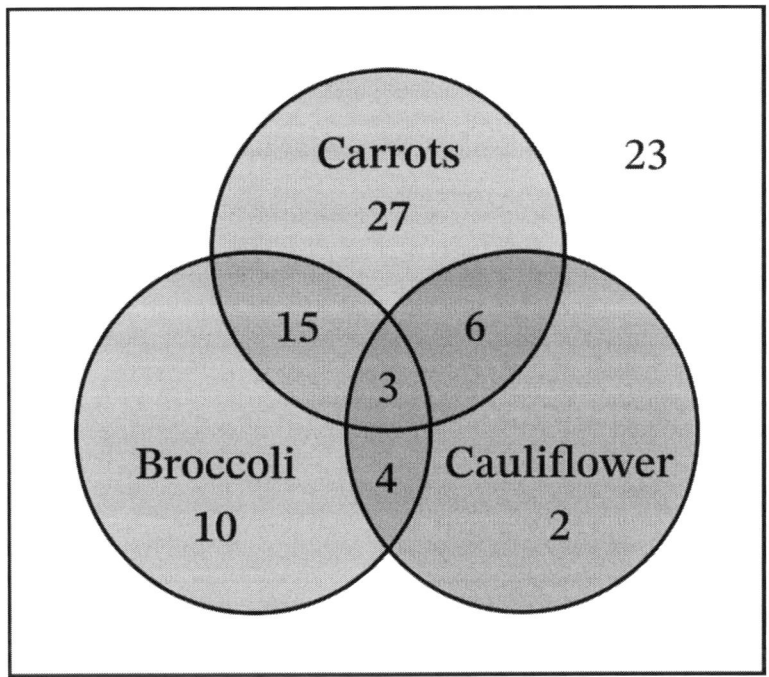

a. A student chosen at random likes broccoli.
b. Given a student chosen at random likes carrots, they will also like at least one other vegetable.
c. Given a student chosen at random likes cauliflower and broccoli, they will also like carrots.
d. A student chosen at random does not like carrots, broccoli, or cauliflower.

8. An exam has 30 questions. A student gets 1 point for each correctly answered question and loses $\frac{1}{2}$ point for each incorrectly answered question. The student neither gains nor loses any points for a question left blank. If $C$ is the number of questions a student gets right and $B$ is the number of questions the student leaves blank, which of the following represents the student's score on the exam?

a. $C - \frac{1}{2}B$
b. $C - \frac{1}{2}(30 - B)$
c. $C - \frac{1}{2}(30 - B - C)$
d. $(30 - C) - \frac{1}{2}(30 - B)$

*Refer to the following for questions 9–10:*

**Consider the following graphic showing demographics of a high school with 1,219 total students:**

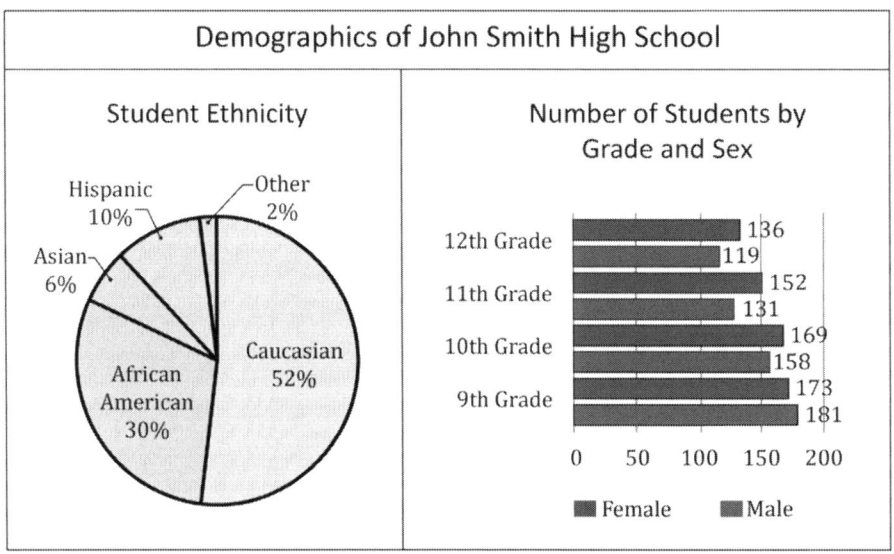

9. Which of these is the smallest quantity?
   a. The average number of African American students in the 9th and 10th grades
   b. The number of Asian female students at the school
   c. The difference in the number of male and female students at the school
   d. The difference in the number of 10th and 12th grade students at the school

10. Which of these is the greatest quantity?
    a. The average number of male students in the 11th and 12th grades
    b. The number of Hispanic students at the school
    c. The difference in the number of male and female students at the school
    d. The difference in the number of 9th and 12th grade students at the school

11. Alan has a large number of cubical building blocks 4 cm on a side. He wants to use them to make a larger solid cube 20 cm on a side. How many building blocks will he need for this?
    a. 25
    b. 94
    c. 125
    d. 150

12. A building has a number of floors of equal height, as well as a thirty-foot spire on top. If the height of each floor in feet is $h$, and there are $n$ floors in the building, which of the following represents the building's total height in feet?
    a. $n + h + 30$
    b. $nh + 30$
    c. $30n + h$
    d. $30h + n$

13. A car moves at a constant velocity. Which of the following accurately describes the appearance of the position-time graph?
    a. It is a line with a positive slope.
    b. It is a line with a negative slope.
    c. It is a curve with an increasing slope.
    d. It is a curve with a decreasing slope.

14. At a school carnival, three students spend an average of $10. Six other students spend an average of $4. What is the average amount of money spent by all nine students?
    a. $5
    b. $6
    c. $7
    d. $8

15. A particular map has a scale of 1 inch = 5 miles. On the map, Lost Canyon Road is one foot long. How long is the actual road?
    a. 2.4 miles
    b. 6 miles
    c. 24 miles
    d. 60 miles

16. What is $\frac{|2|+|-2|}{|3|-|-1|}$?
    a. 0
    b. 1
    c. 2
    d. 4

17. If $x + 2y = 3$ and $-x - 3y = 4$, then what is the value of $x$?
    a. 1
    b. 5
    c. 7
    d. 17

18. Simplify the expression $\frac{\sqrt{2}}{\sqrt{6}}$.
    a. $2\sqrt{3}$
    b. $\sqrt{3}$
    c. $\frac{\sqrt{3}}{2}$
    d. $\frac{\sqrt{3}}{3}$

19. Prizes are to be awarded to the best pupils in each class of an elementary school. The number of students in each grade is shown in the table, and the school principal wants the number of prizes awarded in each grade to be proportional to the number of students. If there are twenty prizes, how many should go to fifth-grade students?

| Grade | 1 | 2 | 3 | 4 | 5 |
|---|---|---|---|---|---|
| Students | 35 | 38 | 38 | 33 | 36 |

   a. 3
   b. 4
   c. 5
   d. 7

20. Which of the following graphs represents the inequality $-2 < x \leq 4$?

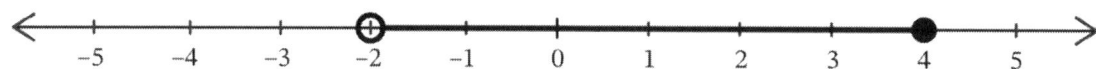
a.

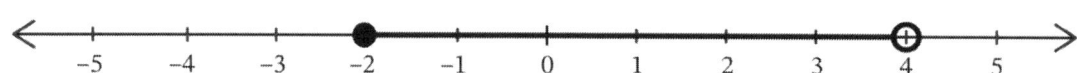
b.

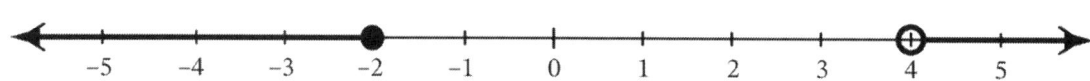
c.

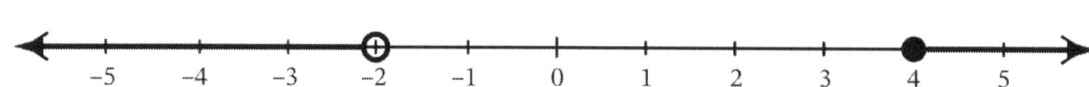
d.

## Advanced Algebra and Functions Placement Test

1. The formula for the volume of a pyramid is $\frac{1}{3}Bh$, where $B$ is the area of the base and $h$ is the height. The Pyramid of Khafre in Giza has a square base about 700 feet on a side and is about 450 feet high. Which of the following is closest to its volume?
   a. 18 million cubic feet
   b. 55 million cubic feet
   c. 75 million cubic feet
   d. 220 million cubic feet

2. Suppose the area of the square in the diagram below is 64 in². (The square is not shown as its actual size.) What is the area of the circle?

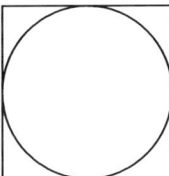

   a. $16\pi$ in²
   b. $64\pi$ in²
   c. $\frac{64}{\pi}$ in²
   d. $\frac{128}{\pi}$ in²

3. Expand the following expression: $(x+2)(x-3)$
   a. $x^2 - 1$
   b. $x^2 - 6$
   c. $x^2 - x - 6$
   d. $x^2 - 5x - 1$

4. If $f(x) = \frac{x^3 - 2x + 1}{3x}$, what is $f(2)$?
   a. $\frac{1}{3}$
   b. $\frac{1}{2}$
   c. $\frac{5}{6}$
   d. $\frac{5}{2}$

5. Every person attending a meeting hands out a business card to every other person at the meeting. If a total of 30 cards are handed out, how many people are at the meeting?
   a. 5 people
   b. 6 people
   c. 10 people
   d. 15 people

6. What is the expanded form of $(x+6)(x-6)$?
   a. $x^2 - 12x - 36$
   b. $x^2 + 12x - 36$
   c. $x^2 + 12x + 36$
   d. $x^2 - 36$

7. Solve $\sqrt{2x} - 3 = \sqrt{2x - 15}$.
   a. $x = 0$
   b. $x = 4$
   c. $x = 8$
   d. $x = 10$

8. If $\cos\theta + 1 = 0$, which of the following is a possible value of $\theta$?
   a. $-180°$
   b. $-90°$
   c. $0°$
   d. $135°$

9. A chest is filled with large gold and silver coins, weighing a total of 30 pounds. If each gold coin weighs 12 ounces, each silver coin weighs 8 ounces, and there are 50 coins in all, how many gold coins does the chest contain? (There are 16 ounces in a pound.)
   a. 10 coins
   b. 15 coins
   c. 20 coins
   d. 30 coins

10. What is $\log_5(5^3)$?
    a. $-2$
    b. 1
    c. 3
    d. 243

11. Given the function $p(y) = \frac{4y}{2} + 5$, what is the value of $p(4)$?
    a. 9
    b. 7
    c. 13
    d. 37

12. Lisa is selling brownies and cupcakes at a bake sale. Brownies cost $2 each and cupcakes cost $3 each. Lisa must sell at least $150 worth of baked goods to break even on baking costs and the cost of renting the booth. If the x-axis represents the number of brownies sold and the y-axis represents the number of cupcakes sold, which of the following graphs shows the amount of baked goods Lisa must sell to break even or make a profit?

a.
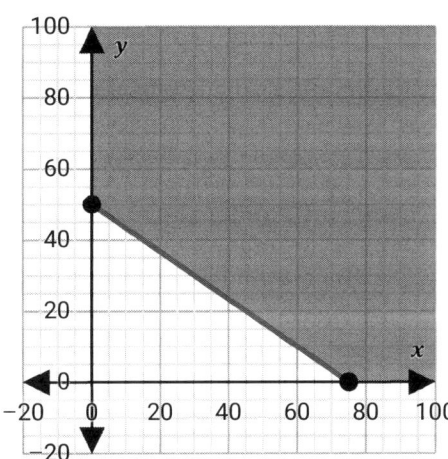

c.
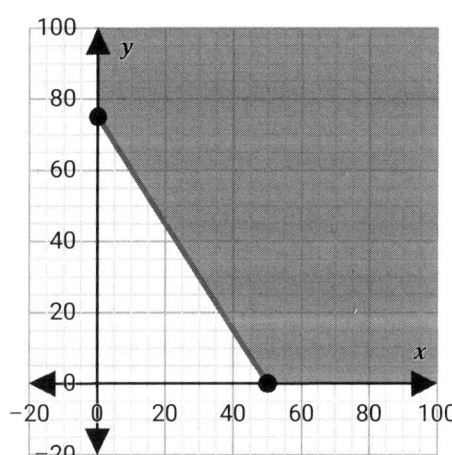

b.
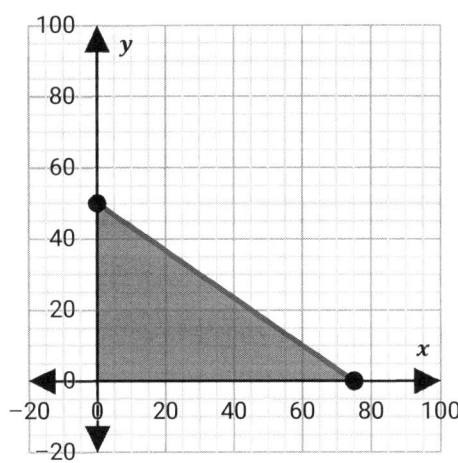

d.
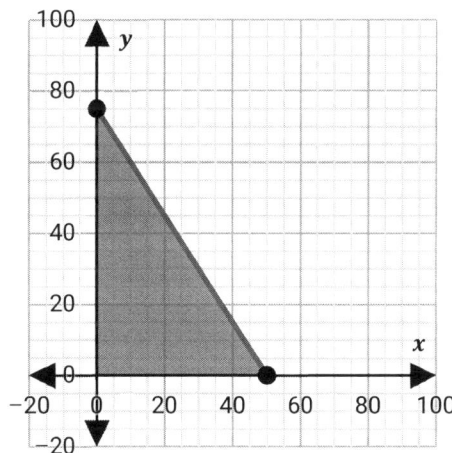

13. Which of the following is the correct graph of the system of inequalities below?
$$\begin{cases} x - y > 1 \\ 2x + y > 2 \end{cases}$$

a.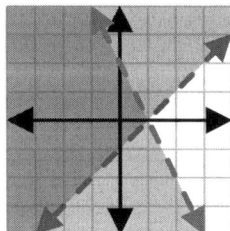
b.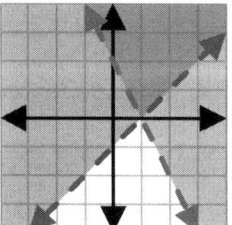

c.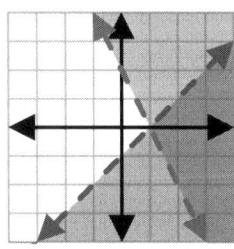
d.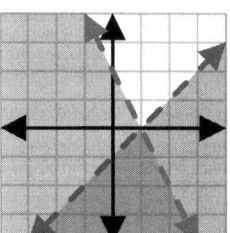

14. Subtract the polynomials: $(2x^2 + 3x + 2) - (x^2 + 2x - 3)$
    a. $x^2 + x + 5$
    b. $x^2 + x - 1$
    c. $x^2 + 5x + 5$
    d. $x^2 + 5x - 1$

15. If the lines $y = ax + b$ and $y = bx + 2a$ intersect at the point $(2, 3)$, then what is the value of $a$?
    a. $\frac{2}{3}$
    b. $1$
    c. $\frac{3}{2}$
    d. $3$

16. Simplify the expression: $\frac{x^7 + 2x^6 + x^5}{x^4 - x^2}$
    a. $x^3 + 2x$
    b. $x^3 + x + 1$
    c. $\frac{x^5 + x^3}{x^2}$
    d. $\frac{x^4 + x^3}{x - 1}$

17. If $3^x = 2$, then what is the value of $x$?
    a. $9$
    b. $\sqrt{3}$
    c. $\sqrt[3]{2}$
    d. $\log_3 2$

18. Which of the following represents the factored form of the expression $x^2 - 3x - 40$?
    a. $(x-8)(x+5)$
    b. $(x-7)(x+4)$
    c. $(x+10)(x-4)$
    d. $(x+6)(x-9)$

19. Which of the following correctly represents the solution to the inequality?
$$x^2 + 2x \geq x + 6$$

a.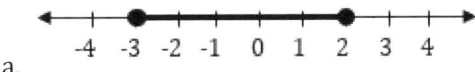

b. 

c. 

d. 

20. If $\sec\theta = 2$, then which of the following is a possible value for $\sin\theta$?
    a. $-\frac{\sqrt{3}}{2}$
    b. $-\frac{1}{2}$
    c. 0
    d. 1

# Answer Key and Explanations for Test #1

## Reading Placement Test

**1. D:** Choice C is close to being the answer, but choice D is the best answer because the narrator can enter the consciousness of both the man and the dog, making it third person omniscient. Choices A and B can be ruled out because the narrator does not use the pronouns *I* or *we*.

**2. A:** Choice A offers the best interpretation. The passage refers to immortality and man's place in the universe; the man does not have the imagination to contemplate such issues, and he does not seem to realize the frailty of humans on the planet. Choices B and C contradict or misinterpret the meaning of the passage. Choice D is not really implied by the passage; in fact, the dog's instincts make it seem more intelligent than the man in a certain sense.

**3. C:** Choice C can be supported by the following quotation: "[The dog's] instinct told it a truer tale than was told to the man by the man's judgment." Choice A may sound possible, but it does not really capture the narrator's main point of comparison. Choice B can be contradicted by the following quotation: "In its brain there was no sharp consciousness of a condition of very cold such as was in the man's brain." There is nothing in the passage to support the claim in choice D.

**4. C:** Only interpretation III fits with the meaning of the passage. The narrator's statement that the man lacked imagination means that he did not have the foresight to realize that he was risking his life. Interpretation I is incorrect because the passage reads, "He was quick and alert in the things of life." Interpretation II is incorrect because the quote shows lack of imagination as a danger, not something unneeded.

**5. D:** Choice D is not a supporting detail because it is a definition of salvage logging. The other choices are supporting details of the forest manager's argument.

**6. B:** Plot A was salvage logged and burned worse than the unmanaged plot (Plot B). This study supports the professor's view that salvage logging increases the risk and severity of fire.

**7. A:** The question asks which option is the chief argument regarding fire prevention. Choices B and D are not helpful for fire prevention. Choice C is incorrect because logging decreases soil temperature. Choice B is a supporting detail from the passage but is not the main idea. Choice C contradicts the passage. Choice D is not mentioned in the passage.

**8. C:** Both the manager and the professor discuss the importance of seedling growth after a fire. So, a study looking at the regrowth of seedlings in logged and unmanaged forests would potentially provide support for both arguments (as well as possibly showing problems with both arguments).

**9. C:** Although the passage does describe some of the symptoms encephalitis caused by the West Nile virus as well as the incident in which the birds died at Alexander's feet, these descriptions are incidental to the paragraph's main purpose. The main idea of the paragraph is that Alexander may have died of encephalitis.

**10. D:** The passage describes the loss of these coastal barrier lands to erosion. The fifth sentence then states, "the result is that recent hurricane seasons have been the most expensive on record." This establishes the cause-and-effect between barrier island erosion and monetary losses due to great storms.

**11. B:** The author plainly is not attempting to entertain (A). Nor is he unemotionally sharing information (B) or meekly apologizing (D). The use of words such as *outrageous*, *undemocratic*, and *absolutely* imparts a strongly emotional tone to the passage, which can be described as antagonistic, irate, or angry.

**12. D:** Since space restriction is one of the major problems encountered in planting trees in urban sites, the author implies that dwarf trees–since they are small–would prove successful in this cramped environment.

**13. C:** The passage explores the wide variety of self-improvement classes offered. As such, it touches upon the variety of content and subject matter, different venues in which the classes may be taught, and the range of enrollment sizes that may be encountered.

**14. D:** The first sentence introduces the topic, the contributions made to the patent literature by women. The remainder of the paragraph is dedicated to giving examples of these contributions, beginning with Lady Lovelace two centuries ago and continuing through present day contributions to biomedicine. The passage does not describe any causes or effects, so the passage cannot be considered an analysis.

**15. D:** The author presents the problems of global warming and the rapid depletion of the planet's natural resources and offers several practical suggestions for how to stop global warming and use remaining resources judiciously.

**16. C:** This is stated in the fifth and final sentence of the passage. Barbed wire led to disputes between farmers and ranchers, rather than ending them (A). Choice B was not disputed in the article. Choice D does not follow from the message of the passage.

**17. C:** Answer choice C best combines the main points into a unified thought: scientists do not necessarily know the causes or even the results of geomagnetic reversal, but there is enough evidence to indicate that they should be paying close attention to it. The passage states that the earth could be "potentially unprotected from the sun's radiation," so it is inaccurate to state that negative effects will be limited (choice A). While the passage indicates that geomagnetic reversals have occurred, there is no mention of mankind (choice B). And while the author might agree that studies should be conducted, he does not state this nor mention government funding (choice D).

**18. B:** Inclement weather is rough, severe, or stormy weather. The context of the sentence suggests that the weather is bad, so tourists are forced to make the best of the situation. Balmy weather is pleasant and warm, so this choice does not appear appropriate. Weather seldom is described as "ugly," and Choice D, "insipid," does not make sense.

**19. C:** To *deplete* means *to decrease significantly* or *to exhaust the abundance of a thing*. The effect of drought is to decrease the abundance of water in the aquifer. This word is stronger than merely *to use* (Choice A): it means *to diminish* or *to use up*. Choices B and D are not logical choices for this scenario.

**20. A:** To *castigate* means *to criticize severely, to rebuke*. The use of the word *fault* in the sentence implies that Evan was chastised for detrimental events for which he bore no responsibility. As a result, lauded, which means to praise (choice B), is not an appropriate choice. *Interrogated* (choice C) is closer but does not give the connotation of unwarranted blame. *Rescinded* (choice D) does not make sense in this context.

## Writing Placement Test

**1. C:** Choice C begins with a subject and verb and is followed by a clause. It is also clear and concise. Choice A is incorrect because the words are out of order and don't logically follow the previous sentence. Sentence 2 should begin with "She says" because it is the school principal's opinion being expressed. This choice is also incorrect because it uses the words *not appropriate* instead of *inappropriate*. Choice B is incorrect because the clause "that students wear to school" should come after the word *outfits*. Choice D is incorrect because the word order changes the meaning of the sentence by stating that any outfits are distracting and inappropriate.

**2. A:** Answer choice A uses correct punctuation and a logical conjunction. Because the conjunction *and* connects two independent clauses (meaning that they can stand on their own as sentences), there must be a comma before the conjunction. Therefore, choices B and D are incorrect because they are missing this comma.

While choice C does have a comma before the conjunction, it uses the conjunction *but* rather than *and*. *But* implies that the two clauses contradict each other. *And* is a better choice because the two clauses are connected and support each other.

**3. C:** The plural verb *are* does not match the singular subject, *self expression*. Choice A is incorrect because *expression* is already written with the correct spelling. Choice B is incorrect because the conjunction *and* is connecting an independent clause with a dependent clause. When *and* is used in this way, there should not be a comma before the conjunction. Choice D is incorrect because an article is not needed before the name of the school, which is a proper noun.

**4. B:** The word *furthermore* shows that the sentence will present additional support for the writer's argument. Choice A is incorrect because *however* indicates that the following sentence will contradict what came before. Choice C is incorrect because the sentence is not presenting the first point in the writer's argument. Choice D is incorrect because the sentence is not presenting a conclusion, but an additional point

**5. C:** *Teacher's* is not being used as a possessive. Instead, it is being used as a plural noun and therefore should not have an apostrophe. Choice A is incorrect because *however* is a better transition to sentence (22) due to the sentence showing a contrast with a previous point. Choice B is incorrect because the word *of* should not follow *several*. Choice D is incorrect because the comma correctly separates a dependent clause from an independent clause.

**6. B:** *Sophisticated* is the correct spelling. Choice A is incorrect because *pilots* is not a possessive in this context. Choice C is incorrect because a comma is not needed to separate a list that only has two items. Choice D is incorrect because *their* is a possessive, which fits the sentence. *They're* refers to *they are*, which does not work in this sentence.

**7. D:** The word order in answer choice D best conveys the meaning of the sentence in a concise manner. Choice B is incorrect because *Nungesser and Coli* is a nonessential phrase and needs to be separated from the rest of the sentence with commas. Choice C inverts the order of the sentence and makes it more awkward; it is better to have a simple subject and verb at the beginning of a sentence. Choice A is incorrect because the word order confuses the sentence's meaning.

**8. C:** A comma is rarely needed after the word *and*. A comma would only be required if a nonessential phrase followed *and*. However, the word *and* in this sentence simply separates a two-item series. The other commas are correct because commas should be used both before and after a state's name.

**9. D:** This answer choice uses the correct punctuation and verb tense. Choice A is incorrect because the conjunction *and* separates two independent clauses; when the conjunction is used in this way, a comma must come before it. Choice B is incorrect because there is no conjunction between the two independent clauses, making the answer choice a run-on sentence. Choice C is incorrect because the passage is written in the past tense but *says* is incorrectly written in the present tense.

**10. A:** This is the best answer choice because *subsequently* sums up the essay and leads into the final paragraph. Choices B and D are incorrect because the words *furthermore* and *additionally* indicate that an additional argument will be made. Choice C is incorrect because the word *therefore* should be used as a conclusion to a specific point rather than the conclusion of an entire essay.

**11. B:** *Saw* is the correct past tense of the verb *see*. Choice A is not correct because *blackened* is the correct adjective. Choice C is not correct because a comma is needed to separate adjectives when each adjective separately describes the noun. Choice D is not correct because *into* is spelled correctly.

**12. D:** *Stares* is in the present tense, while the rest of the essay is in the past tense. *Stared* is the correct past tense of stare. Choice B is not correct because *me* is the object of the sentence as it is the recipient of the action *stares*. *I* is traditionally used as a subject. Choice C is not correct because *with hard eyes* is an introductory clause, and a comma is needed after the clause.

**13. D:** The quotation marks after *out* indicate dialogue. Quotation marks are needed before *Shut* to begin the dialogue. Choice A is not correct because when used as a noun, *everything* is one word. Choice B is not correct because a comma is needed before the closing quotation when the sentence is not completed with the quotation. Choice C is not correct because the sentence is not completed with the quotation, and therefore it needs a comma rather than a period before the closing quotation.

**14. D:** Choice D is grammatically correct. Choice B is not correct because when using the pronoun *me* in a series, it is always placed at the end of the series. Choice C is not correct because the repetition of *and* is not grammatically correct. The nouns need to be separated using commas in a series of more than two items.

**15. C:** A proper transition into the next sentence involves the acknowledgement that time has passed. Choice A is not correct because *however* is not a good transition into this sentence, as it does not require a shift in ideas. Choice B is not correct because *consequentially* is not a good transition into this sentence, as it presents no cause and effect. Choice D is not correct because *therefore* is not a good transition into this sentence, as it also presents no cause and effect.

**16. B:** This sentence is the most grammatically correct, and does not change the meaning of the original sentence. Answer choice A repeats the grammatical errors. Choices C and D change the meaning of the original sentence.

**17. B:** Emphasis and clarity are not needed for this split infinitive. So, it is best to place the verb directly after the infinitive *to*. Choice D is not correct because the author understands that the Revolutionary War had multiple purposes, but the author chooses to note that this was the primary purpose. Choice C is not correct because this is an essential modifier. Choice A is not correct because the split infinitive needs to be corrected.

**18. C:** This sentence directly supports the idea in the previous sentence about people taking their voting rights for granted. It shows that people don't have personal experience with being denied this right, and sets up the next sentence. Answer choices A and D do not make sense in the context of the discussion in this paragraph. Choice B does not support sentence (10) or lead into sentence (11) as effectively as choice C.

**19. A:** This revision mirrors the concise and more formal tone of the rest of the essay. Choices B and D are too short, and do not provide the context and explanation of the author's ideas like the other sentences in the essay do. Choice C is too formal and passive, whereas the rest of the essay has some conversational aspects to the language, and is, for the most part, active.

**20. B:** This sentence is a personal aside by the author, which is unnecessary and does not help with the argument being put forth by the author. It is best to remove this sentence to maintain a focus on the author's argument that more people need to exercise their right to vote.

**21. D:** This informal statement from the author shifts from the formal tone that has been established and is necessary for the addressed reader.

**22. B:** The verb *could* means that something might happen; the word *potentially* means the same thing and is redundant. Removing *soft* would make it unclear what type of drinks Elyse is referring to. The word *us* is required to know whom Elyse is talking about. The word *not* adds crucial meaning to the sentence; without the word, the reader would think Elyse was talking about drinking soft drinks in the high school.

**23. B:** This sentence explains the benefits of the education that Elyse proposes. The other choices are incorrect because they don't relate to the education plan that Elyse is proposing. These sentences might work better in the introductory or concluding paragraphs.

**24. D:** A colon is used to set off a list. The phrase *including those chocolate chip cookies* is a non-essential phrase that should be separated from the sentence in some way, such as parentheses. Deleting the comma after *drinks* is incorrect because the comma is required to separate the dependent clause from the independent clause. Changing *higher* to *high* is incorrect because using the word *high* changes the meaning of the sentence; Elyse is not proposing that the prices for should be high; instead, she is proposing that certain items should cost more (or have higher prices) than others. Changing *nutritional* to *nutrition* is incorrect because *nutritional* is an adjective while *nutrition* is a noun.

**25. A:** Sentence (18) supports Elyse's previous point with an additional point. The word *furthermore* correctly connects these two points. *However* and *although* are incorrect because these transition words are used for contrasting points, but Elyse is presenting two points that support each other. *In conclusion* is incorrect because Elyse is not done with her argument at this point.

## Arithmetic Placement Test

**1. B:** One way to compare fractions is to convert them to equivalent fractions with common denominators. In this case, the lowest common denominator of the three fractions is $7 \times 12 = 84$. Convert each of the fractions to this denominator: $\frac{1}{3} = \frac{1 \times 28}{3 \times 28} = \frac{28}{84}$, $\frac{2}{7} = \frac{2 \times 12}{7 \times 12} = \frac{24}{84}$, and $\frac{5}{12} = \frac{5 \times 7}{12 \times 7} = \frac{35}{84}$. Since $24 < 28 < 35$, it must be the case that $\frac{2}{7} < \frac{1}{3} < \frac{5}{12}$.

**2. A:** Evaluate the expression using the order of operations. Start by simplifying the operations inside parentheses.

$$\frac{2}{3}(3-2) + \frac{1}{2}(2-4)$$

$$\frac{2}{3}(1) + \frac{1}{2}(-2)$$

Then, simplify the multiplication.

$$\frac{2}{3} - \frac{2}{2}$$

Next, simplify the fraction $\frac{2}{2}$.

$$\frac{2}{3} - 1$$

Since we are subtracting fractions, change 1 to the equivalent fraction $\frac{3}{3}$ so the two fractions have the same denominator, and subtract the two fractions.

$$\frac{2}{3} - \frac{3}{3} = -\frac{1}{3}$$

**3. D:** There are 16 empty chairs. This gives $\frac{2}{5}$ of the total enrollment. So, the full class must be:

$$\text{Class} = \frac{5}{2} \times 16 = 40 \text{ students}$$

Another option is to use proportions.

$$\frac{2}{5} = \frac{16}{x}$$

First, cross multiply to get: $2x = 80$. Then, divide each side by 2 to solve for $x$. So, $x = 40$, which means there are 40 students in the entire class.

**4. D:** Taking a percent of a number means multiplying by that percent: if 50 is $P\%$ of 40, then $50 = 40 \times P\%$. That means $P\%$ is just $\frac{50}{40}$. We can write that as a decimal by dividing, putting a decimal point after the dividend and adding zeroes as necessary.

$$\begin{array}{r} 1.25 \\ 40 \overline{)50.00} \\ -40\phantom{.00} \\ \hline 100\phantom{0} \\ -80\phantom{0} \\ \hline 200 \\ -200 \\ \hline 0 \end{array}$$

So $\frac{50}{40} = 1.25$. To convert to a percent, we can multiply by 100, which is equivalent to moving the decimal point two places to the right: $1.25 = 125\%$.

**5. D:** If the dress's price is 20% off, it is $(100\% - 20\%) = 80\%$ of the regular price. So, the sales price of the dress, \$40, is 80% of what price? To find the answer, divide 40 by 80%, which is equivalent to the fraction $\frac{80}{100}$. Dividing by the fraction $\frac{80}{100}$ is the same as multiplying by its reciprocal, $\frac{100}{80}$. $40 \times \frac{100}{80} = 40 \times \frac{5}{4} = \frac{200}{4} = 50$, so, the original price was \$50.00.

**6. C:** Recall that "percent" just means "divided by 100." Find the equivalent fraction for each number:

I. $\frac{58}{67}$

II. $0.58\% = \frac{0.58}{100} = \frac{58}{10,000}$

III. $58\% = \frac{58}{100}$

IV. $5.8\% = \frac{5.8}{100} = \frac{58}{1,000}$

All of the fractions share the same numerator. Among fractions with the same numerator, the largest fraction has the smallest denominator. We can order these fractions from greatest to least by ordering the denominators from least to greatest. The correct order is $\frac{58}{67} > \frac{58}{100} > \frac{58}{1,000} > \frac{58}{10,000}$.

**7. A:** To multiply a fraction by a decimal, it is helpful to either convert both numbers to decimals or both numbers to fractions. If we convert $\frac{2}{5}$ to a fraction, we divide 2 by 5, putting a decimal point after the 2 and keeping track of where the digits of the quotient are relative to the decimal point.

$$\underline{0.4}$$

$$5\overline{)2.0}$$
$$\underline{-2\ 0}$$
$$0$$

So $\frac{2}{5} = 0.4$, and $\frac{2}{5} \times 2.5 = 0.4 \times 2.5$. $4 \times 25 = 100$, and since 0.4 and 2.5 each have one digit after the decimal point, the product should have two digits after the decimal point, so the answer is 1.00, or simply 1.

**8. C:** To find out how much more milk he needs, subtract the amount he has from the amount he needs: $2\frac{1}{4} - 1\frac{1}{2}$. To add or subtract mixed numbers, first convert them to improper fractions. We can do this by multiplying the integer part by the denominator and adding that to the numerator. So, $2\frac{1}{4} = \frac{2 \times 4 + 1}{4} = \frac{9}{4}$, and $1\frac{1}{2} = \frac{1 \times 2 + 1}{2} = \frac{3}{2}$. Now convert both fractions so that they share the lowest common denominator, which in this case is 4. $\frac{9}{4}$ already has a denominator of 4, so we need to convert $\frac{3}{2}$: $\frac{3}{2} = \frac{3 \times 2}{2 \times 2} = \frac{6}{4}$. We can now subtract: $\frac{9}{4} - \frac{6}{4} = \frac{3}{4}$. Therefore, Brian needs $\frac{3}{4}$ cup of milk in order to make the cookies.

**9. B:** Remember the order of operations: parentheses, exponents, multiplication and division, addition and subtraction.

Perform the operations inside the parentheses first.

$$5(10) + (5) - (45)$$

Then, do any multiplication and division, working from left to right. Remember, a number next to parentheses tells you to multiply the two values.

$$50 + 5 - 45$$

Finally, do any adding or subtracting, working from left to right.

$$55 - 45 = 10$$

**10. B:** The number of people who voted for the proposition is 9.5% of 51,623. If we only require an approximation, we can round 9.5% to 10%, and 51,623 to 50,000. Then 9.5% of 51,623 is about 10% of 50,000, or $0.1 \times 50,000 = 5,000$. Therefore, about 5,000 people voted for the proposition.

**11. B:** While we could multiply together all the numbers in the numerator and all the numbers in the denominator and then simplify, it would be easier to cancel what we can first. There is a factor of 7 in both the numerator and the denominator; we can cancel those. The same goes for a factor of 3. That leaves us with $\frac{1}{8} \times \frac{2}{1} \times \frac{4}{5} \times \frac{1}{1}$. We can go further, though; since $2 \times 4 = 8$, the 2 and the 4 in the numerator cancel the 8 in the denominator, leaving us with just $\frac{1}{1} \times \frac{1}{1} \times \frac{1}{5} \times \frac{1}{1}$, or simply $\frac{1}{5}$.

**12. C:** To solve, use the percentage increase formula.

$$\text{Percentage Increase} = \frac{\text{new} - \text{initial}}{\text{initial}} \times 100$$

In this case, the initial value is $80, and the new value is $120.

$$\text{Percentage Increase} = \frac{120 - 80}{80} \times 100 = \frac{40}{80} \times 100 = 50\%$$

Therefore, the total amount in her account increased by 50%.

**13. B:** To find the best estimate for this, start by rounding each number to the nearest whole number. To round 23.97124, look at the tenths place (9). Since this number is greater than or equal to 5, 23.97124 rounds up to 24. To round 8.023 to the nearest whole number, look again at the tenths place (0). Since it is less than 5, 8.023 rounds down to 8. Now these rounded numbers can be divided to find the best estimate. $24 \div 8 = 3$, so 3 is the best estimate for $23.79124 \div 8.023$.

**14. D:** To add or subtract fractions, first convert them to equivalent fractions with the lowest common denominator, which in this case is 15. So $\frac{2}{3} + \frac{2}{5} = \frac{2 \times 5}{3 \times 5} + \frac{2 \times 3}{5 \times 3} = \frac{10}{15} + \frac{6}{15} = \frac{16}{15}$. To convert this to a mixed number, divide the numerator by the denominator; the quotient is the integer part of the mixed number and the remainder is the numerator of the fractional part of the mixed number. $16 \div 15 = 1$ with a remainder of 1, so $\frac{16}{15} = 1\frac{1}{15}$.

**15. B:** To find the number of miles per hour over the speed limit, divide the fine by the cost for each mile over the speed limit: $882 \div 49 = 18$.

$$\begin{array}{r} 18 \\ 49\overline{)882} \\ -49\phantom{0} \\ \hline 392 \\ -392 \\ \hline 0 \end{array}$$

Therefore, Tina was traveling 18 mph over the speed limit.

**16. C:** In order to add decimal numbers, write them one above the other with the decimal points aligned, and then carry out the addition normally, placing the decimal point in the same position in the result.

$$\begin{array}{r} 2.220 \\ 0.100 \\ +0.623 \\ \hline 2.943 \end{array}$$

**17. B:** To multiply decimals, first multiply the numbers normally ignoring the decimal point; then, position the decimal point in the answer so that the number of digits after the decimal point in the product is equal to the sum of the number of digits after the decimal point in both factors. Performing the multiplication without regard to the decimal point first, we get $22 \times 313 = 6,886$. Since there is one digit after the decimal point in 2.2 and one digit after the decimal point in 31.3, there should be two digits after the decimal point in the product, which is therefore 68.86.

**18. A:** To find the value of the expression $0.924 - 0.439$, we will line the two numbers at the decimal point vertically with 0.924 above 0.439. Since 4 is smaller than 9, we will borrow 1 from the hundredths column to make the 4 into 14, then we subtract 9 from 14 to get 5. Since we had to turn the 2 into a 1 to borrow, we now must subtract 3 from 1. Since 1 is smaller than 3, we will again borrow 1 from the tenths place to make the 1 into an 11 and subtract 3 from it to get 8. Since we had to borrow from the tenths place and changed the 9 into an 8, we will subtract 4 from 8 to get 4. Therefore, the value of the expression $0.924 - 0.439$ is $0.485$.

$$\begin{array}{r} 0.9\overset{8}{\cancel{2}}\overset{11}{\cancel{4}}^{14} \\ -0.439 \\ \hline 0.48\,5 \end{array}$$

**19. C:** One way to compare two fractions is by converting them to a common denominator and then comparing the numerators. The fraction $\frac{2}{3}$ may be multiplied by $\frac{2}{2}$ to get a common denominator with $\frac{5}{6}$. $\frac{2\times 2}{3\times 2} = \frac{4}{6}$, and $4 < 5$, so $\frac{4}{6} < \frac{5}{6}$. This means that $\frac{2}{3} < \frac{5}{6}$, and the correct operation is $<$.

**20. B:** If he has covered $\frac{1}{2}$ the distance after two hours, and $\frac{2}{3}$ the distance after four hours, and he does not backtrack, then the fraction of the distance he has covered after three hours must be between $\frac{1}{2}$ and $\frac{2}{3}$. To compare fractions, we can convert them to equivalent fractions with the least common denominator. The least common denominator across all the fractions is 60, so the distances become $\frac{1}{2} = \frac{1\times 30}{2\times 30} = \frac{30}{60}$ and $\frac{2}{3} = \frac{2\times 20}{3\times 20} = \frac{40}{60}$. Now convert each of the answer options.

$$\frac{2}{5} = \frac{2 \times 12}{5 \times 12} = \frac{24}{60}$$
$$\frac{3}{5} = \frac{3 \times 12}{5 \times 12} = \frac{36}{60}$$
$$\frac{3}{4} = \frac{3 \times 15}{4 \times 15} = \frac{45}{60}$$
$$\frac{4}{5} = \frac{4 \times 12}{5 \times 12} = \frac{48}{60}$$

Only $\frac{36}{60}$ is between $\frac{30}{60}$ and $\frac{40}{60}$, so $\frac{3}{5}$ is the answer.

## Quantitative Reasoning, Algebra, and Statistics Placement Test

**1. D:** The volume of a right rectangular prism—that is, a box shape—is equal to the product of its length, width, and height. So, the volume of the given box is equal to $(20\text{ cm})(30\text{ cm})(15\text{ cm}) = 9{,}000\text{ cm}^3$.

**2. C:** Six hours is equal to $6 \times 60 = 360$ minutes. If Alice can create 1 ring in 12 minutes, then in 360 minutes she can create $\frac{360}{12} = 30$ rings.

Here is another way to solve the problem. A rate of 1 ring in 12 minutes is equivalent to a rate of $\frac{1 \text{ ring}}{12 \text{ minutes}} \times \frac{60 \text{ minutes}}{1 \text{ hour}} = \frac{5 \text{ rings}}{1 \text{ hour}}$. Therefore, in 6 hours Alice can create $5 \times 6 = 30$ rings.

**3. D:** To determine the probability of Susan's drawing two left and two right socks from the drawer, we can determine the total number of possible sets of two left socks and two right socks, and divide by the total number of possible sets of four socks. If there are eight pairs of socks in the drawer, then there are eight left socks, so the total number of possible sets of two left socks that can be drawn is $_8C_2 = \binom{8}{2} = \frac{8!}{2!(8-2)!} = \frac{8\times 7\times 6!}{2!\times 6!} =$

$\frac{56}{2} = 28$. By the same logic, there are also 28 possible sets of two right socks that can be drawn. Since there are 16 socks in the drawer in all, the total number of possible sets of four socks that can be drawn is:

$$_{16}C_4 = \binom{16}{4} = \frac{16!}{4!\,(16-4)!} = \frac{16 \times 15 \times 14 \times 13 \times 12!}{4! \times 12!} = 4 \times 5 \times 7 \times 13 = 1{,}820$$

The probability of her drawing two left socks and two right socks is therefore $\frac{28 \times 28}{1{,}820} = \frac{28}{65}$.

**4. B:** The charge is \$1.20 for each minute after the first ten minutes. The number of minutes after the first ten minutes is $m - 10$, so \$1.20 per minute charged for the part of the phone call exceeding 10 minutes is $1.2(m - 10)$. Adding this to the \$5.00 charge for the first ten minutes gives $d = 5 + 1.2(m - 10)$.

**5. D:** When a number is raised to a power, you multiply the number by itself the number of times indicated by the power. For example, $2^3 = 2 \times 2 \times 2 = 8$. A number raised to the power of 0 is always equal to 1. So, $6^0$ is the smallest number shown. Similarly, for the other numbers:

$$9 = 9;\ 10^1 = 10;\ 4^2 = 4 \times 4 = 16$$

Since $1 < 8 < 9 < 10 < 16$, we can write the order as $6^0, 2^3, 9, 10^1, 4^2$.

**6. D:** The probability of a woman from Department 1 being chosen is $\frac{11}{100}$ and the probability of a man from Department 2 is $\frac{15}{99}$, since there are only 99 employees left to choose from after the first employee has been selected. The probability of that pair being chosen is equal to the product of the two probabilities, since the picks are independent of one another. So, the product of the probabilities is $\frac{11}{100} \times \frac{15}{99} = \frac{165}{9{,}900}$, which simplifies to $\frac{1}{60}$.

**7. B:** Determine the probability of each choice.

For choice A, this is the total number of students in the broccoli circle of the Venn diagram divided by the total number of students surveyed:

$$\frac{10 + 4 + 3 + 15}{90} = \frac{32}{90} \approx 35.6\%$$

For choice B, this is the total number of students in the carrots circle and also in at least one other circle divided by the total number in the carrots circle:

$$\frac{15 + 3 + 6}{15 + 3 + 6 + 27} = \frac{24}{51} \approx 47.1\%$$

For choice C, this is the number of students in the intersection of all three circles divided by the total number in the overlap of the broccoli and cauliflower circles:

$$\frac{3}{3 + 4} = \frac{3}{7} \approx 42.9\%$$

For choice D, this is the number of students outside of all the circles divided by the total number of students surveyed:

$$\frac{23}{90} \approx 25.6\%$$

Since choice B has the highest percentage, it is the choice that is most probable.

**8. C:** If the exam has 30 questions, and the student answered $C$ questions correctly and left $B$ questions blank, then the number of questions the student answered incorrectly must be $30 - B - C$. The student gets 1 point for each correct question, or $1 \times C = C$ points, and loses $\frac{1}{2}$ point for each incorrect question, or $\frac{1}{2}(30 - B - C)$ points. Since the blank questions do not affect the student's score, one way to express his total score is $C - \frac{1}{2}(30 - B - C)$.

**9. B:** The average number of African American students in the 9th and 10th grades is approximately 204 (30% of 681). There are approximately 38 Asian females at the school ($0.06 \times 630$). The difference in the number of male and female students at the school is $630 - 589 = 41$, and the difference in the number of 9th and 12th grade students at the school is $354 - 255 = 99$. Therefore, the smallest quantity is the number of Asian female students at the school.

**10. A:** The average number of male students in the 11th and 12th grades is $\frac{131 + 119}{2} = 125$. The number of Hispanic students at the school is 10% of 1,219, which is $0.10 \times 1,219 = 121.9 \approx 122$ students. The difference in the number of male and female students at the school is $630 - 589 = 41$, and the difference in the number of 9th and 12th grade students at the school is $354 - 255 = 99$.

**11. C:** The ratio of volumes on two objects of the same shape is equal to the cube of the ratio of their lengths. Therefore, if the ratio of the length of the large cube to that of a building block is $\frac{20 \text{ cm}}{4 \text{ cm}} = 5$, the ratio of the volume of the large cube to that of a building block is $5^3 = 125$. Therefore, it will take 125 building blocks to make the large cube.

**12. B:** If there are $n$ floors and each floor has a height of $h$ feet, then to find the total height of the floors, we just multiply the number of floors by the height of each floor: $nh$. To find the total height of the building, we must also add the height of the spire, 30 feet. The building's total height in feet is $nh + 30$.

**13. A:** The position of the car is changing according to a constant speed. Thus, the graph will show a straight line with a positive but constant slope.

**14. B:** The average is the total amount spent divided by the number of students. The first three students spend an average of $10, so the total amount they spend is $3 \times \$10 = \$30$. The other six students spend an average of $4, so the total amount they spend is $6 \times \$4 = \$24$. The total amount spent by all nine students is $\$30 + \$24 = \$54$, and the average amount they spend is $\$54 \div 9 = \$6$.

**15. D:** 1 foot is equal to 12 inches, so the road is 12 inches long on the map. If the map's scale is 1 inch = 5 miles, then we can find the road's actual length by solving the proportion $\frac{12 \text{ inches}}{x \text{ miles}} = \frac{1 \text{ inch}}{5 \text{ miles}}$, or simply $\frac{12}{x} = \frac{1}{5}$. Solve this is by cross-multiplying: $12 \times 5 = x \times 1$, so $x = 60$. Therefore, the actual road is 60 miles long.

**16. C:** Start by evaluating each absolute value. Remember, absolute value shows the distance between the value and 0. In other words, it always makes the value positive.

$$\frac{2+2}{3-1}$$

From here, simplify the numerator and denominator.

$$\frac{4}{2}$$

Remember, a fraction bar represents division, so divide 4 by 2 to get the final answer.

$$4 \div 2 = 2$$

**17. D:** There are several ways to solve a system of equations like this. In this case, the simplest way to solve is by elimination. Add the two equations together to cancel out the $x$-values.

$$(x + 2y = 3) + (-x - 3y = 4)$$
$$x + 2y - x - 3y = 3 + 4$$
$$-y = 7$$
$$y = -7$$

Now, put that value for $y$ back into one of the original equations.

$$x + 2(-7) = 3$$
$$x - 14 = 3$$
$$x = 17$$

Therefore, the value of $x$ is 17.

**18. D:** To rationalize the denominator of a ratio of radicals, multiply both sides of the fraction by the radical in the denominator and reduce if necessary: $\frac{\sqrt{2}}{\sqrt{6}} = \frac{\sqrt{2} \times \sqrt{6}}{\sqrt{6} \times \sqrt{6}} = \frac{\sqrt{12}}{6} = \frac{2\sqrt{3}}{6} = \frac{\sqrt{3}}{3}$.

**19. B:** First, determine the proportion of students in Grade 5. Since the total number of students is 180, this proportion is $\frac{36}{180} = 0.2$, or 20%. Then, determine the same proportion of the total prizes, which is 20% of 20, or $0.2 \times 20 = 4$. Therefore, 4 prizes should go to fifth-grade students.

**20. A:** When graphing an inequality, a solid circle at an endpoint means that the number at that endpoint is included in the range, while a hollow circle means it is not. Since the inequality says that $x$ is strictly greater than –2, the circle at –2 should be hollow. Since the inequality says that $x$ is less than or equal to 4, the circle at 4 should be solid. $-2 < x \leq 4$ indicates that $x$ is between –2 and 4, so the area between the circles should be shaded.

## Advanced Algebra and Functions Placement Test

**1. C:** The area of the square base is just the square of the side length: $(700 \text{ ft})^2 = 490,000 \text{ ft}^2$. Since we only need an approximation, we can round that to $500,000 \text{ ft}^2$, or half a million square feet. The volume is therefore $\frac{1}{3}Bh \approx \frac{1}{3}\left(\frac{1}{2} \text{ million ft}^2\right)(450 \text{ ft}) = \frac{450}{6} \text{ million ft}^3 = 75 \text{ million ft}^3$.

**2. A:** The area of a square is equal to the square of the length of one side. If the area is 64 in², the side length must therefore be $\sqrt{64 \text{ in}^2} = 8$ in. The circle is inscribed in the square, so the side length of the square is the same as the circle's diameter. If the circle's diameter is 8 in, then the circle's radius must be half of that, or 4 in. The area of a circle is equal to $A = \pi r^2 = \pi(4 \text{ in})^2 = 16\pi \text{ in}^2$.

**3. C:** A method commonly taught to multiply binomials is the FOIL method, an acronym for *first, outer, inner, last*: multiply the first terms of each factor, then the outer terms, then the inner terms, and finally, the last terms.

$$(x+2)(x-3)$$
$$(x)(x) + (x)(-3) + (2)(x) + (2)(-3)$$

From here, simplify and combine like terms.

$$x^2 - 3x + 2x - 6$$
$$x^2 - x - 6$$

**4. C:** Substitute 2 for each $x$ and simplify.

$$f(2) = \frac{(2)^3 - 2(2) + 1}{3(2)} = \frac{8 - 4 + 1}{6} = \frac{5}{6}$$

**5. B:** Call the number of people present at the meeting $x$. If each person hands out a card to every other person (that is, every person besides himself), then each person hands out $x - 1$ cards. The total number of cards handed out is therefore $x(x - 1)$. Since we are told there are a total of 30 cards handed out, we have the equation $x(x - 1) = 30$, which we can rewrite as the quadratic equation $x^2 - x - 30 = 0$. We can solve this equation by factoring the quadratic expression. One way to do this is to find two numbers that add up to the coefficient of $x$ (in this case, –1) and that multiply to the constant term (in this case, –30). Those two numbers are 5 and –6. Our factored equation is therefore $(x + 5)(x - 6) = 0$. To make the equation true, one or both of the factors must be zero: either $x + 5 = 0$, in which case $x = -5$, or $x - 6 = 0$, in which case $x = 6$. Obviously, the number of people at the meeting cannot be negative, so the second solution, $x = 6$, must be correct. There are 6 people at the meeting.

**6. D:** Use the difference of squares rule that states that $(a + b)(a - b) = a^2 - b^2$, or multiply the binomials using the FOIL method: multiply together the *first* term of each factor, then the *outer* terms, then the *inner* terms, and finally the *last* terms. Then add the products together.

$$(x+6)(x-6) = x \times x + x \times (-6) + 6 \times x + 6 \times (-6)$$
$$= x^2 - 6x + 6x - 36$$
$$= x^2 - 36$$

**7. C:** When solving radical equations, check for extraneous solutions.

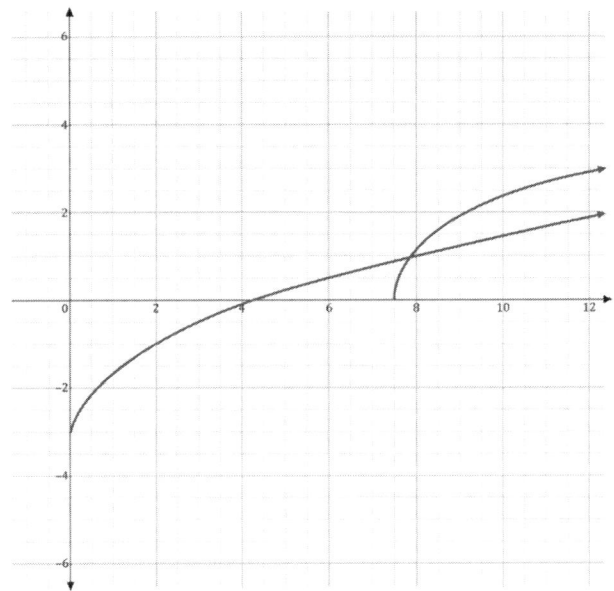

$$\sqrt{2x} - 3 = \sqrt{2x - 15}$$
$$\left(\sqrt{2x} - 3\right)^2 = \left(\sqrt{2x - 15}\right)^2$$
$$2x - 6\sqrt{2x} + 9 = 2x - 15$$
$$-6\sqrt{2x} + 9 = -15$$
$$-6\sqrt{2x} = -24$$
$$\sqrt{2x} = 4$$
$$2x = 16$$
$$x = 8$$

Check: 
$$\sqrt{2(8)} - 3 = \sqrt{2(8) - 15}$$
$$\sqrt{16} - 3 = \sqrt{16 - 15}$$
$$4 - 3 = \sqrt{1}$$
$$1 = 1$$

Since the solution checks, it is a valid solution. Notice that the graphs $y = \sqrt{2x} - 3$ and $y = \sqrt{2x - 15}$ intersect, which confirms there is a solution.

**8. A:** If $\cos \theta + 1 = 0$, then $\cos \theta = -1$. This has only one solution in the interval $0° \leq \theta < 360°$, namely $\theta = 180°$. This is not one of the answer choices; however, the cosine function has a period of $360°$, which means that adding or subtracting any multiple of $360°$ to the argument does not change the result. Since $180° - 360° = -180°$, $\cos(-180°) = \cos(180°) = -1$, so $-180°$ is also a solution to the equation.

**9. C:** We can write the problem as a system of two linear equations. Let $x$ be the number of gold coins and $y$ be the number of silver coins. Since there are fifty coins total, we have $x + y = 50$ as one of the equations. If each gold coin weighs 12 ounces, then the total weight in ounces of the gold coins is $12x$. Similarly, the total weight in ounces of the silver coins is $8y$. Since all the coins together weigh 30 pounds, which is equal to $30 \times 16 = 480$ ounces, we have $12x + 8y = 480$. Because each term in this equation is divisible by 4, we can divide the whole equation by 4 to get $3x + 2y = 120$. This is not a required step, but does make the numbers a little smaller and more manageable.

We now have two equations: $x + y = 50$ and $3x + 2y = 120$. There are a number of ways to solve a system of equations like this. One is to the substitution method. We can solve the first equation for $y$ to get $y = 50 - x$, and then substitute this into the second equation to get $3x + 2(50 - x) = 120$. After distributing the 2, we get $3x + 100 - 2x = 120$. Combining like terms gives $x + 100 = 120$. Finally, subtracting 100 from both sides yields $x = 20$. Thus, the number of gold coins is 20.

**10. C:** For any base $b$, $\log_b x$ and $b^x$ are inverse functions, so $\log_b(b^x) = b^{\log_b x} = x$. It is also true that $a^c = b$ is equivalent to $\log_a c = b$ for any positive $a$ and $c$. Therefore, $\log_5(5^3) = 3$.

**11. C:** The equation describes a functional relationship between $y$ and $p(y)$. To solve the equation, substitute 4 as the value of $y$.

$$p(4) = \frac{4(4)}{2} + 5 = \frac{16}{2} + 5 = 8 + 5 = 13$$

**12. A:** The equation for this scenario is $2b + 3c \geq 150$, where $b$ is the number of brownies that must be sold and $c$ is the number of cupcakes that must be sold. Solve for the intercepts of the inequality by momentarily changing the inequality sign to an equal sign, substituting 0 for $b$ and solving for $c$, and then substituting 0 for $c$ and solving for $b$. The intercepts of this linear inequality are $b = 75$ and $c = 50$. The $x$-axis represents the number of brownies sold, so the $x$-intercept is $(75, 0)$. The $y$-axis represents the number of cupcakes sold, so the $y$-intercept is $(0, 50)$. The solid line through the two intercepts, $(75,0)$ and $(0,50)$, represents the minimum number of each type of baked good that must be sold to offset production costs. Since you are breaking even or making a profit, shade above the line.

**13. C:** The four choices all have the two lines that mark the boundaries of the inequalities plotted identically; the only difference is which sides are shaded. It's therefore not necessary to check that the lines are correct; simply determine which of the areas bounded by the lines pertain to the system of inequalities. One way to do that is to pick a point in each region and check whether it satisfies the inequalities. For instance, in the region on the left, we can pick the origin, $(0, 0)$. Since $0 - 0 \not> 1$ and $2(0) + 0 \not> 2$, this does not satisfy either inequality, so the point $(0,0)$ is not in the shaded area. From the top region we can choose the point $(0, 3)$. $0 - 3 \not> 1$, so this fails to satisfy the first inequality. Therefore, the point $(0,3)$ is not in the shaded area. From the bottom region we can choose $(0, -2)$. $0 - (-2) > 1$, so the first inequality is satisfied, but $2(0) + (-2) \not> 2$, so the second is not. Therefore, $(0, -2)$ is not in the shaded area. Finally, from the rightmost region we can choose the point $(2, 0)$. $2 - 0 > 1$ and $2(2) + 0 > 2$, so both inequalities are satisfied; this is the only region that should be shaded.

**14. A:** Note that $(2x^2 + 3x + 2) - (x^2 + 2x - 3) = (2x^2 + 3x + 2) + (-1)(x^2 + 2x - 3)$. Distribute the $-1$ to remove the parentheses: $2x^2 + 3x + 2 - x^2 - 2x + 3$. Next, combine like terms.

$$(2x^2 - x^2) + (3x - 2x) + (2 + 3) = x^2 + x + 5$$

**15. C:** If the two lines intersect at the point $(2, 3)$, that means $x = 2$, $y = 3$ is a solution to both equations, and we can substitute in those values for $x$ and $y$ to yield $3 = 2a + b$ and $3 = 2b + 2a$. We now have two equations and two unknowns. There are many ways to solve this system of equations, including the substitution method. We can solve the first equation for $2a$ and substitute the result into the second equation, which also contains the term $2a$. The first equation solved for $2a$ is $2a = 3 - b$, and when this value for $2a$ is substituted into the second equation, we can solve for $b$.

$$3 = 2b + (3 - b)$$
$$3 = b + 3$$
$$b = 0$$

Since we already know $2a = 3 - b$, we can substitute the found value in for $b$ and solve for $a$.

$$2a = 3 - (0)$$
$$2a = 3$$
$$a = \frac{3}{2}$$

**16. D:** To simplify this rational expression, we can first factor out the largest common power of $x$ in both the numerator and denominator.

$$\frac{x^7 + 2x^6 + x^5}{x^4 - x^2} = \frac{x^5(x^2 + 2x + 1)}{x^2(x^2 - 1)}$$
$$= \frac{x^5}{x^2} \times \frac{x^2 + 2x + 1}{x^2 - 1}$$
$$= x^3 \times \frac{x^2 + 2x + 1}{x^2 - 1}$$

Now, we can factor both the numerator and denominator of the fraction. The numerator is a quadratic equation that can be factored by recognizing it as the square of a binomial: $(a + b)^2 = a^2 + 2ab + b^2$, so $x^2 + 2x + 1 = x^2 + 2(x)(1) + 1^2 = (x + 1)^2$. Similarly, the denominator is a difference of squares: $(a + b)(a - b) = a^2 - b^2$, so $x^2 - 1 = x^2 - 1^2 = (x + 1)(x - 1)$. The expression becomes:

$$x^3 \times \frac{(x+1)^2}{(x+1)(x-1)} = x^3 \times \frac{x+1}{x-1}$$
$$= \frac{x^3(x+1)}{x-1}$$
$$= \frac{x^4 + x^3}{x-1}$$

**17. D:** To solve the equation $3^x = 2$, we need to take the logarithm base three of both sides of the equation. ($b^x$ and $\log_b x$ are inverse functions and cancel each other out for any positive base $b$.) Then we have $\log_3(3^x) = \log_3 2$, or simply $x = \log_3 2$. Alternatively, just keep in mind that $a^b = c$ is equivalent to $\log_a c = b$ for any positive $a$ and $c$, so $3^x = 2$ is equivalent to $\log_3 2 = x$.

**18. A:** The expression may be factored as $(x - 8)(x + 5)$. The factorization may be checked by distributing each term in the first factor to each term in the second factor by using the FOIL method. Doing so gives $x^2 + 5x - 8x - 40$, which can be rewritten as $x^2 - 3x - 40$.

**19. B:** To simplify the inequality $x^2 + 2x \geq x + 6$, we can first move all the terms to the left-hand side.

$$x^2 + 2x - x - 6 \geq 0$$
$$x^2 + x - 6 \geq 0$$

We can now factor the left-hand side. Since the leading coefficient is 1, one way to do this is to look for two numbers that add to the coefficient of $x$ (1) and multiply to the constant term (–6). The two numbers that qualify are –2 and 3, so $x^2 + x - 6 = (x - 2)(x + 3)$.

$$(x - 2)(x + 3) \geq 0$$

We know the dividing points for the regions that do and do not satisfy the inequality are then at $x - 2 = 0$ and at $x + 3 = 0$, that is at $x = 2$ and at $x = -3$. Consider the sign in each region: when $x < -3$, then $x - 2$ and $x + 3$ are both negative, and their product is positive. When $-3 < x < 2$, then $x - 2$ is negative and $x + 3$ is positive, so their product is negative. When $x > 2$, then then $x - 2$ and $x + 3$ are both positive, and their product is positive: $(x - 2)(x + 3) \geq 0$ when $x \leq -3$ or $x \geq 2$.

**20. A:** $\sec \theta = \frac{1}{\cos \theta}$, or, equivalently, $\cos \theta = \frac{1}{\sec \theta}$. Therefore, if $\sec \theta = 2$, then $\cos \theta = \frac{1}{2}$. $\cos \theta = \frac{1}{2}$ when $\theta = 60°$ or $\theta = 300°$; $\sin 60° = \frac{\sqrt{3}}{2}$ and $\sin 300° = -\frac{\sqrt{3}}{2}$. Alternatively, use the Pythagorean identity $\sin^2 \theta + \cos^2 \theta = 1$ to find $\sin \theta$, so $\sin^2 \theta = 1 - \cos^2 \theta$, and $\sin \theta = \pm\sqrt{1 - \cos^2 \theta} = \pm\sqrt{1 - \left(\frac{1}{2}\right)^2} = \pm\sqrt{1 - \frac{1}{4}} = \pm\sqrt{\frac{3}{4}} = \pm\frac{\sqrt{3}}{2}$.

(Whether the sine is positive or negative depends on what quadrant the angle is in. There is not enough information given in the problem to determine that, which is why the problem only asks which of the answer choices is a *possible* value for $\sin \theta$.)

# Practice Test #2

## Reading Placement Test

*Refer to the following for questions 1–4:*

*[The Time Traveller is talking to his friends. He has just explained that while three dimensions—length, breadth, and thickness— are typically accepted, a "fourth dimension" should also be considered. ]*

'Well, I do not mind telling you I have been at work upon this geometry of Four Dimensions for some time. Some of my results are curious. For instance, here is a portrait of a man at eight years old, another at fifteen, another at seventeen, another at twenty-three, and so on. All these are evidently sections, as it were, Three-Dimensional representations of his Four-Dimensioned being, which is a fixed and unalterable thing.

'Scientific people,' proceeded the Time Traveller, after the pause required for the proper assimilation of this, 'know very well that Time is only a kind of Space. Here is a popular scientific diagram, a weather record. This line I trace with my finger shows the movement of the barometer. Yesterday it was so high, yesterday night it fell, then this morning it rose again, and so gently upward to here. Surely the mercury did not trace this line in any of the dimensions of Space generally recognized? But certainly it traced such a line, and that line, therefore, we must conclude was along the Time-Dimension.'

'But,' said the Medical Man, staring hard at a coal in the fire, 'if Time is really only a fourth dimension of Space, why is it, and why has it always been, regarded as something different? And why cannot we move in Time as we move about in the other dimensions of Space?'

The Time Traveller smiled. 'Are you sure we can move freely in Space? Right and left we can go, backward and forward freely enough, and men always have done so. I admit we move freely in two dimensions. But how about up and down? Gravitation limits us there.'

'Not exactly,' said the Medical Man. 'There are balloons.'

'But before the balloons, save for spasmodic jumping and the inequalities of the surface, man had no freedom of vertical movement.'

'Still they could move a little up and down,' said the Medical Man.

'Easier, far easier down than up.'

'And you cannot move at all in Time, you cannot get away from the present moment.'

'My dear sir, that is just where you are wrong. That is just where the whole world has gone wrong..."

[Adapted from H. G. Wells, *The Time Machine* (1895)]

1. **Which of the following best summarizes the above selection?**
   a. It is a conversation involving the age of men and space.
   b. It is a conversation about the nature of time and space.
   c. It is a dialogue from two friends about their medical ideas.
   d. It is a dialogue from two colleagues about time and distance.

2. As referred to in paragraph 6 above, what is a synonym for the word "spasmodic"?
   a. Required
   b. Impromptu
   c. Occasional
   d. Surprising

3. What effect does the point-of-view in this story have on its development?
   a. It makes the reader feel intelligent.
   b. It creates confusion.
   c. It builds suspense.
   d. It develops a feeling of contentment.

4. How can you tell that the mens' regular work is important?
   a. The author does not identify them by name, but by occupation.
   b. The author mentions the free movement of an object in space.
   c. The author mentions portraits of an aging person.
   d. None of the above

*Refer to the following for questions 5–8:*

**Passage A**

Black History Month is unnecessary. In a place and time in which we overwhelmingly elected an African American president, we can and should move to a post-racial approach to education. As Detroit Free Press columnist Rochelle Riley wrote in a February 1 column calling for an end to Black History Month, "I propose that, for the first time in American history, this country has reached a point where we can stop celebrating separately, stop learning separately, stop being American separately."

In addition to being unnecessary, the idea that African American history should be focused on in a given month suggests that it belongs in that month alone. It is important to instead incorporate African American history into what is taught every day as American history. It needs to be recreated as part of mainstream thought and not as an optional, often irrelevant, side note. We should focus efforts on pushing schools to diversify and broaden their curricula.

There are a number of other reasons to abolish it: first, it has become a shallow commercial ritual that does not even succeed in its (limited and misguided) goal of focusing for one month on a sophisticated, intelligent appraisal of the contributions and experiences of African Americans throughout history. Second, there is a paternalistic flavor to the mandated bestowing of a month in which to study African American history that is overcome if we instead assert the need for a comprehensive curriculum. Third, the idea of Black History Month suggests that the knowledge imparted in that month is for African Americans only, rather than for all people.

**Passage B**

Black History Month is still an important observance. Despite the election of our first African American president being a huge achievement, education about African American history is still unmet to a substantial degree. Black History Month is a powerful tool in working towards meeting that need. There is no reason to give up that tool now, and it can easily coexist with an effort to develop a more comprehensive and inclusive yearly curriculum.

Having a month set aside for the study of African American history doesn't limit its study and celebration to that month; it merely focuses complete attention on it for that month. There is absolutely no contradiction between having a set-aside month and having it be present in the curriculum the rest of the year.

Equally important is that the debate *itself* about the usefulness of Black History Month can, and should, remind parents that they can't necessarily count on schools to teach African American history as thoroughly as many parents would want.

Although Black History Month has, to an extent, become a shallow ritual, it doesn't have to be. Good teachers and good materials could make the February curriculum deeply informative, thought-provoking, and inspiring. The range of material that can be covered is rich, varied, and full of limitless possibilities.

Finally, it is worthwhile to remind ourselves and our children of the key events that happened during the month of February. In 1926, Woodson organized the first Black History Week to honor the birthdays of essential civil rights activists Abraham Lincoln and Frederick Douglass. W. E. B. DuBois was born on February 23, 1868. The 15th Amendment, which granted African Americans the right to vote, was ratified on February 3, 1870. The first black US senator, Hiram R. Revels, took his oath of office on February 25, 1870. The National Association for the Advancement of Colored People (NAACP) was founded on February 12, 1909. Malcolm X was shot on February 21, 1965.

**5. The author's primary purpose in Passage A is to:**
   a. Argue that Black History Month should not be so commercial.
   b. Argue that Black History Month should be abolished.
   c. Argue that Black History Month should be maintained.
   d. Suggest that African American history should be taught in two months rather than just one.

**6. It can be inferred that the term *post-racial* in the second sentence of Passage A refers to an approach that:**
   a. Treats race as the most important factor in determining an individual's experience
   b. Treats race as one factor, but not the most important, in determining an individual's experience
   c. Considers race after considering all other elements of a person's identity
   d. Is not based on or organized around concepts of race

**7. Which of the following statements is true?**
   a. The author of Passage A thinks that it is important for students to learn about the achievements and experiences of African Americans, while the author of Passage B does not think this is important.
   b. The author of Passage B thinks that it is important for students to learn about the achievements and experiences of African Americans, while the author of Passage A does not think this is important.
   c. Neither author thinks that it is important for students to learn about the achievements and experiences of African Americans.
   d. Both authors think that it is important for students to learn about the achievements and experiences of African Americans.

**8. The author of Passage A argues that celebrating Black History Month suggests that the study of African American history can and should be limited to one month of the year. What is the author of Passage B's response?**
   a. Black History Month is still an important observance.
   b. Black History Month is a powerful tool in meeting the need for education about African American history.
   c. Having a month set aside for the study of African American history does not limit its study and celebration to that month.
   d. Black History Month does not have to be a shallow ritual.

**9. The statements made in the passage support which of the following claims?**

> It is believed that the diamond was originally discovered and extracted in India as much as 6,000 years ago. The word *diamond*, however, derives from the Greek αδαμας, or *adámas*, which means "unbreakable" or even "untamed," and has made its way into Western literature through the Greek tradition. Having heard rumors of exceptionally strong stones, the Greeks developed a mythology about an unbreakable stone that was known as *adamant*. By the Middle Ages, this came to be recognized as the diamond. Over time, the legendary adamant came to take on a mystical quality that passed into certain forms of medieval literature and even today has an allegorical place in some genres.

   a. Given the legendary status of the adamant, it might have been better if the diamond and its actual qualities had remained a mystery.
   b. Because the adamant was originally associated with mythical qualities, it retains figurative attributes that are still valuable for some writers.
   c. The diamond and the adamant are essentially the same gem, and the two terms can be interchanged.
   d. The Greek word *adámas* is based on an ancient word of India that meant the same thing but has now been lost to history.

**10. If the passage is true, which of the following can be inferred from it?**

> Colorblindness is a vision deficiency that limits the ability of the sufferer to see certain colors clearly. The condition may affect a person in varying degrees, ranging from mild colorblindness with a red or green color deficiency to complete colorblindness with no ability to distinguish any colors beside dim shades of brown. The primary cause of colorblindness is believed to be a mutation on the X chromosome. Men carry a single X chromosome, possessing an XY-chromosome makeup, while women carry two X chromosomes, thus having the potential to combat colorblindness with an extra X chromosome.

   a. Colorblindness is a rare condition that affects very few members of the population.
   b. Despite the handicap, those who are colorblind might have certain advantages, particularly in seeing camouflage.
   c. Women alone are capable of passing on a gene for colorblindness.
   d. Because of the way colorblindness affects the X chromosome, men are more likely to be colorblind than women.

**11. What is the main purpose of the paragraph?**

Some of our most delighted *voyageurs* are from Portland, Maine. When they had journeyed some 1,500 miles to Omaha they imagined themselves at least half way across our continent. Then, when they had finished that magnificent stretch of some 1,700 miles more from Omaha to Portland, Oregon, in the palace cars of the Union Pacific, they were quite sure of it. Of course, they confessed a sense of mingled disappointment and eager anticipation when they learned that they were yet less than half way. They learned what is a fact—that the extreme west coast of Alaska is as far west of Sitka as Portland, Maine, is east of Portland, Oregon, and the further fact that San Francisco lacks 4,000 miles of being as far west as Uncle Sam's "Land's End," at extreme Western Alaska.

a. To convey the awe and delight the group felt at seeing the sights of Alaska
b. To describe the people in the group
c. To show the great distance and size of Alaska
d. To explain that San Francisco lacks 4,000 miles of being as far west as Uncle Sam's "Land's End"

**12. If the passage is true, all of the following may be concluded EXCEPT:**

Psychologists have found that there are fascinating differences between children and adults when it comes to learning a new musical instrument. In particular, the piano is an instrument that knows no one age for learning and presents multiple opportunities for the successful attainment of musical skills. It does, however, offer a variety of challenges both to children and to adults – due to the differences in mind development – with children developing certain skills more quickly and more effectively than adults. How quickly children learn is often limited by their motor skills, but they are more likely to remember in detail the pieces they learn and to retain that knowledge over long periods of time. At the same time, adults are more likely to retain the muscle memory of the pieces that they learn and reproduce them blindly, just by allowing their fingers to recall the correct notes.

a. Adult minds learn the skills required to play the piano differently than children's minds.
b. Adults might not recall the exact details of the piece they learned, but the muscle memory in their fingers makes them very likely to remember the notes.
c. The piano is the only instrument that both children and adults can learn to play well.
d. Learning the piano is not limited to children, because adults can learn to play well.

**13. Considering the claims below within the context of the passage, which claim is most likely to be true?**

The climate extremes of the North Atlantic nation of Iceland ensure that little plant growth is able to survive there. The majority of the island is covered in low grasses, with only one tree species known to exist. Deforestation in previous centuries depopulated the entire island of its trees. Because of both the severe cold and the severe heat, plants require a long period of time to grow in Iceland, and modern residents have only just begun replanting the trees. Plant life in Iceland is also notoriously delicate, and off-road vehicles are allowed only in certain areas; in some cases, hikers are required to walk around certain plants to ensure that the plants will survive even during the extreme weather that constantly surrounds Iceland.

a. More developed plant growth exists closer to the island's center, where volcanic warmth allows the plants to survive.
b. The plants that manage to survive in Iceland are extremely hardy.
c. The only type of tree capable of growing successfully in Iceland is the northern birch.
d. Off-road vehicles can cause permanent or long-term damage to the re-growth of some plants.

**14. Which of the following statements best explains the farmer's concern about the high cost of setting up a certified organic farm?**

A local farmer is hoping to establish a certified organic farm but is concerned about the cost of setting it up. A certified organic farm requires far fewer supplies than a non-organic farm, and most of the supplies are less costly in comparison. Also, because an organic farm does not use expensive pesticides or tools, the cost of maintenance is also fairly low in comparison to the maintenance cost of a non-organic farm. But the set-up of the certified organic farm remains expensive, and the farmer is unsure if the return on his investment will justify the cost.

a. There is little demand in the community for more certified organic food.
b. More resources are required for establishing a certified organic farm than a non-organic farm.
c. There are three other certified organic farms in the community that are much larger than the farm the farmer is planning to establish.
d. The licensing fees for the farmer to acquire certification add considerably to the cost of set-up.

**15. Which of the following best summarizes the paragraph?**

Are video games without pitfalls? Certainly not. But many games offer life-improving benefits that are often overlooked. They improve coordination and response time. They enhance logic and reasoning. They fill empty hours productively and create a sense of passion and excitement. Lastly, video games foster a variety of social bonds among players of all types, skill levels, and backgrounds. With so many positive aspects, video games are worth checking out. Try them—you might find you like them!

a. Video games are good for everyone
b. Video games have a number of pitfalls
c. Social bonds are one of the greatest benefits of video games
d. Despite the pitfalls, video games are worth trying

**16. The tone of this passage is**

It is supposed that the Phoenicians, who were an ancient people, famous for carrying on trade, came in ships to these Islands, and found that they produced tin and lead; both very useful things, as you know, and both produced to this very hour upon the sea-coast. The most celebrated tin mines in Cornwall are, still, close to the sea. One of them, which I have seen, is so close to it that it is hollowed out underneath the ocean; and the miners say, that in stormy weather, when they are at work down in that deep place, they can hear the noise of the waves thundering above their heads. So, the Phoenicians, coasting about the Islands, would come, without much difficulty, to where the tin and lead were.

a. humorous
b. informative
c. angry
d. bored

**17. What is the author's purpose in writing this passage?**

Many of the concepts utilized in crew resource management (CRM) have been successfully applied to single-pilot operations which led to the development of single-pilot resource management (SRM). Defined as the art and science of managing all the resources (both on board the aircraft and from outside resources) available to a single pilot (prior to and during flight), SRM ensures the successful outcome of the flight. SRM training helps the pilot maintain situational awareness by managing automation, associated control, and navigation tasks. This enables the pilot to accurately assess hazards, manage resulting risk potential, and make good decisions. To make informed decisions during flight operations, a pilot must be aware of the resources found both inside and outside the cockpit. Resources must not only be identified, but a pilot must also develop the skills to evaluate whether he or she has the time to use a particular resource and the impact its use has upon the safety of flight.

a. To describe single-pilot resource management
b. To compare single-pilot resource management to crew resource management
c. To persuade readers to use single-pilot resource management
d. To answer objections to single-pilot resource management

**18. Since Glenda was short on money, she decided that her current appliances were ____ for the present.**

a. ephemeral
b. imperious
c. pestilent
d. sufficient

**19. The varsity basketball team's perfect season ____ in a championship win over their biggest rival.**

a. alleviated
b. culminated
c. dispersed
d. lamented

**20. The forecaster said that the high winds would ____ around midnight and that the next day would have light breezes.**

a. capitulate
b. dispatch
c. intensify
d. subside

# Writing Placement Test

*Refer to the following for questions 1–5:*

(1) My favorite song is "imagine" by John Lennon. (2) It was released in 1971. (3) It is one of the few famous songs that John Lennon recorded and sang alone. (4) For the majority of his career, John Lennon was a member of an iconic rock band called the Beatles, a band that changed the music industry. (5) The Beatles accepted a lot of success in their career, with popular songs such as "I Want to Hold Your Hand," "Come Together," "Let it Be," and "Here Comes the Sun." (6) After the band decided to separate, John Lennon became a solo artist as well as a promoter for peace.

(7) "Imagine" tells the story of Lennons dream of peace in the world. He asks the listener to imagine different situations. (8) He says to imagine that there are no countries, religions, or possessions. (9) He says, "I wonder if you can." (10) This line strikes me the most I try to imagine such a world. (11) When talking about no possessions, he continues and says, "No need for greed or hunger." (12) It is a great line. (13) Throughout the

song, he says, "Imagine all the people." (14) And he gives examples. (15) At first he says, "living for today," and then moves on to say, "living life in peace," and finally, "sharing all the world."

(16) My favorite part of the song is the chorus. (17) Lennon says, "You may say I'm a dreamer, but I'm not the only one. (18) I hope someday you'll join us, and the world will be as one." (19) When I really listen to the words of this song, I realize that "Imagine" is so much more than something that sounds nicely. (20) Lennon is saying something very important and suggesting ways in which the world can live in peace. (21) Because of this song, I am a dreamer as well, and I join John Lennon in the fight for world peace.

**1. Which is the best version of sentence (2)?**
 a. NO CHANGE
 b. The song is just as popular today as it was in 1971.
 c. The song was released in 1971.
 d. Although it was released in 1971, the lyrics are still important today.

**2. What is the best verb to replace *accepted* in sentence (5)?**
 a. Lasted
 b. Liked
 c. Had
 d. Watched

**3. Which is the best version of sentence (10)?**
 a. NO CHANGE
 b. This line strikes me the most, I try to imagine such a world.
 c. This line strikes me, the most. I try to imagine such a world.
 d. This line strikes me the most as I try to imagine such a world.

**4. Which is the best way to combine sentences (13) and sentence (14)?**
 a. Throughout the song he says "Imagine all the people" and he gives examples.
 b. Throughout the song, he says, "Imagine all the people," and he gives examples.
 c. Throughout the song he says Imagine all the people, and he gives examples.
 d. Throughout the song he says Imagine all the people and he gives examples.

**5. What correction should be made to sentence (19)?**
 a. Delete the comma after *song*
 b. Change *something* to *some thing*
 c. Change *nicely* to *nice*
 d. Change *realize* to *realized*

*Refer to the following for questions 6–10:*

(1) In Ruth Campbell's book *Exploring the Titanic*, the events of the famous ship's only journey and sinking are brought to life. (2) In 1912, Titanic was built and was the largest passenger steamship at the time. (3) On what would be its first and only journey, the ship departed from Southampton in England and was supposed to arrive in New York City. (4) The ship hit an iceberg late at night on April 14, 1912, and sunked less than three hours later.

(5) Titanic was designed by some of the best engineers and had the latest technology of the time. (6) The ship was made to carry over three and a half thousand passengers and crew members, but had only twenty lifeboats. (7) There was not enough lifeboats for all of the people onboard, and as a result, only seven hundred six people survived.

(8) One interesting thing about Titanic, is that the ship was divided into classes. (9) The most expensive tickets were first class, and first class passengers had the biggest and much luxurious rooms. (10) The first class rooms were the closest to the ship's deck. (11) Because this the majority of survivors came from first class. (12) They were able to reach the deck fastest to get a seat on a lifeboat. (13) The third class rooms were located the farthest below deck, and the majority of the third class passengers did not survive.

(14) Ruth Campbell's book was very interesting but also sad because the story of Titanic is true. (15) However, Campbell ended the book by talking about the positive things that have happened because of this tragedy. (16) Most importantly, experts now recommend that ships' carry enough lifeboats for all passengers onboard. (17) This would have saved a lot of lifes. (18) It was a good book, and it displayed a good message in history that lessons should be learned from mistakes.

**6. What correction should be made to sentence (1)?**
  a. Change ship's to ships
  b. Insert a comma after book
  c. Change are to is
  d. Change brought to bring

**7. Which of the following options improves the precision of language in sentence 7 without adding new information?**
  a. Due to the limited number of lifeboats on board, only seven hundred six individuals were able to survive the sinking of the Titanic.
  b. Titanic had insufficient lifeboats to rescue all passengers, causing the death of more than half of those on board.
  c. The lifeboats provided were scarce, with the majority of passengers and crew succumbing to the freezing waters.
  d. As a result of inadequate safety measures, only seven hundred six people were rescued from the sinking ship, despite having thousands on board.

**8. What correction should be made to sentence (8)?**
  a. NO CHANGE
  b. Delete the comma after Titanic
  c. Change divided into divide
  d. Change was to were

**9. What is the BEST way to revise and combine sentence 11 and sentence 12?**
  a. Because, the majority of survivors came from first class as they were able to reach the deck fastest to get a seat on a lifeboat.
  b. Because of this, the majority of survivors came from first class, as they were able to reach the deck fastest to get a seat on a lifeboat.
  c. Because this, the majority of survivors came from first class, they were able to reach the deck fastest to get a seat on a lifeboat.
  d. Because of this, the majority of survivors came from first class as they were able to reach the deck fastest to get a seat on a lifeboat.

**10. What is the BEST transition that could be added to the beginning of sentence 13?**
  a. Lastly
  b. For example
  c. On the other hand
  d. Therefore

*Refer to the following for questions 11–15:*

### The Beginnings of Basketball

(1) One of the most popular and exciting sports of our time, is basketball. (2) Behind this fast-paced sport, however, is a rich history. (3) There have been many changes made to the game over the years, but the essence remains the same. (4) From its humble beginnings in 1891, basketball has grown to have worldwide appeal.

(5) In 1891, Dr. James Naismith, a teacher and Presbyterian minister, needed an indoor game to keep college students busy during long winter days in Springfield, Massachusetts at the Springfield YMCA Training School. (6) This need prompted the creation of basketball, which was originally played by tossing a soccer ball into an empty peach basket nailed to the gym wall. (7) Additionally, there was two teams but only one basket in the original game.

(8) Because of the simplicity of basketball, the game spread across the nation within 30 years of its invention in Massachusetts. (9) As more teams formed, the need for a league became apparent. (10) The smaller National Basketball League (NBL) formed soon after. (11) On June 6, 1946 the Basketball Association of America (BAA) was formed. (12) In 1948, the BAA merged with the NBL, and the National Basketball Association (NBA) was born. (13) The NBA played its first full season in 1948–49 and is still going strong today.

(14) Though much has changed in our world since 1891, the popularity of the sport of basketball has remained strong. (15) From it's humble start in a YMCA gym to the multi-million-dollar empire it is today, the simple fun of the sport has endured. (16) Although many changes have been made over the years, the essence of basketball has remained constant. (17) Its rich history and simplicity ensure that basketball will always be a popular sport around the world.

**11. Which is the best way to combine sentences (2) and (3)?**
   a. Behind this fast-paced sport is a rich history; however, there have been many changes made to the game over the years.
   b. Over the years the essence remains the same for this fast-paced sport with its rich history.
   c. Behind this fast-paced sport is a rich history, but the essence remains the same.
   d. Though there have been many changes made to the game over the years, the essence remains the same for this fast-paced sport with its rich history.

**12. Consider the following excerpt from the passage.**

Sentence (5): In 1891, Dr. James Naismith, a teacher and <u>Presbyterian minister, needed</u> an indoor game to keep college students busy during long winter days in Springfield, Massachusetts at the Springfield YMCA Training School.

**Select the best version of the underlined portion.**
   a. NO CHANGE
   b. Presbyterian Minister needed
   c. presbyterian minister, needed
   d. a Presbyterian Minister, founded

13. **Where should this sentence be located to achieve the best organization and clarity for the paragraph?**

   <u>The smaller National Basketball League (NBL) formed soon after.</u>

   a. It should remain where it is.
   b. It should be moved one sentence earlier.
   c. It should be moved one sentence later.
   d. It should be moved to the end of the paragraph.

14. **Consider the following excerpt from the passage.**

   Sentence (15): From <u>it's humble start in a YMCA gym to the multi-million-dollar empire</u> it is today, the simple fun of the sport has endured.

   **Select the best version of the underlined portion.**

   a. NO CHANGE
   b. it's humble start in a YMCA gymnasium to the multi-million-dollar
   c. it's humble start in a YMCA gym to the multi-million dollar
   d. its humble start in a YMCA gym to the multi-million-dollar

15. **The author wants to add the following statement to the passage:**

   *One thing that sets the history of basketball apart from other major sports is the fact that it was created with the intent of playing indoors.*

   **Where should this sentence be added?**

   a. After sentence (3)
   b. After sentence (4)
   c. After sentence (8)
   d. After sentence (14)

*Refer to the following for questions 16–20:*

(1) Most scientists agree that while the scientific method is an invaluable methodological tool, it is not a failsafe method for arriving at objective truth. (2) It is debatable, for example, whether a hypothesis can actually be confirmed by evidence.

(3) When the hypothesis is of a form, "All x are y," which is commonly believed that a piece of evidence that is both x and y confirms the hypothesis. (4) For example, for the hypothesis "All monkeys are hairy," a particular monkey that is hairy is thought to be a confirming piece of evidence for the hypothesis. (5) A problem arises when one encounters evidence that disproves a hypothesis: while no scientist would argue that one piece of evidence proves a hypothesis, it is possible for one piece of evidence to disprove a hypothesis. (6) To return to the monkey example, one hairless monkey out of one billion hairy monkeys disproves the hypothesis "All monkeys are hairy." (7) Single pieces of evidence, then, seem to affect a given hypothesis in radically different ways. (8) For this reason, the confirmation of hypotheses is better described as probabilistic.

(9) Hypotheses that can only be proven or disproven based on evidence need to be based on probability because sample sets for such hypotheses are too large. (10) In the monkey example, every single monkey in the history of monkeys would need to be examined before the hypothesis could be proven. (11) By making confirmation a function of probability, one may make provisional or working conclusions that allow for the possibility of a given hypothesis being dissipated in the future. (12) In the monkey case, then, encountering a hairy monkey would slightly raise the probability that "all monkeys are hairy," while encountering a hairless monkey would slightly decrease the probability that "all monkeys are hairy." (13) This method of confirming

hypotheses is both counterintuitive and controversial, but it allowed for evidence to equitably effect hypotheses and it does not require infinite sample sets for confirmation or disconfirmation.

**16. Which is the best placement for sentence (4) in this passage?**
a. NO CHANGE
b. After sentence (5)
c. After sentence (6)
d. Before sentence (7)

**17. Consider the following excerpt from the passage.**

Sentences 7-8: Single pieces of evidence, then, seem to affect a given hypothesis in radically <u>different ways. For this reason, the confirmation</u> of hypotheses is better described as probabilistic.

**Select the best version of the underlined portion.**
a. different ways, but the confirmation
b. different ways; therefore, the confirmation
c. different ways—the confirmation
d. different ways; however, for this reason, the confirmation

**18. Consider the following excerpt from the passage.**

Sentence 11: By making confirmation a function of probability, one may make provisional or working conclusions that allow for the possibility of a given hypothesis being <u>dissipated</u> in the future.

**Select the best version of the underlined portion.**
a. NO CHANGE
b. distilled
c. disconfirmed
d. destroyed

**19. Consider the following excerpt from the passage.**

Sentence 13: This method of confirming hypotheses is both counterintuitive and controversial, <u>but it allowed for evidence to equitably effect hypotheses</u> and it does not require infinite sample sets for confirmation or disconfirmation.

**Select the best version of the underlined portion.**
a. NO CHANGE
b. but it allows for evidence to equitably effect hypotheses,
c. but it allowed for evidence to equitably affect hypotheses,
d. but it allows for evidence to equitably affect hypotheses,

**20. This passage ends with, "...it does not require infinite sample sets for confirmation or disconfirmation." This statement refers to information found where in the passage?**
a. Most specifically in the initial sentence in this same paragraph
b. Most specifically in the second sentence of the same paragraph
c. Most specifically the fourth sentence of the previous paragraph
d. The information is not found in any paragraph.

*Refer to the following for questions 21–25:*

### New Zealand Inhabitants

(1) The islands of New Zealand are among the most remote of all the Pacific islands. (2) New Zealand is an archipelago, with two large islands, and a number of smaller ones. (3) Its climate is far cooler than the rest of Polynesia. (4) Nevertheless, according to Maori legends, it was colonized in the early fifteenth century by a wave of Polynesian voyagers who traveled southward in their canoes and settled on North Island. (5) At this time, New Zealand will already be known to the Polynesians, who had probably first landed there some 400 years earlier.

(6) The Polynesian southward migration was limited by the availability of food. (7) Traditional Polynesian tropical crops such as taro and yams will grow on North Island, but the climate of the South Island is too cold for them. (8) The first settlers were forced to rely on hunting and gathering, and, of course, fishing. (9) Especially on the South Island, most settlements remained close to the sea. (10) At the time of the Polynesian incursion, enormous flocks of moa birds had their rookeries on the island shores. (11) These flightless birds were easy prey for the settlers, and within a few centuries had been hunted to extinction. (12) Fish, shellfish and the roots of the fern were other important sources of food, but even these began to diminish in quantity as the human population increased. (13) The Maori had few other sources of meat: dogs, smaller birds, and rats. (14) Archaeological evidence shows that human flesh was also eaten, and that tribal warfare increased markedly after the moa disappeared.

(15) By far the most important farmed crop in prehistoric New Zealand was the sweet potato. (16) This tuber is hearty enough to grow throughout the islands, and could be stored to provide food during the winter months, when other food-gathering activities were difficult. (17) The availability of the sweet potato made possible a significant increase in the human population. (18) Thus, Maori tribes were often located near the most fertile farmlands in encampments called pa, which were fortified with earthen embankments.

**21. What is the BEST way to revise and combine sentence 2 and sentence 3?**
   a. Its climate is far cooler than the rest of Polynesia because New Zealand is an archipelago, with two large islands and a number of smaller ones.
   b. New Zealand is an archipelago, with two large islands and a number of smaller ones, and its climate is far cooler than the rest of Polynesia.
   c. Its climate is far cooler than the rest of Polynesia; however, New Zealand is an archipelago, with two large islands and a number of smaller ones.
   d. New Zealand is an archipelago, with two large islands and a number of smaller ones; thus, its climate is far cooler than the rest of Polynesia.

**22. Consider the following excerpt from the passage.**
   Sentence (5): <u>At this time, New Zealand will already be known to the Polynesians</u>, who had probably first landed there some 400 years earlier.

**Select the best version of the underlined portion.**
   a. NO CHANGE
   b. New Zealand is already known by the Polynesians
   c. New Zealand has already been known to the Polynesians
   d. New Zealand was already known to the Polynesians

**23. What is the best replacement for the word *incursion* as used in sentence 10?**
   a. NO CHANGE
   b. Import
   c. Influx
   d. Gathering

24. **Consider the following excerpt from the passage.**

> Sentences (8-9): The first settlers were forced to rely on hunting, gathering, and <u>fishing. Especially on the South Island</u>, most settlements remained close to the sea.

**Select the best version of the underlined portion.**
   a. fishing, but especially on South Island
   b. fishing; however, on South Island
   c. fishing: especially on South Island
   d. fishing; therefore, on South Island

25. **Which is the best placement for sentence 17 in this passage?**
   a. Before sentence 16
   b. After sentence 12
   c. After sentence 18
   d. In its current place

## Arithmetic Placement Test

1. **Which of the following fractions is closest to $\frac{15,012}{19,938}$?**
   a. $\frac{1}{4}$
   b. $\frac{3}{4}$
   c. $\frac{4}{5}$
   d. $\frac{5}{9}$

2. **In an election in Kimball County, Candidate A obtained 36,800 votes. His opponent, Candidate B, obtained 32,100 votes. Write-in candidates obtained 2,100 votes. What percentage of the vote went to Candidate A?**
   a. 45.2%
   b. 46.8%
   c. 51.8%
   d. 53.4%

3. **Which of the following is largest?**
   a. 0.55
   b. 0.500
   c. 0.505
   d. 0.0555

4. **A regular toilet uses 3.2 gallons of water per flush. A low-flow toilet uses 1.6 gallons of water per flush. What is the difference between the number of gallons used by the regular toilet and the low-flow toilet after 375 flushes?**
   a. 100 gallons
   b. 525 gallons
   c. 600 gallons
   d. 1,200 gallons

5. Which of the following is NOT equal to the others?
   a. $\frac{10}{3}$
   b. $\frac{30}{9}$
   c. $2\frac{4}{3}$
   d. $3\frac{2}{3}$

6. What is $-\frac{3}{2}\left(\frac{1}{2}+\frac{1}{3}\right)-\frac{2}{3}\left(\frac{1}{2}-\frac{3}{4}\right)$?
   a. $-1\frac{5}{12}$
   b. $-1\frac{1}{12}$
   c. $-1\frac{1}{2}$
   d. $1\frac{5}{12}$

7. What is $783 - 124$?
   a. 559
   b. 584
   c. 619
   d. 659

8. What is $156 \div 4$?
   a. 13
   b. 27
   c. 35
   d. 39

9. Three treasure hunters decide to split up their haul. The first treasure hunter gets $\frac{1}{3}$ of the treasure. The second treasure hunter gets $\frac{1}{4}$ of the treasure. What fraction of the treasure does the third treasure hunter get?
   a. $\frac{1}{2}$
   b. $\frac{1}{5}$
   c. $\frac{5}{7}$
   d. $\frac{5}{12}$

10. Find the value of $100 \div (9 + 1) \times 2$.
    a. 5
    b. 15
    c. 20
    d. 76

11. What is $6.32 - 3.5$?
    a. 2.82
    b. 3.18
    c. 3.27
    d. 5.97

12. What is the proper ordering (from greatest to least) of the following numbers?

   I. $0.071\%$
   II. $0.71$
   III. $7.1\%$
   IV. $\frac{71}{101}$

   a. II, III, I, IV
   b. II, IV, III, I
   c. III, II, I, IV
   d. IV, I, III, II

13. A fruit vendor has 52 mangoes, 88 kiwis, 48 pineapples, and 45 papayas. How many pieces of fruit does the vendor have?

   a. 221
   b. 231
   c. 233
   d. 243

14. A reporter for a school newspaper surveys the students at the school to ask if they prefer chocolate, vanilla, or strawberry ice cream. Of the students who answer her question, 35% prefer vanilla, and 40% prefer chocolate. What percent of the students she surveyed prefer strawberry?

   a. 15%
   b. 25%
   c. 35%
   d. 40%

15. What is $1\frac{3}{4} \div \frac{7}{10}$?

   a. $2\frac{1}{2}$
   b. $2\frac{1}{14}$
   c. $1\frac{11}{14}$
   d. $\frac{4}{10}$

16. Which of the following inequalities is true?

   a. $\frac{4}{5} < \frac{5}{7}$
   b. $\frac{5}{7} > \frac{3}{5}$
   c. $\frac{2}{3} > \frac{4}{5}$
   d. $\frac{1}{2} < \frac{2}{5}$

17. A local theater group rents an auditorium with 25 rows of 40 seats each. How many seats does the auditorium contain?

   a. 800 seats
   b. 900 seats
   c. 1,000 seats
   d. 1,200 seats

18. What is $3\frac{1}{4} + 2\frac{5}{6}$?

    a. $5\frac{1}{2}$
    b. $5\frac{3}{5}$
    c. $6\frac{1}{12}$
    d. $6\frac{1}{2}$

19. What is 10% of 40%?

    a. 4%
    b. 30%
    c. 50%
    d. 400%

20. What is $2.62 \times 7.1$?

    a. 1.462
    b. 14.62
    c. 16.062
    d. 18.602

# Quantitative Reasoning, Algebra, and Statistics Placement Test

1. Freshmen and sophomore students at a high school were asked which caffeinated beverage they prefer. Given the two-way frequency table shown below with a summary of their responses, what is the probability that a student is a sophomore or prefers lattes?

|  | Cappuccino | Latte | Frappuccino | Total |
|---|---|---|---|---|
| Freshman | 20 | 29 | 22 | 71 |
| Sophomore | 19 | 26 | 22 | 67 |
| Total | 39 | 55 | 44 | 138 |

a. $\frac{48}{59}$
b. $\frac{37}{51}$
c. $\frac{16}{23}$
d. $\frac{39}{50}$

2. The variables $x$ and $y$ have a linear relationship. The table below shows a few sample values. Which of the following graphs correctly represents the linear equation relating $x$ and $y$?

| $x$ | $y$ |
|---|---|
| −2 | −11 |
| −1 | −8 |
| 0 | −5 |
| 1 | −2 |
| 2 | 1 |

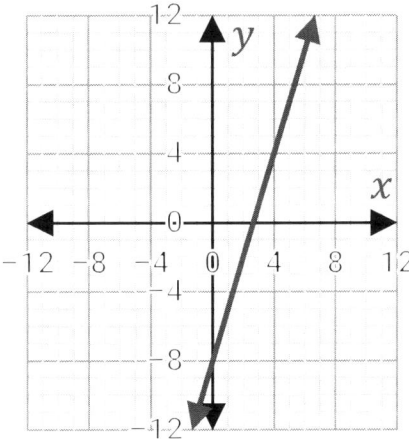
a.

b.

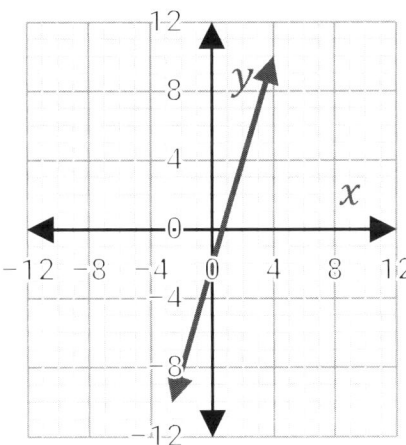
c.

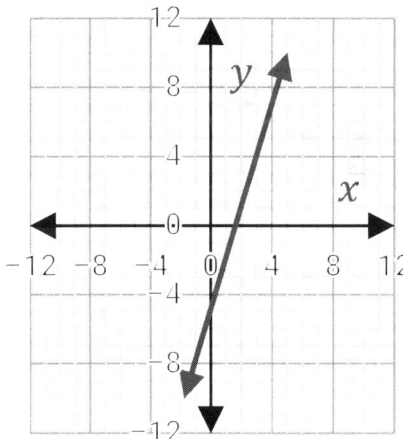
d.

3. A rectangular lot is three yards wide and four yards long. What is the area of the lot in square feet?
 a. $4 \text{ ft}^2$
 b. $12 \text{ ft}^2$
 c. $36 \text{ ft}^2$
 d. $108 \text{ ft}^2$

4. Which of the following is the solution to $3 - 2x < 5$ ?
 a. $x < 1$
 b. $x > 1$
 c. $x < -1$
 d. $x > -1$

5. Last year, Jenny tutored students in math, in chemistry, and for the ACT. She tutored 10 students in math, 8 students in chemistry, and 7 students for the ACT. She tutored 5 students in math and chemistry, and she tutored 4 students in chemistry and for the ACT, and 5 students in math and for the ACT. She tutored 3 students in all three subjects. How many students did Jenny tutor last year?
   a. 34
   b. 25
   c. 23
   d. 14

*Refer to the following for question 6:*

Kyle bats third in the batting order for the Badgers baseball team. The table below shows the number of hits that Kyle had in each of 7 consecutive games played during one week in July.

| Day | Monday | Tuesday | Wednesday | Thursday | Friday | Saturday | Sunday |
|---|---|---|---|---|---|---|---|
| Hits | 1 | 2 | 3 | 1 | 1 | 4 | 2 |

6. What is the mean of the numbers in the distribution shown in the table?
   a. 1
   b. 2
   c. 3
   d. 4

7. There are twelve inches in a foot, and three feet in a yard. How many inches are in five yards?
   a. 20
   b. 41
   c. 75
   d. 180

8. $|x| > x$ for what values of $x$?
   a. $x < 0$
   b. $x > 0$
   c. $|x| > x$ for all real values of $x$.
   d. There is no real number $x$ such that $|x| > x$.

9. Which of the following is equal to 0.0023?
   a. $2.3 \times 10^{-3}$
   b. $2.3 \times 10^{-2}$
   c. $2.3 \times 10^{2}$
   d. $2.3 \times 10^{3}$

10. What is $\frac{x^3+2x}{x+3}$ when $x = -1$ ?
   a. $-\frac{3}{2}$
   b. $-\frac{2}{3}$
   c. $\frac{1}{2}$
   d. $\frac{3}{4}$

11. A school is selling tickets to its production of *Annie Get Your Gun*. Student tickets cost $3 each, and non-student tickets are $5 each. To offset the costs of the production, the school must earn at least $300 in ticket sales. Which graph shows the number of tickets the school must sell to offset production costs?

a.

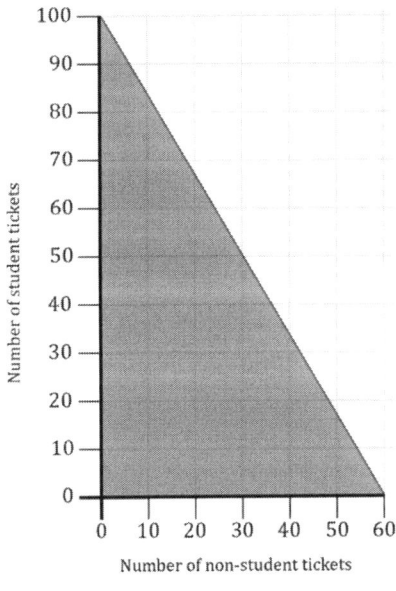

c.

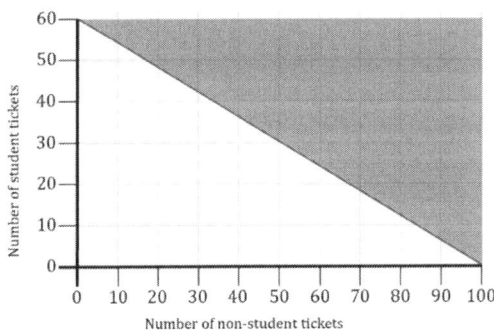

b.

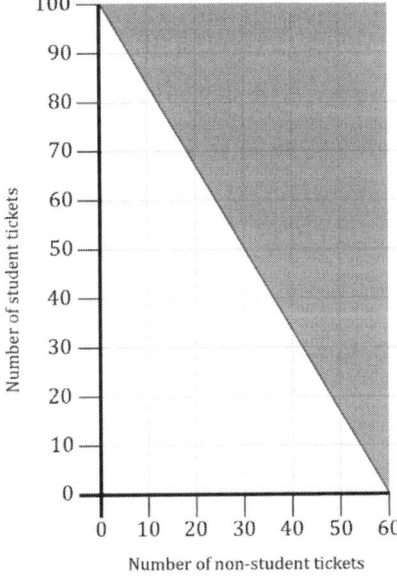

d.

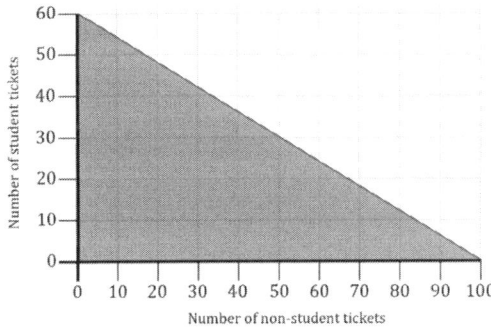

*Refer to the following for question 12:*

Kyle bats third in the batting order for the Badgers baseball team. The table below shows the number of hits that Kyle had in each of 7 consecutive games played during one week in July.

| Day | Monday | Tuesday | Wednesday | Thursday | Friday | Saturday | Sunday |
|---|---|---|---|---|---|---|---|
| Hits | 1 | 2 | 3 | 1 | 1 | 4 | 2 |

12. What is the median of the numbers in the distribution shown in the table?

   a. 1
   b. 2
   c. 3
   d. 4

13. What is $|x| + |x - 2|$ when $x = 1$?

   a. 0
   b. 1
   c. 2
   d. 3

14. The two shortest sides of a right triangle are 6 and 8 units long, respectively. What is the perimeter of the triangle?

   a. 10 units
   b. 14 units
   c. 18 units
   d. 24 units

15. Sam runs for fifteen minutes at eight miles per hour, and then jogs for forty-five minutes at four miles per hour. What is his average speed during this time?

   a. 5 miles per hour
   b. 5.5 miles per hour
   c. 6 miles per hour
   d. 7 miles per hour

16. Mandy can buy 4 containers of yogurt and 3 boxes of crackers for $9.55. She can buy 2 containers of yogurt and 2 boxes of crackers for $5.90. How much does one box of crackers cost?

   a. $1.75
   b. $2.00
   c. $2.25
   d. $2.50

17. Which of the following exponential expressions represents the smallest number?

   a. $8^{\frac{3}{2}}$
   b. $16$
   c. $4^{\frac{5}{2}}$
   d. $2^{\frac{7}{2}}$

18. Joanie is playing songs on her MP3 player from a 15-song playlist in which every song is equally likely to be played next. Three of the 15 songs are by Beyonce. What is the probability that the next two songs will both be by an artist who is not Beyonce?

 a. $\frac{1}{25}$
 b. $\frac{9}{25}$
 c. $\frac{16}{25}$
 d. $\frac{24}{25}$

19. Attending a summer camp are 12 six-year-olds, 15 seven-year-olds, 14 eight-year-olds, 12 nine-year-olds, and 10 ten-year-olds. If a camper is randomly selected to participate in a special event, what is the probability that he or she is at least eight years old?

 a. $\frac{2}{9}$
 b. $\frac{22}{63}$
 c. $\frac{4}{7}$
 d. $\frac{3}{7}$

20. Water drains from a bathtub at a rate of one gallon every fifteen seconds. If the bathtub initially has twelve gallons of water in it, how long will it take to drain completely?

 a. 48 seconds
 b. 1 minute 15 seconds
 c. 3 minutes
 d. 4 minutes

## Advanced Algebra and Functions Placement Test

1. A function $f(x)$ is defined by $f(x) = 2x^2 + 7$. What is the value of $2f(x) - 3$?

 a. $4x^2 + 11$
 b. $4x^4 + 11$
 c. $x^2 + 11$
 d. $4x^2 + 14$

2. Solve the system of equations.

$$3x + 4y = 2$$
$$2x + 6y = -2$$

 a. $\left(0, \frac{1}{2}\right)$
 b. $\left(\frac{2}{5}, \frac{1}{5}\right)$
 c. $(2, -1)$
 d. $\left(-1, \frac{5}{4}\right)$

3. The two legs of a right triangle have side lengths of 5 and 12. What is the length of the hypotenuse?

 a. 13
 b. 17
 c. $\sqrt{60}$
 d. $\sqrt{119}$

4. Simplify $\frac{x^6}{y^4} \cdot x^2 y^3$.

   a. $x^4 y$
   b. $\frac{x^4}{y}$
   c. $x^8 y$
   d. $\frac{x^8}{y}$

5. Consider the function $f$, whose graph appears here, and the function $g$, defined by $g(x) = -x^2 + 8x - 15$. Which of the following statements correctly describes properties these two functions have in common?

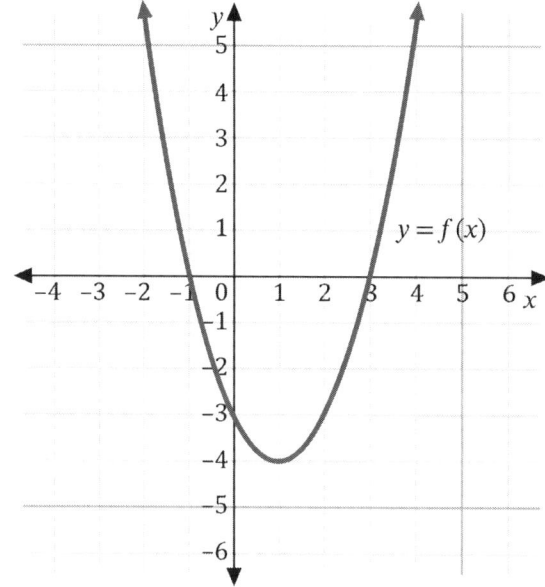

   a. They have the same vertex.
   b. They have the same two roots.
   c. They have the same $y$-intercept.
   d. They have exactly one common root.

6. Which of the following is NOT a factor of $x^3 - 3x^2 - 4x + 12$?

   a. $x - 2$
   b. $x + 2$
   c. $x - 3$
   d. $x + 3$

7. Two companies offer monthly cell phone plans, both of which include free text messaging. Company A charges a $25 monthly fee plus five cents per minute of phone conversation, while Company B charges a $50 monthly fee and offers unlimited calling. At what total duration of monthly calls do both companies charge the same amount?

   a. 500 hours
   b. 8 hours and 33 minutes
   c. 8 hours and 20 minutes
   d. 5 hours

*Refer to the following for question 8:*

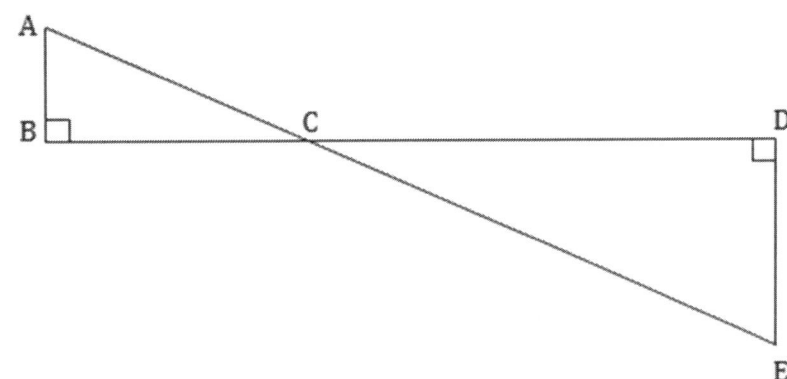

8. In the figure above, $\overline{BC}$ is 4 units long. Segment $\overline{CD}$ is 8 units long. Segment $\overline{DE}$ is 6 units long. What is the length of segment $\overline{AC}$?

   a. 7 units
   b. 5 units
   c. 3 units
   d. 2.5 units

9. In the triangle, which of the following is equal to $\sin \theta$?

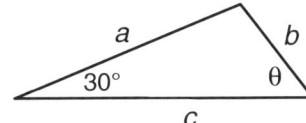

   a. $\frac{a}{2b}$
   b. $\frac{2b}{a}$
   c. $\frac{a}{2c}$
   d. $\frac{b}{ac}$

10. The table below shows the cost of renting a bicycle for 1, 2, or 3 hours. Which answer choice shows the equation that best represents the data? Let $C$ represent the cost of the rental and $h$ stand for the number of hours of rental time.

| Hours | 1 | 2 | 3 |
|---|---|---|---|
| Cost | $3.60 | $7.20 | $10.80 |

   a. $C = 3.60h$
   b. $C = h + 3.60$
   c. $C = 3.60h + 10.80$
   d. $C = \frac{10.80}{h}$

11. The population of the town of Wrassleton has tripled every ten years since 1950. If $P_0$ is the town's population in 1950 and $t$ is the number of years since 1950, which of the following describes the town's growth during this time?

   a. $P(t) = 10 P_0^{3t}$
   b. $P(t) = P_0^{\frac{3}{10}t}$
   c. $P(t) = P_0 \times 3^{\frac{t}{10}}$
   d. $P(t) = P_0 \times \left(\frac{3}{10}\right)^t$

12. Factor the following expression: $x^2 + x - 12$

   a. $(x - 2)(x + 6)$
   b. $(x + 6)(x - 2)$
   c. $(x - 4)(x + 3)$
   d. $(x + 4)(x - 3)$

13. Ben is purchasing notebooks and boxes of pencils for a class he is teaching. Notebooks cost $1 each and pencils cost $3 per box. If the $x$-axis represents boxes of pencils, the $y$-axis represents notebooks, and Ben can spend a maximum of $30, which of the following graphs shows the number of notebooks and pencils Ben can purchase?

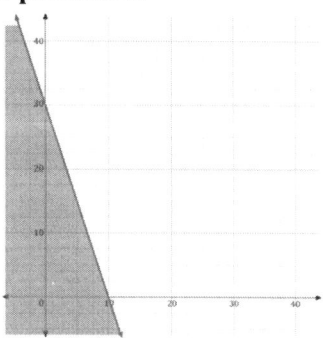
a.

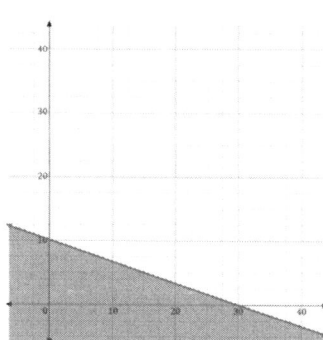
c.

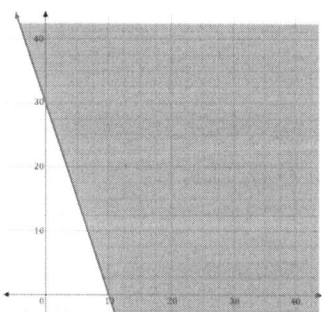
b.

d.

14. Solve in the complex number system: $7x^2 + 6x = -2$.

   a. $x = \frac{-3 \pm \sqrt{23}}{7}$
   b. $x = \pm i\sqrt{5}$
   c. $x = \pm \frac{2i\sqrt{2}}{7}$
   d. $x = \frac{-3 \pm i\sqrt{5}}{7}$

15. If $2\sec\theta = \tan^2\theta$, which of the following is a possible value for $\sec\theta$?
   a. 2
   b. $1+\sqrt{2}$
   c. $\sqrt{2}-1$
   d. $2-\sqrt{2}$

16. What is $(2+\sqrt{3}) \div (2-\sqrt{3})$?
   a. 2
   b. $\sqrt{3}$
   c. $7+4\sqrt{3}$
   d. $1+4\sqrt{3}$

17. Which of the following is equivalent to $x^2 + 3 > 2x + 2$?
   a. $x < -1$
   b. $x \neq 1$
   c. $x > 1$
   d. $x < -1$ or $x > 1$

18. If $x > 2$, then what is the value of $\left(\frac{x^2-5x+6}{x+1}\right) \times \left(\frac{x+1}{x-2}\right)$?
   a. $x+1$
   b. $x-3$
   c. $\frac{x^2+2x+1}{x-2}$
   d. $\frac{x^2-2x-3}{x+1}$

19. Given the diagram below, which of the following theorems may be used to verify that lines $a$ and $b$ are parallel?

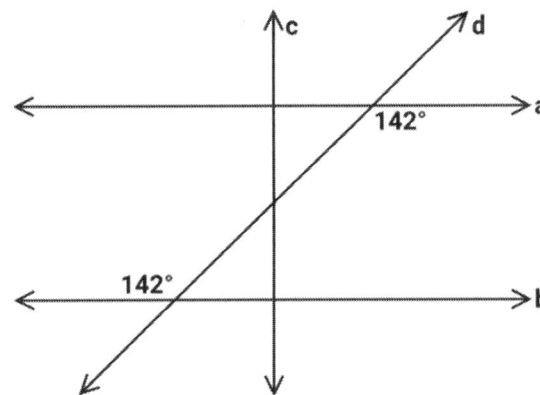

   a. Alternate interior angles converse theorem
   b. Alternate exterior angles converse theorem
   c. Consecutive interior angles converse theorem
   d. Corresponding angles converse theorem

20. Which of the following represents the graph of $y = (x-4)^2 + 3$?

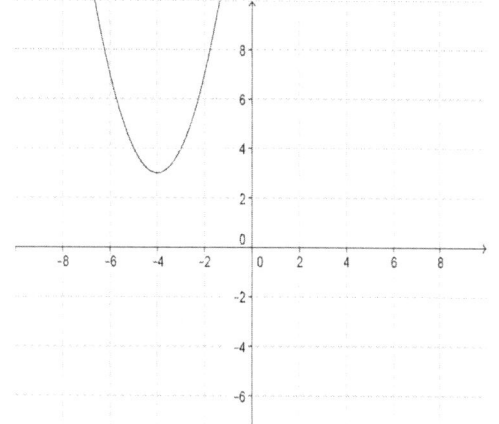

a.

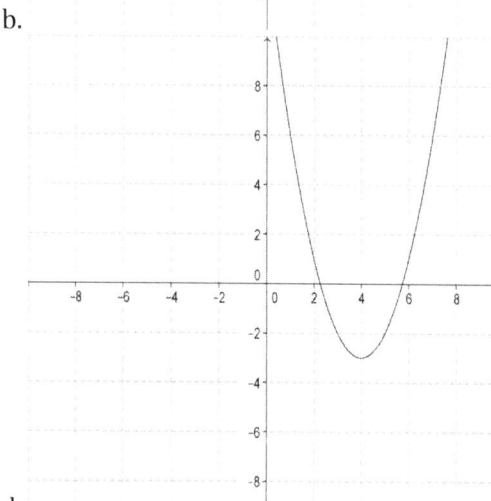

b.

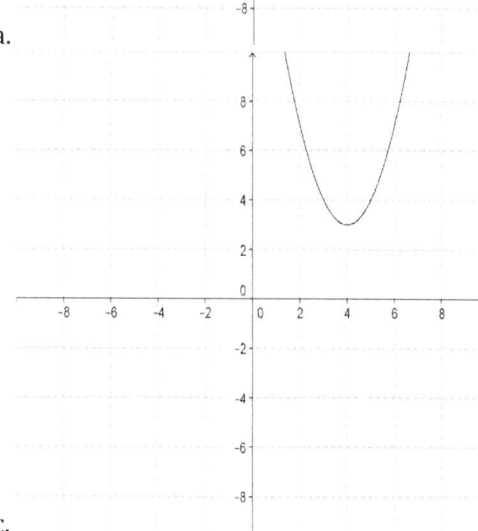

c.

d.

# Answer Key and Explanations for Test #2

## Reading Placement Test

**1. B:** The two men are talking about four possible dimensions and their ability to move through them.

**2. C:** "Occasional" is very similar in meaning to "spasmodic."

**3. C:** It builds suspense because the Time Traveller already knows about the outcome of his experiments with time travel, and he is only leading his audience along by explaining the thought process behind it.

**4. A:** The characters in the selection are not given names, but occupation titles. The Time Traveller and the Medical Man are discussing their ideas here to give the reader a quick insight into their characters.

**5. B:** Passage A begins with the sentence "Black History Month is unnecessary," then goes on to make the argument that Black History Month should be abolished and offers numerous reasons for why this is the best course of action. The passage does mention that it has become "a shallow commercial ritual," but this is one of the many reasons given for abolishing it, not the primary purpose of the passage. The author wants to abolish Black History Month, not maintain or expand it.

**6. D:** The context of the sentence suggests that *post-racial* refers to an approach in which race is not a useful or positive organizing principle. The term *post-racial* refers to a time period when racial discrimination no longer exists. The author of Passage A believes that we are in a post-racial time and that it is time to remove race from education, which includes ending Black History Month.

**7. D:** Clearly both authors think it is important for students to learn about the achievements and experiences of African Americans; their debate is whether observing Black History Month is the best way to achieve this goal.

**8. C:** The author of Passage B points out that just because there is a month focused on African American history, this doesn't mean that African American history must be ignored for the rest of the year.

**9. B:** Choice B accurately provides an inference that has clear antecedent in the passage. The author of the passage claims, "By the Middle Ages, this came to be recognized as the diamond. Over time, the legendary adamant came to take on a mystical quality that passed into certain forms of medieval literature and, even today, has an allegorical place in some genres." This means that the inference and claim made in choice B are correct: the adamant *was* originally associated with mythical qualities, and as a result, writers still utilize it in literature for its figurative (or allegorical) attributes.

**10. D:** At the end of the passage, the author notes, "Men carry a single X chromosome, possessing an XY-chromosome makeup, while women carry two X chromosomes, thus having the potential to combat colorblindness with an extra X chromosome." This suggests that men are more likely to be colorblind than women because men have only a single X chromosome. Of all the options, choice D can best be inferred from the passage, so it is correct.

**11. C:** Paragraph 7 mostly gives specific details showing how far away Alaska is from the mainland (such as in the phrase that says *they were yet less than half way*). Choice A is incorrect because the group is not yet in Alaska. Instead, they are journeying towards the territory and learning how big it is. Although the paragraph does give some details about people in the group, such as the hometown of some of the travelers, the majority of the paragraph focuses on the location and size of Alaska. Choice D is incorrect because this just a detail listed at the end of the paragraph. The main part of the paragraph talks about the size and distance of the territory.

**12. C:** The author states early in the passage, "the piano is an instrument that knows no one age for learning and presents multiple opportunities for the successful attainment of musical skills." This suggests that the piano is *one* instrument that both adults and children can learn to play. This does not imply, however, that the piano is the *only* instrument that adults and children can learn to play. Choice C cannot be concluded from the passage, so it is the correct answer.

**13. D:** Of all the options, choice D is the only one that can correctly be inferred from the information in the passage. The author states that "little plant growth will be able to survive" in Iceland, that "plants require a long period of time to grow in Iceland," and that "the plant life in Iceland is also notoriously delicate." This suggests that off-road vehicles have the potential to destroy plant life, leaving plants unable to grow back for long periods of time or, in some cases, unable to grow back at all.

**14. D:** Answer choice (D) most clearly explains the reason for the farmer's concerns about cost. Although the cost of supplies and maintenance might be lower than that of a non-organic farm, the cost of the certification itself is very high, creating a financial burden for the farmer as he tries to establish the certified organic farm. Answer choice (D) is correct.

**15. D:** The paragraph discusses the benefits of playing video games but also acknowledges that they have issues.

**16. B:** The author describes the history of the islands and gives informative details about the islands and the people who lived there in the past. Choice A is incorrect because the author does not make jokes during the article; instead, he simply describes facts. Choice C is incorrect because the author does not display anger or any other emotions; he simply describes facts. Choice D is incorrect because the author proves that he's very interested in the topic by giving many descriptive details. Therefore, he is the opposite of bored.

**17. A:** The passage is a broad overview of single-pilot resource management (SRM). The passage only briefly mentions CRM and does not fully compare it to SRM (B). Given the passage's characterization as an overview of SRM, there is no persuasive element to the passage (C), nor does it discuss objections to SRM (D).

**18. D:** "Short on money" is a clue that Glenda could not afford new appliances. Sufficient means adequate or tolerable. If Glenda is not able to buy new appliances, then her current appliances will have to be satisfactory until she can afford new ones.

**19. B:** *Culminate* means to come to completion. The words "perfect season" and "championship win" allude to the happy ending of the basketball season. *Culminate* is the only choice that fits.

**20. D:** The only word choices which make any sense at all are subside and intensify. The next day's light breezes indicate that the winds would decrease, or subside, making subside the best choice. While it is possible that the already high winds could intensify, it is far more likely that the next day's "light breezes" indicate the opposite.

## Writing Placement Test

**1. D:** The sentence as written is a fact that is not essential to this passage. To maintain the focus of the passage, the author should note a reason for including this information. Choice D is the best option because the fact remains and the focus can continue with explaining the reason for the importance of the lyrics. Choice B is not the best option because it is not the focus of the passage on whether the song is popular. Instead, the focus is on how the song is impactful to an individual. Choice C is not the option because it does not correct the shift in focus. Choice A is not correct because the sentence should be revised.

**2. C:** The missing verb in this sentence must have something to do with possession since it discusses the band's success. *Had* indicates possession. A, B, and D are incorrect, because these verbs do not fit within the sentence.

**3. D:** The sentence is missing the article *as*. This is the simplest way to express the idea of the sentence. B is incorrect because this sentence is not grammatically correct. C is incorrect because the first sentence is grammatically incorrect.

**4. B:** This is the simplest way to express the idea in a grammatically correct sentence. A is incorrect because a comma is missing after *song* and after *people*. C is incorrect because a comma is missing after *song*, and quotation marks are missing around the quotation, *"Imagine all the people."* D is not correct. A comma is missing after *song* and after *people*, and quotation marks are missing around the quotation, *"Imagine all the people."*

**5. C:** In this sentence *nice* is an adjective rather than an adverb. It describes the noun, *sounds*, not the verb. A is not correct. *When I really listen to the words of this song* is an introductory clause, and a comma is needed after the clause. B is not correct. *Something* is one word when used as a noun. D is not correct. Although most of the essay is in the past tense, the final paragraph is in the present tense. *Realized* is in the past tense.

**6. B:** A comma is needed to separate the interjection of the book title. *Ship* in the sentence is possessive and requires the apostrophe. *Are* is the plural of *is*. The subject, *events*, is plural and therefore the verb needs to be plural in subject-verb agreement. *Are brought* is in the past participle, and *bring* is in the present tense.

**7. A:** Choice A provides a more precise explanation of the reason why only a limited number of people were able to survive the sinking of the Titanic. It replaces the vague phrase *not enough* with *limited*, which is a more specific term that clearly identifies the issue. Additionally, the revised sentence maintains the original meaning and accurately conveys the fact that the insufficient number of lifeboats was the main reason why so many people died. Choice B introduces new information by suggesting that more than half of the passengers on board died, which is not mentioned in the original sentence. The word *insufficient* can also be interpreted in several ways, which does not contribute to a more precise meaning. Choice C uses the improved word *scarce* but also adds new information about the freezing waters, which is not relevant to the sentence. Choice D uses the term *inadequate safety measures*, which is not specifically mentioned in the original sentence and introduces a new idea that may not be entirely accurate.

**8. B:** There is no need for a comma. As it stands, the comma disrupts the normal flow of thought in the sentence. The subject, *ship*, is singular, and the verb also must be singular in subject-verb agreement. *Was divided* is in the past participle. *Divide* is in the present tense, and the rest of the essay is in the past.

**9. B:** Choice B is the simplest way to express the idea in a grammatically correct sentence. *Because of this* refers to the content of the previous sentence.

**10. C:** Choice C shows the contrast between first-class and third-class passengers. The previous sentences explained why majority of the survivors were a part of the first class passengers. Sentence 13 shifts to explain explains why most of the third class passengers did not survive. "On the other hand" clearly signals this contrast. "Lastly" is not an appropriate transition word, as there was not a series of listed facts. "For example" is not an appropriate transition to use since it is not giving an example. "Therefore" is not an appropriate transition word because the new information does not involve cause and effect with the previous sentences.

**11. D:** The incorrect choices all remove an essential element of the sentence. It is also incorrect to set up a contrast that did not exist in the original passage. The correct answer choice does not remove a key part of the sentence or change the intent of the original. It merely revises the two original sentences by combining them.

**12. A:** The capitalization and punctuation in the sentence is correct as written.

**13. C:** This sentence refers to the "smaller National Basketball League." This needs to be located after the sentence about the BAA's formation for comparison.

**14. D:** The error in the sentence is with the contraction *it's*. The author should replace it with the possessive pronoun *its*.

**15. B:** After sentence (4) is the best choice because this sentence effectively introduces the paragraph that discusses the origins of the game. After sentence (3) is not the best option because the introduction is highlighting broad topics that will be discussed in the body paragraphs. After sentence (8) is not the best option because the focus of this paragraph is on the spread of the game after its invention and the development of organized basketball. After sentence (14) is not the best option because new information should not be introduced in the conclusion.

**16. A:** Sentence (4) is already in its best place for this passage. Following sentence (3), the fourth sentence provides a needed example. So, it is best served in its current place.

**17. B:** Choice B is the best choice because it correctly transitions from sentence 7 to sentence 8 and maintains the author's original meaning.

**18. C:** In terms of determining their validity, hypotheses are confirmed or disconfirmed. None of the other options are meaningful.

**19. D:** Since the sentence begins in the present tense, it should continue in the present tense as well. The proper verb to be used in this clause is *affect*, meaning to have an impact, not *effect*, meaning to bring about.

**20. B:** The second sentence of the same paragraph states, "In the monkey example, every single monkey in the history of monkeys would need to be examined before the hypothesis could be proven or disproven." In the passage's last sentence, "...infinite sample sets for confirmation or disconfirmation" refers directly to that second sentence (quoted above here). The initial sentence of this paragraph (A) states that evidence-based hypotheses must use probability because sample sets are too large, which agrees with the sentence following it, but it does not specifically identify infinite sample sets as the sentence following it does. The fourth sentence of the previous paragraph (C) shows how even one piece of evidence out of a very large—but NOT infinite—sample size of one billion can disprove a hypothesis rather than showing how infinite sample sizes are required.

**21. B:** Although it is a simple combination, the connection of sentence 2 and sentence 3 outlined in choice B is the one that remains grammatically correct, maintains the author's original intent, and is logical.

**22. D:** A past tense verb is needed for this sentence.

**23. C:** The passage speaks of New Zealand being colonized, where previously it was not occupied, so *incursion* is not an accurate word to describe the coming of the settlers. *Influx* is a more appropriate description.

**24. D:** The two sentences are cause and effect. The first sentence gives the cause (that the settlers depended on hunting, gathering, and fishing), and the second sentence gives the effect (that the settlers stayed close to the sea where fish were abundant). *Therefore* is a good transition between cause and effect, so this choice is correct.

**25. D:** This sentence functions best in its current place, as sentence 15 functions as a topic sentence on the sweet potato, and sentence 17 logically comes after sentence 16 stating how the sweet potato could grow in many areas and survive the winter months as well.

# Arithmetic Placement Test

**1. B:** If each number is rounded to the nearest thousand, 15,012 rounds to 15,000, and 19,938 rounds to 20,000. We would therefore expect $\frac{15,012}{19,938}$ to be close to $\frac{15,000}{20,000}$, which can be simplified to $\frac{15,000 \div 1,000}{20,000 \div 1,000} = \frac{15}{20} = \frac{15 \div 5}{20 \div 5} = \frac{3}{4}$.

**2. C:** Candidate A's vote percentage is determined by the number of votes that he obtained divided by the total number of votes cast, and then multiplied by 100 to convert the decimal into a percentage.

$$\text{Candidate A's vote percentage} = \frac{36,800}{36,800 + 32,100 + 2,100} \times 100 = 51.8\%$$

Therefore, 51.8% of the vote went to Candidate A.

**3. A:** When comparing decimals, compare them one decimal place at a time. First compare the part before the decimal point; whichever has the largest whole part is largest. If the whole parts are equal, compare the tenths place, the place just after the decimal point. If the digits in the tenths place are the same, compare the hundredths place, the second place after the decimal point, and so on. In this case, all the decimals have a zero before the decimal point, so we'll start by comparing the tenths place. 0.55, 0.500, and 0.505 all have a 5 in the tenths place, while 0.0555 has a zero in the tenths place. So, 0.55, 0.500, and 0.505 are larger than 0.0555. Now, compare the hundredths place of the remaining choices, discarding the 0.0555 that we now know is smallest. 0.55 has a 5 in the hundredths place, while 0.500 and 0.505 both have zeroes. So, 0.55 is the largest of the choices.

**4. C:** To solve this problem, first calculate how many gallons each toilet uses in 375 flushes.

$$3.2 \times 375 = 1,200 \text{ gallons}$$
$$1.6 \times 375 = 600 \text{ gallons}$$

The problem is asking for the difference, so find the difference between the regular toilet and the low-flow toilet: $1,200 - 600 = 600$ gallons. Note that you could also find the difference in water use for one flush, and then multiply that amount by 375.

$$3.2 - 1.6 = 1.6$$
$$1.6 \times 375 = 600$$

With both methods of solving, the regular toilet uses 600 gallons more than the low-flow toilet after 375 flushes.

**5. D:** Multiplying both the numerator and denominator by the same constant does not change the value of a fraction; for instance, $\frac{10}{3} = \frac{10 \times 3}{3 \times 3} = \frac{30}{9}$. To convert a mixed number to a fraction, multiply the integer part by the denominator and add the product to the numerator; this becomes the numerator of the improper fraction, while the denominator remains the same. So, $2\frac{4}{3} = \frac{2 \times 3 + 4}{3} = \frac{10}{3}$. Note that $2\frac{4}{3}$ is a nonstandard mixed number because it has an improper fractional component; nevertheless, it is equivalent to $\frac{10}{3}$ and $\frac{30}{9}$. $3\frac{2}{3}$ is a nonequivalent mixed number: $3\frac{2}{3} = \frac{3 \times 3 + 2}{3} = \frac{11}{3} \neq \frac{10}{3}$. As a standard mixed number, $\frac{10}{3}$ would be equal to $3\frac{1}{3}$.

**6. B:** Begin by converting the fractions inside the parentheses to common denominators and then simplify.

$$-\frac{3}{2}\left(\frac{1}{2}+\frac{1}{3}\right)-\frac{2}{3}\left(\frac{1}{2}-\frac{3}{4}\right) = -\frac{3}{2}\left(\frac{3}{6}+\frac{2}{6}\right)-\frac{2}{3}\left(\frac{2}{4}-\frac{3}{4}\right)$$
$$= -\frac{3}{2}\left(\frac{5}{6}\right)-\frac{2}{3}\left(-\frac{1}{4}\right)$$
$$= -\frac{15}{12}+\frac{2}{12}$$
$$= -\frac{13}{12}$$

Finally, to convert this to a mixed number, divide the numerator by the denominator; the quotient is the integer part, and the remainder is the new numerator, while the denominator remains the same. $13 \div 12 = 1$ with a remainder of 1, so $-\frac{13}{12} = -1\frac{1}{12}$.

**7. D:** First, place 783 on top of 124 to subtract vertically. Then, subtract from right to left. $3 - 4$ is negative, so borrow from the 8 to make 3 become 13 and 8 is reduced to 7. $13 - 4 = 9$, so write a 9 under the 4. $7 - 2 = 5$, so write a 5 under the 2. $7 - 1 = 6$, so write a 6 under the 1. This gives a final answer of 659.

$$\begin{array}{r} 783 \\ -124 \\ \hline \end{array} \quad \begin{array}{r} 7\,13 \\ 7\cancel{8}\cancel{3} \\ -124 \\ \hline 9 \end{array} \quad \begin{array}{r} 7\,13 \\ 7\cancel{8}\cancel{3} \\ -124 \\ \hline 59 \end{array} \quad \begin{array}{r} 7\,13 \\ 7\cancel{8}\cancel{3} \\ -124 \\ \hline 659 \end{array}$$

**8. D:** The correct answer is 39. This can be found by using long division.

$$\begin{array}{r} 39 \\ 4\overline{)156} \\ -12 \\ \hline 36 \\ -36 \\ \hline 0 \end{array}$$

**9. D:** The total must be 1, so the fraction that goes to the third treasure hunter is $1 - \frac{1}{3} - \frac{1}{4}$. To subtract these fractions, convert them all to fractions with the least common denominator, which is in this case 12.

$$\frac{12}{12} - \frac{4}{12} - \frac{3}{12} = \frac{8}{12} - \frac{3}{12} = \frac{5}{12}$$

Therefore, the third treasure hunter gets $\frac{5}{12}$ of the treasure.

**10. C:** Parentheses must be completed first. Here, $9 + 1 = 10$, so we can rewrite our expression as $100 \div 10 \times 2$. When dealing with multiplication and division, we must solve the operations in the order in which they appear, from left to right. Because division appears before multiplication, we must divide 100 by 10 before we multiply by 2. The quotient of 100 and 10 is 10, simplifying our expression to $10 \times 2$, or 20. Our final answer is 20.

**11. A:** In order to subtract decimal numbers, write them one above the other with the decimal points aligned, filling in zeroes as necessary, and then carry out the subtraction normally, placing the decimal point in the same position in the result.

$$\begin{array}{r} \overset{5\ 13}{6.\cancel{3}2} \\ -3.50 \\ \hline 2.82 \end{array}$$

**12. B:** Recall that percent just means "divided by 100." Each of the given numbers can be represented as fractions.

I. $0.071\% = \frac{0.071}{100} = \frac{71}{100,000}$, II. $0.71 = \frac{71}{100}$, III. $7.1\% = \frac{7.1}{100} = \frac{71}{1,000}$, IV. $\frac{71}{101}$

All the fractions share the same numerator. Among fractions with the same numerator, the largest fraction has the smallest denominator. We can order these fractions from greatest to least by ordering the denominators from least to greatest. The correct order is $\frac{71}{100} > \frac{71}{101} > \frac{71}{1,000} > \frac{71}{100,000}$. Therefore, the ordering from greatest to least is II, IV, III, I.

**13. C:** The number of pieces of fruit that the vendor has is equal to the sum of the numbers of individual types of fruit. The number equals $52 + 88 + 48 + 45$, or 233 pieces of fruit.

**14. B:** Since all students who answered her survey said they prefer one of the three flavors, the percentages must add up to 100%. Therefore, the percentage of students who prefer strawberry must be $100\% - (35\% + 40\%) = 100\% - 75\% = 25\%$.

**15. A:** To multiply or divide mixed numbers, first convert them to improper fractions. To get the numerator of the equivalent improper fraction, multiply the denominator of the mixed number's fractional component by the whole number component and add this product to the numerator of the fractional component. Keep the denominator of the improper fraction the same as the denominator of the fractional component of the mixed number. So $1\frac{3}{4} = \frac{1 \times 4 + 3}{4} = \frac{7}{4}$. Dividing by a fraction is the same as multiplying by its reciprocal, so $\frac{7}{4} \div \frac{7}{10} = \frac{7}{4} \times \frac{10}{7} = \frac{70}{28}$, which reduces to $\frac{70 \div 7}{28 \div 7} = \frac{10}{4} = \frac{10 \div 2}{4 \div 2} = \frac{5}{2}$. Convert this back to a mixed number by dividing the numerator by the denominator. The quotient is the integer part of the mixed number, and the remainder is the numerator of the fractional part of the mixed number. $5 \div 2 = 2$ with a remainder of 1, so $\frac{5}{2} = 2\frac{1}{2}$.

**16. B:** When comparing fractions, it is necessary to find common denominators.

$$\frac{28}{35} = \frac{4}{5} > \frac{5}{7} = \frac{25}{35}$$
$$\frac{25}{35} = \frac{5}{7} > \frac{3}{5} = \frac{21}{35}$$
$$\frac{10}{15} = \frac{2}{3} < \frac{4}{5} = \frac{12}{15}$$
$$\frac{5}{10} = \frac{1}{2} > \frac{2}{5} = \frac{4}{10}$$

Once all the fractions have been represented using common denominators, it is easy to determine which of each pair is greater since the greater is the one with the larger numerator. Among the four choices, the only valid inequality is $\frac{5}{7} > \frac{3}{5}$.

**17. C:** The number of seats in the auditorium is equal to the product of the number of rows and the number of seats per row. The number of seats equals $25 \times 40$, or 1,000 seats.

**18. C:** When adding mixed numbers, add the whole number parts and the fractional parts together separately. Start by adding the fractional parts by first converting to common denominators and then adding the numerators.

$$\frac{1}{4} + \frac{5}{6} = \frac{3}{12} + \frac{10}{12} = \frac{13}{12} = 1\frac{1}{12}$$

Now, add the whole number parts. Since there is a whole number part from adding the fractional parts, add that part to the original whole numbers.

$$3 + 2 + 1 = 6$$

Now, combine the whole number part and the fractional part to get a sum of $6\frac{1}{12}$.

**19. A:** Remember that $x\%$ is the same thing as $\frac{x}{100}$, and finding $x\%$ of a number is the same as multiplying that number by $x\%$. This is true even when the number is itself a percentage. So, 10% of 40% is $40\% \times 10\% = \frac{40}{100} \times \frac{10}{100} = \frac{400}{10,000} = \frac{4}{100} = 4\%$.

**20. D:** To multiply decimals, first multiply the numbers normally ignoring the decimal point. Then, position the decimal point in the answer so that the number of digits after the decimal point in the product is equal to the sum of the number of digits after the decimal point in both factors.

$$262 \times 71 = 18,602$$

There are two digits after the decimal point in 2.62 and one digit after the decimal point in 7.1, so there should be three digits after the decimal point in the product, which is therefore 18.602.

## Quantitative Reasoning, Algebra, and Statistics Placement Test

**1. C:** We can find the probability by adding the distinct probabilities that a given student is a sophomore and that a given student prefers lattes. However, we must also remember to subtract off the probabilities that a student is a Sophomore and prefers lattes. Our previous calculation double counted these students. The probability may be written as: $P(S \text{ or } L) = \frac{67}{138} + \frac{55}{138} - \frac{26}{138}$. Thus, the probability a student is a Sophomore or prefers Lattes is $\frac{96}{138}$, which simplifies to $\frac{16}{23}$.

**2. D:** We can use the table to find the linear equation in slope-intercept form, $y = mx + b$, where $m$ is the slope and $b$ is the $y$-intercept. The table shows the $y$-intercept (the $y$-value at $x = 0$) to be $-5$. The slope is the ratio of the change in $y$-values to the corresponding change in $x$-values. As the $x$-value increases by 1, the $y$-value increases by 3. Thus, the slope is $\frac{3}{1}$, or 3. So the equation is $y = 3x - 5$.

Only the graphs in choices B and D have a $y$-intercept at $-5$. Of these two graphs, only choice D has a $y$-value increase of 3 for each $x$-value increase of 1, indicating a slope of 3.

**3. D:** There are three feet in a yard. In feet, the lot is $3 \times 3 = 9$ feet wide, and $4 \times 3 = 12$ feet long. So, its area is $9 \text{ ft} \times 12 \text{ ft} = 108 \text{ ft}^2$.

As an alternate way of solving the problem, first find the lot's area in square yards: $3 \text{ yd} \times 4 \text{ yd} = 12 \text{ yd}^2$. Then, convert square yards to square feet: since there are 3 feet in a yard, there are $3^2 = 9$ square feet in a square yard. So, the lot's area in square feet is $12 \times 9 = 108$ square feet.

**4. D:** To solve the inequality $3 - 2x < 5$, we can first subtract 3 from both sides to get $-2x < 2$. Now we can divide both sides of the inequality by $-2$. When an inequality is multiplied or divided by a negative number, its direction changes ($<$ becomes $>$, $\leq$ becomes $\geq$, and vice versa). So $-2x < 2$ becomes $\frac{-2x}{-2} > \frac{2}{-2}$, or $x > -1$.

**5. D:** Use a Venn diagram to help organize the given information. Start by filling in the space where the three circles intersect: Jenny tutored three students in all three areas. Use that information to fill in the spaces where two circles intersect. For example, she tutored 4 students in chemistry and for the ACT, and 3 of those were students she tutored in all three areas, so 1 student was tutored in chemistry and for the ACT but not for math. Once the diagram is completed, add the number of students who were tutored in all areas to the number of students tutored in only two of the three areas to the number of students tutored in only one area. The total number of students tutored was $3 + 2 + 2 + 1 + 3 + 2 + 1 = 14$.

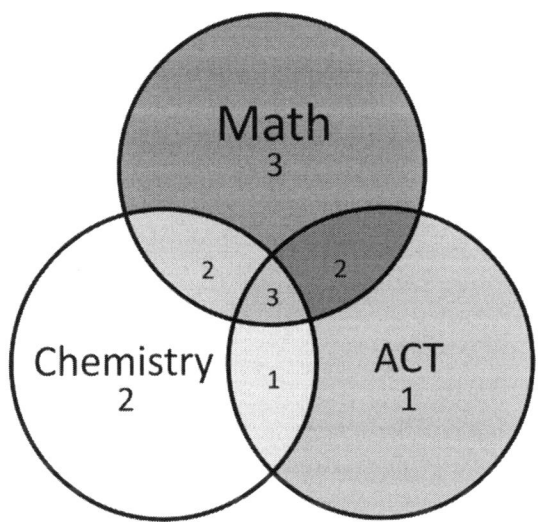

**6. B:** The mean, or average, is the sum of the numbers in a data set divided by the total number of items in the set. This data set has 7 items (one for each day of the week). The total number of hits that Kyle had during the week is the sum of the numbers in the bottom row. The sum is 14, so the mean is 2 because $14 \div 7 = 2$.

**7. D:** If there are three feet in a yard, then to convert yards to feet we just multiply by 3. So five yards is equal to $5 \times 3 = 15$ feet. Likewise, since there are twelve inches in a foot, to convert feet to inches, we just multiply by 12. So 15 feet is equal to $15 \times 12 = 180$ inches.

**8. A:** When $x \geq 0$, $|x| = x$, so it is not true that $|x| > x$. However, when $x < 0$, $|x| = -x$. This means $x$ is negative and $|x|$ is positive, and since any positive number is greater than any negative number, $|x| > x$ when $x < 0$.

**9. A:** To convert a number to scientific notation, move the decimal point until there is just one digit before it (not counting leading zeroes), and rewrite the number as the result times a power of ten. The exponent of the power of ten is equal to the number of places the decimal point was moved—positive if the decimal was moved left, and negative if the decimal was moved right. Starting with 0.0023, to put only one digit before the decimal point, we have to move the decimal point three places to the right. Therefore, $0.0023 = 2.3 \times 10^{-3}$.

**10. A:** To evaluate $\frac{x^3+2x}{x+3}$ at $= -1$, substitute in $-1$ for $x$ in the expression.

$$\frac{(-1)^3 + 2(-1)}{(-1) + 3} = \frac{(-1) + (-2)}{2} = \frac{-3}{2} = -\frac{3}{2}$$

**11. B:** The inequality that represents this scenario is $5n + 3s \geq 300$, where $n$ is the number of non-student tickets that must be sold, and $s$ is the number of student tickets that must be sold. The intercepts of this linear inequality can be found by substituting 0 for $s$ and solving for $n$ and then by substituting 0 for $n$ and solving for $s$. The intercepts are $n = 60$ and $s = 100$. The solid line through the two intercepts represents the minimum number of each type of ticket that must be sold to offset production costs. The shading above the line represents sales which result in a profit for the school.

**12. B:** The median of a data set is the middle element of the set after it is sorted in numerical order.

$$1, 1, 1, 2, 2, 3, 4$$

In this example the median is 2.

**13. C:** Substitute 1 for $x$ in the expression and solve.

$$|x| + |x - 2| = |1| + |1 - 2|$$
$$= |1| + |-1|$$
$$= 1 + 1$$
$$= 2$$

**14. D:** The longest side of a right triangle, called the hypotenuse, $H$, can be calculated using the Pythagorean theorem, together with the lengths of the other two sides, which are given as 6 and 8 units.

$$H^2 = (S_1)^2 + (S_2)^2$$
$$H^2 = 6^2 + 8^2$$
$$H^2 = 36 + 64$$
$$H^2 = 100$$
$$\sqrt{H^2} = \sqrt{100}$$
$$H = 10$$

Therefore, using $H = 10$, the perimeter, $P$, can be calculated as follows: $P = 10 + 6 + 8 = 24$. The perimeter of the triangle is 24 units.

**15. A:** To find Sam's average speed, we have to divide the total distance he travelled by the total travel time. Note that fifteen minutes is $\frac{1}{4}$ hour, and forty-five minutes is $\frac{3}{4}$ hour. During the first fifteen minutes, therefore, the distance Sam runs is 8 mph $\times \frac{1}{4}$ hour $= 2$ miles. During the next forty-five minutes, he jogs 4 mph $\times \frac{3}{4}$ hours $= 3$ miles. So, the total distance he runs is $2 + 3 = 5$ miles. The time he runs is $\frac{1}{4}$ hour $+ \frac{3}{4}$ hours $= 1$ hour, so his average speed is 5 miles $\div 1$ hour $= 5$ miles per hour.

**16. C:** The situation may be modeled by this system of equations:

$$\begin{cases} 4y + 3c = 9.55 \\ 2y + 2c = 5.90 \end{cases}$$

Multiplying the bottom equation by −2 gives:

$$\begin{cases} 4y + 3c = 9.55 \\ -4y - 4c = -11.80 \end{cases}$$

Adding the two equations gives $-c = -2.25$, or $c = 2.25$. Thus, one box of crackers costs $2.25.

**17. D:** Each of the base numbers in these expressions is a power of 2. If we express each of them in terms of 2, it will be easier to compare them.

$$8^{\frac{3}{2}} = (2^3)^{\frac{3}{2}} = 2^{\frac{9}{2}}$$
$$16 = 2^4 = 2^{\frac{8}{2}}$$
$$4^{\frac{5}{2}} = (2^2)^{\frac{5}{2}} = 2^{\frac{10}{2}}$$
$$2^{\frac{7}{2}} = 2^{\frac{7}{2}}$$

Once each of the choices has been expressed as a power of 2, we can see that $2^{\frac{7}{2}}$ is the smallest.

**18. C:** Since 3 of the 15 songs are by Beyonce, the probability that any one song will be by Beyonce is $\frac{3}{15} = \frac{1}{5}$. The probability that the next song is not by Beyonce is $\frac{4}{5}$. Therefore, the probability that the next two songs are both not by Beyonce is $\frac{4}{5} \times \frac{4}{5} = \frac{16}{25}$.

**19. C:** If all possible outcomes are equally likely, then the probability of an event is the number of outcomes in which that event occurs, divided by the number of possible outcomes. A camper who is at least eight years old can be eight, nine, or ten years old, so the probability of randomly selecting a camper at least eight years old is:

$$\frac{\text{number of eight-, nine-, and ten-year-old campers}}{\text{total number of campers}} = \frac{14 + 12 + 10}{12 + 15 + 14 + 12 + 10} = \frac{36}{63} = \frac{4}{7}$$

**20. C:** We can start by rewriting the rate of drainage in gallons per minute. $\frac{1 \text{ gallon}}{15 \text{ seconds}} \times \frac{60 \text{ seconds}}{1 \text{ minute}} = \frac{60 \text{ gallons}}{15 \text{ minutes}} =$ 4 gallons/minute. This means that in $t$ minutes, the tub will have drained $4t$ gallons. We are asked to find how long the tub will take to drain 12 gallons, so $4t = 12$. Dividing both sides by 4, we find $t = 3$. Therefore, it takes 3 minutes to drain the bathtub.

## Advanced Algebra and Functions Placement Test

**1. A:** Start by substituting the function $f(x)$ into the expression $2f(x) - 3$.

$$2(2x^2 + 7) - 3$$

From here, simplify the expression using the distributive property.

$$4x^2 + 14 - 3$$

Finally, combine like terms.

$$4x^2 + 11$$

**2. C:** A system of linear equations can be solved by using matrices or by using the graphing, substitution, or elimination (also called linear combination) method. The elimination method is shown here:

$$3x + 4y = 2$$
$$2x + 6y = -2$$

In order to eliminate $x$ by linear combination, multiply the top equation by 2 and the bottom equation by $-3$ so that the coefficients of the $x$-terms will be additive inverses.

$$2(3x + 4y = 2)$$
$$-3(2x + 6y = -2)$$

Then, add the two equations and solve for $y$.

$$6x + 8y = 4$$
$$\underline{-6x - 18y = 6}$$
$$-10y = 10$$
$$y = -1$$

Substitute $-1$ for $y$ in either of the given equations and solve for $x$.

$$3x + 4y = 2$$
$$3x + 4(-1) = 2$$
$$3x - 4 = 2$$
$$3x = 6$$
$$x = 2$$

The solution to the system of equations is $(2, -1)$.

**3. A:** The legs and hypotenuse of a right triangle are related through the Pythagorean theorem, $a^2 + b^2 = c^2$, where $a$ and $b$ are the lengths of the legs and $c$ is the length of the hypotenuse. In this case, $a = 5$ and $b = 12$ (or vice-versa; it doesn't matter which leg we call $a$ and which leg we call $b$). Substitute these values into the Pythagorean theorem and solve for $c$.

$$(5)^2 + (12)^2 = c^2$$
$$25 + 144 = c^2$$
$$169 = c^2$$
$$13 = c$$

Therefore, the length of the hypotenuse is 13.

**4. D:** When variables are multiplied, their exponents are added together. First, move any variables out of the denominator by reversing the sign on their exponents.

$$\frac{x^6}{y^4} \cdot x^2 y^3 = x^6 y^{-4} \cdot x^2 y^3$$

Next, group sets of like variables to make it easier to combine them accurately.

$$= (x^6 x^2)(y^{-4} y^3)$$

Finally, add the exponents and simplify.

$$= x^{6+2}y^{-4+3}$$
$$= x^8 y^{-1}$$
$$= \frac{x^8}{y}$$

**5. D:** By inspection of the graph, the function $f$ has roots $x = -1$ and $x = 3$. We can factor $g$ as $g(x) = -x^2 + 8x - 15 = -(x^2 - 8x + 15) = -(x - 3)(x - 5)$. To find the roots, set each factor equal to 0 and solve for $x$. The roots are $x = 3$ and $x = 5$. Thus functions $f$ and $g$ share the root $x = 3$ but not a second root. The $y$-intercept of $f$ can be found by determining the point where the graph crosses the $y$-axis, which is at the point $(0, -3)$. The $y$-intercept of $g$ can be found by determining $g(0)$, which is $-15$, so the $y$-intercept is at the point $(0, 15)$. Therefore, the functions $f$ and $g$ have different $y$-intercepts.

**6. D:** Note that the first two terms and the last two terms of $x^3 - 3x^2 - 4x + 12$ are each divisible by $x - 3$, meaning $x - 3$ can be factored from each set of terms.

$$x^3 - 3x^2 - 4x + 12$$
$$x^2(x - 3) - 4(x - 3)$$
$$(x^2 - 4)(x - 3)$$

The term $x^2 - 4$ is a difference of squares, and since $x^2 - a^2 = (x + a)(x - a)$, we know $x^2 - 4 = (x + 2)(x - 2)$. The full factorization of $x^3 - 3x^2 - 4x + 12$ is therefore $(x + 2)(x - 2)(x - 3)$. Thus, all the answer choices except $x + 3$ are factors.

Alternatively, instead of factoring the polynomial, we could have divided the polynomial $x^3 - 3x^2 - 4x + 12$ by the expression contained in each answer choice. Of the expressions listed, only $x + 3$ yields a nonzero remainder when divided into $x^3 - 3x^2 - 4x + 12$, so it is not a factor.

**7. C:** The expression representing the monthly charge for Company A is $\$25 + \$0.05m$, where $m$ is the time in minutes spent talking on the phone. Set this expression equal to the monthly charge for Company B, which is $\$50$. Solve for $m$ to find the number of minutes the two companies charge the same amount.

$$\$25 + \$0.05m = \$50$$
$$\$0.05m = \$25$$
$$m = 500$$

Notice that the answer choices are given in hours, not in minutes. Since there are 60 minutes in an hour, $m = \frac{500}{60}$ hours $= 8\frac{1}{3}$ hours. One-third of an hour is 20 minutes, so $m$ is 8 hours and 20 minutes.

**8. B:** The two right triangles are similar because they share a pair of vertical angles. Vertical angles are always congruent (e.g., $\angle ACB$ and $\angle DCE$). Both right angles (e.g., $\angle B$ and $\angle D$) are also congruent. So, $\angle A$ and $\angle E$ are congruent because of the triangular sum theorem.

With similar triangles, corresponding sides will be proportional. $\overline{BC}$ is $\frac{1}{2}$ the length of $\overline{CD}$. So, $\overline{AC}$ will be $\frac{1}{2}$ the length of $\overline{CE}$. The length of $\overline{CE}$ can be computed from the Pythagorean theorem because it is the hypotenuse of a right triangle where the lengths of the other two sides are known.

$$\overline{CE} = \sqrt{6^2 + 8^2} = \sqrt{36 + 64} = \sqrt{100} = 10$$

The length of $\overline{AC}$ will be $\frac{1}{2}$ of this value, or 5 units.

**9. A:** This problem is most easily solved using the law of sines, which states that the ratio of the sine of each angle in a triangle to the length of the opposite side is equal: $\frac{\sin A}{a} = \frac{\sin B}{b} = \frac{\sin C}{c}$. In this case, angle $\theta$ is opposite side $a$, and the angle with a measure of 30° is opposite side $b$, so we can write $\frac{\sin \theta}{a} = \frac{\sin 30°}{b}$. Since $\sin 30° = \frac{1}{2}$, this becomes $\frac{\sin \theta}{a} = \frac{\frac{1}{2}}{b}$, or $\sin \theta = \frac{a}{2b}$.

**10. A:** This equation is a linear relationship that has a slope of 3.60 and passes through the origin. The table shows that for each hour of rental, the cost increases by $3.60. This matches with the slope of the equation. Of course, if the bicycle is not rented at all (0 hours), there will be no charge ($0). If plotted on the Cartesian plane, the line would have a $y$-intercept of 0. The first choice is the only one that meets these requirements.

**11. C:** If the town's population triples every ten years, this is an example of exponential growth, which is described by the equation $P = P_0 e^{kt}$, where $P$ is the population at time $t$, $P_0$ is the initial population, and $k$ is growth rate. To find $k$, we can use the fact that ten years after 1950 the town's population will be three times what it started with: i.e., when $t = 10$, $P = 3P_0$. So, $3P_0 = P_0 e^{10k}$; we can cancel out the $P_0$ from both sides to get $3 = e^{10k}$. Taking the natural logarithm of both sides, we get $\ln 3 = 10k$, so $k = \frac{1}{10} \ln 3$. So the equation is $P(t) = P_0 e^{\left(\frac{1}{10} \ln 3\right)t} = P_0 e^{\ln 3 \left(\frac{t}{10}\right)}$; using the fact that $a^{bc} = (a^b)^c$, we can rewrite this as $P(t) = P_0 (e^{\ln 3})^{\frac{t}{10}}$. But $e^x$ and $\ln x$ are inverse functions, so $e^{\ln 3} = 3$, and this becomes $P(t) = P_0 \times 3^{\frac{t}{10}}$.

**12. D:** Recall that the general form of a quadratic expression is $ax^2 + bx + c$. A great way to factor quadratic expression like this, where $a = 1$ and all the answer choices are integer factors, would be to consider the factors of the last term, $c$. Specifically, any two factors of $c$ that would add to $b$. Essentially: $f_1 \times f_2 = -12$ and $f_1 + f_2 = 1$. We can check the factors of –12.

| $f_1$ | $f_2$ | $f_1 + f_2$ |
|---|---|---|
| 12 | –1 | 11 |
| 6 | –2 | 4 |
| 4 | –3 | 1 |
| 3 | –4 | –1 |
| 2 | –6 | –4 |
| 1 | –12 | –11 |

The only option from this table that works is 4 and –3, which means the expression factors as $(x + 4)(x - 3)$.

**13. A:** The inequality that represents this scenario is $n + 3p \leq 30$, where $n$ is the number of notebooks and $p$ is the number of boxes of pencils. To graph this inequality, find the intercepts of this linear inequality by making the inequality an equality and setting $n$ and $p$ equal to 0 and solving for the other variable.

$$(0) + 3p = 30$$
$$3p = 30$$
$$p = 10$$

$$n + 3(0) = 30$$
$$n = 30$$

The intercepts are $n = 30$ and $p = 10$. The solid line through the two intercepts represents the maximum number of each item that may be purchased. Since this inequality represents the maximum he can purchase, all first-quadrant points below the line are also possible amounts within Ben's budget.

**14. D:** There are many ways to solve quadratic equations in the form $ax^2 + bx + c = 0$. However, some methods, such as graphing and factoring, are not useful for equations with irrational or complex roots. Solve this equation by using the quadratic formula, $x = \frac{-b \pm \sqrt{b^2-4ac}}{2a}$. Set the given equation equal to zero, so $7x^2 + 6x + 2 = 0$. Substitute the values $a = 7$, $b = 6$, and $c = 2$ into the quadratic formula.

$$x = \frac{-b \pm \sqrt{b^2 - 4ac}}{2a}$$
$$x = \frac{-6 \pm \sqrt{6^2 - 4(7)(2)}}{2(7)}$$
$$x = \frac{-6 \pm \sqrt{36 - 56}}{14}$$
$$x = \frac{-6 \pm \sqrt{-20}}{14}$$
$$x = \frac{-6 \pm 2i\sqrt{5}}{14}$$
$$x = \frac{-3 \pm i\sqrt{5}}{7}$$

**15. B:** The simplest way to solve this problem is to first use a trigonometric identity.

$$\sec^2 \theta = \tan^2 \theta + 1$$
$$\tan^2 \theta = \sec^2 \theta - 1$$

Replacing $\tan^2 \theta$ with $\sec^2 \theta - 1$, the given equation becomes $2 \sec \theta = \sec^2 \theta - 1$. Moving everything to one side of the equation, we get $\sec^2 \theta - 2 \sec \theta - 1 = 0$. If we let $x = \sec \theta$, it becomes a simple quadratic equation, $x^2 - 2x - 1 = 0$. We can solve this using the quadratic formula.

$$x = \frac{-(-2) \pm \sqrt{(-2)^2 - 4(1)(-1)}}{2(1)}$$
$$= \frac{2 \pm \sqrt{4 - (-4)}}{2}$$
$$= \frac{2 \pm \sqrt{8}}{2}$$
$$= \frac{2 \pm 2\sqrt{2}}{2}$$
$$= 1 \pm \sqrt{2}$$

So, $\sec \theta = 1 \pm \sqrt{2}$.

**16. C:** We can write the quotient as a fraction: $\frac{2+\sqrt{3}}{2-\sqrt{3}}$. Now, we need to rationalize the denominator. In other words, convert this fraction to a form without any radicals in the denominator. To do this, we multiply both sides of the fraction by the conjugate of the denominator: $\frac{(2+\sqrt{3})\times(2+\sqrt{3})}{(2-\sqrt{3})\times(2+\sqrt{3})}$. We can simplify both the numerator and the denominator by using the FOIL method.

$$\frac{2+\sqrt{3}}{2-\sqrt{3}} = \frac{(2+\sqrt{3})\times(2+\sqrt{3})}{(2-\sqrt{3})\times(2+\sqrt{3})}$$
$$= \frac{(2\times 2)+(2\times\sqrt{3})+(\sqrt{3}\times 2)+(\sqrt{3}\times\sqrt{3})}{(2\times 2)+(2\times\sqrt{3})+[(-\sqrt{3})\times 2]+[(-\sqrt{3})\times\sqrt{3}]}$$
$$= \frac{4+2\sqrt{3}+2\sqrt{3}+3}{4+2\sqrt{3}-2\sqrt{3}-3}$$
$$= \frac{7+4\sqrt{3}}{1}$$
$$= 7+4\sqrt{3}$$

**17. B:** To simplify the given inequality, first move all the terms to one side.

$$x^2+3 > 2x+2$$
$$x^2+3-2x-2 > 0$$
$$x^2-2x+1 > 0$$

Now, factor the left-hand side.

$$x^2-2x+1 = (x-1)(x-1) = (x-1)^2$$

The original inequality is equivalent to $(x-1)^2 > 0$. Since the square of a negative number is positive, $(x-1)^2 > 0$ everywhere except where $x-1 = 0$, i.e. at $x = 1$. Therefore, $x \neq 1$ is equivalent to $x^2+3 > 2x+2$.

**18. B:** Before carrying out the multiplication of the polynomials, notice that there is a factor of $x+1$ in both the right numerator and left denominator, so this term can be canceled out. The expression then multiplies to $\frac{x^2-5x+6}{x-2}$. We can simplify further by factoring the numerator.

One way to factor a quadratic expression with a leading coefficient of 1 is to look for two numbers that add up to the coefficient of $x$ (in this case –5) and multiply to the constant term (in this case 6). Two such numbers are –2 and –3: $(-2)+(-3) = -5$ and $(-2)\times(-3) = 6$. So $x^2-5x+6 = (x-2)(x-3)$. That means $\frac{x^2-5x+6}{x-2} = \frac{(x-2)(x-3)}{x-2}$. The $x-2$ in the numerator and denominator can cancel, so we are left with just $x-3$. (Note that if $x = -1$ or $x = 2$, the obtained simplified expression would not be true: either value of $x$ would result in a denominator of zero in the original expression, so the whole expression would be undefined. Therefore, it is necessary to state that these values of $x$ are excluded from the domain. For a domain of $x > 2$, both $x = -1$ and $x = 2$ would be excluded.)

**19. A:** The alternate interior angles have congruent angle measures, each measuring 142°. According to the alternate interior angles converse theorem, two lines are parallel if a transversal, intersecting the lines, forms congruent alternate interior angles.

**20. C:** This graph is shifted 4 units to the right and 3 units up from that of the parent function, $y = x^2$.

# Six Additional Practice Tests

To take these additional ACCUPLACER practice tests, visit our online resources page: **mometrix.com/resources719/accuplacer-28992**

# How to Overcome Test Anxiety

Just the thought of taking a test is enough to make most people a little nervous. A test is an important event that can have a long-term impact on your future, so it's important to take it seriously and it's natural to feel anxious about performing well. But just because anxiety is normal, that doesn't mean that it's helpful in test taking, or that you should simply accept it as part of your life. Anxiety can have a variety of effects. These effects can be mild, like making you feel slightly nervous, or severe, like blocking your ability to focus or remember even a simple detail.

If you experience test anxiety—whether severe or mild—it's important to know how to beat it. To discover this, first you need to understand what causes test anxiety.

## Causes of Test Anxiety

While we often think of anxiety as an uncontrollable emotional state, it can actually be caused by simple, practical things. One of the most common causes of test anxiety is that a person does not feel adequately prepared for their test. This feeling can be the result of many different issues such as poor study habits or lack of organization, but the most common culprit is time management. Starting to study too late, failing to organize your study time to cover all of the material, or being distracted while you study will mean that you're not well prepared for the test. This may lead to cramming the night before, which will cause you to be physically and mentally exhausted for the test. Poor time management also contributes to feelings of stress, fear, and hopelessness as you realize you are not well prepared but don't know what to do about it.

Other times, test anxiety is not related to your preparation for the test but comes from unresolved fear. This may be a past failure on a test, or poor performance on tests in general. It may come from comparing yourself to others who seem to be performing better or from the stress of living up to expectations. Anxiety may be driven by fears of the future—how failure on this test would affect your educational and career goals. These fears are often completely irrational, but they can still negatively impact your test performance.

## Elements of Test Anxiety

As mentioned earlier, test anxiety is considered to be an emotional state, but it has physical and mental components as well. Sometimes you may not even realize that you are suffering from test anxiety until you notice the physical symptoms. These can include trembling hands, rapid heartbeat, sweating, nausea, and tense muscles. Extreme anxiety may lead to fainting or vomiting. Obviously, any of these symptoms can have a negative impact on testing. It is important to recognize them as soon as they begin to occur so that you can address the problem before it damages your performance.

The mental components of test anxiety include trouble focusing and inability to remember learned information. During a test, your mind is on high alert, which can help you recall information and stay focused for an extended period of time. However, anxiety interferes with your mind's natural processes, causing you to blank out, even on the questions you know well. The strain of testing during anxiety makes it difficult to stay focused, especially on a test that may take several hours. Extreme anxiety can take a huge mental toll, making it difficult not only to recall test information but even to understand the test questions or pull your thoughts together.

# Effects of Test Anxiety

Test anxiety is like a disease—if left untreated, it will get progressively worse. Anxiety leads to poor performance, and this reinforces the feelings of fear and failure, which in turn lead to poor performances on subsequent tests. It can grow from a mild nervousness to a crippling condition. If allowed to progress, test anxiety can have a big impact on your schooling, and consequently on your future.

Test anxiety can spread to other parts of your life. Anxiety on tests can become anxiety in any stressful situation, and blanking on a test can turn into panicking in a job situation. But fortunately, you don't have to let anxiety rule your testing and determine your grades. There are a number of relatively simple steps you can take to move past anxiety and function normally on a test and in the rest of life.

# Physical Steps for Beating Test Anxiety

While test anxiety is a serious problem, the good news is that it can be overcome. It doesn't have to control your ability to think and remember information. While it may take time, you can begin taking steps today to beat anxiety.

Just as your first hint that you may be struggling with anxiety comes from the physical symptoms, the first step to treating it is also physical. Rest is crucial for having a clear, strong mind. If you are tired, it is much easier to give in to anxiety. But if you establish good sleep habits, your body and mind will be ready to perform optimally, without the strain of exhaustion. Additionally, sleeping well helps you to retain information better, so you're more likely to recall the answers when you see the test questions.

Getting good sleep means more than going to bed on time. It's important to allow your brain time to relax. Take study breaks from time to time so it doesn't get overworked, and don't study right before bed. Take time to rest your mind before trying to rest your body, or you may find it difficult to fall asleep.

Along with sleep, other aspects of physical health are important in preparing for a test. Good nutrition is vital for good brain function. Sugary foods and drinks may give a burst of energy but this burst is followed by a crash, both physically and emotionally. Instead, fuel your body with protein and vitamin-rich foods.

Also, drink plenty of water. Dehydration can lead to headaches and exhaustion, especially if your brain is already under stress from the rigors of the test. Particularly if your test is a long one, drink water during the breaks. And if possible, take an energy-boosting snack to eat between sections.

Along with sleep and diet, a third important part of physical health is exercise. Maintaining a steady workout schedule is helpful, but even taking 5-minute study breaks to walk can help get your blood pumping faster and clear your head. Exercise also releases endorphins, which contribute to a positive feeling and can help combat test anxiety.

When you nurture your physical health, you are also contributing to your mental health. If your body is healthy, your mind is much more likely to be healthy as well. So take time to rest, nourish your body with healthy food and water, and get moving as much as possible. Taking these physical steps will make you stronger and more able to take the mental steps necessary to overcome test anxiety.

# Mental Steps for Beating Test Anxiety

Working on the mental side of test anxiety can be more challenging, but as with the physical side, there are clear steps you can take to overcome it. As mentioned earlier, test anxiety often stems from lack of preparation, so the obvious solution is to prepare for the test. Effective studying may be the most important weapon you have for beating test anxiety, but you can and should employ several other mental tools to combat fear.

First, boost your confidence by reminding yourself of past success—tests or projects that you aced. If you're putting as much effort into preparing for this test as you did for those, there's no reason you should expect to fail here. Work hard to prepare; then trust your preparation.

Second, surround yourself with encouraging people. It can be helpful to find a study group, but be sure that the people you're around will encourage a positive attitude. If you spend time with others who are anxious or cynical, this will only contribute to your own anxiety. Look for others who are motivated to study hard from a desire to succeed, not from a fear of failure.

Third, reward yourself. A test is physically and mentally tiring, even without anxiety, and it can be helpful to have something to look forward to. Plan an activity following the test, regardless of the outcome, such as going to a movie or getting ice cream.

When you are taking the test, if you find yourself beginning to feel anxious, remind yourself that you know the material. Visualize successfully completing the test. Then take a few deep, relaxing breaths and return to it. Work through the questions carefully but with confidence, knowing that you are capable of succeeding.

Developing a healthy mental approach to test taking will also aid in other areas of life. Test anxiety affects more than just the actual test—it can be damaging to your mental health and even contribute to depression. It's important to beat test anxiety before it becomes a problem for more than testing.

# Study Strategy

Being prepared for the test is necessary to combat anxiety, but what does being prepared look like? You may study for hours on end and still not feel prepared. What you need is a strategy for test prep. The next few pages outline our recommended steps to help you plan out and conquer the challenge of preparation.

## STEP 1: SCOPE OUT THE TEST

Learn everything you can about the format (multiple choice, essay, etc.) and what will be on the test. Gather any study materials, course outlines, or sample exams that may be available. Not only will this help you to prepare, but knowing what to expect can help to alleviate test anxiety.

## STEP 2: MAP OUT THE MATERIAL

Look through the textbook or study guide and make note of how many chapters or sections it has. Then divide these over the time you have. For example, if a book has 15 chapters and you have five days to study, you need to cover three chapters each day. Even better, if you have the time, leave an extra day at the end for overall review after you have gone through the material in depth.

If time is limited, you may need to prioritize the material. Look through it and make note of which sections you think you already have a good grasp on, and which need review. While you are studying, skim quickly through the familiar sections and take more time on the challenging parts. Write out your plan so you don't get lost as you go. Having a written plan also helps you feel more in control of the study, so anxiety is less likely to arise from feeling overwhelmed at the amount to cover.

## STEP 3: GATHER YOUR TOOLS

Decide what study method works best for you. Do you prefer to highlight in the book as you study and then go back over the highlighted portions? Or do you type out notes of the important information? Or is it helpful to make flashcards that you can carry with you? Assemble the pens, index cards, highlighters, post-it notes, and any other materials you may need so you won't be distracted by getting up to find things while you study.

If you're having a hard time retaining the information or organizing your notes, experiment with different methods. For example, try color-coding by subject with colored pens, highlighters, or post-it notes. If you learn better by hearing, try recording yourself reading your notes so you can listen while in the car, working out, or simply sitting at your desk. Ask a friend to quiz you from your flashcards, or try teaching someone the material to solidify it in your mind.

## STEP 4: CREATE YOUR ENVIRONMENT

It's important to avoid distractions while you study. This includes both the obvious distractions like visitors and the subtle distractions like an uncomfortable chair (or a too-comfortable couch that makes you want to fall asleep). Set up the best study environment possible: good lighting and a comfortable work area. If background music helps you focus, you may want to turn it on, but otherwise keep the room quiet. If you are using a computer to take notes, be sure you don't have any other windows open, especially applications like social media, games, or anything else that could distract you. Silence your phone and turn off notifications. Be sure to keep water close by so you stay hydrated while you study (but avoid unhealthy drinks and snacks).

Also, take into account the best time of day to study. Are you freshest first thing in the morning? Try to set aside some time then to work through the material. Is your mind clearer in the afternoon or evening? Schedule your study session then. Another method is to study at the same time of day that you will take the test, so that your brain gets used to working on the material at that time and will be ready to focus at test time.

## STEP 5: STUDY!

Once you have done all the study preparation, it's time to settle into the actual studying. Sit down, take a few moments to settle your mind so you can focus, and begin to follow your study plan. Don't give in to distractions or let yourself procrastinate. This is your time to prepare so you'll be ready to fearlessly approach the test. Make the most of the time and stay focused.

Of course, you don't want to burn out. If you study too long you may find that you're not retaining the information very well. Take regular study breaks. For example, taking five minutes out of every hour to walk briskly, breathing deeply and swinging your arms, can help your mind stay fresh.

As you get to the end of each chapter or section, it's a good idea to do a quick review. Remind yourself of what you learned and work on any difficult parts. When you feel that you've mastered the material, move on to the next part. At the end of your study session, briefly skim through your notes again.

But while review is helpful, cramming last minute is NOT. If at all possible, work ahead so that you won't need to fit all your study into the last day. Cramming overloads your brain with more information than it can process and retain, and your tired mind may struggle to recall even previously learned information when it is overwhelmed with last-minute study. Also, the urgent nature of cramming and the stress placed on your brain contribute to anxiety. You'll be more likely to go to the test feeling unprepared and having trouble thinking clearly.

So don't cram, and don't stay up late before the test, even just to review your notes at a leisurely pace. Your brain needs rest more than it needs to go over the information again. In fact, plan to finish your studies by noon or early afternoon the day before the test. Give your brain the rest of the day to relax or focus on other things, and get a good night's sleep. Then you will be fresh for the test and better able to recall what you've studied.

## STEP 6: TAKE A PRACTICE TEST

Many courses offer sample tests, either online or in the study materials. This is an excellent resource to check whether you have mastered the material, as well as to prepare for the test format and environment.

Check the test format ahead of time: the number of questions, the type (multiple choice, free response, etc.), and the time limit. Then create a plan for working through them. For example, if you have 30 minutes to take a 60-question test, your limit is 30 seconds per question. Spend less time on the questions you know well so that you can take more time on the difficult ones.

If you have time to take several practice tests, take the first one open book, with no time limit. Work through the questions at your own pace and make sure you fully understand them. Gradually work up to taking a test under test conditions: sit at a desk with all study materials put away and set a timer. Pace yourself to make sure you finish the test with time to spare and go back to check your answers if you have time.

After each test, check your answers. On the questions you missed, be sure you understand why you missed them. Did you misread the question (tests can use tricky wording)? Did you forget the information? Or was it something you hadn't learned? Go back and study any shaky areas that the practice tests reveal.

Taking these tests not only helps with your grade, but also aids in combating test anxiety. If you're already used to the test conditions, you're less likely to worry about it, and working through tests until you're scoring well gives you a confidence boost. Go through the practice tests until you feel comfortable, and then you can go into the test knowing that you're ready for it.

# Test Tips

On test day, you should be confident, knowing that you've prepared well and are ready to answer the questions. But aside from preparation, there are several test day strategies you can employ to maximize your performance.

First, as stated before, get a good night's sleep the night before the test (and for several nights before that, if possible). Go into the test with a fresh, alert mind rather than staying up late to study.

Try not to change too much about your normal routine on the day of the test. It's important to eat a nutritious breakfast, but if you normally don't eat breakfast at all, consider eating just a protein bar. If you're a coffee drinker, go ahead and have your normal coffee. Just make sure you time it so that the caffeine doesn't wear off right in the middle of your test. Avoid sugary beverages, and drink enough water to stay hydrated but not so much that you need a restroom break 10 minutes into the test. If your test isn't first thing in the morning, consider going for a walk or doing a light workout before the test to get your blood flowing.

Allow yourself enough time to get ready, and leave for the test with plenty of time to spare so you won't have the anxiety of scrambling to arrive in time. Another reason to be early is to select a good seat. It's helpful to sit away from doors and windows, which can be distracting. Find a good seat, get out your supplies, and settle your mind before the test begins.

When the test begins, start by going over the instructions carefully, even if you already know what to expect. Make sure you avoid any careless mistakes by following the directions.

Then begin working through the questions, pacing yourself as you've practiced. If you're not sure on an answer, don't spend too much time on it, and don't let it shake your confidence. Either skip it and come back later, or eliminate as many wrong answers as possible and guess among the remaining ones. Don't dwell on these questions as you continue—put them out of your mind and focus on what lies ahead.

Be sure to read all of the answer choices, even if you're sure the first one is the right answer. Sometimes you'll find a better one if you keep reading. But don't second-guess yourself if you do immediately know the answer. Your gut instinct is usually right. Don't let test anxiety rob you of the information you know.

If you have time at the end of the test (and if the test format allows), go back and review your answers. Be cautious about changing any, since your first instinct tends to be correct, but make sure you didn't misread any of the questions or accidentally mark the wrong answer choice. Look over any you skipped and make an educated guess.

At the end, leave the test feeling confident. You've done your best, so don't waste time worrying about your performance or wishing you could change anything. Instead, celebrate the successful completion of this test. And finally, use this test to learn how to deal with anxiety even better next time.

> **Review Video: Test Anxiety**
> Visit mometrix.com/academy and enter code: 100340

## Important Qualification

Not all anxiety is created equal. If your test anxiety is causing major issues in your life beyond the classroom or testing center, or if you are experiencing troubling physical symptoms related to your anxiety, it may be a sign of a serious physiological or psychological condition. If this sounds like your situation, we strongly encourage you to seek professional help.

# Online Resources

Due to our efforts to try to keep this book to a manageable length, we've created a link that will give you access to all of your online resources:

mometrix.com/resources719/accuplacer-28992